2

HOW AMERICA WAS LOST

HOW AMERICA WAS LOST

FROM 9/11 TO THE POLICE/WARFARE STATE

PAUL CRAIG ROBERTS

CLARITY PRESS, INC.

© 2014 Paul Craig Roberts
ISBN: 0-9860362-9-3
    978-0-9860362-9-3

In-house editor: Diana G. Collier
Cover: R. Jordan P. Santos
Cover photo: european pressphoto agency

THE COVER IMAGE: Tanks deployed on the streets of
Boston during the mandatory "shelter in place" military curfew
that put the entire city on lockdown after the Marathon bombing.
All public transportation in and out of Boston was suspended and
schools were shut down as authorities conducted helicopter and
warantless house-to-house searches throughout the city for the
wounded 19-year-old alleged perpetrator.

Library of Congress Cataloging-in-Publication Data

Roberts, Paul Craig, 1939-
  How America was lost : from 9/11 to the police/warfare state / by Paul
Craig Roberts.
      pages cm
  Includes bibliographical references and index.
  ISBN 978-0-9860362-9-3 (alk. paper)
  1. United States--Politics and government--21st century. 2. United
States--Foreign relations--21st century. I. Title.
  E907.R63 2014
  973.93--dc23
                            2014002447

Clarity Press, Inc.
Ste. 469, 3277 Roswell Rd. NE
Atlanta, GA. 30305 , USA
http://www.claritypress.com

TABLE OF CONTENTS

Dedicated to:
Bradley Manning
Glenn Greenwald
Julian Assange
Edward Snowden
William Binney
and all others
who stand for truth, justice, mercy

INTRODUCTION

The demonization of the Soviet Union in the post-World War II era was the basis for America's reputation as the defender of freedom and democracy. Some historians and commentators deny that the United States deserved its reputation. They point to America's destruction of native inhabitants, to the theft of Spanish territories in Texas and what became the Southwest of the United States, to the internment of Japanese-American citizens during World War II, to the apartheid existence of black Americans who participated very little in freedom and democracy for most of American history, and to Washington's refusal to tolerate the rise of reformist governments in Central America.

Whether or not America ever deserved its reputation, during the last few years of the 20th century under the Bill Clinton regime and during the 21st century neoconservative regimes of George W. Bush and Barak Obama, Washington threw away America's reputation in order to better pursue its agenda of hegemony over the world.

The Soviet Union had constrained and limited American power. The collapse of the Soviet Union unleashed American hubris and arrogance. Having declared itself to be the "world's only superpower," Washington began reorganizing the world in its own interest, which Washington disguised as "bringing freedom and democracy to the world."

The September 11, 2001, attacks on the World Trade Center and on the Pentagon provided the "new Pearl Harbor" that the neoconservatives had written was necessary in order to launch their wars of conquest. The history of the 21st century has been the consequence of 9/11.

The government's account of 9/11 has been effectively challenged by 2,000 high-rise architects and structural engineers, by physicists and chemists, by firefighters and first responders, by pilots, and by numerous former government officials. No aware and informed person believes that the US national security state and the intelligent services of Washington's NATO allies and Israel's Mossad were outsmarted by a handful of Arabs operating independently of any government and intelligence service.

Washington's argument has been that terrorists must be killed "over there" before they come "over here" and attack America again. This argument has never made any sense, because Washington acknowledges that terrorists are stateless. According to Washington, almost all of the 9/11 terrorists were Saudi Arabians. Yet, Washington attacked Afghanistan and Iraq. Washington arranged the overthrow of Gaddafi in Libya despite the absence of any relationship to 9/11. Almost every day Washington murders with drones people in Pakistan and Yemen, countries with which America is not at war. Washington has sent Kenyan troops to fight Islamists in Somalia, and has sent French and Nigerian troops to Mali to fight the Washington-armed Islamists who drifted there after helping to overthrow Gaddafi.

Mao said power comes out of the barrel of a gun. Washington says freedom and democracy come out of bombings. Mao is reviled, but Washington is praised or praises itself.

The second part of Washington's argument is that in order to be safe, Americans must give up the civil liberties granted to them by the US Constitution. In order to be safe, Americans must consent to citizens being thrown into prison indefinitely without any evidence presented to a court and without any executive branch accountability to due process.

Americans must also consent to their government's murder of citizens without due process of law. Mere suspicion or unproven accusation by some unaccountable executive branch official is enough to snuff out the life and liberty of American citizens and to confiscate all of their property and assets.

To be safe, Americans must also consent to being spied on—every email, every Internet site visited, every telephone call, every letter written, every credit card used and purchase made, as William Binney and Edward Snowden have proven. On September 28, 2013, *The New York Times* reported that the NSA is even mapping the social connections of US citizens. Washington's argument is that unless Americans accept the most complete police state in human history, they are not safe.

Consequently, today no American is safe from his own government.

In public discourse in the United States facts are no longer permitted. Propaganda reigns. Washington, despite conclusive evidence to the contrary, ruled that Saddam Hussein in Iraq possessed "weapons of mass destruction" and that his possession of such weapons justified Washington's invasion of Iraq.

When chemical weapons were used in Syria, Washington instantly blamed the Assad government and attempted to organize support for intervening against the secular Syrian government in behalf of the Islamists. Washington claimed to have conclusive evidence but refused to share it. The ploy did not work. The world saw through it. The Russian government challenged it.

The British Parliament, long an American puppet, voted against Obama's war against Syria, declaring that Great Britain would not serve as cover for another American war crime. All of NATO except the French "socialist" president abandoned Obama's war scheme, as did the American people and the US Congress.

Putin, the President of Russia, stated publicly that US Secretary of State John Kerry "is lying and knows that he is lying. It is sad."

At this time of writing, the world seems to be coming to the conclusion that the US is not what it pretends to be. Instead, America is a malevolent force that brings the threat of a Third World War to humanity.

Russia, the voice for peace, has tied down the US government in a UN resolution that ratifies Syria's agreement to turn over all chemical weapons for destruction and that prevents the use of force against Syria. The criminal Obama regime fought this peace initiative with all its power and with all its purchased governments; yet Russia prevailed.[1]

The columns in this collection from August 2008 through December 2013 document America's descent into a Stasi Police State domestically and into a warfare state whose aim is world domination. The individual incidents and travesties presented in this collection are most likely forgotten, assuming Americans ever knew of them. When massed together they document the descent of the US into the lawlessness of tyranny. There is some repetition. I was faced with the decision to eliminate the repetition so that the individual selections would read more like chapters in a book or to leave the repetition so that the individual selections could stand independently of the book as a whole. I decided to retain the individual selections largely as written as that presents the reader both with a book and with a collection of essays.

As I write the President of Brazil, an enormous and rich country, has denounced Washington before the United Nations for "violations of international law." The presidents of Bolivia and Venezuela are bringing a lawsuit against the US for "human rights violations." Russia distrusts every word said by Washington, and China regards Washington as a crazed entity.

Only a few of the bought-and-paid-for British and European politicians stand by Washington. But can the governments of NATO members, who are subject to the International Criminal Court, afford to take the risk of being in the dock for their complicity in Washington's war crimes?

These foolish politicians allied with Washington need to wake up. Washington does not represent the American people. Washington represents about six powerful private interest groups. Washington cannot even govern America, must less the world. As I write, the US government has been shut down, because the two corrupt political parties cannot agree who pays in order to close an annual budget deficit that requires the Federal Reserve to create new money with which to purchase $1,000 billion bonds per annum.

The Republicans want the poor to pay. The Democrats partly agree, but want to issue more debt with which to pay. America's power resides in being the world reserve currency, but America is printing dollars at a rate that vastly exceeds the demand for new dollars. As neither party is willing to terminate America's multi-trillion dollar wars, it is only a matter of time before flight from the US dollar begins. With this flight comes the end of American power. The end of American power is a prerequisite for world peace.

AMERICAN INSOUCIANCE

August 7, 2008

Now that military officers selected by the Bush Pentagon have reached a split verdict convicting Salim Hamdan, a one-time driver for Osama bin Laden, of supporting terrorism, but innocent of terrorist conspiracy, do you feel safe?

Or are we superpower Americans still at risk until we capture bin Laden's dentist, barber, and the person who installed the carpet in his living room?

The Bush Regime with its comic huffings and puffings is unaware that it has made itself the laughing stock of the world, a comedy version of the Third Reich.

Hamdan was not defended by the slick lawyers that got O.J. Simpson off, and he most certainly did not have a jury of his peers. Hamdan was defended by a Pentagon appointed US Navy officer, and his jurors were all Pentagon appointed US military officers with an eye on their careers. Even in this Kangaroo Court, Hamdan was cleared of the main charge.

The US Navy officer who was Hamdan's appointed attorney is certainly no terrorist sympathizer. Yet even this United States officer said that the rules Bush designed for the military tribunals were designed to achieve convictions.[2] He also said that the judge allowed evidence that would not have been admitted by any civilian or military US court. He said that the interrogations of Hamdan, which comprised the basis of the Bush Regime's case, were tainted by coercive tactics, including sleep deprivation and solitary confinement.

Does this make you a proud American?

Do you think you are made more safe when you stand there while "your" government implements its own version of Joseph Stalin's show trials?

The trial and conviction of Hamdan has made every American very unsafe.

The one certain fact about US law is that it is expanded until it applies to everyone. Consider RICO, for example, the asset freeze law that was intended only in criminal cases involving the Mafia; it wasn't long before RICO found its way into civil divorce proceedings.

Bush's multi-year, multi-billion dollar "war on terror" has been reduced to railroading a low-level employee, a driver, for "terrorism."

One would hope that the Hamdan verdict would be enough shame and ridicule for the US in one day. But no, Bush didn't stop there. On his way to the Beijing Olympics, President Bush expressed "deep concerns" for the state of human rights in China.

But not in Guantanamo, nor in Abu Ghraib, nor in the CIA's torture dungeons used for "renditions," nor in Iraq and Afghanistan where the US is expert at bombing weddings, funerals, children's soccer games, and every assortment of civilians imaginable.

As the good book says, clean the beam from your own eye before pointing to the mote in your brother's eye.

But Americans, the salt of the earth, have neither beams nor motes. We are the virtuous few, ordained by God to impose our hegemony on the world. It is written, or so say the neocons.

What would President Bush say if, heaven forbid, the Chinese were as rude as he is and asked Mr. Superpower why the land of "freedom and democracy" has one million names on a watch list. China with a population four times as large doesn't have a watch list with one million names.

What would President Bush say if China asked him why the US, with a population one-fourth the size of China's has hundreds of thousands more of its citizens in prison? The percentage of Americans in prison is far higher than in China and is a larger absolute number.

What would President Bush say if China asked him why he used lies and deception to justify his invasion of Iraq. China, unlike Bush, is not responsible for 1.2 million dead Iraqis and 4 million displaced Iraqis.

China's human rights policy is not perfect. China's greatest human rights failing is that China is the Bush Regime's prime enabler of its war crimes and human rights abuses in Iraq and Afghanistan. By financing Bush's budget deficit, China is financing Bush's gratuitous wars. Indeed, China can be said to finance the weaponry that the US gives Israel to enable the suppression of the Palestinians and with which to bomb the civilian population of Lebanon.

China is a serious human rights abuser, because China is complicit in Bush's human rights abuses.

If we are honest about who is actually murdering and abusing people, it is the US, Israel, and the UK. There's your "axis of evil."

WHO WILL STAND UP TO AMERICA AND ISRAEL?

May 28, 2009

"Obama Calls on World to 'Stand Up to' North Korea" read the headline.[2] The United States, Obama said, was determined to protect "the peace and security of the world."

Shades of doublespeak, doublethink, *1984*.

North Korea is a small place. China alone could snuff it out in a few minutes. Yet the president of the U.S. thinks that nothing less than the entire world is a match for North Korea.

We are witnessing the Washington gangsters construct yet another threat like Slobodan Milosevic, Osama bin Laden, Saddam Hussein, John Walker Lindh, Yaser Hamdi, José Padilla, Sami al-Arian, Hamas, Mahmoud Ahmadinejad, and the hapless detainees demonized by former secretary of defense Rumsfeld as "the 760 most dangerous terrorists on the face of the earth," who were tortured for six years at Gitmo only to be quietly released. Just another mistake, sorry.

The military/security complex that rules America, together with the Israel Lobby and the banksters, needs a long list of dangerous enemies to keep the taxpayers' money flowing into its coffers.

The Homeland Security lobby is dependent on endless threats to convince Americans that they must forgo civil liberty in order to be safe and secure.

The real question: who is going to stand up to the American and Israeli governments?

Who is going to protect Americans' and Israelis' civil liberties, especially those of Israeli dissenters and Israel's Arab citizens?

Who is going to protect Palestinians, Iraqis, Afghans, Lebanese, Iranians, and Syrians from Americans and Israelis?

Not Obama, and not the right-wing brownshirts who today rule Israel.

Obama's notion that it takes the entire world to stand up to North Korea is mind-boggling, but this mind-boggling idea pales in comparison to Obama's guarantee that America will protect "the peace and security of the world."

Is this the same America that bombed Serbia, including Chinese diplomatic offices and civilian passenger trains, and pried Kosovo loose from Serbia and gave it to a gang of Muslim drug lords, lending them NATO troops to protect their operation?

Is this the same America that is responsible for approximately 1 million dead Iraqis, leaving orphans and widows everywhere and turning one-fifth of the Iraqi population into refugees?

Is this the same America that blocked the rest of the world from condemning Israel for its murderous attack on Lebanese civilians in 2006 and on Gazans most recently, the same America that has covered up for Israel's theft of Palestine over the past 60 years, a theft that has produced 4 million Palestinian refugees driven by Israeli violence and terror from their homes and villages?

Is this the same America that is conducting military exercises in former constituent parts of Russia and ringing Russia with missile bases?

Is this the same America that has bombed Afghanistan into rubble with massive civilian casualties?

Is this the same America that has started a horrific new war in Pakistan, a war that in its first few days has produced 1 million refugees?

"The peace and security of the world"? Whose world?

On his return from his consultation with Obama in Washington, the brownshirted Israeli Prime Minister Benjamin Netanyahu declared that it was Israel's responsibility to "eliminate" the "nuclear threat" from Iran.

What nuclear threat? The U.S. intelligence agencies are unanimous in their conclusion that Iran has had no nuclear weapons program since 2003. The inspectors of the International Atomic Energy Agency report that there is no sign of a nuclear weapons program in Iran.

Whom is Iran bombing? How many refugees is Iran sending fleeing for their lives?

Whom is North Korea bombing?

The two great murderous, refugee-producing countries are the U.S. and Israel. Between them, they have murdered and dislocated millions of people who were a threat to no one.

No countries on earth rival the U.S. and Israel for barbaric, murderous violence.

But Obama gives assurances that the U.S. will protect "the peace and security of the world." And the brownshirt Netanyahu assures the world that Israel will save it from the "Iranian threat."

Where is the media?

Why aren't people laughing their heads off?

ARE THE IRANIAN PROTESTS ANOTHER US ORCHESTRATED "COLOR" REVOLUTION?

June 19, 2009

A number of commentators have expressed their idealistic belief in the purity of Mousavi, Montazeri, and the westernized youth of Tehran. The CIA destabilization plan, announced two years ago (see below) has somehow not contaminated unfolding events.

The claim is made that Ahmadinejad stole the election, because the outcome was declared too soon after the polls closed for all the votes to have been counted. However, Mousavi declared his victory several hours before the polls closed. This is classic CIA destabilization designed to discredit a contrary outcome. It forces an early declaration of the vote. The longer the time interval between the preemptive declaration of victory and the release of the vote tally, the longer Mousavi has to create the impression that the authorities are using the time to fix the vote. It is amazing that people don't see through this trick.

As for the grand ayatollah Montazeri's charge that the election was stolen, he was the initial choice to succeed Khomeini, but lost out to the current Supreme Leader. He sees in the protests an opportunity to settle the score with Khamenei. Montazeri has the incentive to challenge the election whether or not he is being manipulated by the CIA, which has a successful history of manipulating disgruntled politicians.

There is a power struggle among the ayatollahs. Many are aligned against Ahmadinejad because he accuses them of corruption, thus playing to the Iranian countryside where Iranians believe the ayatollahs' lifestyles indicate an excess of power and money. In my opinion, Ahmadinejad's attack on the ayatollahs is opportunistic. However, it does make it odd for his American detractors to say he is a conservative reactionary lined up with the ayatollahs.

Commentators are "explaining" the Iranian elections based on their own illusions, delusions, emotions, and vested interests. Whether or not the poll results predicting Ahmadinejad's win are sound, there is, so far, no evidence beyond surmise that the election was stolen. However, there are credible reports that the CIA has been working for two years to destabilize the Iranian government.

On May 23, 2007, Brian Ross and Richard Esposito reported on ABC News: "The CIA has received secret presidential approval to mount a covert "black" operation to destabilize the Iranian government, current and former officials in the intelligence community tell ABC News."

On May 27, 2007, the London *Telegraph* independently reported: "Mr. Bush has signed an official document endorsing CIA plans for a propaganda and disinformation campaign intended to destabilize, and eventually topple, the theocratic rule of the mullahs."

A few days previously, the *Telegraph* reported on May 16, 2007, that Bush administration neocon warmonger John Bolton told the *Telegraph* that a US military attack on Iran would "be a 'last option' after economic sanctions and attempts to foment a popular revolution had failed."

On June 29, 2008, Seymour Hersh reported in *The New Yorker*: "Late last year, Congress agreed to a request from President Bush to fund a major escalation of covert operations against Iran, according to current and former military, intelligence, and congressional sources. These operations, for which the President sought up to four hundred million dollars, were described in a Presidential Finding signed by Bush, and are designed to destabilize the country's religious leadership."

The protests in Tehran no doubt have many sincere participants. The protests also have the hallmarks of the CIA orchestrated protests in Georgia and Ukraine. It requires total blindness not to see this.

Daniel McAdams has made some telling points.[3] For example, neoconservative Kenneth Timmerman wrote the day before the election that "there's talk of a 'green revolution' in Tehran." How would Timmerman know that unless it was an orchestrated plan? Why would there be a 'green revolution' prepared prior to the vote, especially if Mousavi and his supporters were as confident of victory as they claimed? This looks like definite evidence that the US is involved in the election protests.

Timmerman goes on to write that "the National Endowment for Democracy has spent millions of dollars promoting 'color' revolutions . . . Some of that money appears to have made it into the hands of pro-Mousavi groups, who have ties to non-governmental organizations outside Iran that the National Endowment for Democracy funds." Timmerman's own neocon Foundation for Democracy is "a private, non-profit organization established in 1995 with grants from the National Endowment for Democracy (NED), to promote democracy and internationally-recognized standards of human rights in Iran."

WHY NOT CRIPPLING SANCTIONS FOR ISRAEL AND THE US?

August 31, 2009

In Israel, a country stolen from the Palestinians, fanatics control the government. One of the fanatics is the prime minister, Benjamin Netanyahu. Last week Netanyahu called for "crippling sanctions" against Iran.

The kind of blockade that Netanyahu wants qualifies as an act of war. Israel has long threatened to attack Iran on its own but prefers to draw in the US and NATO.

Why does Israel want to initiate a war between the United States and Iran?

Is Iran attacking other countries, bombing civilians and destroying civilian infrastructure? No. These are crimes committed by Israel and the US. Is Iran evicting peoples from lands they have occupied for centuries and herding them into ghettoes? No, that's what Israel has been doing to the Palestinians for 60 years.

What is Iran doing?

Iran is developing nuclear energy, which is its right as a signatory to the Non-Proliferation Treaty. Iran's nuclear energy program is subject to inspections by the International Atomic Energy Agency (IAEA), which consistently reports that its inspections find no diversion of enriched uranium to a weapons program.

The position taken by Israel, and by Israel's puppet in Washington, is that Iran must not be allowed to have the rights as a signatory to the Non-Proliferation Treaty that every other signatory has, because Iran might divert enriched uranium to a weapons program.

In other words, Israel and the US claim the right to abrogate Iran's right to develop nuclear energy. The Israeli/US position has no basis in international law or in anything other than the arrogance of Israel and the United States.

The hypocrisy is extreme. Israel is not a signatory to the Non-Proliferation Treaty and developed its nuclear weapons illegally on the sly, with, as far as we know, US help.

As Israel is an illegal possessor of nuclear weapons and has a fanatical government that is capable of using them, crippling sanctions should be applied to Israel to force it to disarm.

Israel qualifies for crippling sanctions for another reason. It is an apartheid state, as former US President Jimmy Carter demonstrated in his book, *Palestine: Peace Not Apartheid.*

The US led the imposition of sanctions against South Africa because of South Africa's apartheid practices. The sanctions forced the white government to hand over political power to the black population. Israel practices a worse form of apartheid than did the white South African government. Yet, Israel maintains that it is "anti-semitic" to criticize Israel for a practice that the world regards as abhorrent. What remains of the Palestinian West Bank that has not been stolen by Israel consists of isolated ghettoes. Palestinians are cut off from hospitals, schools, their farms, and from one another. They cannot travel from one ghetto to another without Israeli permission enforced at checkpoints.

The Israeli government's explanation for its gross violation of human rights comprises the greatest collection of lies in world history. No one, with the exception of American Christian Zionists and Zionist Jews believes one word of it.

The United States also qualifies for crippling sanctions. Indeed, the US is over-qualified. On the basis of lies and intentional deception of the US Congress, the US public, the UN and NATO, the US government invaded Afghanistan and Iraq, and used the "war on terror" that Washington orchestrated to overturn US civil liberties enshrined in the US Constitution. One million Iraqis have paid with their lives for America's crimes and four million are displaced. Iraq and its infrastructure are in ruins, and Iraq's professional elites, necessary to a modern organized society, are dead or dispersed. The US government has committed a war crime on a grand scale. If Iran qualifies for sanctions, the US qualifies a thousand times over.

No one knows how many women, children, and village elders have been murdered by the US in Afghanistan. However, the American war of aggression against the Afghan people is now in its ninth year. According to the US military, an American victory is still a long ways away. Admiral Michael Mullen, Chairman of the US Joint Chiefs of Staff, declared in August that the military situation in Afghanistan is "serious and deteriorating."

Older Americans can look forward to the continuation of this war for the rest of their lives, while their Social Security and Medicare rights are reduced in order to free up funds for the US armaments industry. Bush/Cheney and Obama/Biden have made munitions the only safe stock investment in the United States.

What is the purpose of the war of aggression against Afghanistan? Soon after his inauguration, President Obama promised to provide an answer but did not. Instead, Obama quickly escalated the war in Afghanistan and launched a new one in Pakistan that has already displaced 2 million Pakistanis. Obama has sent 21,000 more US troops into Afghanistan and already the US commander in Afghanistan, General Stanley McChrystal, is requesting 20,000 more.

Obama is escalating America's war of aggression against the Afghani people despite three high profile opinion polls that show that the American public is firmly opposed to the continuation of the war against Afghanistan.

Sadly, the ironclad agreement between Israel and Washington to make war against Muslim peoples is far stronger than the connection between the American public and the American government.

At a farewell dinner party last Thursday for Israel's military attaché in Washington, who is returning to Israel to become deputy chief of staff of the Israeli military, Admiral Mike Mullen, chairman of the US Joint Chiefs of Staff, Undersecretary of Defense Michele Flournoy, and Dan Shapiro, who is in charge of Middle East Affairs on the National Security Council, were present to pay their respects.

Admiral Mullen declared that the US will always stand with Israel. No matter how many war crimes Israel commits. No matter how many women and children Israel murders. No matter how many Palestinians Israel drives from their homes, villages, and lands.

If truth could be told, the true axis-of-evil is the United States and Israel.

Millions of Americans are now homeless because of foreclosures. Millions more have lost their jobs, and even more millions have no access to health care. Yet, the US government continues to squander hundreds of billions of dollars on wars that serve no US purpose. President Obama and General McChrystal have taken the position that they know best, the American public be damned.

It could not be made any clearer that the President of the United States and the US military have no regard whatsoever for democracy, human rights, and international law. This is yet another reason to apply crippling sanctions against Washington, a government that has emerged under Bush/ Obama as a brownshirt state that deals in lies, torture, murder, war crimes, and deception.

Many governments are complicit in America's war crimes. With Obama's budget deep in the red, Washington's wars of naked aggression are dependent on financing by the Chinese, Japanese, Russians, Saudis, South Koreans, Indians, Canadians and Europeans through their purchase of US debt. The second this foreign financing of American war crimes stops, America's wars of aggression against Muslims stop.

The US is not a forever "superpower" that can indefinitely ignore its own laws and international law. The US will eventually fall as a result of its hubris, arrogance, and imperial overreach. When the American Empire collapses, will its enablers also be held accountable in the war crimes court?

ANOTHER WAR IN THE WORKS: AMERICA IS LED AND INFORMED BY LIARS

September 29, 2009

Does anyone remember all the lies that they were told by President Bush and the "mainstream media" about the grave threat to America from weapons of mass destruction in Iraq? These lies were repeated endlessly in the print and TV media despite the reports from the weapons inspectors, who had been sent to Iraq, that no such weapons existed.

The weapons inspectors did an honest job in Iraq and told the truth, but the mainstream media did not emphasize their findings. Instead, the media served as a Ministry of Propaganda, beating the war drums for the US government.

Now the whole process is repeating itself. This time the target is Iran.

As there is no real case against Iran, Obama took a script from Bush's playbook and fabricated one.

First the facts: As a signatory to the non-proliferation treaty, Iran's nuclear facilities are open to inspection by the International Atomic Energy Agency, which carefully monitors Iran's nuclear energy program to make certain that no material is diverted to nuclear weapons.

The IAEA has monitored Iran's nuclear energy program and has announced repeatedly that it has found no diversion of nuclear material to a weapons program. Every US intelligence agency has affirmed and reaffirmed that Iran abandoned interest in nuclear weapons years ago.

In keeping with the safeguard agreement that the IAEA be informed before an enrichment facility comes online, Iran informed the IAEA on September 21 that it had a new nuclear facility under construction. By informing the IAEA, Iran fulfilled its obligations under the safeguards agreement. The IAEA will inspect the facility and monitor the nuclear material produced to make sure it is not diverted to a weapons program.

Despite these unequivocal facts, Obama announced on September 25 that Iran has been caught with a "secret nuclear facility" with which to produce a bomb that would threaten the world.

The Obama regime's claim that Iran is not in compliance with the safeguards agreement is disinformation. Between the end of 2004 and early 2007, Iran voluntarily complied with an additional protocol (Code 3.1) that was never ratified and never became a legal part of the safeguards agreement. The additional protocol would have required Iran to notify the IAEA prior to beginning construction of a new facility, whereas the safeguards agreement in force requires notification prior to completion of a new facility. Iran ceased its voluntary compliance with the unratified additional protocol in March 2007,[4] most likely because of the American and Israeli misrepresentations of Iran's existing facilities and military threats against them.

By accusing Iran of having a secret "nuclear weapons program" and demanding that Iran "come clean" about the nonexistent program, adding that he does not rule out a military attack on Iran, Obama mimics the discredited Bush regime's use of nonexistent Iraqi "weapons of mass destruction" to set up Iraq for invasion.

The US media, even the "liberal" National Public Radio, quickly fell in with the Obama lie machine. Steven Thomma of the McClatchy Newspapers declared the non-operational facility under construction, which Iran reported to the IAEA, to be "a secret nuclear facility."

Thomma reported incorrectly that the world didn't learn of Iran's "secret" facility, the one that Iran had reported to the IAEA the previous Monday, until Obama announced it in a joint appearance in Pittsburgh the following Friday with British Prime Minister Gordon Brown and French President Nicolas Sarkoszy.

Obviously, Thomma has no command over the facts, a routine inadequacy of "mainstream media" reporters. The new facility was revealed when Iran voluntarily reported the facility to the IAEA on September 21.

Ali Akbar Dareini, an Associated Press writer, reported, incorrectly, over AP: "The presence of a second uranium-enrichment site that could potentially produce material for a nuclear weapon has provided one of the strongest indications yet that Iran has something to hide."

Dareini goes on to write that "the existence of the secret site was first revealed by Western intelligence officials and diplomats on Friday." Dareini is mistaken. We learned of the facility when the IAEA announced that Iran had reported the facility the previous Monday in keeping with the safeguards agreement.

Dareini's untruthful report of "a secret underground uranium enrichment facility whose existence has been hidden from international inspectors for years" helped to heighten the orchestrated alarm.

There you have it. The president of the United States and his European puppets are doing what they do best—lying through their teeth. The US "mainstream media" repeats the lies as if they were facts. The US "media" is again making itself an accomplice to wars based on fabrications. Apparently, the media's main interest is to please the US government and hopefully obtain a taxpayer bailout of its failing print operations.

Dr. Mohamed ElBaradei, Director General of the International Atomic Energy Agency, a rare man of principle who has not sold his integrity to the US and Israeli governments, refuted in his report (September 7, 2009) the baseless "accusations that information has been withheld from the Board of Governors about Iran's nuclear programme. I am dismayed by the allegations of some Member states, which have been fed to the media, that information has been withheld from the Board. These allegations are politically motivated and totally baseless. Such attempts to influence the work of the Secretariat and undermine its independence and objectivity are in violation of Article VII.F. of the IAEA Statute and should cease forthwith."

As there is no legal basis for action against Iran, the Obama regime is creating another hoax, like the non-existent "Iraqi weapons of mass destruction." The hoax is that a facility, reported to the IAEA by Iran, is a secret facility for making nuclear weapons.

Just as the factual reports from the weapons inspectors in Iraq were ignored by the Bush Regime, the factual reports from the IAEA are ignored by the Obama Regime.

Like the Bush Regime, the Middle East policy of the Obama Regime is based on lies and deception.

Who is the worst enemy of the American people, Iran or the government in Washington and the media whores who serve it?

WARMONGER WINS PEACE PRIZE

October 10, 2009

It took 25 years longer than George Orwell thought for the slogans of *1984* to become reality.

"War is Peace," "Freedom is Slavery," "Ignorance is Strength."

I would add, "Lie is Truth."

The Nobel Committee has awarded the 2009 Peace Prize to President Obama, the person who started a new war in Pakistan, upped the war in Afghanistan, and continues to threaten Iran with attack unless Iran does what the US government demands and relinquishes its rights as a signatory to the non-proliferation treaty.

The Nobel committee chairman, Thorbjoern Jagland, said, "Only very rarely has a person to the same extent as Obama captured the world's attention and given its people hope for a better future." Obama, the committee gushed, has created "a new climate in international politics."

Tell that to the 2 million displaced Pakistanis and the unknown numbers of dead ones that Obama has racked up in his few months in office. Tell that to the Afghans where civilian deaths continue to mount as Obama's "war of necessity" drones on interminably.

No Bush policy has changed. Iraq is still occupied. The Guantanamo torture prison is still functioning. Rendition and assassinations are still occurring. Spying on Americans without warrants is still the order of the day. Civil liberties are continuing to be violated in the name of Oceania's "war on terror."

Apparently, the Nobel committee is suffering from the delusion that, being a minority, Obama is going to put a stop to Western hegemony over darker-skinned peoples.

The non-cynical can say that the Nobel committee is seizing on Obama's rhetoric to lock him into the pursuit of peace instead of war. We can all hope that it works. But the more likely result is that the award has made "War is Peace" a reality.

Obama has done nothing to hold the criminal Bush regime to account, and the Obama administration has bribed and threatened the

Palestinian Authority to go along with the US/Israeli plan to deep-six the UN's Goldstone Report on Israeli war crimes committed during Israel's inhuman military attack on the defenseless civilian population in the Gaza Ghetto during Operation Cast Lead.

The US Ministry of Truth is delivering the Obama administration's propaganda that Iran only notified the IAEA of its "secret" new nuclear facility because Iran discovered that US intelligence had discovered the "secret" facility. This propaganda is designed to undercut the fact of Iran's compliance with the Safeguards Agreement and to continue the momentum for a military attack on Iran.

The Nobel committee has placed all its hopes on a bit of skin color.

"War is Peace" is now the position of the formerly antiwar organization, Code Pink.

Code Pink has decided that women's rights are worth a war in Afghanistan.

When justifications for war become almost endless—oil, hegemony, women's rights, democracy, revenge for 9/11, denying bases to al Qaeda and protecting against terrorists—war becomes the path to peace.

The Nobel committee has bestowed the prestige of its Peace Prize on Newspeak and Doublethink.

THE EVIL EMPIRE

November 7, 2009

The US government is now so totally under the thumbs of organized interest groups that "our" government can no longer respond to the concerns of the American people who elect the president and the members of the House and Senate. Will voters vent their frustrations over their impotence on the president, which implies a future of one-term presidents? Will our presidents soon be as ineffective as Roman emperors in the final days of that empire?

Obama promised change, but has delivered none. His health care bill is being written by the private insurance companies seeking greater profits. The most likely outcome will be cuts in Medicare in order to help fund ObamaCare and wars that enrich the military/security complex and the many companies created by privatizing services that the military once provided for itself at lower costs. It would be interesting to know the percentage of the $700+ billion "defense" spending that goes to private companies. In American "capitalism," an amazing amount of taxpayers' earnings go to private firms via the government. Yet, Republicans scream about "socializing" health care.

Republicans and Democrats saw opportunities to create new sources of campaign contributions by privatizing as many military functions as possible. There are now a large number of private companies that have never made a dollar in the market, feeding instead at the public trough that drains taxpayers of dollars while loading Americans with debt service obligations.

Obama inherited an excellent opportunity to bring US soldiers home from the Bush regime's illegal wars of aggression. In its final days, the Bush regime realized that it could "win" in Iraq by putting the Sunni insurgents on the US military payroll. Once Bush had 80,000 insurgents collecting US military pay, violence, although still high, dropped in half. All Obama had to do was to declare victory and bring our boys home, thanking Bush for winning the war. It would have shut up the Republicans.

But this sensible course would have impaired the profits and share prices of those firms that comprise the military/security complex. So instead of doing what he said he would do and what the voters elected him to do,

Obama restarted the war in Afghanistan and launched a new one in Pakistan. Soon Obama was echoing Bush and Cheney's threats to attack Iran.

In place of health care for Americans, there will be more profits for private insurance companies.

In place of peace there will be more war.

Voters are already recognizing the writing on the wall and are falling away from Obama and the Democrats. Independents who gave Obama his comfortable victory have now swung against him, recently electing Republican governors in New Jersey and Virginia to succeed Democrats. This is a protest vote, not a confidence vote in Republicans.

Obama's credibility is shot. And so is that of Congress, assuming it ever had any. The US House of Representatives has just voted to show the entire world that the US House of Representatives is nothing but the servile, venal, puppet of the Israel Lobby. The House of Representatives of the American "superpower" did the bidding of its master, AIPAC, and voted 344 to 36 to condemn the Goldstone Report.

In case you don't know, the Goldstone Report is the Report of the United Nations Fact Finding Mission on the Gaza Conflict. The "Gaza Conflict" is the Israeli military attack on the Gaza ghetto, where 1.5 million dispossessed Palestinians, whose lands, villages, and homes were stolen by Israel, are housed. The attack was on civilians and civilian infrastructure. It was without any doubt a war crime under the Nuremberg standard that the US established in order to execute Nazis.

Goldstone is not only a very distinguished Jewish jurist who has given his life to bringing people to accountability for their crimes against humanity, but also a Zionist. However, the Israelis have demonized him as a "self-hating Jew" because he wrote the truth instead of Israeli propaganda.

US Representative Dennis Kucinich, who is now without a doubt a marked man on AIPAC's political extermination list, asked the House if the members had any realization of the shame that the vote condemning Goldstone would bring on the House and the US government. The entire rest of the world accepts the Goldstone report.

The House answered with its lopsided vote that the rest of the world doesn't count as it doesn't give campaign contributions to members of Congress.

This shameful, servile act of "the world's greatest democracy" occurred the very week that a court in Italy convicted 23 US CIA officers for kidnapping a person in Italy. The CIA agents are now considered "fugitives from justice" in Italy, and indeed they are.

The kidnapped person was renditioned to the American puppet state of Egypt, where the victim was held for years and repeatedly tortured. The case against him was so absurd that even an Egyptian judge ordered his release.

One of the convicted CIA operatives, Sabrina deSousa, an attractive young woman, says that the US broke the law by kidnapping a person and sending him to another country to be tortured in order to manufacture another "terrorist" in order to keep the terrorist hoax going at home. Without the terrorist hoax, America's wars for special interest reasons would become transparent even to Fox "News" junkies.

Ms. deSousa says that "everything I did was approved back in Washington," yet the government, which continually berates us to "support the troops," did nothing to protect her when she carried out the Bush regime's illegal orders.

Clearly, this means that the crime that Bush, Cheney, the Pentagon, and the CIA ordered is too heinous and beyond the pale to be justified, even by memos from the despicable John Yoo and the Republican Federalist Society.

Ms. deSousa is clearly worried about herself. But where is her concern for the innocent person that she sent into an Egyptian hell to be tortured until death or admission of being a terrorist? The remorse deSousa expresses is only for herself. She did her evil government's bidding and her evil government that she so faithfully served turned its back on her. She has no remorse for the evil she committed against an innocent person.

Perhaps deSousa and her 22 colleagues grew up on video games. It was great fun to plot to kidnap a real person and fly him on a CIA plane to Egypt. Was it like a fisherman catching a fish or a deer hunter killing a beautiful 8-point buck? Clearly, they got their jollies at the expense of their renditioned victim.

The finding of the Italian court, and keep in mind that Italy is a bought-and-paid-for US puppet state, indicates that even our bought puppets are finding the US too much to stomach.

Moving from the tip of the iceberg down, we have Ambassador Craig Murray, rector of the University of Dundee and until 2004 the UK Ambassador to Uzbekistan, which he describes as a Stalinist totalitarian state courted and supported by the Americans.

As ambassador, Murray saw the MI5 intelligence reports from the CIA that described the most horrible torture procedures. "People were raped with broken bottles, children were tortured in front of their parents until they [the parents] signed a confession, people were boiled alive."

"Intelligence" from these torture sessions was passed on by the CIA to MI5 and to Washington as proof of the vast al Qaeda conspiracy.

Ambassador Murray reports that the people delivered by CIA flights to Uzbekistan's torture prisons "were told to confess to membership in Al Qaeda. They were told to confess they'd been in training camps in Afghanistan. They were told to confess they had met Osama bin Laden in person. And the CIA intelligence constantly echoed these themes."

"I was absolutely stunned," says the British ambassador, who thought that he served a moral country that, along with its American ally, had moral integrity. The great Anglo-American bastion of democracy and human rights, the homes of the Magna Carta and the Bill of Rights, the great moral democracies that defeated Nazism and stood up to Stalin's gulags, were prepared to commit any crime in order to maximize profits.

Ambassador Murray learned too much and was fired when he vomited it all up. He saw the documents that proved that the motivation for US and UK military aggression in Afghanistan had to do with the natural gas deposits in Uzbekistan and Turkmenistan. The Americans wanted a pipeline that bypassed Russia and Iran and went through Afghanistan. To insure this, an invasion was necessary. The idiot American public could be told that the invasion was necessary because of 9/11 and to save them from "terrorism," and the utter fools would believe the lie.

"If you look at the deployment of US forces in Afghanistan, as against other NATO country forces in Afghanistan, you'll see that undoubtedly the US forces are positioned to guard the pipeline route. It's what it's about. It's about money, it's about energy, it's not about democracy."

Guess who the consultant was who arranged with then Texas governor George W. Bush the agreements that would give to Enron the rights to Uzbekistan's and Turkmenistan's natural gas deposits and to Unocal to develop the trans-Afghanistan pipeline. It was Karzai, the US-imposed "president" of Afghanistan, who has no support in the country except for American bayonets.

Ambassador Murray was dismissed from the UK Foreign Service for his revelations. No doubt on orders from Washington to our British puppet.

KHALID SHEIKH MOHAMMED'S TRIAL WILL CONVICT US ALL

November 24, 2009

Republican members of Congress and what masquerades as a "conservative" media are outraged that the Obama administration intends to try in federal court Khalid Sheikh Mohammed, the alleged mastermind of 9/11, and four alleged co-conspirators.

The Republican and right-wing rant that a trial is too good for these people proves what I have written for a number of years: Republicans and many Americans who think of themselves as conservatives have no regard for the US Constitution or for civil liberties.

They have no appreciation for the point made by Thomas Paine in his *Dissertations on First Principles of Government* (1790):

> An avidity to punish is always dangerous to liberty. It leads men to stretch, to misinterpret, and to misapply even the best of laws. He that would make his own liberty secure must guard even his enemy from oppression; for if he violates this duty he establishes a precedent that will reach to himself.

Republicans and American conservatives regard civil liberties as coddling devices for criminals and terrorists. They assume that police and prosecutors are morally pure and, in addition, never make mistakes. An accused person is guilty or government wouldn't have accused him. All of my life I have heard self-described conservatives disparage lawyers who defend criminals. Such "conservatives" live in an ideal, not real, world.

Even some of those, such as Stuart Taylor in the *National Journal*, who defend giving Mohammed a court trial do so on the grounds that there are no risks as Mohammed is certain to be convicted and that "a civilian trial will show Americans and the rest of the world that our government is sure it can prove the 9/11 defendants guilty in the fairest of all courts."

Taylor agrees that Mohammed deserves "summary execution," but that it is a good Machiavellian ploy to try Mohammed in civilian court, while dealing with cases that have "trickier evidentiary problems" in "more flexible military commissions, away from the brightest spotlights."

In other words, Stuart Taylor and the *National Journal* endorse Mohammed's trial as a show trial that will prove both America's honorable respect for fair trials and Muslim guilt for 9/11.

If, as Taylor writes, "the government's evidence is so strong," why wasn't Mohammed tried years ago? Why was he held for years and tortured–apparently water boarded 183 times–in violation of US law and the Geneva Conventions? How can the US government put a defendant on trial when its treatment of him violates US statutory law, international law, and every precept of the US legal code? Mohammed has been treated as if he were a captive of Hitler's Gestapo or Stalin's NKVD, the predecessor of the KGB. And now we are going to finish him off in a show trial.

If the barbaric treatment Mohammed has received during his captivity hasn't driven him insane, how do we know he hasn't decided to confess in order to obtain for himself for evermore the glory of the deed? How many people can claim to have outwitted the CIA, the National Security Agency and all 16 US intelligence agencies, NORAD, the Pentagon, the National Security Council, airport security (four times on one morning), US air traffic control, the US Air Force, the military Joint Chiefs of Staff, all the neocons, Mossad, and even the supposedly formidable Dick Cheney?

Considering that some Muslims will blow themselves up in order to take out a handful of Israelis or US and NATO occupation troops, the payoff that Mohammed will get out of a guilty verdict is enormous. Are we really sure we want to create a Muslim Superhero of such stature?

Originally, according to the US government, Osama bin Laden was the mastermind of 9/11. To get bin Laden is the excuse given for the US invasion of Afghanistan, which set up the invasion of Iraq. But after eight years of total failure to catch Osama bin Laden, it became absolutely necessary to convict some culprit, so the government switched Mohammed for bin Laden.

The prosecution doesn't need any evidence in order to convict Mohammed, because no judge and no jury is going to let the demonized "mastermind of 9/11" off. No judge or juror wants to be forever damned by the brainwashed American public or assassinated by right-wing crazies. Keep in mind that the kid, John Walker Lindh, termed "the American Taliban" by an ignorant and propagandistic US media, was guilty of nothing except being in the wrong place at the wrong time. Despite the complete trampling of his every right, he got 20 years on a coerced plea bargain.

The price that Mohammed will pay will be small compared to the price we Americans will pay. The outcome of Mohammed's trial will complete the transformation of the US legal system from a shield of the people into a weapon in the hands of the state. David Feige (*Slate*, Nov. 19, 2009) writes that Mohammed's statements obtained by torture will not be suppressed, that witnesses against him will not be produced ("national security"), that documents that compromise the prosecution will be redacted. At each stage of Mohammed's appeals process, higher courts will enshrine into legal precedents the denial of the Constitutional right to a speedy trial, thus enshrining indefinite detention, the denial of the right against damning pretrial publicity, thus allowing demonization prior to trial, and the denial of the right to have witnesses and documents produced, thus eviscerating a defendant's rights to exculpatory evidence and to confront adverse witnesses, The twisted logic necessary to disentangle Mohammed's torture from his confession will also be upheld and will "provide a blueprint for the government, giving them the prize they've been after all this time—a legal way both to torture and to prosecute."

It took Hitler a while to corrupt the German courts. Hitler first had to create new courts, like President George W. Bush's military tribunals, that did not require evidence, using in place of evidence hearsay, secret charges, and self-incrimination obtained by torture.

Every American should be concerned that the Obama administration has decided to use Mohammed's trial to complete the corruption of the American court system. When Mohammed's trial is over, an American Joe Stalin or Adolf Hitler will be able to convict America's Founding Fathers on charges of treason and terrorism. No one will be safe.

THE OBAMA
PUPPET

December 3, 2009

It didn't take the Israel Lobby very long to bring President Obama to heel regarding his prohibition against further illegal Israeli settlements on occupied Palestinian land. Obama discovered that a mere American president is powerless when confronted by the Israel Lobby and that the United States simply is not allowed a Middle East policy separate from Israel's.

Obama also found out that he cannot change anything else either, if he ever intended to do so.

The military/security lobby has war and a domestic police state on its agenda, and a mere American president can't do anything about it.

President Obama can order the Guantanamo torture chamber closed and kidnapping and rendition and torture to be halted, but no one carries out the order.

Essentially, Obama is irrelevant.

President Obama can promise that he is going to bring the troops home, and the military lobby says, "No, you are going to send them to Afghanistan, and in the meantime start a war in Pakistan and maneuver Iran into a position that will provide an excuse for a war there, too. Wars are too profitable for us to let you stop them."

And the mere president has to say, "Yes, Sir!"

Obama can promise health care to 50 million uninsured Americans, but he can't override the veto of the war lobby and the insurance lobby. The war lobby says its war profits are more important than health care and that the country can't afford both the "war on terror" and "socialized medicine."

The insurance lobby says health care has to be provided by private health insurance; otherwise, we can't afford it.

The war and insurance lobbies rattled their campaign contribution pocketbooks and quickly convinced Congress and the White House that the real purpose of the health care bill is to save money by cutting Medicare benefits, thereby "getting entitlements under control."

Entitlements is a right-wing word used to cast aspersion on the few things that the government did, in the distant past, for citizens. Social Security and Medicare, for example, are denigrated as "entitlements." The right-wing goes on endlessly about Social Security and Medicare as if they were welfare giveaways to shiftless people who refuse to look after themselves, whereas in actual fact citizens are vastly overcharged for the meager benefits with a 15% tax on their wages and salaries.

Indeed, for decades now the federal government has been funding its wars and military budgets with the surplus revenues collected by the Social Security tax on labor.

To claim, as the right-wing does, that we can't afford the only thing in the entire budget that has consistently produced a revenue surplus indicates that the real agenda is to drive the mere citizen into the ground.

The real entitlements are never mentioned. The "defense" budget is an entitlement for the military/security complex about which President Eisenhower warned us 50 years ago. A person has to be crazy to believe that the United States, "the world's only superpower," protected by oceans on its East and West and by puppet states on its North and South, needs a "defense" budget larger than the military spending of the rest of the world combined.

The military budget is nothing but an entitlement for the military/security complex. To hide this fact, the entitlement is disguised as protection against "enemies" and passed through the Pentagon.

I say cut out the middleman and simply allocate a percentage of the federal budget to the military/security complex. This way we won't have to concoct reasons for invading other countries and go to war in order for the military/security complex to get its entitlement. It would be a lot cheaper just to give them the money outright, and it would save a lot of lives and grief at home and abroad.

The US invasion of Iraq had nothing whatsoever to do with American national interests. It had to do with armaments profits and with eliminating an obstacle to Israeli territorial expansion. The cost of the war, aside from the $3 trillion, was over 4,000 dead Americans, over 30,000 wounded and maimed Americans, tens of thousands of broken American marriages and lost careers, one million dead Iraqis, four million displaced Iraqis, and a destroyed country.

All of this was done for the profits of the military/security complex and to make paranoid Israel, armed with 200 nuclear weapons, feel "secure."

My proposal would make the military/security complex even more wealthy as the companies would get the money without having to produce the weapons. Instead, all the money could go for multi-million dollar bonuses and dividend payouts to shareholders. No one, at home or abroad, would have to be killed, and the taxpayer would be better off.

No American national interest is served by the war in Afghanistan. As the former UK Ambassador Craig Murray disclosed, the purpose of the war is to protect Unocal's interest in the Trans-Afghanistan pipeline. The cost of the war is many times greater than Unocal's investment in the pipeline. The obvious solution is to buy out Unocal and give the pipeline to the Afghans as partial compensation for the destruction we have inflicted on that country and its population, and bring the troops home.

The reason my sensible solutions cannot be effected is that the lobbies think that their entitlements would not survive if they were made obvious. They think that if the American people knew that the wars were being fought to enrich the armaments and oil industries, the people would put a halt to the wars.

In actual fact, the American people have no say about what "their" government does. Polls of the public show that half or more of the American people do not support the wars in Iraq or Afghanistan and do not support President Obama's escalation of the war in Afghanistan. Yet, the occupations and wars continue. According to General Stanley McChrystal, the additional 40,000 troops are enough to stalemate the war, that is, to keep it going forever, the ideal situation for the armaments lobby.

The people want health care, but the government does not listen.

The people want jobs, but Wall Street wants higher priced stocks and forces American firms to offshore the jobs to countries where labor is cheaper.

The American people have no effect on anything. They can affect nothing. They have become irrelevant like Obama. And they will remain irrelevant as long as organized interest groups can purchase the US government.

The inability of the American democracy to produce any results that the voters want is a demonstrated fact. The total unresponsiveness of government to the people is conservatism's contribution to American democracy. Some years ago there was an effort to put government back into the hands of the people by constraining the ability of organized interest groups to pour enormous amounts of money into political campaigns and, thus, obligate the elected official to those whose money elected him. Conservatives said that any restraints would be a violation of the First Amendment's guarantee of free speech.

The same "protectors" of "free speech" had no objection to the Israel Lobby's passage of a "hate speech" bill, which tried to criminalized criticism of Israel's genocidal treatment of the Palestinians and continuing theft of their lands.

In less than one year, President Obama has betrayed all of his supporters and broken all of his promises. He is the total captive of the oligarchy of the ruling interest groups.

America's reputation is suffering. Russia's Putin has already compared the US to Nazi Germany, and the Chinese premier has likened the US to an irresponsible, profligate debtor.

Increasingly the rest of the world sees the US as the source of all of its problems. Germany has lost the chief of its armed forces and its defense minister, because the US convinced or pressured, by hook or crook, the German government to violate its Constitution and to send troops to fight for Unocal's interest in Afghanistan. The Germans had pretended that their troops were not really fighting, but were engaged in a "peace-keeping operation." This more or less worked until the Germans called in an air strike that murdered 100 women and children lined up for a fuel allotment.

The British are investigating their leading criminal, former prime minister Tony Blair, and his deception of his own cabinet in order to do Bush's bidding and provide some cover for Bush's illegal invasion of Iraq. The UK investigators have been denied the ability to bring criminal charges, but the issue of war based entirely on orchestrated deception and lies is getting a hearing. It will reverberate throughout the world, and the world will note that there is no corresponding investigation in the US, the country that originated the False War.

Meanwhile, the US investment banks, which have wrecked the financial stability of many governments, including that of the US, continue to control, as they have done since the Clinton administration, US economic and financial policy. The world has suffered terribly from the Wall Street gangsters, and now looks upon America with a critical eye.

The United States no longer commands the respect it enjoyed under President Ronald Reagan or President George Herbert Walker Bush. World polls show that the US and Israel are regarded as the two greatest threats to peace. Washington and Israel outrank on the most dangerous list the crazy regime in North Korea.

The world is beginning to see America as a country that needs to go away. When the dollar is over-inflated by a Washington unable to pay its bills, will the world be motivated by greed and try to save us in order to save its investments, or will it say, thank God, good riddance.

FOR PALESTINIANS, EVERY DAY IS KRISTALLNACHT

December 15, 2009

"Settlers attack West Bank mosque and burn holy Muslim books" was a London *Times* headline on December 11, 2009.

These attacks, together with the demolition of Palestinian homes, the uprooting of Palestinians' olive groves, the innumerable checkpoints that prevent Palestinians from accessing schools, work, and medical care, the Israeli Wall that denies Palestinians access to the land stolen from them, and the isolation and blockade of the Gaza Ghetto, are part of the Israeli government's policy of genocide for the Palestinians.

Note that nearly 10 years of aggressive land grabbing by Israel has taken place since this map was last updated. The question is: Who is really

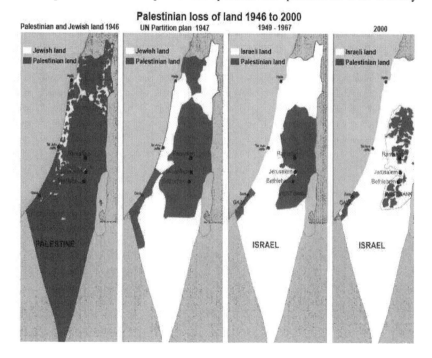

Palestinian loss of land 1946 to 2000

Palestinian and Jewish land 1946	UN Partition plan 1947	1949 - 1967	2000

wiping who off the map? The Israel Lobby has such power over America that even former President Jimmy Carter, a good friend of Israel, is demonized for using the polite term—apartheid—for the genocide that has occurred over the decades during which American "Christian" preachers, together with bought-and-paid-for politicians, justified Israel's policy of slow genocide for Palestine.

Israelis who still have a moral conscience—a small part of the population—endeavor to use moral protests against the inhumanity of the Israeli government. Israelis Jeff Halper and Angela Godfrey-Goldstein lead the Israeli Committee Against House Demolition (ICAHD), a non-violent, direct-action group established to oppose and resist Israeli demolition of Palestinian homes in the Occupied Territories.

Under international law an occupier by military force is forbidden to steal the occupied land. The US, however, has protected Israel's violation of international law for decades by vetoing UN resolutions. Israel has been able to steal Palestine from the Palestinians, because the US government used its power to prevent Israel from being held accountable under international law.

In March 2003 American citizen Rachel Corrie stood in front of an Israeli bulldozer, made by Caterpillar and sent to destroy a Palestinian home. Her courageous act of defiance was regarded as an annoyance, and she was run over and murdered by the Israeli bulldozer operator. Israel suffered no consequences for its murder of an American citizen who had a moral conscience.

In the Israeli-controlled American media, we hear endlessly that Palestinians are terrorists who strap on explosives in order to kill innocent Israelis and who terrorize Israeli towns by firing rockets into them. One look at the maps above is enough to make clear who the real terrorist is. The success of Israeli propaganda in the face of totally obvious facts damns the ignorance and unconcern of the American people.

The Israeli newspaper, *Haaretz*, which also has a moral conscience and is intelligent to boot, wrote on December 4, 2009: "Every appointee to the American government must endure a thorough background check by the American Jewish community."[5]

Haaretz notes that any American that the President of the United States proposes for an appointment to his government is subject to the approval of the Israel Lobby, which can blackball appointees at will.

Haaretz gives the example of Charles Freeman, whom President Obama intended to appoint as head of the National Intelligence Council. The Israel Lobby proved, again, that it was more powerful than a mere American President and prevented the appointment, citing Freeman's "anti-Israel leaning." In other words, because Freeman was not an overboard apologist for Israel's crimes he was unacceptable to the Israel Lobby.

Haaretz reports: "The next attempt to appoint an intelligence aide, in this case, former Republican senator Chuck Hagel, also resulted in vast criticism over his not having a pro-Israel record." The Israel Lobby is trying to block Hagel's appointment by President Obama. Hagel doesn't want to start a war with Iran for Israel's_benefit and was blackballed by Morton A. Klein, the president of the Zionist Organization of America. Hagel, it seems, "refused to sign a letter calling on then-president George Bush to speak about Iran's nuclear program at the G8 summit that year."

Now it is a Jewish daughter of a Holocaust survivor, Hannah Rosenthal, whose appointment to head the US Office to Monitor and Combat Anti-Semitism, an office that is another indication of America's puppet state status, who is under attack. Rosenthal was the head of the Jewish Council for Public Affairs during 2000-2005. Her black mark came from serving on the advisory board of the J Street Lobby, an American Jewish organization recently formed in opposition to AIPAC's murderous militarism.

The Israel Lobby's opposition to Hannah Rosenthal shows that no moral person can survive the Israel Lobby's blackball.

The US, "the world's only superpower," has no independent voice in Middle Eastern affairs. The real power rests in the hands of the settler thug, Avigdor Lieberman, Deputy Prime Minister of Israel and Minister of Foreign Affairs. This is the man who controls the Obama government's Middle East policy. Lieberman forced the "all-powerful President of the US, Barack Omama," to rescind his order to Israel to halt the illegal settler settlements on occupied Palestinian land. Obama was given the bird and submitted to his master.

Macho Americans who prance around as if they owned the world are nothing but the puppets of Israel. The US is not a country. It is a colony.

AMERICANS SUBMIT TO TYRANNY

December 29, 2009

"A nation of sheep will beget a government of wolves."

Obama's dwindling band of true believers has taken heart that their man has finally delivered on one of his many promises—the closing of the Guantanamo prison. But the prison is not being closed. It is being moved to Illinois, *if* the Republicans permit. In truth, Obama has handed his supporters another defeat. Closing Guantanamo meant ceasing to hold people in violation of our legal principles of habeas corpus and due process and ceasing to torture them in violation of US and international laws.

All Obama would be doing would be moving 100 people, against whom the US government is unable to bring a case, from the prison in Guantanamo to a prison in Thomson, Illinois.

Are the residents of Thomson despondent that the US government has chosen their town as the site on which to continue its blatant violation of US legal principles? No, the residents are happy. It means jobs.

The hapless prisoners had a better chance of obtaining release from Guantanamo. Now the prisoners are up against two US senators, a US representative, a mayor, and a state governor who have a vested interest in the prisoners' permanent detention in order to protect the new prison jobs in the hamlet devastated by unemployment.

Neither the public nor the media have ever shown any interest in how the detainees came to be incarcerated. Most of the detainees were unprotected people who were captured by Afghan war lords and sold to the Americans as "terrorists" in order to collect a proffered bounty. It was enough for the public and the media that the Defense Secretary at the time, Donald Rumsfeld, declared the Guantanamo detainees to be the "760 most dangerous people on earth."

The vast majority have been released after years of abuse. The 100 who are slated to be removed to Illinois have apparently been so badly abused that the US government is afraid to release them because of the testimony the prisoners could give to human rights organizations and foreign media about their mistreatment.

Our British allies are showing more moral conscience than Americans are able to muster. Former PM Tony Blair, who provided cover for President Bush's illegal invasion of Iraq, is being damned for his crimes by UK officialdom testifying before the Chilcot Inquiry.

The London *Times* on December 14 summed up the case against Blair in a headline: "Intoxicated by Power, Blair Tricked Us Into War." Two days later the British *First Post* declared: "War Crime Case Against Tony Blair Now Rock-solid." In an unguarded moment Blair let it slip that he favored a conspiracy for war regardless of the validity of the excuse [weapons of mass destruction] used to justify the invasion.

The movement to bring Blair to trial as a war criminal is gathering steam, but is not likely to succeed. Writing in the *First Post* Neil Clark reported: "There is widespread contempt for a man [Blair] who has made millions [his reward from the Bush regime] while Iraqis die in their hundreds of thousands due to the havoc unleashed by the illegal invasion, and who, with breathtaking arrogance, seems to regard himself as above the rules of international law." Clark notes that the West's practice of shipping Serbian and African leaders off to the War Crimes Tribunal, while exempting itself, is wearing thin.

In the US, of course, there is no such attempt to hold to account Bush, Cheney, Condi Rice, Rumsfeld, Wolfowitz, and the large number of war criminals that comprised the Bush Regime. Indeed, Obama, whom Republicans love to hate, has gone out of his way to protect the Bush cohort from being held accountable.

Here in Great Moral America we only hold accountable celebrities and politicians for their sexual indiscretions. Tiger Woods is paying a bigger price for his girlfriends than Bush or Cheney will ever pay for the deaths and ruined lives of millions of people. The consulting company, Accenture Plc, which based its marketing program on Tiger Woods, has removed Woods from its website. Gillette announced that the company is dropping Woods from its print and broadcast ads. AT&T says it is re-evaluating the company's relationship with Woods.

Apparently, Americans regard sexual infidelity as far more serious than invading countries on the basis of false charges and deception, invasions that have caused the deaths and displacement of millions of innocent people. Remember, the House impeached President Clinton not for his war crimes in Serbia, but for lying about his affair with Monica Lewinsky.

Americans are more upset by Tiger Woods' sexual affairs than they are by the Bush and Obama administrations' destruction of US civil liberty. Americans don't seem to mind that "their" government for the last 8 years has resorted to the detention practices of 1,000 years ago—simply grab a person and throw him into a dungeon forever without bringing charges and obtaining a conviction.

According to polls, Americans support torture, a violation of both US and international law, and Americans don't mind that their government violates the Foreign Intelligence Surveillance Act and spies on them without obtaining warrants from a court. Apparently, the brave citizens of the "sole remaining superpower" are so afraid of terrorists that they are content to give up liberty for safety, an impossible feat.

With stunning insouciance, Americans have given up the rule of law that protected their liberty. The silence of law schools and bar associations indicates that the age of liberty has passed. In short, the American people support tyranny. And that's where they are headed.

LIBERTY
HAS BEEN LOST

January 6, 2010

I had just finished reading the uncensored edition of Aleksandr Solzhenitsyn's book, *In The First Circle*,[6] when I came across Chris Hedges article, "One Day We'll All Be Terrorists".[7] In Hedges' description of the U.S. government's treatment of American citizen Syed Fahad Hashmi, I recognized the Stalinist legal system as portrayed by Solzhenitsyn.

Hashmi has been held in solitary confinement going on three years. Guantanamo's practices have migrated to the Metropolitan Correction Center in Manhattan, where Hashmi is held in the Special Housing Unit. His access to attorneys, family and other prisoners is prevented or severely curtailed. He must clean himself and use toilet facilities on camera. He is let out of solitary for one hour every 24 hours to exercise in a cage.

Hashmi is a U.S. citizen, but his government has violated every right guaranteed to him by the Constitution. The U.S. government, in violation of U.S. law, is also subjecting Hashmi to psychological torture known as extreme sensory deprivation. The bogus "evidence" against him is classified and denied to him. Like Joseph K. in Kafka's *The Trial*, Hashmi is under arrest on secret evidence. As the case against him is unknown or nonexistent, defense is impossible.

Hashmi's rights have been abrogated by his government with the allegation that he is a potential terrorist or perhaps just a terrorist sympathizer. Another American citizen, Junaid Babar stayed with Hashmi for two weeks and allegedly delivered ponchos and socks to Al Qaeda in Pakistan. Allegedly Babar used Hashmi's cell phone to reach others aiding terrorists. The U.S. government says that this suffices to implicate Hashmi in Babar's activities.

Babar made a plea bargain to five counts of "material support" for terrorism, but is working off his prison sentence by testifying as a government witness in other terror trials, including in Canada and the U.K., and as the U.S. government's only evidence against Hashmi.

Hashmi's real offense is that he is a Muslim activist defending Muslim civil liberties and making provocative statements about the U.S. As Michael Ratner, president of the Center for Constitutional Rights, has pointed out, federal courts have given the U.S. government wide latitude to use Hashmi's exercise of his constitutionally protected rights to free speech and association as evidence of a terrorist frame of mind and, thereby, of intent to commit terrorism.

Brooklyn College professor Jeanne Theoharis warns us that an American citizen can now be tried on secret evidence.

> You can spend years in solitary confinement before you are convicted of anything. There has been attention paid to extraordinary rendition, Guantanamo and Abu Ghraib with this false idea that if people are tried in the United States things will be fair.   But what allowed Guantanamo to happen was the devolution of the rule of law here at home, and this is not only happening to Hashmi.

Indeed, Hedges reports that "radical activists in the environmental, (anti)-globalization, anti-nuclear, sustainable agriculture and anarchist movements are already being placed by the state in special detention facilities with Muslims charged with terrorism." Hedges warns: "This corruption of our legal system will not be reserved by the state for suspected terrorists or even Muslim Americans. In the coming turmoil and economic collapse, it will be used to silence all who are branded as disruptive or subversive. Hashmi endures what many others, who are not Muslim, will endure later."

The silence of bar associations and law schools indicates an astounding insouciance to Thomas Paine's warning: "He that would make his own liberty secure must guard even his enemy from oppression; for if he violates this duty, he establishes a precedent that will reach to himself."

Some of my Republican and conservative acquaintances are even gleeful that, finally, we are going to get tough and deal forcibly with "these people." They naively believe that they themselves will remain safe when law ceases to be a shield of the people and becomes a weapon in the hands of government.

In "A Man for All Seasons," Sir Thomas More cautions against cutting the law down in order to chase after devils, for with the law cut down, where do we stand when the devil turns on us?

Clearly, these fundamental questions are of no concern to the U.S. Department of Justice (*sic*), to Congress or the White House, to the "mainstream media," to the American people or even to very much of the federal judiciary.

Glenn Greenwald pointed out in *Salon*[8] that the Convention Against Torture, championed and signed by President Ronald Reagan and ratified by the U.S. Senate, states:

Each State Party is required either to prosecute torturers who are found in its territory or to extradite them to other countries for prosecution. No exceptional circumstances whatsoever, whether a state of war or threat of war, internal political instability or any other public emergency may be invoked as a justification of torture. Each State Party shall ensure that all acts of torture are offenses under its criminal law.

Two decades later, the U.S. government tortures at will. Justice Department officials write memos authorizing torture despite the ratified Convention Against Torture, U.S. law and the Geneva Conventions. The Pew Poll reports that 67 percent of Republicans and 47 percent of Democrats support the use of torture.

And Americans think they have freedom and democracy and live under the protection of the rule of law.

The law is lost, and with it American liberty.

IS ANYONE TELLING US
THE TRUTH?

January 8, 2010

What are we to make of the failed Underwear Bomber plot, the Toothpaste, Shampoo, and Bottled Water Bomber plot, and the Shoe Bomber plot? These blundering and implausible plots to bring down an airliner seem far removed from Al Qaeda's expertise in allegedly pulling off 9/11.

If we are to believe the U.S. government, Khalid Sheikh Mohammed, Washington's replacement for Osama bin Laden as the alleged Al Qaeda "mastermind" behind 9/11, outwitted the CIA, the NSA, indeed all 16 U.S. intelligence agencies as well as those of all U.S. allies including Mossad, the National Security Council, NORAD, Air Traffic Control, Airport Security four times on one morning, and Dick Cheney, and with untrained and inexperienced pilots pulled off skilled piloting feats of crashing hijacked airliners into the World Trade Center towers, and the Pentagon.

After such amazing success, Al Qaeda would have attracted the best minds in the business, but, instead, it has been reduced to amateur stunts.

The Underwear Bomb plot is being played to the hilt on the TV media and especially on Fox News. After reading recently that the *Washington Post* allowed a lobbyist to write a news story that preached the lobbyist's interest, I wondered if the manufacturers of full body scanners were behind the heavy coverage of the Underwear Bomber, if not behind the plot itself. In America, everything is for sale. Integrity is gone with the wind.

Recently I read a column by an author who has a "convenience theory" about the Underwear Bomber being a Nigerian allegedly trained by Al Qaeda in Yemen. As the U.S. is involved in an undeclared war in Yemen, about which neither the American public nor Congress were informed or consulted, the Underwear Bomb plot provided a convenient excuse for Washington's new war, regardless of whether it was a real attack or a put-up job.

Once you start to ask yourself about whose agenda is served by events and their news spin, other things come to mind. For example, last July there was a news report that the government in Yemen had disbanded a terrorist cell, which was operating under the supervision of Israeli intelligence

53

services. According to the news report, Yemeni President Ali Abdullah Saleh told Saba news agency that a terrorist cell was arrested and that the case was referred to judicial authorities "for its links with the Israeli intelligence services."

Could the Underwear Bomber have been one of the Israeli terrorist recruits? Certainly Israel has an interest in keeping the US fully engaged militarily against all potential foes of Israel's territorial expansion.

The thought brought back memory of my Russian studies at Oxford University where I learned that the Tsar's secret police set off bombs so that they could blame those whom they wanted to arrest.

I next remembered that Francesco Cossiga, the president of Italy from 1985-1992, revealed the existence of Operation Gladio, a false flag operation under NATO auspices that carried out bombings across Europe in the 1960s, 1970s, and 1980s. The bombings were blamed on communists and were used to discredit communist parties in elections.

An Italian parliamentary investigation unearthed the fact that the attacks were overseen by the CIA. Gladio agent Vincenzo Vinciguerra stated in sworn testimony that the attacks targeted innocent civilians, including women and children, in order "to force the public to turn to the state to ask for greater security."

What a coincidence. That is exactly what 9/11 succeeded in accomplishing in the U.S.

Among the well-meaning and the gullible in the West, the supposition still exists that government represents the public interest. Political parties keep this myth alive by fighting over which party best represents the public's interest. In truth, government represents private interests, those of the office holders themselves and those of the lobby groups that finance their political campaigns. The public is in the dark as to the real agendas.

The U.S. and its puppet state allies were led to war in the Middle East and Afghanistan entirely on the basis of lies and deception. Iraqi weapons of mass destruction did not exist and were known by the U.S. and British governments not to exist. Forged documents, such as the "yellowcake documents," were leaked to newspapers in order to create news reporting that would bring the public along with the government's war agenda.

Now the same thing is happening in regard to the nonexistent Iranian nuclear weapons program. Forged documents leaked to the *Times* (London) that indicated Iran was developing a "nuclear trigger" mechanism have been revealed as forgeries.

Who benefits? Clearly, attacking Iran is on the Israeli-U.S. agenda, and someone is creating the "evidence" to support the case, just as the leaked secret "Downing Street Memo" to the British cabinet informed Prime Minister Tony Blair's government that President Bush had already made the decision to invade Iraq and "the intelligence and facts were being fixed around the policy."

The willingness of people to believe their rulers and the propaganda ministries that serve the rulers is astonishing. Many Americans believe Iran has a nuclear weapons program despite the unanimous conclusion of 16 U.S. intelligence agencies to the contrary.

Vice President Dick Cheney and the neoconservatives fought hard with limited success to change the CIA's role from intelligence agency to a political agency that manufactures facts in support of the neoconservative agenda. For the Bush Regime creating "new realities" was more important than knowing the facts.

Recently I read a proposal from a person purporting to favor an independent media that stated that we must save the print media from financial failure with government subsidies. Such a subsidy would complete the subservience of the media to government.

Even in Stalinist Russia, a totalitarian political system where everyone knew that there was no free press, a gullible or intimidated public and Communist Party enabled Joseph Stalin to put the heroes of the Bolshevik Revolution on show trial and execute them as capitalist spies.

In the U.S. we are developing our own show trials. Sheikh Mohammed's will be a big one. As Chris Hedges recently pointed out, once government uses demonized Muslims to get the new "justice" system going, the rest of us will be next.

INSOUCIANT AMERICANS

January 11, 2010

The Underwear Bomber case indicates that whoever is behind these bomb scares is laughing at our gullibility.

How realistic is it that Al Qaeda, an organization that allegedly pulled off the most fantastic terror attack in world history, would in these days of heightened security choose for an attack on an airliner a person who is the most conspicuous of all? Umar Farouk Mutallab had a one-way ticket, no luggage, no passport, and his father, reportedly a CIA and Mossad asset, had reported him to the CIA and Mossad. Does anyone really believe that Al Qaeda would choose as an airliner bomber a person waving every red flag imaginable?

This obvious question has escaped the U.S. media, a collection of salespersons marketing full body scanning machines for airports: would Al Qaeda, with its extensive knowledge of explosives, have armed Umar with a "bomb" that experts say couldn't have blown up his own seat? It is difficult to imagine a more gullible population than America's, but do even Americans believe this story? Since 9/11 the FBI has been busy enticing people, who lack organizational skills, into "terrorist plots" that consist of FBI initiated hot air talk. These ridiculous stings are then taken to trial, and the media fans the flames of fear of "home-grown terrorist plots against Americans." There is little doubt that those interested in leading the U.S. deeper into a police state and deeper into a "war on terror" are active in adding orchestrated events to whatever real ones real terrorists manage to accomplish. The paucity of real terrorists has caused the U.S. government and its Ministry of Truth to promote the Taliban to terrorist rank. The problem is that these "terrorist acts" are taking place thousands of miles away in lands that the average American cannot find on a map and, thus, lack scare value. To keep the peril alive for Americans, we have the Underwear Bomb Plot.

What will be next? An elaborate head of hair laced with nano-thermite?

The "war on terror" is a far greater threat to Americans than all the terrorists in the world combined. This is so because the "war on terror" has destroyed the U.S. Constitution and the Bill of Rights. American citizens are now helpless in the event someone in government decides that some constitutionally protected behavior, such as free speech, or a contribution to a children's hospital in Gaza, where Hamas, a U.S.-declared "terrorist organization," happens to be the elected government, constitutes aiding and abetting terrorism.

On Jan. 5 a ruling by the Federal Appeals Court in the District of Columbia gave away the most essential protection of liberty by declaring that the U.S. government is not bound by law during war. The ruling absolves Washington from complying with America's own laws and from complying with international laws, such as the Geneva Conventions. It makes a mockery of all war crime trials everywhere. By elevating the executive branch above the law, the court gave the government carte blanche.

The rationale offered by the court for refusing to uphold the law came from Judge Janice Rogers Brown, who said that America had been pushed by war past "the leading edge of a new and frightening paradigm, one that demands new rules be written. War is a challenge to law, and the law must adjust."[9] By "adjust" she means "be set aside" or "be thrown out."

The U.S. Supreme Court has refused to defend both the Constitution and the principle that government is not above the law. Last Dec.14 the Supreme Court refused to review a ruling by the Federal Appeals Court in the District of Columbia, which dismissed a torture case with the argument that "torture is a foreseeable consequence of the military's detention of suspected enemy combatants." In other words, neither U.S. nor international laws against torture can be enforced in U.S. courts. The opinion[10] was written by Judge Karen Lecraft Henderson.

The "war on terror," which is enriching Halliburton, Blackwater (now operating under an alias), and the military/security complex, while denying Americans health care, is running up debt that is a threat to Americans' purchasing power and living standards. The contrast between America's sanctimonious rhetoric and the murder of civilians and torture of prisoners has destroyed America's reputation and caused Europeans as well as Muslims to despise the United States.

The sacrifice of the Constitution and rule of law to a hyped "terrorist threat" has destroyed the heart and soul of America herself.

As a poet wrote, "our world in stupor lies."

IT IS NOW OFFICIAL:
THE US IS A POLICE STATE

February 10, 2010

Americans have been losing the protection of law for years. In the 21st century the loss of legal protections accelerated with the Bush administration's "war on terror," which continues under the Obama administration and is essentially a war on the Constitution and U.S. civil liberties.

The Bush regime was determined to vitiate habeas corpus in order to hold people indefinitely without bringing charges. The regime had acquired hundreds of prisoners by paying a bounty for "terrorists." Afghan warlords and thugs responded to the financial incentive by grabbing unprotected people and selling them to the Americans.

The Bush regime needed to hold the prisoners without charges because it had no evidence against the people and did not want to admit that the U.S. government had stupidly paid warlords and thugs to kidnap innocent people. In addition, the Bush regime needed "terrorists" prisoners in order to prove that there was a terrorist threat.

As there was no evidence against the "detainees" (most have been released without charges after years of detention and abuse), the U.S. government needed a way around U.S. and international laws against torture in order that the government could produce evidence via self-incrimination. The Bush regime found inhumane and totalitarian-minded lawyers and put them to work at the U.S. Department of Justice (*sic*) to invent arguments that the Bush regime did not need to obey the law.

The Bush regime created a new classification for its detainees that it used to justify denying legal protection and due process to the detainees. As the detainees were not U.S. citizens and were demonized by the regime as "the 760 most dangerous men on earth," there was little public outcry over the regime's unconstitutional and inhumane actions.

As our Founding Fathers and a long list of scholars warned, once civil liberties are breached, they are breached for all. Soon U.S. citizens were being held indefinitely in violation of their habeas corpus rights. Dr. Aafia Siddiqui, an American citizen of Pakistani origin, might have been the first. Dr. Siddiqui, a scientist educated at MIT and Brandeis University, was seized in Pakistan for no known reason, sent to Afghanistan, and was held secretly for five years in the U.S. military's notorious Bagram prison in Afghanistan. Her three young children were with her at the time she was abducted, one an eight-month-old baby. She has no idea what has become of her two youngest children. Her oldest child, 7 years old, was also incarcerated in Bagram and subjected to similar abuse and horrors.

Siddiqui has never been charged with any terrorism-related offense. A British journalist, hearing her piercing screams as she was being tortured, disclosed her presence.[11] An embarrassed U.S. government responded to the disclosure by sending Siddiqui to the U.S. for trial on the trumped-up charge that while a captive, she grabbed a U.S. soldier's rifle and fired two shots attempting to shoot him. The charge apparently originated as a U.S. soldier's excuse for shooting Dr. Siddiqui twice in the stomach resulting in her near death.

On February 4, Dr. Siddiqui was convicted by a stupid and utterly immoral New York jury for attempted murder. The only evidence presented against her was the charge itself and an unsubstantiated claim that she had once taken a pistol-firing course at an American firing range. No evidence was presented of her fingerprints on the rifle that this frail and broken 100-pound woman had allegedly seized from an American soldier. No evidence was presented that a weapon was fired, no bullets, no shell casings, no bullet holes. Just an accusation.

Wikipedia has this to say about the trial: "The trial took an unusual turn when an FBI official asserted that the fingerprints taken from the rifle, which was purportedly used by Aafia to shoot at the U.S. interrogators, did not match hers."

An ignorant and bigoted American jury convicted her for being a Muslim. This is the kind of "justice" that always results when the state hypes fear and demonizes a group.

The people who should have been on trial are the people who abducted her, disappeared her young children, shipped her across international borders, violated her civil liberties, tortured her apparently for the fun of it, raped her, and attempted to murder her with two gunshots to her stomach. Instead, the victim was put on trial and convicted.

This is the unmistakable hallmark of a police state. And this victim is an American citizen.

Anyone can be next. Indeed, on February 3, Dennis Blair, director of National Intelligence told the House Intelligence Committee that it was now "defined policy" that the U.S. government can murder its own citizens on the sole basis of the judgment of someone in the government that an American is a threat. No arrest, no trial, no conviction, just execution on suspicion of being a threat.

This shows how far the police state has advanced. A presidential appointee in the Obama administration tells an important committee of Congress that the executive branch has decided that it can murder American citizens abroad if it thinks they are a threat. I can hear readers saying the government might as well kill Americans abroad as it kills them at home—Waco, Ruby Ridge, the Black Panthers.

Yes, the U.S. government has murdered its citizens, but Dennis Blair's "defined policy" is a bold new development. The government, of course, denies that it intended to kill the Branch Davidians, Randy Weaver's wife and child, or the Black Panthers. The government says that Waco was a terrible tragedy, an unintended result brought on by the Branch Davidians themselves. The government says that Ruby Ridge was Randy Weaver's fault for not appearing in court on a day that had been miscommunicated to him, The Black Panthers, the government says, were dangerous criminals who insisted on a shoot-out.

In no previous death of a U.S. citizen at the hands of the U.S. government has the government claimed the right to kill Americans without arrest, trial, and conviction of a capital crime.

In contrast, Dennis Blair has told the U.S. Congress that the executive branch has assumed the right to murder Americans whom it deems a "threat."

What defines "threat"? Who will make the decision? What it means is that the government will murder whomever it chooses.

There is no more complete or compelling evidence of a police state than the government announcing that it will murder its own citizens if it views them as a "threat."

Ironic, isn't it, that "the war on terror" to make us safe ends in a police state with the government declaring the right to murder American citizens.

THE ROAD TO ARMAGEDDON

THE INSANE DRIVE FOR AMERICAN HEGEMONY THREATENS LIFE ON EARTH

February 26, 2010

The Washington Times is a newspaper that looks with favor upon the Bush/Cheney/Obama/neocon wars of aggression in the Middle East and favors making terrorists pay for 9/11. Therefore, I was surprised to learn on February 24 that the most popular story on the paper's website for the past three days was the "Inside the Beltway" report, "Explosive News," about the 31 press conferences in cities in the US and abroad on February 19 held by Architects and Engineers for 9/11 Truth, an organization of professionals which now has 1,000 members. [Editor's note: as of 2013 the membership is 2,000.]

I was even more surprised that the news report treated the press conference seriously.

How did three World Trade Center skyscrapers suddenly disintegrate into fine dust? How did massive steel beams in three skyscrapers suddenly fail as a result of short-lived, isolated, and low temperature fires? "A thousand architects and engineers want to know, and are calling on Congress to order a new investigation into the destruction of the Twin Towers and Building 7," reports *The Washington Times*.

The paper reports that the architects and engineers have concluded that the Federal Emergency Management Agency and the National Institute of Standards and Technology provided "insufficient, contradictory and fraudulent accounts of the circumstances of the towers' destruction" and are "calling for a grand jury investigation of NIST officials."

The newspaper reports that Richard Gage, the spokesperson for the architects and engineers said: "Government officials will be notified that 'Misprision of Treason,' U.S. Code 18 (Sec. 2382) is a serious federal offense, which requires those with evidence of treason to act. The implications are enormous and may have profound impact on the forthcoming Khalid Sheikh Mohammed trial."

There is now an organization, Firefighters for 9/11 Truth. At the main press conference in San Francisco, Eric Lawyer, the head of that organization, announced the firefighters' support for the architects and engineers' demands. He reported that no forensic investigation was made of the fires that are alleged to have destroyed the three buildings and that this failure constitutes a crime.

Mandated procedures were not followed, and instead of being preserved and investigated, the crime scene was destroyed. He also reported that there are more than one hundred first responders who heard and experienced explosions and that there is radio, audio and video evidence of explosions.

Also at the press conference, physicist Steven Jones presented the evidence of nano-thermite in the residue of the WTC buildings found by an international panel of scientists led by University of Copenhagen nano-chemist Professor Niels Harrit. Nano-thermite is a high-tech explosive/pyrotechnic capable of instantly melting steel girders.

Before we yell "conspiracy theory," we should be aware that the architects, engineers, firefighters, and scientists offer no theory. They provide evidence that challenges the official theory. This evidence is not going to go away.

If expressing doubts or reservations about the official story in the 9/11 Commission Report makes a person a conspiracy theory kook, then we have to include both co-chairmen of the 9/11 Commission and the Commission's legal counsel, all of whom have written books in which they clearly state that they were lied to by government officials when they conducted their investigation, or, rather, when they presided over the investigation conducted by executive director Philip Zelikow, a member of President George W. Bush's transition team and Foreign Intelligence Advisory Board and a co-author of the propaganda lie delivered by Bush Secretary of State Condi "Mushroom Cloud" Rice.

There will always be Americans who will believe whatever the government tells them no matter how many times they know the government has lied to them. Despite expensive wars that threaten Social Security and Medicare, wars based on non-existent Iraqi weapons of mass destruction, non-existent Saddam Hussein connections to al Qaida, non-existent Afghan participation in the 9/11 attacks, and the non-existent Iranian nukes that are being hyped as the reason for the next American war of aggression in the Middle East, more than half of the U.S. population still believes the fantastic story that the government has told them about 9/11, that the events were due to a Muslim conspiracy that outwitted the entire Western world.

Moreover, it doesn't matter to these Americans how often the government changes its story. For example, Americans first heard of Osama bin Laden because the Bush regime pinned the 9/11 attacks on him. Over the years video after video was served up to the gullible American public of bin Laden's pronouncements. Experts dismissed the videos as fakes, but Americans remained their gullible selves. Then suddenly last year a new 9/11 "mastermind" emerged to take bin Laden's place, the captive Khalid Sheikh Mohammed, the detainee waterboarded 183 times until he confessed to masterminding the 9/11 attack.

In the Middle Ages confessions extracted by torture constituted evidence, but self-incrimination has been a no-no in the U.S. legal system since our founding. But with the Bush regime and the Republican federal judges, whom we were assured would defend the U.S. Constitution, the self-incrimination of Sheikh Mohammed stands today as the only evidence the U.S. government has that Muslim terrorists pulled off 9/11.

If a person considers the feats attributed to Khalid Sheikh Mohammed, they are simply unbelievable. Sheikh Mohammed is a more brilliant, capable superhero than V in the fantasy movie, "V for Vendetta." Sheikh Mohammed outwitted all 16 U.S. intelligence agencies along with those of all U.S. allies or puppets, including Israel's Mossad. No intelligence service on earth or all of them combined was a match for Sheikh Mohammed.

Sheikh Mohammed outwitted the U.S. National Security Council, Dick Cheney, the Pentagon, the State Department, NORAD, the U.S. Air Force, and Air Traffic Control.

He caused Airport Security to fail four times in one morning. He caused all defenses of the National Security State to fail, allowing a hijacked airliner, which was off course all morning while the U.S. Air Force, for the first time in history, was unable to get aloft intercepter aircraft, to crash into the Pentagon.

Sheikh Mohammed was able to perform these feats with unqualified pilots.

Sheikh Mohammed, even as a waterboarded detainee, has managed to prevent the FBI from releasing the many confiscated videos that would show, according to the official story, the hijacked airliner hitting the Pentagon.

How naive do you have to be to believe that any human, or for that matter Hollywood fantasy character, is this powerful and capable?

If Sheikh Mohammed has these superhuman capabilities, how did the incompetent Americans catch him? This guy is a patsy tortured into confession in order to keep the American naifs believing the government's conspiracy theory.

What is going on here is that the U.S. government has to bring the 9/11 mystery to an end. The government must put on trial and convict a culprit so that it can close the case before it explodes. Anyone waterboarded 183 times would confess to anything.

The U.S. government has responded to the evidence being arrayed against its outlandish 9/11 conspiracy theory by redefining the war on terror from external to internal enemies. Homeland Security Secretary Janet Napolitano said on February 21 that American extremists are now as big a concern as international terrorists. Extremists, of course, are people who get in the way of the government's agenda, such as the 1,000 Architects and Engineers for 9/11 Truth. The group used to be 100, now it is 1,000. What if it becomes 10,000?

Cass Sunstein, an Obama regime official, has a solution for the 9/11 skeptics: infiltrate them and provoke them into statements and actions that can be used to discredit or to arrest them. But get rid of them at all cost.

Why employ such extreme measures against alleged kooks if they only provide entertainment and laughs? Is the government worried that they are on to something?

Instead, why doesn't the U.S. government simply confront the evidence that is presented and answer it?

If the architects, engineers, firefighters, and scientists are merely kooks, it would be a simple matter to acknowledge their evidence and refute it. Why is it necessary to infiltrate them with police agents and to set them up?

Many Americans would reply that "their" government would never even dream of killing Americans by hijacking airliners and destroying buildings in order to advance a government agenda. But on February 3, National Intelligence Director Dennis Blair told the House Intelligence Committee that the U.S. government can assassinate its own citizens when they are overseas. No arrest, trial, or conviction of a capital crime is necessary. Just straight out murder.

Obviously, if the U.S. government can murder its citizens abroad it can murder them at home, and has done so. For example, 100 Branch Davidians were murdered in Waco, Texas, by the Clinton administration for no legitimate reason. The government just decided to use its power knowing that it could get away with it, which it did.

Americans who think "their" government is some kind of morally pure operation would do well to familiarize themselves with Operation Northwoods. Operation Northwoods was a plot drawn up by the U.S. Joint Chiefs of Staff for the CIA to commit acts of terrorism in American cities and fabricate evidence blaming Castro so that the U.S. could gain domestic and international support for regime change in Cuba. The secret plan was nixed by President John F. Kennedy and was declassified by the John F. Kennedy Assassination Records Review Board. It is available online in the National Security Archive. There are numerous online accounts available, including

Wikipedia. James Bamford's book, *Body of Secrets*, also summarizes the plot:

> Operation Northwoods, which had the written approval of
> the Chairman [Gen. Lemnitzer] and every member of the
> Joint Chiefs of Staff, called for innocent people to be shot
> on American streets; for boats carrying refugees fleeing
> Cuba to be sunk on the high seas; for a wave of violent
> terrorism to be launched in Washington, D.C., Miami, and
> elsewhere. People would be framed for bombings they
> did not commit; planes would be hijacked. Using phony
> evidence, all of it would be blamed on Castro, thus giving
> Lemnitzer and his cabal the excuse, as well as the public
> and international backing, they needed to launch their war.

Prior to 9/11 the American neoconservatives were explicit that the wars of aggression that they intended to launch in the Middle East required "a new Pearl Harbor."

For their own good and that of the wider world, Americans need to pay attention to the growing body of experts who are telling them that the government's account of 9/11 fails their investigation. 9/11 launched the neoconservative plan for U.S. world hegemony. As I write the U.S. government is purchasing the agreement of foreign governments that border Russia to accept U.S. missile interceptor bases. The U.S. intends to ring Russia with U.S. missile bases from Poland through central Europe and Kosovo to Georgia, Azerbaijan and central Asia.[12] U.S. envoy Richard Holbrooke declared on February 20 that al Qaida is moving into former central Asian constituent parts of the Soviet Union, such as Tajikistan, Kyrgyzstan, Uzbekistan, Turkmenistan, and Kazakhstan. Holbrooke is soliciting U.S. bases in these former Soviet republics under the guise of the ever-expanding "war on terror."

The U.S. has already encircled Iran with military bases. The U.S. government intends to neutralize China by seizing control over the Middle East and cutting China off from oil.

This plan assumes that Russia and China, nuclear armed states, will be intimidated by U.S. anti-missile defenses and acquiesce to U.S. hegemony and that China will lack oil for its industries and military.

The U.S. government is delusional. Russian military and political leaders have responded to the obvious threat by declaring NATO a direct threat to the security of Russia and by announcing a change in Russian war doctrine to the pre-emptive launch of nuclear weapons. The Chinese are too confident to be bullied by a washed up American "superpower."

The sociopaths in Washington are pushing the envelope of nuclear war. The insane drive for American hegemony threatens life on earth. The American people, by accepting the lies and deceptions of "their" government, are facilitating this outcome.

AMERICAN NAIFS BRINGING RUIN TO OTHER LANDS

March 18, 2010

According to news reports, the U.S. military is shipping "bunker-buster" bombs to the U.S. Air Force base at Diego Garcia in the Indian Ocean. The *Herald Scotland* reports that experts say the bombs are being assembled for an attack on Iran's nuclear facilities.[13] The newspaper quotes Dan Piesch, director of the Centre for International Studies and Diplomacy at the University of London: "They are gearing up totally for the destruction of Iran."

Will the next step be a staged "terrorist attack," a "false flag" operation as per Operation Northwoods, for which Iran will be blamed? As Iran and its leadership have already been demonized, a "false flag" attack would suffice to obtain US and European public support for bombing Iran. The bombing would include more than the nuclear facilities and would continue until the Iranians agree to regime change and the installation of a puppet government. The corrupt American and European media would present the new puppet as "freedom and democracy."

If the past is a guide, Americans would fall for the deception. In the February issue of the *American Behavioral Scientist*, a scholarly journal, Professor Lance DeHaven-Smith writes that state crimes against democracy (SCAD) involve government officials, often in combination with private interests, that engage in covert activities in order to implement an agenda. Examples include McCarthyism or the fabrication of evidence of communist infiltration, the Gulf of Tonkin Resolution based on false claims of President Johnson and Pentagon chief McNamara that North Vietnam attacked a U.S. naval vessel, the burglary of the office of Daniel Ellsberg's psychiatrist in order to discredit Ellsberg (the Pentagon Papers) as "disturbed," and the falsified "intelligence" that Iraq possessed weapons of mass destruction in order to justify the U.S. invasion of Iraq.

There are many other examples. I have always regarded the 1995 bombing of the Murrah Federal Office Building in Oklahoma City as a SCAD. Allegedly, a disturbed Tim McVeigh used a fertilizer bomb in a truck parked outside the building. More likely, McVeigh was a patsy, whose fertilizer bomb was a cover for explosives planted inside the building.

A number of experts dismissed the possibility of McVeigh's bomb producing such structural damage. For example, General Benton K. Partin, who was in charge of U.S. Air Force munitions design and testing, produced a thick report on the Murrah building bombing which concluded that the building blew up from the inside out. Gen. Partin concluded that "the pattern of damage would have been technically impossible without supplementary demolition charges at some of the reinforced concrete bases inside the building, a standard demolition technique. For a simplistic blast truck bomb, of the size and composition reported, to be able to reach out on the order of 60 feet and collapse a reinforced column base the size of column A7 is beyond credulity."

Gen. Partin dismissed the official report as "a massive cover-up of immense proportions."[14]

Of course, the general's unquestionable expertise had no bearing on the outcome.

One reason is that his and other expert voices were drowned out by media pumping the official story. Another reason is that public beliefs in a democracy run counter to suspicion of government as a terrorist agent. Professor Laurie Manwell of the University of Guelph says that "false flag" operations have the advantage over truth: "research shows that people are far less willing to examine information that disputes, rather than confirms, their beliefs." Professor Steven Hoffman agrees: "Our data shows substantial support for a cognitive theory known as 'motivated reasoning,' which suggests that rather than search rationally for information that either confirms or disconfirms a particular belief, people actually seek out information that confirms what they already believe. In fact, for the most part people completely ignore contrary information." Even when hard evidence turns up, it can be discredited as a "conspiracy theory."

All that is necessary for success of "false flag" or "black ops" events is for the government to have its story ready and to have a reliable and compliant media. Once an official story is in place, thought and investigation are precluded. Any formal inquiry that is convened serves to buttress the already provided explanation.

An explanation ready-at-hand is almost a give-away that an incident is a "black ops" event. Notice how quickly the U.S. government, allegedly so totally deceived by al Qaida, provided the explanation for 9/11. When President Kennedy was assassinated, the government produced the culprit immediately. The alleged culprit was conveniently shot inside a jail by a civilian before he could be questioned. But the official story was ready, and it held.

Professors Manwell and Hoffman's research resonates with me. I remember reading in my graduate studies that the Czarist secret police set off bombs in order to create excuses to arrest their targets. My inclination was to dismiss the accounts as anti-Czarist propaganda by pro-communist historians. It was only later when Robert Conquest confirmed to me that this was indeed the practice of the Czarist secret police that the scales fell from my eyes.

Former CIA official Philip Giraldi in his article, "The Rogue Nation,"[15] makes it clear that the U.S. government has a hegemonic agenda that it is pursuing without congressional or public awareness. The agenda unfolds piecemeal as a response to "terrorism," and the big picture is not understood by the public or by most in Congress. Giraldi protests that the agenda is illegal under both U.S. and international law, but that the illegality of the agenda does not serve as a barrier. Only a naif could believe that such a government would not employ "false flag" operations that advance the agenda.

The U.S. population, it seems, is comprised of naifs whose lack of comprehension is bringing ruin to other lands and to their own also.

WASHINGTON MURDERED SOVEREIGNTY AT HOME AND ABROAD

March 23, 2010

In the Swiss newspaper *Zeit-Fragen*, Professor Dr. Eberhard Hamer from Germany asks, "How Sovereign is Europe?"

He examines the issue and concludes that Europe has little, if any, sovereignty.

Professor Hamer writes that the sovereign rights of Europeans as citizens of nation states were dissolved with the coming into force of the Lisbon Treaty on Dec. 1, 2009. The rights of the people have been conveyed to a political commissariat in Brussels. The French, Germans, Belgians, Spanish, British, Irish, Italians, Greeks, and so forth, now have "European citizenship whatever this may be."

The result of aggregating nations is to reduce the political participation of people. The authority of parliaments and local councils has been impaired. Power is now concentrated in new hierarchical structures within the European Union. European citizenship means indirect and weak participation by people. Self-rule has given way to authoritarian rule from top to bottom.

Professor Hamer then examines the EU commissariat and concludes that it, too, lacks sovereignty, having submitted to the will of the United States. The problem is not only that Europeans are waging an unconstitutional war ordered by the U.S. in a region of the world where Europe has no interests. Europe's puppet state existence goes far beyond its mercenary service to the American Empire.

The EU has given in to Washington's demand for "free access to the banking data of the central financial service provider, Swift, in Europe. All financial flows in Europe (and between Europe and the rest of the world) will now be monitored by the CIA, NSA and other American and Israeli intelligence services." The monitoring will include transfers within Germany, for example, and within individual cities. "The data, even data of completely innocent citizens, have to be stored for five years, of course, at the expense of the banks and their customers."

How sovereign is the EU when it is unable to protect the financial privacy of its citizens from foreign governments?

For some time *Zeit-Fragen* has been reporting Washington's pressure on the Swiss government to violate Swiss statutory law in order to comply with American demands to monitor financial flows within Switzerland and between Switzerland the world. Writers show their astonishment at the total contempt Washington has for the sovereignty of other countries and the privacy rights of their citizens.

We Americans should not be surprised. Notwithstanding statutory laws, our privacy rights are long gone. In the U.S. privacy has become a cruel and expensive joke. It means that parents cannot find out about the college grades of a son or daughter without the permission of the son or daughter. It means that credit card companies, banks and other financial institutions are required to waste money sending a steady stream of "privacy notices" to customers about the use of the customer's information. It means an American cannot get information about his account with a credit card company, telephone, cable, and Internet provider, bank, utility company or make any alteration in his account without providing a stranger with his Social Security number or other private information over and beyond one's name, address, and account number. This routine is a joke when the government has access to everything. It is part of our Orwellian world that privacy is protected by the requirement to give strangers private information over the telephone.

The American sheeple quietly accepted the complete destruction of their right to privacy. Encouraged by success in smiting the American people, Washington has now destroyed the privacy of Europeans.

Indeed, the "freedom and democracy" government spies on the entire world and sends drones into foreign countries to murder people disapproved by Washington.

Washington denounces other governments for human rights violations while itself violating human rights every day.

Washington puts foreign leaders on trial for war crimes, while committing war crimes every day.

What happens when the dollar collapses and Washington no longer has the money to bribe compliance with its demands? When that day arrives, will sovereignty reemerge?

TRUTH HAS FALLEN AND TAKEN LIBERTY WITH IT

March 24, 2010

This was my final column announcing my resignation as a syndicated columnist. I had come to the conclusion that Americans were too unaware and too unconcerned to be able to protect their liberty or even to know that it was being lost. I concluded that I was pissing into the wind. I did not expect 5,000 emails asking that I reconsider and continue writing. Five thousand is not many in a population of 300 million, but as Margaret Mead said, it only takes a few determined people to change the world. The Bolsheviks were few and so are the neoconservatives who have turned America into a warfare/ police state. I created a website and made a pact with readers that I would continue to write as long as they supported the website.

There was a time when the pen was mightier than the sword. That was a time when people believed in truth and regarded truth as an independent power and not as an auxiliary for government, class, racial, gender, ideological, personal, or financial interest.

Today Americans are ruled by propaganda. Americans have little regard for truth, little access to it, and little ability to recognize it.

Truth is an unwelcome entity. It is disturbing. It is off limits. Those who speak it run the risk of being branded "anti-American," "anti-semite" or "conspiracy theorist."

Truth is an inconvenience for government and for the interest groups whose campaign contributions control government.

Truth is an inconvenience for prosecutors who want convictions, not the discovery of innocence or guilt.

Truth is inconvenient for ideologues.

Today many whose goal once was the discovery of truth are now paid handsomely to hide it. "Free market economists" are paid to sell globalism and jobs offshoring to the American people. High-productivity, high value-added American manufacturing jobs are denigrated as "dirty-fingernail" old industrial jobs. Relics from long ago, we are best shed of them. Their place has been taken by "the New Economy," a mythical economy that allegedly consists of high-tech white collar jobs in which Americans innovate and finance activities that occur offshore. All Americans need in order to participate in this "new economy" are finance degrees from Ivy League universities, and then they will work on Wall Street at million dollar jobs.

Economists who were once respectable took money to contribute to this myth of "the New Economy."

And not only economists sell their souls for filthy lucre. Recently we have had reports of medical doctors who, for money, have published in peer-reviewed journals concocted "studies" that hype this or that new medicine produced by pharmaceutical companies that paid for the "studies."

The Council of Europe is investigating the drug companies' role in hyping a false swine flu pandemic in order to gain billions of dollars in sales of the vaccine.

The media helped the US military hype its recent Marja offensive in Afghanistan, describing Marja as a city of 80,000 under Taliban control. It turns out that Marja is not urban but a collection of village farms.

And there is the doomsday scenario concocted around global warming by NGOs, the UN, and the nuclear industry in order to make cleaning up pollution a profit center.

Wherever one looks, truth has fallen to money.

Wherever money is insufficient to bury the truth, ignorance, propaganda, and short memories finish the job.

I remember when, following CIA director William Colby's testimony before the Church Committee in the mid-1970s, Presidents Gerald Ford and Ronald Reagan issued executive orders preventing the CIA and U.S. black-op groups from assassinating foreign leaders. In 2010 the US Congress was told by Dennis Blair, head of national intelligence, that the US now assassinates its own citizens in addition to foreign leaders.

When Blair told the House Intelligence Committee that US citizens no longer needed to be arrested, charged, tried, and convicted of a capital crime, and could just be murdered on suspicion of being a "threat" alone, he wasn't impeached. No investigation was pursued. Nothing happened. There was no Church Committee. In the mid-1970s the CIA got into trouble for plots to kill Castro. Today it is American citizens who are on the hit list. Whatever objections there might be don't carry any weight. No one in government is in any trouble over the acknowledged assassination of U.S. citizens by the U.S. government.

As an economist, I am astonished that the American economics profession has no awareness whatsoever that the U.S. economy has been destroyed by the offshoring of U.S. GDP to overseas countries. U.S.

corporations, in pursuit of absolute advantage or lowest labor costs and maximum CEO "performance bonuses," have moved the production of goods and services marketed to Americans to China, India, and elsewhere abroad. When I read economists describe offshoring as free trade based on comparative advantage, I realize that there is no intelligence or integrity in the American economics profession. Economists endorse the corporate line that they must offshore jobs in order to be competitive. What is the point of being competitive if it harms the American people and only benefits corporate executives and shareowners?

Intelligence and integrity have been purchased by money. The transnational or global U.S. corporations pay multi-million dollar compensation packages to top managers, who achieve these "performance awards" by replacing U.S. labor with foreign labor. While Washington worries about "the Muslim threat," Wall Street, U.S. corporations and "free market" shills destroy the U.S. economy and the prospects of tens of millions of Americans.

Americans, or most of them, have proved to be putty in the hands of the police state.

Americans have bought into the government's claim that security requires the suspension of civil liberties and accountable government. Astonishingly, Americans, or most of them, believe that civil liberties, such as habeas corpus and due process, protect "terrorists," and not themselves. Many also believe that the Constitution is a tired old document that prevents government from exercising the kind of police state powers necessary to keep Americans safe and free.

Most Americans are unlikely to hear from anyone who would tell them any different.

I was associate editor and columnist for the *Wall Street Journal*. I was *Business Week*'s first outside columnist, a position I held for 15 years. I was columnist for a decade for Scripps Howard News Service, carried in 300 newspapers. I was a columnist for the *Washington Times* and for newspapers in France and Italy and for a magazine in Germany. I was a columnist for Creators Syndicate in Los Angeles. I was a contributor to *The New York Times* and a regular feature in the *Los Angeles Times*. Today I cannot publish in, or appear on, the American "mainstream media."

For the last six years I have been banned from the "mainstream media." My last column in *The New York Times* appeared in January, 2004, coauthored with Democratic U.S. Senator Charles Schumer representing New York. We addressed the offshoring of U.S. jobs. Our op-ed article, considered "controversial," resulted in a conference at the Brookings Institution in Washington, D.C. and live coverage by C-Span. A debate was launched. No such thing could happen today.

For years I was a mainstay at the *Washington Times*, producing credibility for the Moony newspaper as a *Business Week* columnist, former *Wall Street Journal* editor, and former Assistant Secretary of the U.S. Treasury. But when I began criticizing Bush's wars of aggression, the order came down to Mary Lou Forbes to cancel my column.

The American corporate media does not serve the truth. It serves the government and the interest groups that empower the government.

America's fate was sealed when the public and the anti-war movement bought the government's 9/11 conspiracy theory. The government's account of 9/11 is contradicted by much evidence. Nevertheless, this defining event of our time, which has launched the US on interminable wars of aggression and a domestic police state, is a taboo topic for investigation in the media. It is pointless to complain of war and a police state when one accepts the premise upon which they are based.

These trillion dollar wars have created financing problems for Washington's deficits and threaten the U.S. dollar's role as world reserve currency. The wars and the pressure that the budget deficits put on the dollar's value have put Social Security and Medicare on the chopping block. Former Goldman Sachs chairman and U.S. Treasury Secretary Hank Paulson is after these protections for the elderly. Fed chairman Bernanke is also after them. The Republicans are after them as well. These protections are called "entitlements" as if they are some sort of welfare that people have not paid for in payroll taxes all their working lives.

With over 21 per cent unemployment as measured by the methodology of 1980, with American jobs, GDP, and technology having been given to China and India, with war being Washington's greatest commitment, with the dollar over-burdened with debt, with civil liberty sacrificed to the "war on terror," the liberty and prosperity of the American people have been thrown into the trash bin of history.

The pen is censored and its might extinguished. Truth has fallen and taken liberty with it. The militarism of the U.S. and Israeli states, and Wall Street and corporate greed, will now run their course.

AMERICA'S COMPLICITY IN EVIL

June 3, 2010

As I write at 5pm on Monday, May 31, all day has passed since the early morning reports of the Israeli commando attack on the unarmed ships carrying humanitarian aid to Gaza, and there has been no response from President Obama except to say that he needed to learn "all the facts about this morning's tragic events" and that Israeli Prime Minister Netanyahu had canceled his plans to meet with him at the White House.

Thus has Obama made America complicit once again in Israel's barbaric war crimes. Just as the US Congress voted to deep-six Judge Goldstone's report on Israel's war crimes committed in Israel's January 2009 invasion of Gaza, Obama has deep-sixed Israel's latest act of barbarism by pretending that he doesn't know what has happened.

No one in the world will believe that Israel attacked ships in international waters carrying Israeli citizens, a Nobel Laureate, elected politicians, and noted humanitarians bringing medicines and building materials to Palestinians in Gaza, who have been living in the rubble of their homes without repairs or medicines since January 2009, without first clearing the crime with its American protector. Without America's protection, Israel, a totally artificial state, could not exist.

No one in the world will believe that America's spy apparatus did not detect the movement of the Israeli attack force toward the aid ships in international waters in an act of piracy, killing 20, wounding 50, and kidnapping the rest.

Obama's pretense at ignorance confirms his complicity. Once again the US government has permitted the Israeli state to murder good people known for their moral conscience. The Israeli state has declared that anyone with a moral conscience is an enemy of Israel, and every American president except Eisenhower and Carter has agreed.

Obama's 12-hour silence in the face of extreme barbarity is his signal to the controlled corporate media to remain on the sidelines until Israeli propaganda sets the story.

The Israeli story, preposterous as always, is that the humanitarians on one of the ships took two pistols from Israeli commandos, highly trained troops armed with automatic weapons, and fired on the attack force. The Israeli government claims that the commandos' response (70 casualties at last reporting) was justified self-defense. Israel was innocent. Israel did not do anything except drop commandos aboard from helicopters in order to intercept an arms shipment to Gazans being brought in by ships manned by terrorists.

Many Christian evangelicals, brainwashed by their pastors that it is God's will for Americans to protect Israel, will believe the Israeli story, especially when it is unlikely they will ever hear any other. Conservative Americans, especially on Memorial Day when they are celebrating feats of American arms, will admire Israel for its toughness. Here in north Georgia where I am at the moment, I have heard several say, admiringly, "Them Israelis, they don't put up with nuthin."

Conservative Americans want the US to be like Israel. They do not understand why the US doesn't stop pissing around after nine years and just go ahead and defeat the Taliban in Afghanistan. They don't understand why the US didn't defeat whoever was opposing American forces in Iraq. Conservatives are incensed that America had to "win" the war by buying off the Iraqis and putting them on the US payroll.

Israel murders people and then blames its victims. This appeals to American conservatives, who want the US to do the same.

It is likely that Americans will accept Israeli propagandist Mark Regev's story that Israelis were met by deadly fire when they tried to intercept an arms shipment to Palestinian terrorists from IHH, a radical Turkish Islamist organization hiding under the cover of humanitarian aid. This explanation is crafted to allow Americans to sink back into their stupor.

Americans will never hear from the US media that Turkey's Prime Minister Erdogan declared that the aid ships were carefully inspected before departure from Turkey and that there were no terrorists or arms aboard:

> I want to say to the world, to the heads of state and the governments, that these boats that left from Turkey and other countries were checked in a strict way under the framework of the rules of international navigation and were only loaded with humanitarian aid.

Turkey is a US ally, a member of NATO. Turkey's cooperation is important to American's plan for world hegemony. Turkey now realizes that the Israeli state is comprised of total evil. Erdogan must wonder about the morality of Israel's American protector. According to a report in antiwar.com, the Turkish government declared that "future aid ships will be dispatched with a military escort so as to prevent future Israeli attacks."

Will the CIA assassinate Erdogan or pay the Turkish military to overthrow him?

Murat Mercan, head of Turkey's foreign relations committee, said that Israel's claim that there were terrorists aboard the aid ships was Israel's way of covering up its crime. Mercan declared: "Any allegation that the members of this ship are attached to Al Qaeda is a big lie because there are Israeli civilians, Israeli authorities, Israeli parliamentarians on board the ship."

The criminal Israeli state does not deny its act of piracy. Israeli military spokeswoman, Avital Leibovich, confirmed that the attack took place in international waters: "This happened in waters outside of Israeli territory, but we have the right to defend ourselves."

Americans, and their Western European puppet states and the puppet state in Canada, will be persuaded by the servile media to buy the story fabricated by Israeli propaganda that the humanitarian aid ships were manned by terrorists bringing weapons to the Palestinians in Gaza, and that the terrorists posing as humanitarians attacked the force of Israeli commandos with two pistols, clubs, and knives.

Americans will swallow this story without a hiccup.

HILLARY CLINTON'S TRANSPARENT LIES

July 10, 2010

The BBC reported on July 4 that US Secretary of State Hillary Clinton said that the US ballistic missile base in Poland was not directed at Russia. The purpose of the base, she said, is to protect Poland from the Iranian threat.

Why would Iran be a threat to Poland? What happens to US credibility when the Secretary of State makes such a stupid statement? Does Hillary think she is fooling the Russians? Does anyone on earth believe her? What is the point of such a transparent lie? To cover up an act of American aggression against Russia?

In the same breath Hillary warned of a "steel vise" of repression crushing democracy and civil liberties around the world. US journalists might wonder if she was speaking of the United States. Glenn Greenwald reported in *Salon* on July 4 that the US Coast Guard, which has no legislative authority, has issued a rule that journalists who come closer than 65 feet to BP clean-up operations in the Gulf of Mexico without permission will be punished by a $40,000 fine and one to five years in prison. *The New York Times* and numerous journalists report that BP, the US Coast Guard, Homeland Security, and local police are prohibiting journalists from photographing the massive damage from the continuing flow of oil and toxic chemicals into the Gulf.

On July 5 Hillary Clinton was in Tbilisi, Georgia, where, according to the *Washington Post*, she accused Russia of "the invasion and occupation of Georgia." What is the point of this lie? Even America's European puppet states have issued reports documenting that Georgia initiated the war with Russia that it quickly lost by invading South Ossetia in an effort to destroy the secessionists.

It would appear that the rest of the world and the UN Security Council have given the Americans a pass to lie without end in order to advance Washington's goal of world hegemony. How does this benefit the Security Council and the world? What is going on here?

After President Clinton misrepresented the conflict between Serbia and the Albanians in Kosovo and tricked NATO into military aggression against Serbia and after President Bush, Vice President Cheney, the secretary of state, the national security advisor and just about every member of the Bush regime deceived the UN and the world into thinking that Saddam Hussein had weapons of mass destruction, thus finagling an invasion of Iraq, why did anyone fall for Obama's deception that Iran has a nuclear weapons program?

In 2009 all sixteen US intelligence agencies issued a unanimous report that Iran had abandoned its weapons program in 2003. Was the media ignorant of this report?

The International Atomic Energy Agency's weapons inspectors on the ground in Iran have consistently reported that there is no diversion of uranium from the energy program. Was the UN Security Council ignorant of the IAEA reports?

If not ignorant, why did the UN Security Council approve sanctions on Iran for adhering to its right under the Nuclear Non-proliferation Treaty to have a nuclear energy program? The UN sanctions are lawless. They violate Iran's rights as a signatory to the treaty. Is this the "steel vice" of which Hillary spoke?

As soon as Washington got sanctions from the Security Council, the Obama regime unilaterally added more severe US sanctions. Obama is using the UN sanctions as a vehicle to which to attach his unilateral sanctions. Perhaps this is the "steel vice of oppression" of which Hillary spoke.

Why has the UN Security Council given a green light to the Obama regime to start yet another war in the Middle East?

Why has Russia stepped aside? At Washington's insistence, the Russian government has not delivered the air defense system that Iran purchased. Does Russia view Iran as a greater threat to itself than the Americans, who are ringing Russia with US missile and military bases and financing "color revolutions" in former constituent parts of the Russian and Soviet empires?

Why has China stepped aside? China's growing economy needs energy resources. China has extensive energy investments in Iran. It is US policy to contain China by denying China access to energy. China is America's banker. China could destroy the US dollar in a few minutes.

Perhaps Russia and China have decided to let the Americans over-reach until the country self-destructs.

On the other hand, perhaps everyone is miscalculating and more death and destruction is in the works than the world is counting on.

Like in the Gulf of Mexico.

THE BUSINESS
OF AMERICA
IS WAR

July 27, 2010

The White House is screaming like a stuck pig. WikiLeaks' release of the Afghan War Documents "puts the lives of our soldiers and our coalition partners at risk."

What nonsense. Obama's war puts the lives of American soldiers at risk, and the craven puppet state behavior of "our partners" in serving as US mercenaries is what puts their troops at risk.

Keep in mind that it was someone in the US military that leaked the documents to WikiLeaks. This means that there is a spark of rebellion within the Empire itself.

And rightly so. The leaked documents show that the US has committed numerous war crimes and that the US government and military have lied through their teeth in order to cover up the failure of their policies. These are the revelations that Washington wants to keep secret.

If Obama cared about the lives of our soldiers, he would not have sent them to a war, the purpose of which he cannot identify. Earlier in his regime, Obama admitted that he did not know what the mission was in Afghanistan. He vowed to find out what the mission was and to tell us, but he never did. After being read the riot act by the military/security complex, which recycles war profits into political campaign contributions, Obama simply declared the war to be "necessary." No one has ever explained why the war is necessary.

The government cannot explain why the war is necessary, because it is not necessary to the American people. Any necessary reason for the war has to do with the enrichment of narrow private interests and with undeclared agendas. If the agendas were declared and the private interests being served identified, even the American sheeple might revolt.

The Obama regime has made war the business of America. Escalation in Afghanistan has gone hand in hand with drone attacks on Pakistan and the use of proxy forces to conduct wars in Pakistan and North Africa. Currently, the US is conducting provocative naval exercises off the coasts of China and North Korea and instigating war between Columbia and Venezuela in South

America. Former CIA director Michael Hayden declared on July 25 that an attack on Iran seems unavoidable.

With the print and TV media captive, why doesn't Washington simply tell us that the country is at war without actually going to the trouble of going to war? That way the munitions industry could lay off its workers and put the military appropriations directly into profits. We could avoid the war crimes and wasted lives of our soldiers.

The US economy and the well-being of Americans are being sacrificed to the regime's wars. The states are broke and laying off teachers. Even "rich" California, formerly touted as "the seventh largest economy in the world," is reduced to issuing script and cutting its state workers' pay to the minimum wage.

Supplemental war appropriations have become routine affairs, but the budget deficit is invoked to block any aid to Americans—but not to Israel. On July 25 the Israeli newspaper, *Haaretz,* reported that the US and Israel had signed a multi-billion dollar deal for Boeing to provide Israel with a missile system.

Americans can get no help out of Washington, but the US ambassador to the UN, Susan Rice, declared that Washington's commitment to Israel's security is "not negotiable." Washington's commitment to California and to the security of the rest of us is negotiable. War spending has run up the budget deficit, and the deficit precludes any help for Americans.

With the US bankrupting itself in wars, America's largest creditor, China, has taken issue with America's credit rating. The head of China's largest credit rating agency declared: "The US is insolvent and faces bankruptcy as a pure debtor nation."

On July 12, Niall Ferguson, an historian of empire, warned that the American empire could collapse suddenly from weakness brought on by its massive debts and that such a collapse could be closer than we think.

Deaf, blinkered and bought, Washington policymakers prattle on about "thirty more years of war."

DEATH OF THE
FIRST AMENDMENT

August 26, 2010

Chuck Norris is no pinko-liberal-commie, and *Human Events* is a very conservative publication. The two have come together to produce an important article, "Obama's US Assassination Program."

It seems only yesterday that Americans, or those interested in their civil liberties, were shocked that the Bush regime so flagrantly violated the FISA law against spying on American citizens without a warrant. A federal judge serving on the FISA court even resigned to protest the illegality of the spying.

Nothing was done about it. "National security" placed the president and executive branch above the law of the land. Civil libertarians worried that the US government was freeing its power from the constraints of law, but no one else seemed to care.

Encouraged by its success in breaking the law, the executive branch early this year announced that the Obama regime has given itself the right to murder Americans abroad if such Americans are considered a "threat." "Threat" was not defined and, thus, a death sentence would be issued by a subjective decision of an unaccountable official.

There was hardly a peep out of the public or the media. Americans and the media were content for the government to summarily execute traitors and turncoats, and who better to identify traitors and turncoats than the government with all its spy programs.

The problem with this sort of thing is that once it starts, it doesn't stop. As Norris reports, citing Obama regime security officials, the next stage is to criminalize dissent and criticism of the government. The May 2010 National Security Strategy states: "We are now moving beyond traditional distinctions between homeland and national security. . . This includes a determination to prevent terrorist attacks against the American people by fully coordinating the actions that we take abroad with the actions and precautions that we take at home."

Most Americans will respond that the "indispensable" US government would never confuse an American exercising First Amendment rights with a terrorist or an enemy of the state. But, in fact, governments always have. Even one of our Founding Fathers, John Adams and the Federalist Party, had their "Alien and Sedition Acts" which targeted the Republican press.

Few with power can brook opposition or criticism, especially when it is a simple matter for those with power to sweep away constraints upon their power in the name of "national security." Deputy National Security Adviser John Brennan recently explained that more steps are being taken, because of the growing number of Americans who have been "captivated by extremist ideology or causes." Notice that this phrasing goes beyond concern with Muslim terrorists.

In pursuit of hegemony over both the world and its own subjects, the US government is shutting down the First Amendment and turning criticism of the government into an act of "domestic extremism," a capital crime punishable by execution, just as it was in Hitler's Germany and Stalin's Russia.

Initially German courts resisted Hitler's illegal acts. Hitler got around the courts by creating a parallel court system, like the Bush regime did with its military tribunals. It won't be long before a decision of the US Supreme Court will not mean anything. Any decision that goes against the regime will simply be ignored.

This is already happening in Canada, an American puppet state. Writing for *CounterPunch*, Andy Worthington documents the lawlessness of the US trial of Canadian Omar Khadr. In January of this year, the Supreme Court of Canada ruled that the interrogation of Khadr constituted "state conduct that violates the principles of fundamental justice" and "offends the most basic Canadian standards about the treatment of detained youth suspects." According to the *Toronto Star*, the Court instructed the government to "shape a response that reconciled its foreign policy imperatives with its constitutional obligations to Khadr," but the puppet prime minister of Canada, Stephen Harper, ignored the Court and permitted the US government to proceed with its lawless abuse of a Canadian citizen.

September 11 destroyed more than lives, World Trade Center buildings, and Americans' sense of invulnerability. The event destroyed American liberty, the rule of law and the US Constitution.

THE TRUE COST
OF THE WAR

September 3, 2010

Obama's "end of Iraq war" speech must have shattered any remaining belief in him. Forced to appease both his supporters and the warmonger right-wing, who denounce him as a Muslim and a Marxist, Obama resorted to Orwellian DoubleSpeak. He could only announce an end to the war by praising the president who started it and the troops who fought it. Yet, as most earthlings, if not Americans, surely know by now, the war was based on a lie and on intentional deception. The American troops died for a lie, and so did the Iraqis.

President Obama spoke of the cost to Americans of liberating Iraq. But is Iraq liberated or is Iraq in the hands of American puppet politicians and still occupied by 50,000 American troops and 200,000 private mercenaries and "contractors," governed out of the largest embassy in the world, essentially a fortress?

President Obama did not speak of the cost to Iraqis of being "liberated." The uncounted Iraqi deaths, estimates of which range from 100,000 to 1,000,000, most being women and children, were not mentioned. Neither were the uncounted orphaned and maimed children, the four million displaced Iraqis, the flight from Iraq of the professional middle class, the homes, infrastructure, villages and towns destroyed, along with whatever remained of America's reputation.

All of this was left out of the picture that Obama painted of America's "commitment" to Iraq which brought Iraqis "peace" and liberated Iraqis from Saddam Hussein in order that a destroyed Iraq can now be an American puppet state and take its orders from Washington or alternatively be governed by a Shia dictatorship.

As it is impossible for the U.S. government to any longer pretend that the invasion of Iraq was necessary to save America from weapons of mass destruction and al Qaeda terrorists, the U.S. government's justification for its massive war crime has come down to removing Saddam Hussein, who, like the Americans, tortured his opponents.

Does anyone on earth, even among the most moronic of the flag-waving American super-patriots, believe that the bankrupt United States government spent three trillion borrowed dollars to remove one man, Saddam

Hussein, in order to free Iraq from tyranny? Anyone who believes this is insane.

Saddam Hussein might have resigned for far less money had it been offered to him.

Do Americans see the irony in the "saving Iraq from tyranny" excuse? The greatest price of the neoconservative war against Iraq is not the $3 trillion or the dead and maimed American soldiers and their broken families. The greatest price of this evil war is the destruction of the U.S. Constitution and American civil liberties.

The Bush/Cheney/Obama National Security State has eviscerated the Constitution and civil liberty. Nothing remains. The Republican Federalist Society, with its extreme doctrine of the "unitary executive," has put enough federal judges in the judiciary to rule that the president is above the law. The president doesn't have to obey the law against spying on American citizens without warrants. The president doesn't have to obey U.S. and international laws against torture. The president doesn't have to obey the Constitution that mandates that only Congress can declare war. The president can do whatever he wants as long as he justifies it as "national security" or a wartime measure.

The president's part of the government, the unaccountable executive branch, is supreme. The president can announce, without being impeached, his decision to murder Americans abroad and at home if someone somewhere in the unaccountable executive branch regards such American citizens as "threats."

Murder first. No accountability later.

The executive branch has exercised unilateral, unaccountable power to deep-six the U.S. Constitution, with little interference from the judiciary and with support from Congress. The executive branch has declared foreign opponents of America's illegal invasions and occupations of their countries to be "terrorists," subject neither to the laws of war nor to the criminal laws of the U.S. and, therefore, subject to indefinite torture and detention without charges or evidence.

This is the legacy of the Bush/Cheney regime, and this criminal regime continues under Obama.

America's "war on terror," a fabrication, has resurrected the unaccountable dungeon of the Middle Ages and the raw tyranny that prevailed prior to the Magna Carta.

This is the true cost of "liberating" Iraq.

Who will now liberate Americans from the Bush/Cheney/neoconservative/Obama tyranny?

President Obama asserts that America's war crimes have come to an end in Iraq, but Obama asserts the power to export America's war crimes to Afghanistan in order to rein in what the CIA director says are "fifty or less" Al

Qaeda members remaining in Afghanistan. Bankrupt Americans will now be saddled with another three trillion dollars of debt in order to chase after "fifty or less" alleged terrorists. To cover up this extraordinary waste of borrowed money, Obama, following the dishonest practices of prior American regimes, equated al Qaeda with the Taliban, a home-grown movement of hundreds of thousands of Afghans seeking to unify the country.

The least expensive way to combat "terrorists" would be to stop trying to create an American empire in the Middle East and Central Asia and to stop imposing American puppet states on indigenous populations.

The bought-and-paid-for European puppet states, who preen themselves with their superior morality, fall in line with Washington, obeying their American master who fills their pockets with dollars. The West having fought tyranny since the Magna Carta, now imposes tyranny both on itself and on the rest of the world. If Hitler and Stalin had prevailed, what would be the difference? Is the Obama regime going to eliminate the "enemies of the state," condemned without trial or evidence, by shooting them in the front of the head instead of in the back of the neck, as was the practice in the Lubyanka?

What other difference is there?

THE COLLAPSE OF WESTERN MORALITY

September 23, 2010

Yes, I know, as many readers will be quick to inform me, the West never had any morality. Nevertheless things have gotten worse.

In hopes that I will be permitted to make a point, permit me to acknowledge that the US dropped nuclear bombs on two Japanese cities, fire-bombed Tokyo; that Great Britain and the US fire-bombed Dresden and a number of other German cities, expending more destructive force, according to some historians, against the civilian German population than against the German armies; that President Grant and his Civil War war criminals, Generals Sherman and Sheridan, committed genocide against the Plains Indians; that the US today enables Israel's genocidal policies against the Palestinians, policies that one Israeli official has compared to 19th century US genocidal policies against the American Indians; that the US in the new 21st century invaded Iraq and Afghanistan on contrived pretenses, murdering countless numbers of civilians, and that British Prime Minister Tony Blair lent the British army to his American masters, as did other NATO countries, all of whom find themselves committing war crimes under the Nuremberg standard in lands in which they have no national interests, but for which they receive an American pay check.

I don't mean these few examples to be exhaustive. I know the list goes on and on. Still, despite the long list of horrors, moral degradation is reaching new lows. The US now routinely tortures prisoners, despite its strict illegality under US and international law, and a recent poll shows that the percentage of Americans who approve of torture is rising. Indeed, it is quite high, though still just below a majority.

And we have what appears to be a new thrill: American soldiers using the cover of war to murder civilians. Recently American troops were arrested for murdering Afghan civilians for fun and collecting trophies such as fingers and skulls.

This revelation came on the heels of Pfc. Bradley Manning's alleged leak of a US Army video of US soldiers in helicopters and their controllers thousands of miles away having fun with joy sticks murdering members of the press and Afghan civilians. Manning is cursed with a moral conscience that has been discarded by his government and his military, and Manning has been arrested for obeying the law and reporting a war crime to the American people.

US Rep. Mike Rogers, a Republican, of course, from Michigan, who is on the House Subcommittee on Terrorism, has called for Manning's execution. According to US Rep. Rogers it is an act of treason to report an American war crime.

In other words, calling for government to obey the law constitutes "treason to America."

US Rep. Rogers said that America's wars are being undermined by "a culture of disclosure" and that this "serious and growing problem" could only be stopped by the execution of Manning.

If Rep. Rogers is representative of Michigan, then Michigan is a state that we don't need.

The US government, a font of imperial hubris, does not believe that any act it commits, no matter how vile, can possibly be a war crime. One million dead Iraqis, a ruined country, and four million displaced Iraqis are all justified, because the "threatened" US Superpower had to protect itself from nonexistent weapons of mass destruction that the US government knew for a fact were not in Iraq and could not have been a threat to the US if they were in Iraq.

When other countries attempt to enforce the international laws that the Americans established in order to execute Germans defeated in World War II, the US government goes to work and blocks the attempt. A year ago on October 8, the Spanish Senate, obeying its American master, limited Spain's laws of universal jurisdiction in order to sink a legitimate war crimes case brought against George W. Bush, Barack H. Obama, Tony Blair, and Gordon Brown.

The West includes Israel, and there the horror stories are 60 years long. Moreover, if you mention any of them you are declared to be an anti-semite. I only mention them in order to prove that I am not anti-American, anti-British, and anti-NATO, but am simply against war crimes. It was the distinguished Zionist Jewish Judge, Goldstone, who produced the UN report indicating that Israel committed war crimes when it attacked the civilian population and civilian infrastructure of Gaza. For his efforts, Israel declared the Zionist Goldstone to be "a self-hating Jew," and the US Congress, on instruction from the Israel Lobby, voted to disregard the Goldstone Report to the UN.

As the Israeli official said, we are only doing to the Palestinians what the Americans did to the American Indians.

The Israeli army uses female soldiers to sit before video screens and to fire by remote control machine guns from towers to murder Palestinians who come to tend their fields within 1500 meters of the enclosed perimeter of Ghetto Gaza. There is no indication that these Israeli women are bothered by gunning down young children and old people who come to tend to their fields.

If the crimes were limited to war and the theft of lands, perhaps we could say it is a case of jingoism sidetracking traditional morality, otherwise still in effect.

Alas, the collapse of morality is too widespread. Some sports teams now have a win-at-all-cost attitude that involves plans to injure the star players of the opposing teams. To avoid all these controversies, let's go to Formula One racing where 200 mph speeds are attained.

Prior to 1988, 22 years ago, track deaths were due to driver error, car failure, and poorly designed tracks compromised with safety hazards. World Champion Jackie Stewart did much to improve the safety of tracks, both for drivers and spectators. But in 1988 everything changed. Top driver Ayrton Senna nudged another top driver Alain Prost toward a pit wall at 190 mph. According to *AutoWeek* (August 30, 2010), nothing like this had been seen before. "Officials did not punish Senna's move that day in Portugal, and so a significant shift in racing began." What the great racing driver Stirling Moss called "dirty driving" became the norm.

Nigel Roebuck in *AutoWeek* reports that in 1996 World Champion Damon Hill said that Senna's win-at-all-cost tactic "was responsible for fundamental change in the ethics of the sport." Drivers began using "terrorist tactics on the track." Damon Hill said that "the views that I'd gleaned from being around my dad [twice world champion Graham Hill] and people like him, I soon had to abandon," because you realized that no penalty was forthcoming against the guy who tried to kill you in order that he could win.

When asked about the ethics of modern Formula One racing, American World Champion Phil Hill said: "Doing that sort of stuff in my day was just unthinkable. For one thing, we believed certain tactics were unacceptable."

In today's Western moral climate, driving another talented driver into the wall at 200 mph is just part of winning. Michael Schumacher, born in January 1969, is a seven times World Champion, an unequaled record. On August 1 at the Hungarian Grand Prix, *AutoWeek* reports that Schumacher tried to drive his former Ferrari teammate, Rubens Barrichello, into the wall at 200 mph speeds.

Confronted with his attempted act of murder, Schumacher said: "This is Formula One. Everyone knows I don't give presents."

Neither does the US government, nor state and local governments, nor the UK government, nor the EU, nor the Israeli government.

The deformation of the police, which many Americans, in their untutored existence as naive believers in "law and order," still think are "on their side," has taken on new dimensions with the police militarized to fight "terrorists" and "domestic extremists."

The police have been off the leash since the civilian police boards were nixed by the conservatives. Kids as young as 6 years old have been handcuffed and carted off to jail for school infractions that may or may not have occurred. So have moms with a car full of children.

Anyone who googles videos of acts of gratuitous brutality by US police will call up tens of thousands of examples, and this is after laws that make filming police brutality a felony. A year or two ago such a search would call up hundreds of thousands of videos.

In one of the most recent of the numerous daily acts of gratuitous police abuse of citizens, an 84-year-old man had his neck broken because he objected to a night time towing of his car. The goon cop body-slammed the 84-year old and broke his neck. The Orlando, Florida, police department says that the old man was a "threat" to the well-armed much younger police goon, because the old man clenched his fist.

Americans won't be the first people sent straight to Hell while thinking that they are the salt of the earth, they're just getting in line. The Americans have even devised a title for themselves to rival that of the Israelis' self-designation as "God's Chosen People." The Americans call themselves "the indispensable people."

THE WAR ON TERROR: DOES ANYONE REMEMBER?

October 15, 2010

Does anyone remember the "cakewalk war" that would last six weeks, cost $50-$60 billion, and be paid for out of Iraqi oil revenues?

Does anyone remember that White House economist Lawrence Lindsey was fired by Dubya because Lindsey estimated that the Iraq war could cost as much as $200 billion?

Lindsey was fired for over-estimating the cost of a war that, according to Joseph Stiglitz and Linda Bilmes, has cost 15 times more than Lindsey estimated. And the US still has 50,000 troops in Iraq.

Does anyone remember that just prior to the US invasion of Iraq, the US government declared victory over the Taliban in Afghanistan?

Does anyone remember that the reason Dubya gave for invading Iraq was Saddam Hussein's weapons of mass destruction, weapons that the US government knew did not exist?

Are Americans aware that the same neoconservatives who made these fantastic mistakes, or told these fabulous lies, are still in control of the government in Washington?

The "war on terror" is now in its tenth year. What is it really all about?

The bottom line answer is that the "war on terror" is about creating real terrorists. The US government desperately needs real terrorists in order to justify its expansion of its wars against Muslim countries and to keep the American people sufficiently fearful that they continue to accept the police state that provides "security from terrorists," but not from the government that has discarded civil liberties.

The US government creates terrorists by invading Muslim countries, wrecking infrastructure and killing vast numbers of civilians. The US also creates terrorists by installing puppet governments to rule over Muslims and by using the puppet governments to murder and persecute citizens as is occurring on a vast scale in Pakistan today.

Neoconservatives used 9/11 to launch their plan for US world hegemony. Their plan fit with the interests of America's ruling oligarchies. Wars are good for the profits of the military/security complex, about which President Eisenhower warned us in vain a half century ago. American hegemony is good for the oil industry's control over resources and resource flows. The transformation of the Middle East into a vast American puppet state serves well the Israel Lobby's Zionist aspirations for Israeli territorial expansion.

Most Americans cannot see what is happening because of their conditioning. Most Americans believe that their government is the best on earth, that it is morally motivated to help others and to do good, that it rushes aid to countries where there is famine and natural catastrophes. Most believe that their presidents tell the truth, except about their sexual affairs.

The persistence of these delusions is extraordinary in the face of daily headlines that report US government bullying of, and interference with, virtually every country on earth. The US policy is to buy off, overthrow, or make war on leaders of other countries who represent their peoples' interests instead of American interests. A recent victim was the president of Honduras who had the wild idea that the Honduran government should serve the Honduran people.

The American government was able to have Honduran President Manuel Zelaya discarded, because the Honduran military is trained and supplied by the US military. It is the same case in Pakistan, where the US government has the Pakistani government making war on its own people by invading tribal areas that the Americans consider to be friendly to the Taliban, Al Qaeda, "militants" and "terrorists."

Earlier this year a deputy US Treasury secretary ordered Pakistan to raise taxes so that the Pakistani government could more effectively make war on its own citizens for the Americans. On October 14 US Secretary of State Hillary Clinton ordered Pakistan to again raise taxes or the US would withhold flood aid. Clinton pressured America's European puppet states to do the same, expressing in the same breath that the US government was worried by British cuts in the military budget. God forbid that the hard-pressed British, still reeling from American financial fraud, don't allocate enough money to fight America's wars.

On Washington's orders, the Pakistani government launched a military offensive against Pakistani citizens in the Swat Valley that killed large numbers of Pakistanis and drove millions of civilians from their homes. Last July the US instructed Pakistan to send its troops against the Pakistani residents of North Waziristan. On July 6, Jason Ditz reported on Antiwar.com that "at America's behest, Pakistan has launched offensives against [the Pakistani provinces of] Swat Valley, Bajaur, South Waziristan, Orakzai, and Khyber."[16]

A week later Israel's US Senator Carl Levin (D-MI) called for escalating the Obama Administration's policies of US airstrikes against Pakistan's tribal areas. On September 30, the Pakistani newspaper, *The Frontier Post*, wrote that the American air strikes "are, plain and simple, a naked aggression against Pakistan."

The US claims that its forces in Afghanistan have the right to cross into Pakistan in pursuit of "militants." Recently US helicopter gunships killed three Pakistani soldiers whom they mistook for Taliban. Pakistan closed the main US supply route to Afghanistan until the Americans apologized.

Pakistan warned Washington against future attacks. However, US military officials, under pressure from Obama to show progress in the endless Afghan war, responded to Pakistan's warning by calling for expanding the Afghan war into Pakistan. On October 5 the Canadian journalist, Eric Margolis, wrote that "the US edges closer to invading Pakistan."

In his book, *Obama's Wars*, Bob Woodward reports that America's puppet president of Pakistan, Asif Ali Zardari, believes that terrorist bombing attacks inside Pakistan for which the Taliban are blamed are in fact CIA operations designed to destabilize Pakistan and allow Washington to seize Pakistan's nuclear weapons.

To keep Pakistan in line, the US government changed its position that the "Times Square Bombing" was the work of a "lone wolf." Attorney General Eric Holder switched the blame to the "Pakistani Taliban," and Secretary of State Clinton threatened Pakistan with "very serious consequences" for the unsuccessful Times Square bombing, which possibly was a false flag operation aimed at Pakistan. (The bomb was incompetently made and did not explode.)

To further heighten tensions, on September 1 the eight members of a high-ranking Pakistani military delegation en route to a meeting in Tampa, Florida, with US Central Command, were rudely treated and detained as terrorist suspects at Washington, DC's Dulles Airport.

For decades the US government has enabled repeated Israeli military aggression against Lebanon and now appears to be getting into gear for another Israeli assault on the former American protectorate. On October 14 the US government expressed its "outrage" that the Lebanese government had permitted a visit by Iranian President Ahmadinejad, who is the focus of Washington's intense demonization efforts. Israel's representatives in the US Congress threatened to stop US military aid to Lebanon, forgetting that US Rep. Howard Berman (D-CA) has had aid to Lebanon blocked since last August to punish Lebanon for a border clash with Israel.

Perhaps the most telling headline of all is the October 14 report, "Somalia's New American Prime Minister." An American has been installed as the Prime Minister of Somalia, an American puppet government in Mogadishu backed up by thousands of Ugandan troops paid by Washington.

This barely scratches the surface of Washington's benevolence toward other countries and respect for their rights, borders, and lives of their citizens.

Meanwhile, to silence the whistleblower website WikiLeaks and to prevent any more revelations of American war crimes, the "freedom and democracy" government in DC has closed down WikiLeaks' donations by placing the company that collects its money on its "watch list" and by having the Australian puppet government blacklist WikiLeaks.

WikiLeaks is now akin to a terrorist organization. The American government's practice of silencing critics will spread across the Internet.

Remember, they hate us because we have freedom and democracy, First Amendment rights, habeas corpus, respect for human rights, and show justice and mercy to all.

WHO HAS THE
CRYSTAL BALL?

November 2, 2010

My conservative and Republican acquaintances believe that the "liberal media" is destroying America. When I ask them to identify the liberal media, the usual reply is, "all of it!" I ask them about Fox "News," CNN, and point out that the TV networks are no longer independent but parts of large corporate conglomerates and that all of the "liberal" news anchors have been fired or died off. At that point my acquaintances fall back on *The New York Times* and the *Washington Post*. I remind them that the invasion of Iraq would not have been possible without *The New York Times* leading the way.

Judith Miller filled that newspaper with the neoconservative/ Bush regime propaganda that was orchestrated to make the public accept US aggression toward Iraq. The *Times* later sort of apologized and Miller departed the paper.

That left the *Washington Post*, apparently long a CIA asset, as the "liberal media" that is destroying America, until on October 31 the paper's long-time pundit, David Broder, wrote that Obama should spend the next two years disarming the Republicans and renewing the economy by orchestrating a showdown with Iran. Going to war with Iran, "the greatest threat to the world," would simultaneously unite Republicans with Obama and restore the economy. By following Broder's prescription, Obama "will have made the world safer and may be regarded as one of the most successful presidents in history."

Here we have the "liberal" Broder at the "liberal" *Washington Post* advocating the neoconservative's desired war with Iran. The irony deepens. My acquaintances regard Obama as a Marxist and a Muslim. It does not occur to my acquaintances that the military/security complex and Wall Street would not put a Marxist in the White House, or that AIPAC would not put a Muslim in the White House, or that a Muslim would not have chosen a dual Israeli citizen as his chief of staff and staffed up his government with Zionists friendly to Israel, or that a Muslim would not have renewed the war in Afghanistan and started new ones in Pakistan and Yemen, or that, if a Muslim, Obama would be averse to slaughtering Muslims in behalf of the neocons' world hegemony agenda.

Chris Hedges writes in Truthdig:

The American left is a phantom. It is conjured up by the right wing to tag Barack Obama as a socialist and used by the liberal class to justify its complacency and lethargy. It diverts attention from corporate power. It perpetuates the myth of a democratic system that is influenced by the votes of citizens, political platforms and the work of legislators. It keeps the world neatly divided into a left and a right. The phantom left functions as a convenient scapegoat. The right wing blames it for moral degeneration and fiscal chaos. The liberal class uses it to call for 'moderation.' The corporations that control mass communications conjure up the phantom of a left. They blame the phantom for our debacle. And they get us to speak in absurdities.

But that's America. It seems like people simply cannot put two and two together. Thinking is not a widespread activity among the American public.

Indeed, many Americans are incapable of thought on any subject.

Consider the latest bomb scare initially blamed on a young pro-American female student in Yemen who luckily was released before she was tortured and raped. Allegedly, bombs disguised as printer ink modules passed through lax cargo security and were on their way to blow up something. Everyone immediately endorsed the story. UPS pilots urged US officials to tighten cargo screening worldwide. The US has sent a team into Yemen to take over security.

Somehow the security services that were unable to foil the 9/11 plot were able to penetrate this plot before it succeeded.

Consider the timeliness of the foiled plot. British Airways Chairman Martin Broughton and other European officials recently accused the US of making inane demands on airport passengers, such as removing their shoes and separate examinations of laptop computers. Broughton even declared: "Europe should not have to kowtow to the Americans every time they want something done to beef up security on US bound flights."

The owner of London's Heathrow Airport agreed. The European Union has challenged the US requirement for European passengers to have online checks before boarding flights bound for the US, declaring the requirement a "burdensome measure."

Miraculously, a plot is exposed that brands British Airways, London's Heathrow, and the EU as "soft on terrorism security."

Or what about this motive? The Obama regime wants to send CIA hunter-killer teams into Yemen to murder people suspected of hostility to America. CIA drones would be used to blow up suspects despite the proven fact that the CIA drones used in Afghanistan and in violation of Pakistan's sovereignty mainly kill innocent people.

Yemen's President, Ali Abdullah Saleh said that he opposes America's violation of his country's sovereignty, but, alas, it was the Yemeni President's lax air cargo security that let the bombs through. So his protests, too, are discredited by the lax security that enabled the printer ink plot. Unless US forces are in Yemen eliminating terrorists, the world is not safe.

Americans never ask the old Roman question, "Who benefits?"

Consider, for example, the "underwear bomber." How likely is it that Al Qaeda, allegedly having successfully outwitted all 16 US intelligence agencies, the National Security Council, NORAD, airport security, the Pentagon, and the security agencies of all US allies including Israel and brought down the World Trade towers and successfully attacked the Pentagon itself, would choose as a sequel blowing up a mere airliner with an underwear bomb, a shoe bomb, and a shampoo/toothpaste/underarm deodorant bomb? Having acquired the stature associated with 9/11, blowing up an airliner is a big comedown in prestige. It conveys the image of a washed-up Al Qaeda.

Again, who benefits? The most obvious beneficiary of the underwear bomber is the corporation that manufactures the full body scanners that show people as if they are naked. Obviously, the machines were already produced and awaiting a contract. Without the underwear bomber and the hype and fear the media generated over the new threat, it is unlikely the government could have succeeded with such massive violation of personal privacy.

It would be interesting to know what company manufactures the body scanners and what its relationship is to the US and Israeli governments. But these questions never occur to Americans or to the "liberal media."

As a member of the Congressional staff during the 1970s, both House and Senate and committee and member staffs, I learned that except for rare occurrences, the legislation that Congress passes and the President signs is written either by executive agencies or by lobbyists. Congress did not write the PATRIOT Act. It was written in advance of 9/11 awaiting its opportunity. President Bush's National Security Advisor, Condi Rice, is on record saying that no one ever suspected such an event as 9/11 with terrorists using hijacked airliners as missiles against the World Trade Center and Pentagon. Why then was the voluminous PATRIOT Act sitting waiting?

Whose crystal ball read the future and had the PATRIOT Act drafted in advance?

Whose crystal ball foresaw the underwear bomber and had the full body scanners ready to be deployed?

Are these amazing coincidences or orchestrated events?

THE NEW AMERICAN CREDO: MIGHT IS RIGHT

November 3, 2011

In my last column, "Who Has the Crystal Ball," I questioned the existence of "the liberal media," and I remarked that it would be interesting to know the manufacturer of the full body scanners and the company's relationship to the US and Israeli governments.

Conservative readers wrote to me saying that, as I had not mentioned National Public Radio, I had hidden "the liberal media" under the table. Another reader, well informed on the subject, told me about the full body scanner company and its relationship to the US and Israeli governments.

Let's begin with the latter.

The full body scanners are manufactured by Rapiscan Systems, a firm represented by the Chertoff Group. The Chertoff Group is Michael Chertoff, a dual Israeli/US citizen appointed Secretary of Homeland Security in 2005 by Puppet President George W. Bush. The Transportation Security Administration (TSA) used Obama's economic stimulus, the American Recovery and Reinvestment Act, to purchase 150 Rapiscan machines. Much larger purchases are in the works.

Chertoff has been a federal judge on the US Court of Appeals for the Third Circuit and was the federal prosecutor who convicted and destroyed the Arthur Andersen accounting firm, apparently illegally as the conviction was overturned by the US Supreme Court. But, of course, the firm and the careers of its employees were already destroyed by Chertoff.

Chertoff was also appointed Assistant Attorney General of the Department of Justice by George W. Bush. Chertoff supervised the 9/11 investigation or non-investigation.

Chertoff is also the co-author of the USA PATRIOT Act, a piece of fascist legislation that destroys American civil liberties.

Today Chertoff is using his government credentials to push full body scanners into American airports. A rights group, FlyersRights.org, has criticized Chertoff for abusing "the trust the public has placed in him as a former public servant to privately gain from the sale of full-body scanners."[17]

Now let's have a look at National Public Radio. Once upon a time NPR was an alternative voice. That voice was discarded during the Bush administration when Republican fundraiser Gay Hart Gaines was appointed by Dubya as vice chair for the Corporation for Public Broadcasting, Cheryl Feldman Halpern, was appointed chair of the Corporation by Dubya, and Elizabeth Sembler was appointed by Dubya to the board of the corporation.

These women are certainly not liberals. Gaines is affiliated with right-wing and neoconservative organizations, such as the American Enterprise Institute, the Heritage Foundation and the National Review Institute. According to Common Cause, Gaines was "an ardent fundraiser for Newt Gingrich."[18]

Halpern is a Republican donor and a critic of NPR. Halpern has accused NPR of anti-Israel bias and said that public broadcasting journalists should be penalized for biased programs. Biased programs are those that don't fit Republican and AIPAC agendas. Halpern accompanied President George W. Bush to Jerusalem for the celebration of the 60th anniversary of the Israeli state in May 2008. Halpern is a board member of the Washington Institute for Near East Policy, a spin-off organization from AIPAC tasked with focusing primarily on influencing the US executive branch while AIPAC focuses on Congress. At her confirmation hearing, Halpern expressed her opinion that Public Broadcasting System's Bill Moyers was not objective and regretted that as chair of the corporation she lacked the authority to "remove physically somebody who had engaged in editorialization of the news."[19]

Sembler is director of Jewish Studies at the Jewish Day School in Clearwater, Florida. Her husband is CEO of the Sembler Company, a shopping center development firm.

The Corporation for Public Broadcasting board distributes federal funds to noncommercial radio and TV stations. It became clear to NPR that their funding was in question, and NPR deserted truth for money.

The Republican takeover was completed by an infusion of corporate money into NPR.

Today the station has as many advertisements for corporate donors as a commercial station. It still pretends to be financed by listeners, but NPR is now part of the corporate media and sounds like the voice of Israel.

On November 2, NPR's news broadcast showed its new colors. Reporting on the 40-year sentence handed to Omar Khadr by a Gestapo military tribunal for "war crimes," NPR provided commentary from a widow of a US soldier killed in the firefight that captured the wounded 15-year old Khadr and by a retired US military officer. NPR did not provide any commentary by legal experts who have shown the "trial" to be a travesty of law.

Khadr was captured in wounded condition following a four-hour firefight in the Afghan village of Ayub Kheyl, which came under US attack.

He was accused of throwing a hand grenade that fatally wounded a US soldier. It is impossible to know who threw a grenade during a firefight. Moreover, the use of lethal force in military encounters does not constitute a war crime.

Khadr was held for seven years in Guantanamo where he was tortured into confession. At his trial, his confession became a plea bargain.

What Khadr's trial was about is establishing that "enemy combatants" who resist US aggression are war criminals. The assumption is that only "terrorists" resist American invasion of their countries.

None of this information was revealed by the NPR report. Instead America's "alternative voice" was thoroughly neoconservative. NPR presented its listeners with the self-righteous celebration of the US soldier's widow, who, *The Guardian* reported (Nov. 2) "pumped her fist and cheered 'yes.' The widow said that now, finally, that justice was done she could get on with her life. NPR followed up with a retired US military officer, who said that Khadr's sentence was equivalent to freeing a murderer.

Khadr's prosecutor, Jeffrey Groharing, declared that Khadr's sentence "will send a message to Al Qaeda and others whose aims and goals are to kill and cause chaos around the world." The irony in this assertion escaped the tamed NPR. The deaths that can be attributed to Al Qaeda are tiny in number compared to the deaths inflicted by gratuitous US and Israeli naked aggression against Muslims in Iraq, Afghanistan, Palestine, Lebanon, Pakistan, Yemen, and Somalia. Groharing declared the 15-year old Khadr to have been "an accomplished terrorist" who committed the offense of resisting American aggression.

Now, really, what kind of idiot would interpret NPR's report as a product of "the liberal media."

What message did Khadr's sentence send? To insouciant Americans only that finally a terrorist got his comeuppance despite the liberal media. To the rest of the world the message is: the US is a morally bankrupt, self-righteous country that believes that might is right. The American claim to world leadership is discredited.

AMERICA'S DEVOLUTION INTO DICTATORSHIP

November 12, 2010

The United States Department of Justice (*sic*) routinely charges and convicts innocents with bogus and concocted crimes that are not even on the statute book. The distinguished defense attorney and civil libertarian, Harvey A. Silverglate, published a book last year, *Three Felonies A Day: How the Feds Target the Innocent*, which conclusively proves that today in "freedom and democracy" America we have punishment without crime.

This same Justice Department, which routinely frames and railroads the innocent, argued in Federal Court on November 8 that the US government, if approved by the president, could murder anyone it wishes, citizens or noncitizens, at will. All that is required is that the government declare—without evidence, charges, trial, jury conviction or any of the due process required by the US Constitution—that the government suspects the murdered person or persons to be a "threat."

The US Justice Department even told US Federal District Court Judge John Bates that the US judiciary, formerly a co-equal branch of government, has absolutely no legal authority whatsoever to stick its nose into President "Change" Obama's decision to assassinate Americans. The unaccountability of the president's decision to murder people is, the US Justice Department declared, one of "the very core powers of the president as commander in chief."

The argument by the Justice Department that the executive branch has unreviewable authority to kill Americans, whom the executive branch has unilaterally, without presenting evidence, determined to pose a threat, was challenged by the American Civil Liberties Union and the Center for Constitutional Rights. Attorneys for these organizations understand that once the principle of extra-judicial execution is established, it will be expanded by those who wield law as a weapon. Therefore, they want to nip it in the bud.

The outcome of the case will determine whether the neoconservative and Israeli stooge, President George W. Bush, was correct when he said that the US Constitution was nothing but a "scrap of paper."

It is my opinion that the American people and the US Constitution haven't much chance of winning this case. The Republican Federalist Society has succeeded in appointing many federal district, appeals and supreme court judges, who believe that the powers of the executive branch are superior to the powers of the legislature and judiciary. The Founding Fathers of our country declared unequivocally that the executive, legislative, and judicial branches were co-equal, However, the Republicans who comprise the Federalist Society have implanted the society's demonic ideology in the federal bench and Justice Department. Today the erroneous belief is widespread that the executive branch is supreme and that the other branches of government are less than equal.

If Americans have a greater enemy than neoconservatives, that enemy is the Federalist Society.

Disagree with me as you will, but now let's look at this development from another perspective. I am old enough to remember the Nixon years, and I was a presidential appointee, confirmed by the US senate, in the Reagan administration. For those of you too young to know and those who are too old to remember, President Nixon resigned to avoid impeachment simply because Nixon lied about when he learned about the burglary of the Watergate office of the Democratic Party.

Nixon lied about when he learned of the burglary, because he knew that the *Washington Post* would make an issue of the burglary, if he launched an investigation, to defeat his re-election. The military/security complex and the black ops groups in the US government were angry at Nixon for smoothing US-China relations. The *Washington Post*, long regarded as a CIA asset, hid behind its "liberal" image to bring Nixon down. Woodward and Bernstein wrote thriller-type reports of midnight meetings with "deep throat" in dangerous parking garages to get the scoop on the date of Nixon's knowledge of the meaningless burglary.

Let's assume that I have it all wrong. The fact remains that Nixon was driven from office because of the Watergate burglary. No one was harmed. Nixon did not kill anyone or claim the right to kill, without proof or accountability, or to indefinitely detain American citizens. If the dastardly President Nixon had a Justice Department like the present one and the powers accumulated in the presidency by Bush and Obama, Nixon could have invoked "national security" and/or brought charges against Woodward, Bernstein, and the *Washington Post* to force them to reveal the identity of the leaker, who could have been detained indefinitely and tortured until he confessed that he lied in order to injure the president of the US.

Nixon might be too far in the past for most Americans, so let's look at Ronald Reagan.

The neoconservatives' Iran/Contra scandal almost brought down President Reagan. It is unclear whether President Reagan knew about the neocon operation and, if he did, whether he was kept in the loop. But all of this aside, what do you think would have been President Reagan's fate if he, or his Justice Department, had responded to the scandal by declaring that leaks a la Bradley Manning and Edward Snowden were national security threats and that Reagan had the power as commander in chief to assassinate those who posed a threat to US national security?

Instantly, the media would have been in an uproar, law schools and university faculties would have been in an uproar, the Democrats would have been demanding Reagan's impeachment, and his impeachment would have occurred with the speed of light.

Today in America, approximately 25 years later, the ACLU has to go to federal court in order to attempt to affirm that "if the Constitution means anything, it surely means that the president does not have unreviewable authority to summarily execute any American whom he concludes is an enemy of the state."

In reply, the Justice Department told the court that murdering American citizens is a "political question" that is not subject to judicial review. The "freedom and democracy" government then invoked the "state secrets privilege" and declared that the case against the government's power to commit murder must be dismissed in order to avoid "the disclosure of sensitive information"

If the Obama Regime wins this case, the US will have become a dictatorship.

As far as I can tell, the "liberal media" and most Americans do not care. Indeed, conservative Republicans are cheering it on.

They can't wait for America to be a tyranny in which they can destroy their enemies. The fact that they themselves can be destroyed has not yet occurred to them.

THE STENCH OF AMERICAN HYPOCRISY

November 18, 2010

Ten years of rule by the Bush and Obama regimes have seen the collapse of the rule of law in the United States. Is the American media covering this ominous and extraordinary story? No the American media is preoccupied with the rule of law in Burma (Myanmar).

The military regime that rules Burma just released from house arrest the pro-democracy leader, Aung San Suu Kyi. The American media used the occasion of her release to get on Burma's case for the absence of the rule of law. I'm all for the brave lady, but if truth be known, "freedom and democracy" America needs her far worse than does Burma.

I'm not an expert on Burma, but the way I see it the objection to a military government is that the government is not accountable to law. Instead, such a regime behaves as it sees fit and issues edicts that advance its agenda. Burma's government can be criticized for not having a rule of law, but it cannot be criticized for ignoring its own laws. We might not like what the Burmese government does, but, precisely speaking, it is not behaving illegally.

In contrast, the United States government claims to be a government of laws, not of men, but when the executive branch violates the laws that constrain it, those responsible are not held accountable for their criminal actions. As accountability is the essence of the rule of law, the absence of accountability means the absence of the rule of law.

The list of criminal actions by presidents Bush and Obama, Vice President Cheney, the CIA, the NSA, the US military, and other branches of the government is long and growing. For example, both President Bush and Vice President Cheney violated US and international laws against torture. Amnesty International and the American Civil Liberties Union responded to Bush's recent admission that he authorized torture with calls for a criminal investigation of Bush's crime.

In a letter to Attorney General Eric Holder, the ACLU reminded the US Department of Justice that "a nation committed to the rule of law cannot simply ignore evidence that its most senior leaders authorized torture."

Rob Freer of Amnesty International said that Bush's admission "to authorizing acts which constitute torture under international law" and which constitute "a crime under international law," puts the US government "under obligation to investigate and to bring those responsible to justice."

The ACLU and Amnesty International do not want to admit it, but the US government shed its commitment to the rule of law a decade ago when the US launched its naked aggression—war crimes under the Nuremberg standard—against Afghanistan and Iraq on the basis of lies and deception.

The US government's contempt for the rule of law took another step when President Bush violated the Foreign Intelligence Surveillance Act and had the National Security Agency bypass the FISA court and spy on Americans without warrants. *The New York Times* is on its high horse about the rule of law in Burma, but when a patriot revealed to *The Times* that Bush was violating US law, *The Times'* editors sat on the leak for one year until after Bush was safely re-elected.

Holder, of course, will not attempt to hold Bush accountable for the crime of torture. Indeed, Assistant US Attorney John Durham has just cleared the CIA of accountability for its crime of destroying the videotape evidence of the US government's illegal torture of detainees, a felony under US law.

Last February Cheney said on ABC's This Week that "I was a big supporter of waterboarding."

US law has always regarded waterboarding as torture. The US government executed WWII Japanese for waterboarding American POWs. But Cheney has escaped accountability, which means that there is no rule of law.

Vice president Cheney's office also presided over the outing of a covert CIA agent, a felony. Yet, nothing happened to Cheney, and the underling who took the fall had his sentence commuted by President Bush.

President Obama has made himself complicit in the crimes of his predecessor by refusing to enforce the rule of law. In his criminality, Obama has actually surpassed Bush. Bush is the president of extra-judicial torture, extra-judicial detention, extra-judicial spying and invasions of privacy, but Obama has one-upped Bush. Obama is the president of extra-judicial murder.

Not only is Obama violating the sovereignty of an American ally, Pakistan, by sending in drones and special forces teams to murder Pakistani civilians, but in addition Obama has a list of American citizens whom he intends to murder without arrest, presentation of evidence, trial and conviction.

The most massive change brought by Obama is his assertion of the right of the executive branch to murder whomever it wishes without any interference from US and international law.

The world has not seen such a criminal government as Obama's since

Joseph Stalin's and Hitler's. On November 8, the US Department of Justice told federal district court judge John Bates that president Obama's decision to murder American citizens is one of "the very core powers of the president." Moreover, declared the Justice Department, the murder of American citizens is a "political question" that is not subject to judicial review.

In other words, federal courts exist for one purpose only—to give a faux approval to executive branch actions.

If truth be known, there is more justice in Burma under the military regime than in the USA. The military regime put Aung San Suu Kyi under house arrest in her own home.

The military regime did not throw her into a dungeon and rape and torture her under cover of false allegations and indefinite detention without charges. Moreover, the military "tyrants" released her either as a sign of good will or under pressure from international human rights groups, or some combination of the two.

If only comparable good will existed in the US government or pressure from international human rights groups had equal force in America as in Burma.

But, alas, in America macho tough guys approve the virtual strip search of their wives and daughters by full body scanners and the groping by TSA thugs of three-year-old children screaming in terror.

Unlike in Burma, where Aung San Suu Kyi fights for human rights, the sheeple in America submit to the total invasion of their privacy and to the total destruction of their civil liberties and believe without any evidence that they are at the mercy of "terrorists" in far distant lands who have no armies, navies, or air forces and are armed only with AK-47s and improvised explosive devices.

The ignorant and deceived population of the "Great American Superpower," buried in fear propagated by a Ministry of Truth, has acquiesced in the total destruction of the US Constitution and their civil liberties.

FABRICATING TERROR: THE PORTLAND "BOMB" PLOT

November 29, 2010

Why does the FBI orchestrate fake terror plots?

The latest one snared Osman Mohamud, a Somali-American teenager in Portland, Oregon. The Associated Press report by William Mall and Nedra Pickler (11-27-10) is headlined in Yahoo News: "Somali-born teen plotted car-bombing in Oregon."

This is a misleading headline as the report makes it clear that it was a plot orchestrated by federal agents. Two sentences into the news report we have this: "The bomb was an elaborate fake supplied by the [FBI] agents and the public was never in danger, authorities said." The teenager was supplied with a fake bomb and a fake detonator.

Three sentences later the reporters contradict the quoted authorities with a quote from Arthur Balizan, special agent in charge of the FBI in Oregon: "The threat was very real."

The reporters then contradict Balizan: "White House spokesman Nick Shapiro said Saturday that President Barack Obama was aware of the FBI operation before Friday's arrest. Shapiro said Obama was assured that the FBI was in full control of the operation and that the public was not in danger."

Then Shapiro contradicts himself by declaring: "The events of the past 24 hours underscore the necessity of remaining vigilant against terrorism here and abroad."

The story arrives at its Kafkaesque highpoint when President Obama thanks the FBI for its diligence in saving us from the fake plot the FBI had fabricated.

After vacillating between whether they are reporting a real plot or an orchestrated one, the reporters finally come down on the side of orchestration. Documents released by US Attorney Dwight Holton "show the sting operation began in June." Obviously, the targeted Portland teenager was not hot to trot. The FBI had to work on him for six months. The reporters compare "the Portland sting" to the recent arrest in Virginia of Farooque Ahmed who was ensnared in a "bombing plot that was a ruse conducted over the past six months by federal officials."

Think about this. The FBI did a year's work in order to convince two people to participate in fake plots.

If you are not too bright and some tough looking guys accost you and tell you that they are Al Qaeda and expect your help in a terrorist operation, you might be afraid to say no, or you might be thrilled to be part of a blowback against an American population that is indifferent to their government's slaughter of people of your ethnicity in your country of origin. Whichever way it falls, it is unlikely the ensnared person would ever have done anything beyond talk had the FBI not organized them into action. In other cases the FBI entices people with money to participate in its fake plots.

Since 9/11, the only domestic "terrorist plot" that I recall that was not obviously organized by the FBI is the "Times Square plot" to which Faisal Shahzad pleaded guilty to trying to set off a car bomb in Manhattan. This plot, too, is suspicious. One would think that a real terrorist would have a real bomb, not a smoke bomb.

In the May 19, 2009, online site, sott.net (reprinted Nov. 27, 2010), Joe Quinn collects some of the fake plots,[20] some of which were validated by torture confessions and others by ignorant and fearful juries. The US government comes up with a plot, an accused, and tortures him until he confesses, or the government fabricates a case and takes it to jurors who know that they cannot face their neighbors if they let off a media-declared "terrorist."

Perhaps the most obvious of these cases is "the Miami seven," a hapless group of Christian-Zionist-Muslims that called themselves the "Sea of David" and were quietly living in a Florida warehouse awaiting biblical end times. Along came the FBI posing as Al Qaeda and offered them $50,000 and an Al Qaeda swearing-in ceremony.

The FBI told them that they needed to blow up the Sears Tower in Chicago and various government buildings. An honest reporter at Knight Ridder revealed: "The Justice (*sic*) Department unveiled the arrests with an orchestrated series of news conferences in two cities, but the severity of the charges compared with the seemingly amateurish nature of the group raised concerns among civil libertarians," who noted that the group had "no weapons, no explosives."

The Justice Department and tamed media made a big show out of the "militaristic boots" worn by the hapless "plotters," but the FBI had bought the boots for them.

The biggest piece of evidence against the hapless group was that they had taken photos of "targets" in Florida, but the US government had equipped them with cameras.

The US government even rented cars for its dupes to drive to take the pictures.

It turns out that the group only wanted the $50,000, but an American jury convicted them anyhow.

When the US government has to go to such lengths to create "terrorists" out of hapless people, an undeclared agenda is being served. What could this agenda be?

The answer is many agendas. One agenda is to justify wars of aggression that are war crimes under the Nuremberg standard created by the US government itself. One way to avoid war crimes charges is to create acts of terrorism that justify the naked aggressions against "terrorist countries."

Another agenda is to create a police state. A police state can control people who object to their impoverishment for the benefit of the superrich much more easily than can a democracy endowed with constitutional civil liberties.

Another agenda is to get rich. Terror plots, whether real or orchestrated, have created a market for security. Dual Israeli citizen Michael Chertoff, former head of US Homeland Security, is the lobbyist who represents Rapiscan, the company that manufactures the full body porno-scanners that, following the "underwear bomber" event, are now filling up US airports. Homeland Security has announced that they are going to purchase the porno-scanners for trains, buses, subways, court houses, and sports events. How can shopping malls and roads escape? Recently on Interstate 20 west of Atlanta, trucks had to drive through a similar device. Everyone has forgotten that the underwear bomber lacked required documents and was escorted aboard the airliner by an official.

The "war on terror" provides an opportunity for a few well-connected people to become very rich. If they leave Americans with a third world police state, they will be living it up in Gstaad.

This despite the fact that everyone on the planet knows that it is not lactating mothers, children, elderly people in walkers and wheelchairs, members of Congress, members of the military, nuns, and so on, who are members of Al Qaeda plotting to bring aboard a bomb in their underwear, their shoes, their shampoo and face creams.

Indeed, bombs aboard airliners are a rare event.

What is it really all about? Could it be that the US government needs terrorist events in order to completely destroy the US Constitution? On November 24, National Public Radio broadcast a report by Dina Temple-Raston: "Administration officials are looking at the possibility of codifying detention without trial and are awaiting legislation that is supposed to come out of Congress early next year."[21] Of course, the legislation will not come out of Congress. It will be written by Homeland Security and the Justice Department. The impotent Congress will merely rubber-stamp it.

The obliteration of habeas corpus, the most necessary and important protection of liberty ever institutionalized in law and governing constitution, has become necessary for the US government, because a jury might acquit an alleged or mock "terrorist" or framed person whom the US government has declared prior to the trial will be held forever in indefinite detention even if acquitted in a US court of law. The attorney general of the United States has declared that any "terrorist" that he puts on trial who is acquitted by a jury will remain in detention regardless of the verdict. Such an event would reveal the total lawlessness of American "justice."

The United States of America, "the city upon the hill," "the light unto the world," has become Nazi Germany. It was the practice of the Gestapo to ignore court verdicts and to execute or hold indefinitely the cleared defendant in the camps. The Obama regime is in the process of completing Dick Cheney's dream by legislating the legality of indefinite detention. American law has collapsed to the dungeons of the Dark Ages.

This Nazi Gestapo policy is now the declared policy of the US Department of Justice. Anyone who thinks the United States is a free society where people have liberty, "freedom and democracy" is uninformed.

WHO, PRECISELY, IS ATTACKING THE WORLD?

November 30, 2010

The stuck pigs are squealing. To shift the onus from the U.S. State Department, Hillary Clinton paints WikiLeaks' release of the "diplomatic cables" as an "attack on the international community." To reveal truth is equivalent, in the eyes of the U.S. government, to an attack on the world.

It is WikiLeaks' fault that all those U.S. diplomats wrote a quarter of a million undiplomatic messages about America's allies, a.k.a. puppet states. It is also WikiLeaks' fault that a member of the U.S. government could no longer stomach the cynical ways in which the U.S. government manipulates foreign governments to serve, not their own people, but American interests, and delivered the incriminating evidence to WikiLeaks.

The U.S. government actually thinks that it was WikiLeaks' patriotic duty to return the evidence and to identify the leaker. After all, we mustn't let the rest of the world find out what we are up to. They might stop believing our lies.

The influential German magazine *Der Spiegel* writes: "It is nothing short of a political meltdown for U.S. foreign policy."

This might be more a hope than a reality. The "Soviet threat" during the second half of the 20th century enabled U.S. governments to create institutions that subordinated the interests of other countries to those of the U.S. government. After decades of following U.S. leadership, European "leaders" know no other way to act. Finding out that the boss badmouths and deceives them is unlikely to light a spirit of independence. At least not until America's economic collapse becomes more noticeable.

The question is: how much will the press tell us about the documents? *Spiegel* itself has said that the magazine is permitting the U.S. government to censor, at least in part, what it prints about the leaked material. Most likely, this means the public will not learn the content of the 4,330 documents that "are so explosive that they are labeled 'NOFORN,'" meaning that foreigners, including presidents, prime ministers, and security services that share information with the CIA are not permitted to read the documents. Possibly, also, the content of the 16,652 cables classified as "secret" will not be revealed to the public.

Most likely the press, considering their readers' interests, will focus on gossip and the unflattering remarks Americans made about their foreign counterparts. It will be good for laughs. Also, the U.S. government will attempt to focus the media in ways that advance U.S. policies.

Indeed, it has already begun. On Nov. 29, National Public Radio emphasized that the cables showed that Iran was isolated even in the Muslim world, making it easier for the Israelis and Americans to attack. The leaked cables reveal that the president of Egypt, an American puppet, hates Iran, and the Saudi Arabian government has long been urging the U.S. government to attack Iran. In other words, Iran is so dangerous to the world that even its co-religionists want Iran wiped off the face of the earth.

NPR presented several nonobjective "Iranian experts" who denigrated Iran and its leadership and declared that the U.S. government, by resisting its Middle Eastern allies' call for bombing Iran, was the moderate in the picture. The fact that President George W. Bush declared Iran to be a member of "the axis of evil" and threatened repeatedly to attack Iran, and that President Obama has continued the threats—Adm. Michael Mullen, chairman of the U.S. Joint Chiefs of Staff, has just reiterated that the U.S. hasn't taken the attack option off the table—is not regarded by American "Iran experts" as indications of anything other than American moderation.

Somehow it did not come across in the NPR newscast that it is not Iran but Israel that routinely slaughters civilians in Lebanon, Gaza, and the West Bank, and that it is not Iran but the U.S. and its NATO mercenaries who slaughter civilians in Iraq, Afghanistan, Yemen, and Pakistan.

Iran has not invaded any of its neighbors, but the Americans are invading countries halfway around the globe. The "Iranian experts" treated the Saudi and Egyptian rulers' hatred of Iran as a vindication of the U.S. and Israeli governments' demonization of Iran. Not a single "Iranian expert" was capable of pointing out that the tyrants who rule Egypt and Saudi Arabia fear Iran because the Iranian government represents the interests of Muslims, and the Saudi and Egyptian governments represent the interests of the Americans.

Think what it must feel like to be a tyrant suppressing the aspirations of your own people in order to serve the hegemony of a foreign country, while a nearby Muslim government strives to protect its people's independence from foreign hegemony.

Undoubtedly, the tyrants become very anxious. What if their own oppressed subjects get ideas? Little wonder the Saudi and Egyptian rulers want the Americans to eliminate the independent-minded country that is a bad example for Egyptian and Saudi subjects.

As long as the dollar has enough value that it can be used to purchase foreign governments, information damaging to the U.S. government is unlikely to have much effect. As Alain of Lille said a long time ago, "Money is all."

WIKILEAKS II: A GOVERNMENT CAUGHT UP IN MENDACITY AND LIES

December 1, 2010

The reaction to WikiLeaks and its founder, Julian Assange, tells us all we need to know about the total corruption of our "modern" world, which in fact is a throwback to the Dark Ages.

Some member of the United States government released to WikiLeaks the documents that are now controversial. The documents are controversial, because they are official US documents and show all too clearly that the US government is a duplicitous entity whose raison d'être is to control every other government.

The media, not merely in the US but also throughout the English-speaking world and Europe, has shown its hostility to WikiLeaks. The reason is obvious. WikiLeaks reveals truth, while the media covers up for the US government and its puppet states.

Why would anyone with a lick of sense read the media when they can read original material from WikiLeaks? The average American reporter and editor must be very angry that his/her own cowardice is so clearly exposed by Julian Assange. The American media is a whore, whereas the courageous blood of warriors runs through WikiLeaks' veins.

Just as American politicians want Bradley Manning executed because he revealed crimes of the US government, they want Julian Assange executed. In the past few days the more notorious of the morons that sit in the US Congress have denounced Assange as a "traitor to America." What total ignorance. Assange is an Australian, not an American citizen. To be a traitor to America, one has to be of the nationality. An Australian cannot be a traitor to America any more than an American can be a traitor to Australia. But don't expect the morons who represent the lobbyists to know this much.

Mike Huckabee, the redneck Baptist preacher who was governor of Arkansas and, to America's already overwhelming shame, was third runner up to the Republican presidential nomination, has called for Assange's execution.[22] So here we have a "man of God" calling for the US government to murder an Australian citizen. And Americans wonder why the rest of the world hates their guts.

The material leaked from the US government to WikiLeaks shows that the US government is an extremely disreputable gang of gangsters. The US government was able to get British Prime Minister Brown to "fix" the official Chilcot Investigation[23] into how the former prime minister, Tony Blair, manipulated and lied the British government into being mercenaries for the US invasion of Iraq. One of the "diplomatic" cables released has UK Defense Ministry official Jon Day promising the United States government that Prime Minister Brown's government has "put measures in place to protect your interests."

Other cables show the US government threatening Spanish Prime Minister Zapatero, ordering him to stop his criticisms of the Iraq war or else.[24] I mean, really, how dare these foreign governments to think that they are sovereign.

Not only foreign governments are under the US thumb. So is Amazon.com. Joe Lieberman from Connecticut, who is Israel's most influential senator in the US Senate, delivered sufficiently credible threats to Amazon to cause the company to oust WikiLeaks content from their hosting service.[25]

So there you have it. On the one hand the US government and the prostitute American media declare that there is nothing new in the hundreds of thousands of documents, yet on the other hand both pull out all stops to shut down WikiLeaks and its founder. Obviously, despite the US government's denials, the documents are extremely damaging. The documents show that the US government is not what it pretends to be.

Assange is in hiding. He fears CIA assassination, and to add to his troubles the government of Sweden has changed its mind, perhaps as a result of American persuasion and money, about sex charges that the Swedish government had previously dismissed for lack of credibility. If reports are correct, two women, who possibly could be CIA assets, have brought sex charges against Assange. One claims that she was having consensual sexual intercourse with him, but that he didn't stop when she asked him to when the condom broke.

Think about this for a minute. Other than male porn stars who are bored with it all, how many men can stop at the point of orgasm or when approaching orgasm? How does anyone know where Assange was in the process of the sex act?

Would a real government that had any integrity and commitment to truth try to blacken the name of the prime truth teller of our time on the basis of such flimsy charges? Obviously, Sweden has become another two-bit punk puppet government of the US.

The US government has gotten away with telling lies for so long that it no longer hesitates to lie in the most blatant way. WikiLeaks released a US classified document signed by Secretary of State Hillary Clinton that explicitly orders US diplomats to spy on UN Security Council officials and on the Secretary General of the United Nations. The cable is now in the public record. No one challenges its authenticity. Yet today the Obama regime, precisely White House Press Secretary Robert Gibbs, declared that Hillary had never ordered or even asked US officials to spy on UN officials.

As Antiwar.com asked: Who do you believe, the printed word with Hillary's signature, or the White House?

Anyone who believes the US government about anything is the epitome of gullibility.

2011

"Dissent is what rescues democracy
from a quiet death behind closed doors."
Lewis H. Lapham

The year 2011 will bring Americans a larger and more intrusive police state, more unemployment and home foreclosures, no economic recovery, more disregard by the U.S. government of U.S. law, international law, the Constitution, and truth, more suspicion and distrust from allies, more hostility from the rest of the world, and new heights of media sycophancy.

If not already obvious, 2010 has made clear that the U.S. government does not care a whit for the opinions of citizens. The TSA is unequivocal that it will reach no accommodation with Americans other than the violations of their persons that it imposes by its unaccountable power. As for public opposition to war, the Associated Press reported on December 16 that "Defense Secretary Robert Gates says the U.S. can't let public opinion sway its commitment to Afghanistan." Gates stated bluntly what has been known for some time: the idea is passé that government in a democracy serves the will of the people. If this quaint notion is still found in civics books, it will soon be edited out.

In *Gag Rule*, a masterful account of the suppression of dissent and the stifling of democracy, Lewis H. Lapham writes that candor is a necessary virtue if democracies are to survive their follies and crimes. But where in America today can candor be found? Certainly not in the councils of government. Attorney General John Ashcroft complained of candor-mongers to the Senate Judiciary Committee. Americans who insist on speaking their minds, Ashcroft declared, "scare people with phantoms of lost liberty," "aid terrorists," diminish our resolve," and "give ammunition to America's enemies."

As the Department of Justice (sic) sees it, when the ACLU defends habeas corpus it is defending the ability of terrorists to blow up Americans, and when the ACLU defends the First Amendment it is defending exposures of the lies and deceptions that are the necessary scaffolding for the government's pretense that it is doing God's will while Satan speaks through the voices of dissent.

Neither is candor a trait in which the American media finds comfort. The neoconservative press functions as propaganda ministry for hegemonic American empire, and the "liberal" *New York Times* serves the same master. It was *The New York Times* that gave credence to the Bush regime's lies about Iraqi weapons of mass destruction, and it was the New York Times that guaranteed Bush's re-election by spiking the story that Bush was committing felonies by spying on Americans without obtaining warrants. Conservatives rant about the "liberal media" as if it were a vast subversive force, but they owe their beloved wars and cover-ups of the Bush regime's crimes to *The New York Times*.

With truth the declared enemy of the fantasy world in which the government, media, and public reside, the nation has turned on whistleblowers. Bradley Manning, who allegedly provided the media with the video made by U.S. troops of their wanton, fun-filled slaughter of newsmen and civilians, has been abused in solitary confinement for six months. Murdering civilians is a war crime, and as General Peter Pace, Chairman of the Joint Chiefs of Staff, said at the National Press Club on February 17, 2006, "It is the absolute responsibility of everybody in uniform to disobey an order that is either illegal or immoral" and to make such orders known. If Manning is the source of the leak, he has been wrongfully imprisoned for meeting his military responsibility. The media have yet to make the point that the person who reported the crime, not the persons who committed it, is the one who has been imprisoned, and without a trial.

The lawlessness of the U.S. government, which has been creeping up on us for decades, broke into a full gallop in the years of the Bush/Cheney/Obama regimes. Today the government operates above the law, yet maintains that it is a democracy bringing the same to Muslims by force of arms, only briefly being sidetracked by sponsoring a military coup against democracy in Honduras and attempting to overthrow the democratic government in Venezuela.

As 2011 dawns, public discourse in America has the country primed for a fascist dictatorship. The situation will be worse by 2012. The most uncomfortable truth that emerges from the WikiLeaks saga is that American public discourse consists of cries for revenge against those who tell us truths. The vicious mendacity of the U.S. government knows no restraint. Whether or not international law can save Julian Assange from the clutches of the Americans or death by a government black ops unit, both executive and legislative branches are working assiduously to establish the National Security State as the highest value and truth as its greatest enemy.

America's future is the world of Winston Smith.

AMERICA
HAS GONE AWAY

December 29, 2010

Anyone who doesn't believe that the US is an incipient fascist state needs only to consult the latest assault on civil liberty by Fox "News". Instead of informing citizens, Fox News informs on citizens. Jason Ditz reports that Fox News "no longer content to simply shill for a growing police state," turned in a grandmother to the Department of Homeland Security for making "anti-American comments."[26]

The media have segued into the police attitude, which regards insistence on civil liberties and references to the Constitution as signs of extremism, especially when the Constitution is invoked in defense of dissent or privacy or placarded on a bumper sticker. President George W. Bush set the scene when he declared: "you are with us or against us."

Bush's words demonstrate a frightening decline in our government's respect for dissent since the presidency of John F. Kennedy. In a speech to the Newspaper Publishers Association in 1961, President Kennedy said:

> No president should fear public scrutiny of his program, for from that scrutiny comes understanding, and from that understanding comes support or opposition; and both are necessary. . . . Without debate, without criticism, no administration and no country can succeed, and no republic can survive. That is why the Athenian law makers once decreed it a crime for any citizen to shrink from controversy. And that is why our press was protected by the First Amendment.

The press is not protected, Kennedy told the newspaper publishers, in order that it can amuse and entertain, emphasize the trivial, or simply tell the public what it wants to hear. The press is protected so that it can find and report facts and, thus, inform, arouse "and sometimes even anger public opinion."

In a statement unlikely to be repeated by an American president, Kennedy told the newspaper publishers: "I'm not asking your newspapers to support an administration, but I am asking your help in the tremendous task of informing and alerting the American people, for I have complete confidence in the response and dedication of our citizens whenever they are fully informed."

The America of Kennedy's day and the America of today are two different worlds. In America today the media are expected to lie for the government in order to prevent the people from finding out what the government is up to. If polls can be believed, Americans brainwashed and programmed by O'Reilly, Hannity, Beck, and Limbaugh want Bradley Manning and Julian Assange torn limb from limb for informing Americans of the criminal acts of their government. Politicians and journalists are screeching for their execution.

President Kennedy told the Newspaper Publishers Association that "it is to the printing press, the recorder of man's deeds, the keeper of his conscience, the courier of his news, that we look for strength and assistance, confident that with your help man will be what he was born to be: Free and Independent." Who can imagine a Bill Clinton, a George W. Bush, or a Barack Obama saying such a thing today?

Today the press is a propaganda ministry for the government. Any member who departs from his duty to lie and spin the news is expelled from the fraternity. A public increasingly unemployed, broke and homeless is told that they have vast enemies plotting to destroy them in the absence of annual trillion dollar expenditures for the military/security complex, wars lasting decades, no-fly lists, unlimited spying and collecting of dossiers on citizens supplemented by neighbors reporting on neighbors, full body scanners at airports, shopping centers, metro and train stations, traffic checks, and the equivalent of treason with the uttering of a truth.

Two years ago when he came into office President Obama admitted that no one knew what the military mission was in Afghanistan, including the president himself, but that he would find a mission and define it. On his recent trip to Afghanistan, Obama came up with the mission: to make the families of the troops safe in America, his version of Bush's "we have to kill them over there before they kill us over here."

No one snorted with derision or even mildly giggled. Neither *The New York Times* nor Fox News dared to wonder if perhaps, maybe, murdering and displacing large numbers of Muslims in Iraq, Afghanistan, Pakistan, and Yemen and US support for Israel's similar treatment of Lebanese and Palestinians might be creating a hostile environment that could breed terrorists. If there still is such a thing as the Newspaper Publishers Association, its members are incapable of such an unpatriotic thought.

Today no one believes that our country's success depends on an informed public and a free press. America's success depends on its financial and military hegemony over the world. Any information inconsistent with the indispensable people's god-given right to dominate the world must be suppressed and the messenger discredited and destroyed.

Now that the press has voluntarily shed its First Amendment rights, the government is working to redefine free speech as a privilege limited to the media, not a right of citizens. Thus, the insistence that WikiLeaks is not a media organization and Fox News turning in a citizen for exercising free speech. Washington's assault on Assange and WikiLeaks is an assault on what remains of the US Constitution. When we cheer for WikiLeaks' demise, we are cheering for our own.

EGYPT: THINGS HAVE TO CHANGE IN ORDER TO STAY THE SAME

February 1, 2011

The hypocrisy of the US government is yet again demonstrated in full bore force. The US government invaded Iraq and Afghanistan, laid waste to much of the countries, including entire villages and towns, and massacred untold numbers of civilians in order "to bring democracy" to Iraq and Afghanistan. Now, after days of Egyptians in the streets demanding "Mubarak must go," the US government remains aligned with its puppet Egyptian ruler, even suggesting that Mubarak, after running a police state for three decades, is the appropriate person to implement democracy in Egypt.

On January 30, US Secretary of State Hillary Clinton declared that "freedom and democracy" America neither seeks nor supports the ouster of the Egyptian dictator.

Israeli prime minister Netanyahu told the US and Europe that criticism of Mubarak must be curbed in order "to preserve stability in the region."

By "stability" Netanyahu means the unimpeded ability of Israel to continue oppressing the Palestinians and stealing their country. Mubarak has been for three decades the well-paid enforcer for the US and Israel, sealing off Gaza from the outside world and preventing aid flows across the Egyptian border. Mubarak and his family have become multi-billionaires, thanks to the American taxpayer, and the US government, both Republicans and Democrats, does not want to lose their heavy investment in Mubarak.

The US government has long corrupted Arab governments by paying rulers installed by the US to represent US/Israeli interests rather than the interest of Arab peoples. Arabs put up with American-financed oppression for many years, but now are showing signs of rebellion.

The murderous American-installed dictator in Tunis was overthrown by people taking to the streets. Rebellion has spread to Egypt and there are also street protests against the US-supported rulers in Yemen and Jordan.

These uprisings might succeed in ousting puppet rulers, but will the result be anything more than the exchange of a new American puppet ruler for the old? Mubarak might go, but whoever takes his place is likely to find himself wearing the same American harness.

What dictators do is to eliminate alternative leadership. Potential leaders are either assassinated, exiled, or imprisoned. Moreover, anything short of a full-fledge revolution, such as the Iranian one, leaves in place a bureaucracy accustomed to business as usual. In addition, Egypt and the country's military have grown accustomed to American support and will want the money to keep flowing. It is the flow of this money that ensures the purchase of the replacement government.

Because the US dollar is the world reserve currency, the US government has financial dominance and the ability to financially isolate other countries, such as Iran. To break free of America's grip, one of two things would have to happen. Revolution would have to sweep the Arab world and result in an economic unity that could foster indigenous economic development, or the US dollar has to fail as world currency.

Arab disunity has long been the means by which the Western countries have dominated the Middle East. Without this disunity, Israel and the US could not abuse the Palestinians in the manner in which they have for decades, and without this disunity the US could not have invaded Iraq. It is unlikely that the Arabs will suddenly unite.

The collapse of the dollar is more likely. Indeed, the policy of the US government to maximize both budget and trade deficits, and the policy of the Federal Reserve to monetize the budget deficit and the fraudulent paper assets of the large banks, have the dollar heading for demise.

As the supply of dollars grows, the value diminishes. Perhaps the time is not too many years away when rulers cease to sell out their peoples for American money.

OBAMA'S FY 2012 BUDGET IS A TOOL OF CLASS WAR

February 17, 2011

Obama's new budget is a continuation of Wall Street's class war against the poor and middle class.

Wall Street wasn't through with us when the banksters sold their fraudulent derivatives into our pension funds, wrecked Americans' job prospects and retirement plans, secured a $700 billion bailout at taxpayers' expense while foreclosing on the homes of millions of Americans, and loaded up the Federal Reserve's balance sheet with several trillion dollars of junk financial paper in exchange for newly created money to shore up the banks' balance sheets.

The effect of the Federal Reserve's "quantitative easing" on inflation, interest rates, and the dollar's foreign exchange value are yet to hit. When they do, Americans will get a lesson in poverty.

Now the ruling oligarchies have struck again, this time through the federal budget. The U.S. government has a huge military/security budget. It is almost as large as the budgets of the rest of the world combined. The Pentagon, CIA, and Homeland Security budgets account for the $1.1 trillion federal deficit that the Obama administration forecasts for fiscal year 2012. This massive deficit spending serves only one purpose—the enrichment of the private companies that serve the military/security complex. These companies, along with those on Wall Street, are the ones who elect the U.S. government.

The U.S. has no enemies except those that it creates by bombing and invading other countries and by overthrowing foreign leaders and installing American puppets in their place.

China does not conduct naval exercises off the California coast, but the U.S. conducts war games in the South China Sea off China's coast. Russia does not mass troops on Europe's borders, but the U.S. places missiles on Russia's borders. The U.S. is determined to create as many enemies as possible in order to continue its bleeding of the American population to feed the ravenous military/security complex.

The U.S. government actually spends $56 billion a year, that is, $56,000 million, in order that American air travelers can be porno-scanned and sexually groped so that firms represented by former Homeland Security Secretary Michael Chertoff can make large profits selling the scanning equipment.

With a perpetual budget deficit driven by the military/security complex's desire for profits, the real cause of America's enormous budget deficit is off-limits for discussion.

The U.S. Secretary of War-Mongering, Robert Gates, declared: "We shrink from our global security responsibilities at our peril." The military brass warns of cutting any of the billions of aid to Israel and Egypt, two functionaries for its Middle East "policy."

But what are "our" global security responsibilities? Where did they come from? Why would America be at peril if America stopped bombing and invading other countries and interfering in their internal affairs? The perils America faces are all self-created.

The answer to this question used to be that otherwise we would be murdered in our beds by "the worldwide communist conspiracy." Today the answer is that we will be murdered in our airplanes, train stations, and shopping centers by "Muslim terrorists" and by a newly created imaginary threat—"domestic extremists," that is, war protesters and environmentalists.

The U.S. military/security complex is capable of creating any number of false flag events in order to make these threats seem real to a public whose intelligence is limited to TV, shopping mall experiences, and football games.

So Americans are stuck with enormous budget deficits that the Federal Reserve must finance by printing new money, money that sooner or later will destroy the purchasing power of the dollar and its role as world reserve currency. When the dollar goes, American power goes.

For the ruling oligarchies, the question is: how to save their power.

Their answer is: make the people pay.

And that is what their latest puppet, President Obama, is doing.

With the U.S. in the worst recession since the Great Depression, a great recession that John Williams and Gerald Celente, along with myself, have said is deepening, the "Obama budget" takes aim at support programs for the poor and out-of-work. The American elites are transforming themselves into idiots as they seek to replicate in America the conditions that have led to the overthrow of similarly corrupt elites in Tunisia and Egypt and mounting challenges to U.S. puppet governments elsewhere.

All we need is a few million more Americans with nothing to lose in order to bring the disturbances in the Middle East home to America.

With the U.S. military bogged down in wars abroad, an American revolution would have the best chance of success.

American politicians have to fund Israel as the money returns in campaign contributions.

The U.S. government must fund the Egyptian military if there is to be any hope of turning the next Egyptian government into another American puppet that will serve Israel by continuing the blockade of the Palestinians herded into the Gaza ghetto.

These goals are far more important to the American elite than Pell Grants that enable poor Americans to obtain an education, or clean water, or community block grants, or the low income energy assistance program (cut by the amount that U.S. taxpayers are forced to give to Israel).

There are also $7,700 million of cuts in Medicaid and other health programs over the next five years.

Given the magnitude of the U.S. budget deficit, these sums are a pittance. The cuts will have no effect on U.S. Treasury financing needs. They will put no brakes on the Federal Reserve's need to print money in order to keep the U.S. government in operation.

These cuts serve one purpose: to further the Republican Party's myth that America is in economic trouble because of the poor: The poor are shiftless. They won't work. The only reason unemployment is high is that the poor would rather be on welfare.

A new addition to the welfare myth is that recent middle class college graduates won't take the jobs offered them, because their parents have too much money, and the kids like living at home without having to do anything. A spoiled generation, they come out of university refusing any job that doesn't start out as CEO of a Fortune 500 company. The reason that engineering graduates do not get job interviews is that they do not want them.

What all this leads to is an assault on "entitlements", which means Social Security and Medicare. The elites have programmed, through their control of the media, a large part of the population, especially those who think of themselves as conservatives, to conflate "entitlements" with welfare. America, in their view, is going to hell not because of foreign wars that serve no American purpose, but because people, who have paid 15% of their payroll all their lives for old age pensions and medical care, want "handouts" in their retirement years. The problem is said to be selfish retirees who think that working Americans should be forced through payroll taxes to pay for their pensions and medical care. Why didn't the retirees consume less and prepare for their own retirement?

The elite's line, and that of their hired spokespersons in "think tanks" and universities, is that America is in trouble because of its retirees.

Too many Americans have been brainwashed to believe that

America is in trouble because of its poor and its retirees. America is not in trouble because it coerces a dwindling number of taxpayers to support the military/security complex's enormous profits, American puppet governments abroad, and Israel.

The American elite's solution for America's problems is not merely to foreclose on the homes of Americans whose jobs were sent offshore, but to add to the numbers of distressed Americans with nothing to lose—the sick and the dispossessed retirees, and the university graduates who cannot find jobs that have been sent to China and India.

Of all the countries in the world, none need a revolution as badly as the United States, a country ruled by a handful of selfish oligarchs who have more income and wealth than can be spent in a lifetime.

WAR ÜBER ALLES

February 26, 2011

The United States government cannot get enough of war. With Libyan dictator Muammar Gaddafi's regime falling to a CIA organized overthrow, CNN reports that a Pentagon spokesman said that the U.S. is looking at all options from the military side.

Allegedly, the Pentagon, which is responsible for one million dead Iraqis and an unknown number of dead Afghans and Pakistanis, is concerned about the deaths of 1,000 Libyan protesters.

While the Pentagon tries to figure out how to get involved in the Libyan revolt, the commander of U.S. forces in the Pacific is developing new battle plans to take on China in her home territory. Four-star Admiral Robert Willard thinks the U.S. should be able to whip China in its own coastal waters.

The admiral thinks one way to do this is to add U.S. Marines to his force structure so that the U.S. can eject Chinese forces from disputed islands in the East and South China seas.

It is not the U.S. who is disputing the islands, but if there is a chance for war anywhere, the admiral wants to make sure we are not left out.

The admiral also hopes to develop military ties with India and add that country to his clout. India, the admiral says, "is a natural partner of the United States" and "is crucial to America's 21st-century strategy of balancing China." The U.S. is going to seduce the Indians by selling them advanced aircraft.

If the plan works out, we will have India in NATO helping us to occupy Pakistan and presenting China with the possibility of a two-front war.

The Pentagon needs some more wars so there can be some more "reconstruction." Reconstruction is very lucrative, especially as Washington has privatized so many of the projects, thus turning over to well-placed friends many opportunities to loot. Considering all the money that has been spent, one searches hard to find completed projects. The just released report from the Commission on Wartime Contracting can't say exactly how much of the $200,000 million in Afghan "reconstruction" disappeared in criminal behavior and blatant corruption, but $12,000 million alone was lost to "overt fraud."

War makes money for the politically connected. While the flag-waving population remains proud of the service of their sons, brothers, husbands, fathers, cousins, wives, mothers and daughters, the smart boys who got the fireworks started are rolling in the mega-millions.

As General Smedley Butler told the jingoistic American population, to no avail, "war is a racket." As long as the American population remains proud that their relatives serve as cannon fodder for the military/security complex, war will remain a racket.

OUR TIME OF UNIVERSAL DECEIT NEEDS AN ORWELL

March 13, 2011

If we were to be blessed with a 21st century George Orwell, he would coin a new "speak" to apply to "support the troops." Would he call this "Deceptive Speak"? Or would he be more clever?

The words certainly deserve an Orwellian name. The catch-phrase was rolled out the minute the Iraq war started, which makes one wonder about its public relations origin. Who can oppose supporting the troops, at least before we learned from WikiLeaks and Abu Ghraib of the intentional killing of civilians and torturing of whoever happened to be rounded up in the various sweeps? All for the fun and games of it.

"Support the troops" originated in the public relations department of the military/security complex. What "support the troops" really means is to support the profits of the armaments industry and the neoconservative ideology of US world hegemony.

"Support the troops" is a clever PR slogan that causes Americans to turn a blind eye to the brutal exploitation of our soldiers and military families for profit and for an evil ideology.

Our soldiers and military families are paying for the Bush/Cheney/Obama/neocon wars with lives, limbs, post-traumatic stress, suicides, broken marriages, children without fathers, wives without husbands, and parents without sons and daughters.

"Support the troops" is one of the most cruel hoaxes in human history, and yet the vast majority of the population has fallen for it. "War Is Peace."

When a people are so gullible, it is little wonder that they can be marched off to unaffordable open-ended wars based on nothing but lies, deceptions, and fabrications.

America produces an endless supply of material for a new Orwell. Imagine what an Orwell could do with Hillary's recent speech on America's firm commitment to dissent and the First Amendment. CIA veteran Ray

McGovern stood with his back to Hillary in an act of dissent from the Obama administration's policy of coercing Internet companies into helping to eliminate WikiLeaks as a source of information. McGovern was dragged beaten and bloody from the room, while Hillary continued praising America's commitment to dissent and freedom of information.

To capture this level of hypocrisy requires a George Orwell. "Dissent Is Subversion."

"Globalism" is another doctrine that needs Orwell's illumination. Globalism, which presidents since Clinton have told us we can't do without, enriches transnational corporations and turns workers into serfs who cannot earn enough to pay their bills. "Poverty Is Wealth."

The police state measures that accompany the fake "war on terror" subject Americans to far more danger and insecurity than could ever be realized from terrorists other than those of the state itself. "Captivity Is Freedom."

In his marvelous book, *The Emotional Lives of Animals*, Marc Bekoff describes the devastating impact on animals of being kept in small cages. US soldier Bradley Manning has been kept illegally in an even smaller cage for eight months with no end in sight. At Obama's press conference on March 11, one reporter found the courage to ask President Obama about the conditions of Manning's confinement. The great and noble president of the United States replied that he had asked the Pentagon and was assured that the conditions of Manning's confinement "are appropriate and are meeting our basic standards." Only a George Orwell could do justice to an American president who thinks that keeping a US soldier in conditions worst than those that drive caged animals insane is "appropriate."

The US government, which is profligate in its wars, profligate in tax cuts and bailouts for the mega-rich, and profligate in giving unlimited monopoly power to unregulated financial institutions, blames the resulting financial crisis on "handouts" to the poor and "entitlements" to the elderly. Such deception needs more than exposure. It cries out for a 21st century Orwell.

OBAMA RAISES AMERICAN HYPOCRISY TO A HIGHER LEVEL

March 28, 2011

What does the world think? Obama has been using air strikes and drones against civilians in Afghanistan, Pakistan, Yemen, and Somalia. In his March 28 speech, Obama justified his air strikes against Libya on the grounds that the embattled ruler, Gaddafi, was using air strikes to put down a rebellion.

Gaddafi has been a black hat for as long as I can remember. His black hat is his reward for trying to pursue a foreign policy independent of the US. However murderous Gaddafi might be, there is no doubt whatsoever that the current US president and the predecessor Bush/Cheney regime have murdered many times more people in Iraq, Afghanistan, Pakistan, Yemen and Somalia than Gaddafi has murdered in Libya.

Moreover, Gaddafi is putting down a rebellion against state authority as presently constituted, but Obama and Bush/Cheney initiated wars of aggression based entirely on lies and deception.

Yet Gaddafi is being demonized, and Bush/Cheney/Obama are sitting on their high horse draped in cloaks of morality. Obama described himself as saving Libyans from violence while Obama himself murders Afghans, Pakistanis, and whomever else.

Indeed, the Obama regime has been torturing a US soldier, Bradley Manning, for having a moral conscience. America has degenerated to the point where having a moral conscience is evidence of anti-Americanism and "terrorist activity."

The Bush/Cheney/Obama wars of naked aggression have bankrupted America. Joseph Stiglitz, former chairman of the President's Council of Economic Advisers, concluded that the money wasted on the Iraq war could have been used to fix America's Social Security problem for half a century.[27] Instead, the money was used to boost the obscene profits of the armament industry.

The obscene wars of aggression, the obscene profits of the offshoring

132

corporations, and the obscene bailouts of the rich financial gangsters have left the American public with annual budget deficits of approximately $1.5 trillion. These deficits are being covered by printing money. Sooner or later, the printing presses will cause the US dollar to collapse and domestic inflation to explode. Social Security benefits will be wiped out by inflation rising more rapidly than the cost-of-living adjustments. If America survives, no one will be left but the mega-rich. Unless there is a violent revolution.

Alternatively, if the Federal Reserve puts the brake on monetary expansion, interest rates will rise, sending the economy into a deeper depression.

Washington, focused on its newest war, is oblivious to America's peril. As Stiglitz notes, the costs of the Iraq war alone could have kept every foreclosed family in their home, provided health care for every American child, and wiped out the student loans of graduates who cannot find jobs because they have been outsourced to foreigners. However, the great democratic elected government of "the world's only superpower" prefers to murder Muslims in order to enhance the profits of the military/security complex. More money is spent violating the constitutional rights of American air travelers than is spent in behalf of the needy.

The moral authority of the West is rapidly collapsing. When Russia, Asia, and South America look at Europe, Australia and Canada, they see American puppet states that contribute troops to the aggressive wars of the Empire. The French president, the British prime minister, the "president" of Georgia, and the rest are merely functionaries of the American Empire. The puppet rulers routinely sell out the interests and welfare of their peoples in behalf of American hegemony. And they are well rewarded for their service. One year out of office former British Prime Minister Tony Blair had a net worth of $30 million.

In his war against Libya, Obama has taken America one step further into Caesarism. Obama did Bush one step better and did not even bother to get congressional authorization for his attack on Libya. Obama claimed that his moral authority trumped the US Constitution. In the passage below, Obama's hypocrisy reeks. How the public stands it, I do not know.

> To brush aside America's responsibility as a leader and– more profoundly–our responsibilities to our fellow human beings under such circumstances would have been a betrayal of who we are. Some nations may be able to turn a blind eye to atrocities in other countries. The United States of America is different. And as president, I refused to wait for the images of slaughter and mass graves before taking action.

This from the Great Moral Leader who every day murders civilians in Afghanistan and Pakistan and Yemen and Somalia and now Libya and who turns a blind eye when "the great democracy in the Middle East," Israel, murders more Palestinians.

The American president, whose drones and air force slaughter civilians every day of the year went on to say Libya stands alone in presenting the world with "the prospect of violence on a horrific scale." Obviously, Obama thinks that one million dead Iraqis, four million displaced Iraqis, and an unknown number of murdered Afghans is just a small thing.

The rest of Obama's speech showed a person more capable of DoubleSpeak and DoubleThink than Big Brother and the denizens of George Orwell's *1984*.

THE NEW COLONIALISM: WASHINGTON'S PURSUIT OF WORLD HEGEMONY

April 2, 2011

What we are observing in Libya is the rebirth of colonialism. Only this time it is not individual European governments competing for empires and resources. The new colonialism operates under the cover of "the world community," which means NATO and those countries that cooperate with it. NATO, the North Atlantic Treaty Organization, was once a defense alliance against a possible Soviet invasion of Western Europe. Today NATO provides European troops in behalf of American hegemony.

Washington pursues world hegemony under the guises of selective "humanitarian intervention" and "bringing freedom and democracy to oppressed peoples." On an opportunistic basis, Washington targets countries for intervention that are not its "international partners." Caught off guard, perhaps, by popular revolts in Tunisia and Egypt, there are some indications that Washington responded opportunistically and encouraged the uprising in Libya. Khalifa Hifter, a suspected Libyan CIA asset for the last 20 years, has gone back to Libya to head the rebel army.

Gaddafi got himself targeted by standing up to Western imperialism. He refused to be part of the US Africa Command. Gaddafi saw Washington's scheme for what it is, a colonialist's plan to divide and conquer.

The US Africa Command (AFRICOM) was created by order of President George W. Bush in 2007. AFRICOM describes its objective:

> Our approach is based upon supporting U.S. national security interests in Africa as articulated by the President and Secretaries of State and Defense in the National Security Strategy and the National Military Strategy. The United States and African nations have strong mutual interests in promoting security and stability on the continent

of Africa, its island states, and maritime zones. Advancing these interests requires a unified approach that integrates efforts with those of other U.S. government departments and agencies, as well as our African and other international partners.

Forty-nine countries participate in the US Africa Command, but not Libya, Sudan, Eritrea, Zimbabwe, and Ivory Coast. There is Western military intervention[28] in these non-member countries except for Zimbabwe.

One traditional means by which the US influences and controls a country is by training its military and government officers. The program is called International Military and Education Training (IMET). AFRICOM reports that "in 2009 approximately 900 military and civilian students from 44 African countries received education and training in the United States or their own countries. Many officers and enlisted IMET graduates go on to fill key positions in their militaries and governments."

AFRICOM lists as a key strategic objective the defeat of the "Al Qaeda network." The US Trans Sahara Counter Terrorism Partnership (TSCTP) trains and equips "partner nation forces" to preclude terrorists from establishing sanctuaries and aims to "ultimately defeat violent extremist organizations in the region."

Apparently, far from being defeated after ten years of "the war on terror" an omnipotent Al Qaeda now ranges across Algeria, Burkina Faso, Chad, Mali, Mauritania, Morocco, Niger, Nigeria, Senegal and Tunisia in Africa, across the Middle East, Afghanistan, Pakistan, the UK and is such a threat within the United States itself as to require a $56 billion "Homeland Security" annual budget.

The Al Qaeda threat, a hoax as likely as not, has become Washington's best excuse for intervening in the domestic affairs of other countries and for subverting American civil liberties.

Sixty-six years after the end of World War II and 20 years after the Collapse of the Soviet Union, the US still has a European Command, one of nine military commands and six regional commands.

No other country feels a need for a world military presence. Why does Washington think that it is a good allocation of scarce resources to devote $1.1 trillion annually to military and security "needs"? Is this a sign of Washington's paranoia? Is it a sign that only Washington has enemies?

Or is it an indication that Washington assigns the highest value to empire and squanders taxpayers' monies and the country's credit-worthiness on military footprints, while millions of Americans lose their homes and their jobs?

Washington's expensive failures in Iraq and Afghanistan have not tempered the empire ambition. Washington can continue to rely on the print and TV media to cover up its failures and to hide its agendas, but expensive failures will remain expensive failures. Sooner or later Washington will have to acknowledge that the pursuit of empire has bankrupted the country.

It is paradoxical that Washington and its European "partners" are seeking to extend control over foreign lands abroad while immigration transforms their cultures and ethnic compositions at home. As Hispanics, Asians, Africans, and Muslims of various ethnicities become a larger and larger percentage of the populations of the "First World," support for the white man's empire fades away. Peoples desiring education and in need of food, shelter, and medical care will be hostile to maintaining military outposts in the countries of their origins.

Who exactly is occupying whom?

Parts of the US are reverting to Mexico. For example, demographer Steve Murdock, a former director of the US Census Bureau, reports that two-thirds of Texas children are Hispanics and concludes: "It's basically over for Anglos."

Ironic, isn't it, while Washington and its NATO puppets are busy occupying the world, America and Europe are being occupied by the world.

LIBYA:
THE DC/NATO AGENDA AND THE NEXT GREAT WAR

April 7, 2011

In the 1930s the US, Great Britain, and the Netherlands set a course for World War II in the Pacific by conspiring against Japan. The three governments seized Japan's bank accounts in their countries that Japan used to pay for imports and cut Japan off from oil, rubber, tin, iron and other vital materials. Was Pearl Harbor Japan's response?

Now Washington and its NATO puppets are employing the same strategy against China.

Protests in Tunisia, Egypt, Bahrain, and Yemen arose from the people protesting against Washington's tyrannical puppet governments. However, the protests against Gaddafi, who is not a Western puppet, appear to have been organized by the CIA in the eastern part of Libya where the oil is and where China has substantial energy investments.

Eighty percent of Libya's oil reserves are believed to be in the Sirte Basin in eastern Libya now controlled by rebels supported by Washington.[29] As seventy percent of Libya's GDP is produced by oil, a successful partitioning of Libya would leave Gaddafi's Tripoli-based regime impoverished.

The *People's Daily Online* (March 23) reported that China has 50 large-scale projects in Libya. The outbreak of hostilities has halted these projects and resulted in 30,000 Chinese workers being evacuated from Libya. Chinese companies report that they expect to lose hundreds of millions of yuan.

China is relying on Africa, principally Libya, Angola, and Nigeria, for future energy needs. In response to China's economic engagement with Africa, Washington is engaging the continent militarily with the US African Command (AFRICOM) created by President George W. Bush in 2007. Forty-nine African countries agreed to participate with Washington in AFRICOM, but Gaddafi refused, thus creating a second reason for Washington to target Libya for takeover.

A third reason for targeting Libya is that Libya and Syria are the only two countries with Mediterranean Sea coasts that are not under the control or influence of Washington. Suggestively, protests have also broken out in Syria. Whatever Syrians might think of their government, after watching Iraq's fate and now Libya's, it is unlikely that Syrians would set themselves up for US military intervention. Both the CIA and Mossad are known to use social networking sites to foment protests and to spread disinformation. These intelligence services are the likely conspirators that the Syrian and Libyan governments blame for the protests.

Caught off guard by protests in Tunisia and Egypt, Washington realized that protests could be used to remove Gaddafi and Assad. The humanitarian excuse for intervening in Libya is not credible considering Washington's go-ahead to the Saudi military to crush the protests in Bahrain, the home base for the US Fifth Fleet.

If Washington succeeds in overthrowing the Assad government in Syria, Russia would lose its Mediterranean naval base at the Syrian port of Tartus. Thus, Washington has much to gain if it can use the cloak of popular rebellion to eject both China and Russia from the Mediterranean. Rome's *mare nostrum* ("our sea") would become Washington's *mare nostrum*.

"Gaddafi must go," declared Obama. How long before we also hear, "Assad must go?"

The American captive press is at work demonizing both Gaddafi and Assad, an eye doctor who returned to Syria from London to head the government after his father's death.

The hypocrisy passes unremarked when Obama calls Gaddafi and Assad dictators. Since the beginning of the 21st century, the American president has been a Caesar. Based on nothing more than a Justice Department memo, George W. Bush was declared to be above US statutory law, international law, and the power of Congress as long as he was acting in his role as commander-in-chief in the "war on terror."

Caesar Obama has done Bush one step better. Caesar Obama has taken the US to war against Libya without even the pretense of asking Congress for authorization. This is an impeachable offense, but an impotent Congress is unable to protect its power. By accepting the claims of executive authority, Congress has acquiesced to Caesarism. The American people have no more control over their government than do people in countries ruled by dictators.

Washington's quest for world hegemony is driving the world toward World War III. China is no less proud than was Japan in the 1930s and is unlikely to submit to being bullied and governed by what China regards as the decadent West. Russia's resentment to its military encirclement is rising. Washington's hubris can lead to fatal miscalculation.

OSAMA BIN LADEN'S USEFUL DEATH

May 3, 2011

In a propaganda piece reeking of US Triumphalism, two alleged journalists, Adam Goldman and Chris Brummitt, of the Associated Press or, rather, of the White House Ministry of Truth, write, or copy off a White House or CIA press release that "Osama bin Laden, the terror mastermind killed by Navy SEALs in an intense firefight, was hunted down based on information first gleaned *years ago* (emphasis added) from detainees at secret CIA prison sites in Eastern Europe, officials disclosed Monday."

How many Americans will notice that the first paragraph of the "report" justifies CIA prisons and torture? Without secret prisons and torture "the terror mastermind" would still be running free, despite having in actuality died from renal failure in 2001.

How many Americans will have the wits to wonder why the "terror mastermind"—who in 9/11 defeated not merely the CIA and the FBI, but all 16 US intelligence agencies along with Israel's Mossad and the intelligence services of NATO; who defeated NORAD, the National Security Council, the Pentagon and Joint Chiefs of Staff, the US Air Force, and Air Traffic Control; who caused security procedures to fail four times in US airports in one hour on the same day; and who managed to have three airliners flown into three buildings with pilots who did not know how to fly—has not pulled off any other attack in almost ten years? Do Americans really believe that a government security system that can so totally fail when confronted with a few Saudi Arabians with box cutters can renew itself to perfection overnight?

How many Americans will notice the resurrection of the long missing bin Laden as "terror mastermind" after his displacement by Khalid Sheikh Mohammed, the Guantanamo prisoner who confessed to being the "mastermind of 9/11" after having been water-boarded 183 times?

Americans are too busy celebrating to think, a capability that seems to have been taken out of their education.

Americans are so enthralled over the death of bin Laden that they do not wonder why information gleamed years ago would take so long to locate a person who was allegedly living in a million-dollar building equipped with all the latest communication equipment next to the Pakistani Military Academy. Allegedly, the "most wanted criminal" was not moving from hide-out to hide-out in desolate mountains, but ensconced in luxury quarters in broad daylight. Nevertheless, despite his purported obvious location, it took the CIA years to find him after claiming to have gained information of his whereabouts from captives in secret prisons. This is the image of the CIA as the new Keystone Cops.

In an immediate follow-up to the announcement that the Navy SEALs and CIA mercenaries acted in an exemplary fashion following the rules of engagement while a cowardly bin Laden hid behind a woman shield when the gunfire erupted, we have from the presstitutes that "U.S. officials conceded the risk of renewed attack. The terrorists almost certainly will attempt to avenge bin Laden's death, CIA Director Leon Panetta wrote in a memo. . . . Within a few hours, the Department of Homeland Security warned that bin Laden's death was likely to provide motivation for attacks from 'homegrown violent extremists'."

John Brennan, White House counter-terrorism adviser, told reporters that "it was inconceivable that the terrorist fugitive didn't have support in Pakistan where his hideout had been custom built six years ago in a city with a heavy military presence."

So the claimed murder of bin Laden by the US in a sovereign foreign country with which the US is not at war, a crime under international law, has set up three more self-serving possibilities:

Terrorists will avenge bin Laden's death, says the CIA, setting up another false flag attack to keep the profits flowing into the military/security complex and the power flowing into the unaccountable CIA. Homeland Security can extend the domestic police state, abuse of travelers, and arrests of war protestors. And Pakistan is under the gun of invasion and takeover (for India, of course) for shielding bin Laden.

The Israel Lobby's representatives in the US Congress quickly fell in with the agenda. Senator Carl Levin, Chairman of the Senate Armed Services Committee, declared that the Pakistani Army and intelligence agency "have a lot of questions to answer, given the location, the length of time and the apparent fact that this was actually—this facility was actually build for bin Laden, and its closeness to the central location of the Pakistani army."

The two reporters question nothing in the government's propaganda. Instead, the reporters join in the celebration. Nevertheless they let slip that "officials were weighing the release of at least one photo taken of bin Laden's body as part of what Brennan called an effort to make sure "nobody has any basis to try and deny the death."

As *The Guardian* and European newspapers have revealed, the photo of the dead bin Laden is a fake. As the alleged body has been dumped into the ocean, nothing remains but the word of the US government, which lied about Iraqi weapons of mass destruction and Al Qaeda connections, about yellowcake, about Iranian nukes, and, according to thousands of experts, about 9/11. Suddenly the government is telling us the truth about bin Laden's death? If you believe that, I have a bridge in Brooklyn that I'll let you have for a good price.

My initial interpretation of the faked bin Laden death was that Obama needed closure of the Afghan war and occupation in order to deal with the US budget deficit. Subsequent statements from Obama regime officials suggested that the agenda might be to give Americans a piece of war victory in order to boost their lagging enthusiasm. The military/security complex will become richer and more powerful, and Americans will be rewarded with vicarious pleasure in victory over enemies. However, the real reason for the faked murder of bin Laden is to boost Obama's sagging standing in the polls. There are rumors that the Democrats were thinking of giving the presidential nomination to someone else.

THE AGENDAS BEHIND THE FABRICATED BIN LADEN NEWS EVENT

May 6, 2011

The US government's bin Laden story was so poorly crafted that it did not last 48 hours before being fundamentally altered. Indeed, the new story put out on Tuesday by White House press secretary Jay Carney bears little resemblance to the original Sunday evening story. The fierce firefight did not occur. Osama bin Laden did not hide behind a woman. Indeed, bin Laden, Carney said, "was not armed."

The firefight story was instantly suspicious as not a single SEAL got a scratch, despite being up against Al Qaeda, described by former Pentagon chief Donald Rumsfeld as 'the most dangerous, best-trained, vicious killers on the face of the earth."[30]

Every original story detail has been changed. It wasn't bin Laden's wife who was murdered by the Navy SEALs, but the wife of an aide. It wasn't bin Laden's son, Khalid, who was murdered by the Navy SEALs, but son Hamza.

Carney blamed the changed story on "the fog of war." But there was no firefight, so where did the "fog of war" come from?

The White House has also had to abandon the story that President Obama and his national security team watched tensely as events unfolded in real time (despite the White House having released photos of the team watching tensely), with the operation conveyed into the White House by cameras on the SEALs helmets. If Obama was watching the event as it happened, he would have noticed, one would hope, that there was no firefight and thus would not have told the public that bin Laden was killed in a firefight. Another reason the story had to be abandoned is that if the event was captured on video, every news service in the world would be asking for the video, but if the event was orchestrated theater, there would be no video.

No explanation has been provided for why an unarmed bin Laden, in the absence of a firefight, was murdered by the SEALs with a shot to the head. For those who believe the government's story that "we got bin Laden," the operation can only appear as the most botched operation in history. What kind of incompetence does it require to senselessly and needlessly kill the most valuable intelligence asset on the planet?

According to the US government, the terrorist movements of the world operated through bin Laden, "the mastermind." Perhaps the SEAL was thinking that he could put a notch on his gun and brag for the rest of his life about being the macho tough guy who killed Osama bin Laden?

When such a foundational story as the demise of bin Laden cannot last 48 hours without acknowledged "discrepancies" that require fundamental alternations, there are further grounds for suspicion in addition to those arising from the absence of a dead body, from the absence of any evidence that bin Laden was killed in the raid or that a raid even took place. The entire episode could just be another event like the August 4, 1964, Gulf of Tonkin event that never happened but succeeded in launching open warfare against North Vietnam at a huge cost to Americans and Vietnamese and enormous profits to the military/security complex.

There is no doubt that the US is sufficiently incompetent to have needlessly killed bin Laden instead of capturing him. But who can believe that the US would quickly dispose of the evidence that bin Laden had been terminated? The government's story is not believable that the government dumped the proof of its success into the ocean, but has some photos that might be released, someday.

Governments have known from the beginning of time that they can always deceive citizens and subjects by playing the patriot card. "Remember the Maine," the "Gulf of Tonkin," "weapons of mass destruction," "the Reichstag fire"—the litany of staged events and bogus evidence is endless. If Americans knew any history, they would not be so gullible.

The real question before us is: What agenda(s) is the "death of bin Laden" designed to further?

There are many answers to this question. Many have noticed that Obama was facing re-election with poor approval ratings. Is anyone surprised that *The New York Times*/CBS Poll finds a strong rise in Obama's poll numbers after the bin Laden raid? As the *Times* reported, "the glow of national pride" rose "above partisan politics, as support for the president rose significantly among both Republicans and independents. In all, 57 percent said they now approved of the president's job performance, up from 46 percent."

In Washington-think, a 24% rise in approval rating justifies a staged event.

Another possibility is that Obama realized that the budget deficit and the dollar's rescue from collapse require the end of the expensive Afghan occupation and spillover war into Pakistan. As the purpose of the war was to get bin Laden, success in this objective allows the US to withdraw without loss of face, thus making it possible to reduce the US budget deficit by several hundred billion dollars annually—an easy way to have a major spending cut.

If this is the agenda, then more power to it. However, if indeed this was Obama's agenda, the military/security complex has quickly moved against it. CIA director Leon Panetta opened the door to false flag attacks to keep the war going by declaring that Al Qaeda would avenge bin Laden's killing. Secretary of State Clinton declared that success in killing bin Laden justified more war and more success. Homeland Security declared that the killing of bin Laden would motivate "homegrown violent extremists" into making terrorist attacks. "Homegrown violent extremists" is an undefined term, but this newly created bogyman seems to include environmentalists and war protesters. Like "suspect," the term will include anyone the government wants to pick up.

Various parts of the government quickly seized on the success in killing bin Laden to defend and advance their own agendas, such as torture. Americans were told that bin Laden was found as a result of information gleaned from torturing detainees held in Eastern European CIA secret prisons years ago.

This listing of possible agendas and add-on agendas is far from complete, but for those capable of skepticism and independent thought, it can serve as a starting point. The agendas behind the theater will reveal themselves as time goes on. All you have to do is to pay attention and to realize that most of what you hear from the mainstream media is designed to advance police state/warfare agendas.

AMERICANS
ARE LIVING IN 1984

May 11, 2011

The White House's "death of bin Laden" story has come apart at the seams. Will it make any difference that before 48 hours had passed the story had changed so much that it no longer bore any resemblance to President Obama's Sunday evening broadcast and has lost all credibility?

So far it has made no difference to the once-fabled news organization, the British Broadcasting Corporation (BBC), which on May 9, eight days later, is still repeating the propaganda that the SEALs killed bin Laden in his Pakistani compound, where bin Laden lived next door to the Pakistani Military Academy surrounded by the Pakistani army.

Not even the president of Pakistan finds the story implausible. The BBC reports that the president is launching a full-scale investigation of how bin Laden managed to live for years in an army garrison town without being noticed.

For most Americans the story began and ended with four words: "We got bin Laden." The celebrations, the sweet taste of revenge, of triumph and victory over the demise of "the most dangerous man on the planet" are akin to the thrill experienced by sports fans when their football team defeats the unspeakable rival or their baseball team wins the World Series. No fan wants to hear the next day that it is not so, that it is all a mistake. If these Americans years from now come across a story that the killing of bin Laden was an orchestrated news event to boost other agendas, they will dismiss the report as the ravings of a pinko-liberal-commie.

Everyone knows we killed bin Laden. How could it be otherwise? We—the indispensable people, the virtuous nation, the world's only superpower, the white hats—were destined to prevail. No other outcome was possible.

No one will notice that those who fabricated the story forgot to show the kidney dialysis machine that, somehow, kept bin Laden alive for a decade. No doctors were on the premises.

No one will remember that Fox News reported in December, 2001, that Osama bin Laden had passed away from his illnesses.[31]

If bin Laden beat all odds and managed to live another decade to await, unarmed and undefended, the arrival of the Navy SEALS last week, how it is possible that the "terror mastermind," who defeated not merely the CIA and FBI, but all 16 US intelligence agencies along with those of America's European allies and Israel, the National Security Council, the Pentagon, NORAD, Air Traffic Control, airport security four times on the same morning, etc. etc., never enjoyed another success, not even a little, very minor one? What was the "terror mastermind" doing for a decade after 9/11?

The "death of bin Laden" serves too many agendas that cover the political spectrum for the obvious falsity of the story to be recognized by very many. Patriots are euphoric that America won over bin Laden. Progressives have seized on the story to excoriate the United States for extra-judicial murder that brutalizes us all. Some on the left-wing bought into the 9/11 story because of the emotional satisfaction they received from oppressed Arabs striking back at their imperialist oppressors. These left-wingers are delighted that it took the incompetent Americans an entire decade to find bin Laden, who was hiding in plain view. The American incompetence in finding bin Laden simply, in their minds, proves the incompetence of the US government, which failed to protect Americans against the 9/11 attack.

Those who ordered, and those who wrote, totally incompetent legal memos that torture was permissible under US and international law, thereby setting up George W. Bush and Dick Cheney for the possibility of prosecution, are riding the euphoria of bin Laden's death by declaring that it was torture that led the American assassins to bin Laden. All of a sudden, torture, which had fallen back into the disrepute in which it had been for centuries, is again in the clear. Anything that leads to the elimination of bin Laden is a valid instrument.

Those, who want to increase the pressure on Pakistan to shut up about Americans murdering Pakistani citizens from the air and by troops on the ground, have gained a new club with which to beat the Pakistani government into submission: "You hid bin Laden from us."

Those who want to continue to fatten the profits of the military/ security complex and the powers of Homeland Security, such as Secretary of State Hillary Clinton, use bin Laden's second, or ninth, death as proof that America is succeeding in its war on terror and that the war must continue on such a successful path until all enemies are slain.

Most ominous of all was the statement by the CIA director that bin Laden's death would lead to new attacks on America and new 9/11s from Al Qaeda seeking revenge. This warning, issued within a few hours of President Obama's Sunday evening address, telegraphed the inevitable "Al Qaeda" Internet posting that America would suffer new 9/11s for killing their leader.

If the Taliban knew in December 2001 that bin Laden was dead, does anyone think that Al Qaeda didn't know it? Indeed, no member of the public has any way of knowing if Al Qaeda is anything more than a bogyman organization created by the CIA which issues "Al Qaeda" announcements. The evidence that Al Qaeda's announcements are issued by the CIA is very strong. The various videos of bin Laden for the last nine years have been shown by experts to be fakes. Why would bin Laden issue a fake video? Why did bin Laden cease issuing videos and only issue audios? A person running a worldwide terrorist organization should be able to produce videos. He would also be surrounded by better protectors than a couple of women. Where was Al Qaeda, which according to former Pentagon chief Donald Rumsfeld, consists of "the most dangerous, best-trained, vicious killers on the face of the earth." Had these most dangerous men alive abandoned their leader?

The CIA director's warning of future terrorist attacks, followed by a suspect "Al Qaeda" threat of the same, suggests that if the American public continues to lose its enthusiasm for the government's open-ended wars, which are conducted at the expense of the US budget deficit, the dollar's exchange value, inflation, Social Security, Medicare, income support programs, jobs, recovery, and so forth, "Al Qaeda" will again outwit all 16 US intelligence agencies, those of our allies, NORAD, airport security, Air Traffic Control, etc. etc., and inflict the world's only superpower with another humiliating defeat that will invigorate American support for "the war on terror."

I believe that "Al Qaeda" could blow up the White House or Congress or both and that the majority of Americans would fall for the story, just as the Germans, a better educated and more intelligent population, fell for the Reichstag Fire—as did a number of historians.

The reason I say this is that Americans have succumbed to propaganda that has conditioned them to believe that they are under attack by practically omnipotent adversaries. Proof of this is broadcast every day. For example, on March 9, I heard over National Public Radio in Atlanta that Emory University, a private university of some distinction, treated its 3,500 graduating class to a commencement address by Janet Napolitano, Secretary of Homeland Security.

This is the agency that has goons feeling the genitals of young children and adults and which has announced that it intends to expand this practice from air travelers to shopping malls, bus and train stations. That a serious university invited such a low-lifer, who clearly has no respect for American civil liberty and is devoid of any sort of sense of what is appropriate, to address a graduating class of southern elite is a clear indication that the Ministry of Truth has prevailed. Americans are living in George Orwell's *1984*.

For those who haven't read Orwell's classic prediction of our time, Big Brother, the government, could tell the "citizens" any lie and it was accepted unquestioningly. As a perceptive reader pointed out to me, we Americans, with our "free press," are at this point today: "What is really alarming is the increasingly arrogant sloppiness of these lies, as though the government has become so profoundly confident of its ability to deceive people that they make virtually no effort to even appear credible."

THE WEST IS TRAPPED IN ITS OWN PROPAGANDA

May 12, 2011

One of the wishes that readers often express to me came true today (May 11). I was on the mainstream media. It was a program with a worldwide reach—the BBC World Service. There were others on the program as well, and the topic was Hillary Clinton's remarks (May 10) about the lack of democracy and human rights in China.

I startled the program's host when I compared Hillary's remarks to the pot calling the kettle black. I was somewhat taken aback myself by the British BBC program host's rush to America's defense and wondered about it as the program continued. Surely, he had heard about Abu Ghraib, Guantanamo detainees, CIA secret torture prisons sprinkled around the world, invasion and destruction of Iraq on the basis of lies and deceptions, Afghanistan, Pakistan, Yemen, Somalia, Libya. Surely, he was aware of Hillary's hypocrisy as she demonized China but turned a blind eye to Israel, Mubarak, Bahrain and the Saudis. China's record is not perfect, but is it this bad? Why wasn't the Chinese Minister for Foreign Affairs criticizing America's human rights abuses and rigged elections? How come China minds its own business and we don't?

These questions didn't go down well. None of the other interviewees or guests thought that Hillary had made a good decision, but even the Chinese guests were not free of the common mindset that frames every issue: that the West's standard is the one by which the rest of the world is judged. By pointing out our own shortcomings, I was challenging that standard. The host and other guests could not escape from the restraints imposed on thought by the role of the West as world standard.

What has happened to the West is that it can see itself and others only through the eyes of its own propaganda. There was a great deal of talk about China's lack of democracy. As the BBC program was being broadcast, the news intruded that Greeks had again taken to the streets to protest the costs of the bailout of the banks and Wall Street—the rich—being imposed on ordinary people at the expense of their lives and aspirations. The Irish government announced that it was going to confiscate with a tax part of the Irish people's pension accumulations. It simply did not occur to the host and other guests that these are not democratic outcomes.

It is a strange form of democracy that produces political outcomes that reward the few and punish the many, despite the energetic protests of the many. Political scientists understand that US electoral outcomes are determined by powerful monied interests that finance the political campaigns and that the bills Congress passes and the President signs are written by these interest groups to serve their narrow interests. Such conclusions are dismissed as cynicism and do not alter the mindset. While the program's host and guests were indulging in the West's democratic and human rights superiority, the American Civil Liberties Union was sending out a bulletin urging its members to oppose legislation now before Congress that would give the current and future presidents of the United States expanded war authority to use, on their own initiative, military force anywhere in the world independently of the restraints imposed by the US Constitution and international law.

CREATING THE
BIN LADEN "REALITY"

May 14, 2011

I have heard one dozen times today (May 13) from media that the US killed Osama Bin Laden in Pakistan. I heard it three times from National Public Radio, twice from the BBC, and from every TV and radio station I encountered, even those stations that play the rock and roll music of the 1950s and 1960s. The killing of bin Laden has now entered the legends of our time and, no doubt, the history books.

So...the US government that told us that Saddam Hussein had "weapons of mass destruction" and "Al Qaeda connections" and that Iran has nuclear missiles that require the US to ring Russia with anti-ballistic missile systems, finally told us the truth for once? Obama found Osama and had him murdered, apparently unarmed in his underwear, defended not by Al Qaeda, "the best trained, most dangerous vicious killers on the planet," but by two unarmed women.

As I offered previously, if you believe this, I have a bridge in Brooklyn that I can let you have for a cheap price.

The government has created another reality for us proles. We won again. Us white hats got the black hat, just like in the western movie. Fantasy is better than fact, and us good guys are on a roll. It makes everybody happy, even those who have lost their jobs, their houses, their pensions.

So, who's the next black hat? The military/security complex cannot do without a bad guy, or the budget could be cut and billions of dollars in profits would go missing. Without someone for Americans to hate, the show can't go on.

Homeland Security says the next black hat will be "domestic extremists." The CIA says it will be the next Al Qaeda leader, bin Laden's replacement, who will terrorize us white hats for killing bin Laden. The neocon brownshirts say it is Pakistan, who hid bin Laden from us, thus protecting him from justice being done. Hillary says it is China, and as the US economy continues its collapse, more and more fingers will point at China.

Airport Security will pat down more babies, feel more genitals, and radiate more air travelers.

But without bin Laden, we will feel safer and more secure, which is counterproductive for the military/security complex. Obama has made a fundamental mistake. He has killed Emanuel Goldstein (bin Laden), the hate figure who justified the trillions of dollars we have blown trying to get him.

Once Homeland Security, the CIA, and the White House decide who the new hate figure is to be, we will be off and running again.

It took 10 years to get bin Laden. This proves that all those security experts who say that the war will last for 30 years might be underestimating the necessary commitment. If it takes 10 years each to find and murder the next two leaders, we are faced with conflict that lasts across generations.

As I wrote previously, bin Laden's killing serves so many different agendas that even those who don't believe the story have hooked their wagon to it. Al Qaeda itself can no longer take credit for acts of terrorism without declaring that it was to avenge bin Laden.

The bin Laden story is now set in stone, immune from fact. Global Research has provided us with bin Laden's last known interview, which appeared in a Pakistan newspaper on September 28, 2001 and was translated and made available to the West by the BBC World Monitoring Service on September 29, 2001.

In the interview, bin Laden says: "I have already said that I am not involved in the 11 September attacks in the United States. ... Whoever committed the act of 11 September are not the friends of the American people. I have already said that we are against the American system, not against its people, whereas in these attacks the common American people have been killed ... The Western media is unleashing such a baseless propaganda, which makes us surprised, but it reflects on what is in their hearts and gradually they themselves become captive of this propaganda ... Terror is the most dreaded weapon in the modern age and the Western media is mercilessly using it against its own people."

But who in the West would believe a demonized bin Laden when to do so requires them to disbelieve George W. Bush, Dick Cheney, and the Western media?

We all know, don't we, that in America the government always has the best interest of ordinary people at heart and always tells them the truth? If you don't believe this, you are anti-American.

THE ONGOING BIN LADEN SAGA

May 16, 2011

"The Matrix is a system, Neo. That system is our enemy.
But when you're inside, you look around, what do you see?
Businessmen, teachers, lawyers, carpenters. The very minds of the
people we are trying to save. But until we do, these people are still
a part of that system, and that makes them our enemy. You have to
understand, most of these people are not ready to be unplugged.
And many of them are so inured, so hopelessly dependent on the
system, that they will fight to protect it."

The ever-changing, ever-growing bin Laden story becomes ever
more preposterous. The cowardly bin Laden is now the vain bin Laden,
the terror mastermind who has nothing to do but to sit and watch videos of
himself.

Washington released a video of an alleged bin Laden indulging in self-
admiration, but there is no sound. Why? Was the video made without sound?
Did Washington delete the audio? The video seems to show the alleged bin
Laden speaking to someone in the room. Is the voice not bin Laden's? Is the
alleged bin Laden referring to the image on the screen in the third person, as not
himself? Why would bin Laden have a video made of himself watching videos
of himself? Why is a video of bin Laden watching bin Laden a headline story?
Is it meant to substitute for the absence of a corpse?

As one reader put it, "The government is playing with us,
experimenting to see if there is any tall tale we won't believe."

The story keeps changing as to whether "bin Laden's compound,"
no longer a million dollar luxury mansion, had Internet and communications
or relied on couriers. The latest installment is that bin Laden was online.
Washington says that the raid delivered into its hands bin Laden's emails
and diary, which, Washington claims, show an active bin Laden directing
his terror network to carry out more plots. If bin Laden was online, why did
Obama have to find him by trailing a courier?

Somehow the SEALs grabbed bin Laden's diary and emails, but left all sorts of other documents that allegedly have fallen into Pakistani hands. These left-behind documents now serve as a pretext for more disputes with Pakistan and another excuse for ignoring Pakistan's protests about the military operations the US carries out in Pakistan, violating the sovereignty of the country.

Why would the SEALs leave behind so many precious documents? First they kill for no reason the mastermind who could have revealed the world of terror; then they depart, leaving terror records behind. Some will say that this is typical US government incompetence. So how did such an incompetent government find bin Laden?

Any documents left behind were most likely carried in by the SEALs as plants.

Has anyone independent of Washington examined the alleged bin Laden diary and confirmed that it was in bin Laden's handwriting? These kinds of questions are the kind the media, back when we had one, used to ask.

The bin Laden story is now such a fable with so many contradictory bits that people can pick and choose to suit the telling. *Time* magazine likes it all, except the part about an all-powerful bin Laden, still in control, rejecting an underling's proposal "to fit a tractor with rotating blades to use to 'mow down the enemies of Allah.'" *Time* prefers a bin Laden who was unsettled by his realization that he had lost his "historic significance" prior to losing his life to the US Navy SEALs.

If bin Laden had lost his significance, why did Obama get such a boost in the polls from his claim that he found bin Laden and had him killed?

The American Empire cannot do without bin Laden. Maybe the next installment of the fable will be that bin Laden escaped, leaving behind a double, and is abroad carrying out more terror plots.

As the fable continues, try to rescue from the Memory Hole the fact that we were presented with a death without a corpse and that Washington has no explanation for why an unarmed, undefended, frail man, who was a font of terrorist information, was murdered and not captured.

THE STRAUSS-KAHN FRAME-UP: THE AMERICAN POLICE STATE STRIDES FORWARD

May 18, 2011

The International Monetary Fund's director, Dominique Strauss-Kahn, was arrested last Sunday in New York City on the allegation of an immigrant hotel maid that he attempted to rape her in his hotel room. A New York judge has denied Strauss-Kahn bail on the grounds that he might flee to France.

President Bill Clinton survived his sexual escapades, because he was a servant to the system, not a threat. But Strauss-Kahn, like former New York Governor Eliot Spitzer, was a threat to the system, and, like Eliot Spitzer, Strass-Kahn has been deleted from the power ranks.

Strauss-Kahn was the first IMF director in my lifetime, if memory serves, who disavowed the traditional IMF policy of imposing on the poor and ordinary people the cost of bailing out Wall Street and the Western banks. Strauss-Kahn said that regulation had to be reimposed on the greed-driven, fraud-prone financial sector, which, unregulated, destroyed the lives of ordinary people. Strauss-Kahn listened to Nobel economist Joseph Stiglitz, one of a handful of economists who has a social conscience.

Perhaps the most dangerous black mark in Strauss-Kahn's book is that he was far ahead of America's French puppet, President Sarkozy, in the upcoming French elections. Strauss-Kahn simply had to be eliminated.

It is possible that Strauss-Kahn eliminated himself and saved Washington the trouble. However, as a well-travelled person who has often stayed in New York hotels and in hotels in cities around the world, I have never experienced a maid entering unannounced into my room, much less when I was in the shower.

In the spun story, Strauss-Kahn is portrayed as so deprived of sex that he attempted to rape a hotel maid. Anyone who ever served on the staff of a powerful public figure knows that this is unlikely. On a senator's staff on which I served, there were two aides whose job was to make certain that no woman, with the exception of his wife, was ever alone with the senator. This was done to protect the senator both from female power groupies, who lust after celebrities and powerful men, and from women sent by a rival on missions to compromise an opponent. A powerful man such as Strauss-Kahn would not have been starved for women, and as a multi-millionaire he could certainly afford to make his own discreet arrangements.

As Henry Kissinger said, "power is the ultimate aphrodisiac." In politics, sex is handed out as favors and payoffs, and it is used as a honey trap. Some Americans will remember that Senator Packwood's long career (1969-1995) was destroyed by a female lobbyist, suspected, according to rumors, of sexual conquests of Senators, who charged that Packwood propositioned her in his office. Perhaps what inspired the charge was that Packwood was in the way of her employer's legislative agenda.

Even those who exercise care can be framed by allegations of an event to which there are no witnesses. On May 16 the British *Daily Mail* reported that prior to Strauss-Kahn's fateful departure for New York, the French newspaper, *Liberation*, published comments he made while discussing his plans to challenge Sarkozy for the presidency of France. Strauss-Kahn said that as he was the clear favorite to beat Sarkozy, he would be subjected to a smear campaign by Sarkozy and his interior minister, Glaude Gueant. Strauss-Kahn predicted that a woman would be offered between 500,000 and 1,000,000 euros (more than $1,000,000) to make up a story that he raped her. [32]

The *Daily Mail* reports that Strauss-Kahn's suspicions are supported by the fact that the first person to break the news of Strauss-Kahn's arrest was an activist in Mr Sarkozy's UMP party—who apparently knew about the scandal before it happened. Jonathan Pinet, a politics student, tweeted the news just before the New York Police Department made it public, although he said that he simply had a 'friend' working at the Sofitel where the attack was said to have happened. The first person to re-tweet Mr Pinet was Arnaud Dassier, a spin doctor who had previously publicized details of multi-millionaire Strauss-Kahn's luxurious lifestyle in a bid to dent his left wing credentials.

Strauss-Kahn could just as easily have been set up by rivals inside the IMF, as well as by rivals within the French political establishment.

Michelle Sabban, a senior councilor for the greater Paris region and a Strauss-Kahn loyalist, said: "I am convinced it is an international conspiracy."

She added: "It's the IMF they wanted to decapitate, not so much the Socialist primary candidate. It's not like him. Everyone knows that his weakness is seduction, women. That's how they got him."

Even some of Strauss-Kahn's rivals said they could not believe the news. "It is totally hallucinatory," said centrist Dominique Paille.

"If it is true, this would be a historic moment, but in the negative sense, for French political life. I hope that everyone respects the presumption of innocence. I cannot manage to believe this affair."

And Henri de Raincourt, minister for overseas co-operation in President Nicolas Sarkozy's government, added: "We cannot rule out the thought of a trap."

Michelle Sabban is on to something when she says the IMF was the target. Strauss-Kahn is the first IMF director who is not lined up on the side of the rich against the poor. Strauss-Kahn's suspicions were of Sarkozy, but Wall Street and the US government also had strong reasons to eliminate him. Wall Street is terrified by the prospect of regulation, and Washington was embarrassed by the recent IMF report that China's economy would surpass the US economy within five years. An international conspiracy is not out of the question.

Indeed, the plot is unfolding as a conspiracy. Authorities have produced a French woman who claims she was a near rape victim of Strauss-Kahn a decade ago. It would be interesting to know whether this allegation is the result of a threat or a bribe. As in the case of Julian Assange, there are now two women to accuse Strauss-Kahn. Once the prosecutors get the odds of two females against one male, they win in the media.

It has not been revealed how the authorities knew Strauss-Kahn was on a flight to France. However, by arresting him aboard his scheduled flight just as it was to depart, the authorities created the image of a man fleeing from a crime.

The way American justice (*sic*) works is that prosecutors in about 96 percent of the cases get a plea bargain. US prosecutors are permitted by judges and the public to pay for testimony against the defendant and to put sufficient pressure on innocent defendants to coerce them into making a guilty plea in exchange for lesser charges and a lighter sentence. Unless the hotel maid has a spell of bad conscience and admits she was paid to lie, or gets cold feet about perjuring herself, Strauss-Kahn is likely to find that American criminal justice (*sic*) is organized to produce conviction regardless of innocence or guilt.

On May 16, the day following Strauss-Kahn's arrest, the US Supreme Court threw its weight behind the American police state by destroying the remains of the Fourth Amendment with an 8-1 ruling that, the U.S. Constitution notwithstanding, America's police do not need warrants to invade homes and search persons.

This ruling is more evidence that every American is regarded as a potential enemy of the state, not only by Airport Security but also by the high muckety-mucks in Washington. The conservatives' "war on crime" has created a police state, and conservatives, who originally stood for limited government and civil liberty, are euphoric over the expanded and unaccountable powers that a conservative Supreme Court has handed to the police.

On the same day the federal government reached the $14.3 trillion debt ceiling, which forced the Treasury to "borrow" money from federal employee pensions in order to continue funding America's illegal wars and crimes against humanity. The breached debt ceiling serves as an appropriate marker for a country that has squandered its constitutional heritage and has arrived at moral as well as fiscal bankruptcy

DOMINIQUE STRAUSS-KAHN: THE ESTABLISHMENT ELIMINATES A THREAT

May 20, 2011

The police and the prostitute media have made it impossible for Dominique Strauss-Kahn to get a fair trial. From the moment of the announcement that he had been arrested on suspicion of sexually assaulting a hotel maid, and before he was ever indicted, the accounts given by the police were designed to create the impression that the director of the International Monetary Fund was guilty. For example, the police told the media, which duly regurgitated to the public, that Strauss-Kahn was in such a hurry to flee the scene of the crime that he left behind his cell phone. The police also put out the story that by calling airlines and demanding passenger lists, they managed to catch the fleeing rapist just as his plane was departing for France.

A New York judge denied Strauss-Kahn bail on the basis of police misrepresentation that he was apprehended fleeing the country.

Once he was imprisoned, the police announced that Strauss-Kahn was on suicide watch, which is a way of suggesting to the public that the accused rapist might take his own life in order to avoid the public humiliation of a guilty verdict from a jury.

But what really happened, assuming one can learn anything from press reports, is that Strauss-Kahn, upon arriving at JFK airport for his scheduled flight, discovered that he did not have his cell phone and telephoned the hotel, the scene of the alleged crime. It boggles the mind that anyone could possibly think that a person fleeing from his crime would call the scene of the crime, ask about his left behind cell phone, and tell them where he was.

Then in rapid succession, reeking of orchestration, a French woman steps forward and declares that a decade ago she was nearly raped by Strauss-Kahn. This was followed by Kristin Davis, the Manhattan Madam of the prostitute who did in Eliot Spitzer before he could get the banksters on Wall Street, stepping forward to announce that one of her call girls refused to service Strauss-Kahn a second time because he was too rough in the act.

With hunting season opened, any woman whose career would benefit from publicity, or whose bank account would bless a damage award, can now step forward and claim to have been a victim or near victim of Strauss-Kahn.

This is not to deny that Strauss-Kahn might have an inordinate appetite for sex that did him in. It is to say that long before a jury hears from the maid, or from a prosecutor speaking for the maid, the scene has been set.

Why would he run away if he didn't do it?

Look at all the women he has accosted!

You get the picture.

I have written about the anomalies of the case. One of the most striking is the confirmed reports in the French and British press that a political activist for French President Sarkozy, Jonathan Pinet, tweeted the news of Strauss-Kahn's arrest to Arnaud Dassier, a spin doctor for Sarkozy, before the news was announced by the New York police.

Pinet's explanation for how he was the first to know is that a "friend" in the Sofitel Hotel, where the alleged crime took place, told him. Is it merely a coincidence that the men assigned the task of removing the Strauss-Kahn threat to French President Sarkozy's re-election had a clued-in friend in the Sofitel Hotel? Did the police clue-in the "friend" before they made the public announcement? If so, why?

What bothers me about the Strauss-Kahn affair is that if the police have evidence that supports their insistence on his guilt, it is unnecessary for the police to set up Strauss-Kahn in the media. Generally, set-ups like this occur only when there is no evidence or when the evidence has to be fabricated and cannot withstand examination.

As a person who had a Washington career, I find other aspects of the case disturbing. Strauss-Kahn had emerged as a threat to the establishment. Polls showed that as the socialist candidate, he was the odds-on favorite to defeat the American candidate, Sarkozy, in the upcoming French presidential election. Perhaps it was only electoral posturing to help defeat Sarkozy, but Strauss-Kahn indicated that he intended to move the International Monetary Fund away from its past policy of making the poor pay for the mistakes of the rich. He spoke of strengthening collective bargaining, and of restructuring mortgages, tax and spending policies in order that the economy would serve ordinary people in addition to the banksters. Strauss-Kahn said that regulation needed to be restored[33] to financial markets and implied that a more even distribution of income was required.

These remarks, together with a likely win over Sarkozy in the French election, made Strauss-Kahn a double-barreled challenge to the establishment. The third strike against him was the recent IMF report that said China would surpass the US as the world's first economy within five years.[34]

People who haven't spent their professional life in Washington may not understand the threat to Washington that is in the IMF report. Whether deserved or not, the IMF has a lot of credibility. By placing China as the number one economic power by the end of the next US presidential term, the IMF thrust a dagger through the heart of American hegemony. Washington's power is based on America's economic supremacy. The IMF report said that this supremacy was at its end.

This kind of announcement tells the political world that, as the headline read, although rich and a member of the establishment, and independently of his behavior toward women, Strauss-Kahn made the mistake of revealing that he might have a social conscience. Either this social conscience or the hubris of power led him to challenge American supremacy. This is an unforgivable crime for which he is being punished.

My friend, Alexander Cockburn, an intelligent and civilized person who is derided by right-wingers as a communist, lacks my experience of Washington. Consequently, he thinks that the facts will come out, although he seems to prefer that they come out on the side of the maid and not Strauss-Kahn.

If Alex were the Bolshevik he is said to be, he would know that no high-ranking figure who was serving the establishment would be destroyed on the basis of the word of an immigrant maid living in a sub-let apartment in a building for Aids victims. The very notion that the US establishment craves justice to this extent is a total absurdity. Americans are so indifferent to injustice that the American public shrugs off the hundreds of thousands and millions of women, children, and village elders who are murdered, maimed, dispossessed, and displaced by the US military in Iraq, Afghanistan, Pakistan, Yemen, Libya, Somalia, and wherever Washington and the military/security complex, while feeding on power and profit, can claim to be protecting Americans from "terrorists" or bringing democracy to the heathen.

The American criminal justice system is riddled with wrongful convictions and stinks of injustice. The US has a much higher rate of incarceration than alleged authoritarian regimes such as China, and routinely destroys the lives of young people, and even mothers of small children, for using drugs.

Strauss-Kahn's indictment serves emotional needs of conservatives, left-wingers, and feminists as well as establishment agendas. Conservatives don't like the French, because they did not support the US invasion of Iraq. The left-wing doesn't like rich white guys and IMF officials, and feminists don't like womanizers. But even if the government's case falls apart in the courtroom, Strauss-Kahn has been removed from the French presidential race and from the IMF. This, not justice for an immigrant, is what the case is about.

Many Americans are unable to comprehend that authorities would remove a threat with a frame-up. But far worse has occurred. Francesco Cossiga, a former President of Italy, revealed that many of the bombings in Europe during the 1960s, 70s, and 80s, which were blamed on communists, were in fact "false flag" operations carried out by the CIA and Italian intelligence in order to scare voters away from the communist party. Cossiga's revelations resulted in a parliamentary investigation in which intelligence operative Vincenzo Vinciguerra stated: "You had to attack civilians, the people, women, children, innocent people, unknown people far removed from any political game. The reason was quite simple: to force the public to turn to the state to ask for greater security."

If democratic governments will murder innocents for political reasons, why wouldn't they frame someone? Whether innocent or guilty, Strauss-Kahn has been framed in advance of his trial.

DOES AMERICA
HAVE A CULTURE?

May 23, 2011

The culture of the United States is said to be a youth culture, which is defined in terms of entertainment: sex, rock music or its current equivalent, violent video games, sports, and TV reality shows. This culture has transformed the country and appears on the verge of transforming the rest of the world. There are even indications that secularized Arab and Iranian youth can't wait to be liberated and to partake of this culture of porn-rock.

America's former culture—accountable government, rule of law and presumption of innocence, respect for others, and for principles and manners—has gone by the wayside. Many Americans, especially younger ones, are not aware of what they have lost, because they don't know what they had.

This was brought home to me yet again by some reader responses to my recent columns in which I pointed out that Strauss-Kahn, the IMF director (now former) accused of sexually assaulting a hotel maid, was denied the presumption of innocence. I pointed out that the legal principle of innocent until proven guilty was violated by the police and media, and that Strauss-Kahn was convicted in the media not only prior to trial but also prior to indictment, which became a huge embarrassment to the media and police when the prosecutor was forced by the evidence to drop all charges.

From readers' responses I learned that there are people who do not know that a suspect is innocent until proven guilty by evidence in a public trial. As one wrote, "if he wasn't guilty, he wouldn't be charged." Some thought that by "presumption of innocence" I was saying that Strauss-Kahn was innocent. I was accused of being a woman-hater and received feminist lectures. Some American women are more familiar with feminist mantras than they are with the legal principles that are the foundation of our society.

Many males also confused my defense of the presumption of innocence with a defense of Strauss-Kahn, or if they knew about "innocent until proven guilty," didn't care. Right-wingers wanted Strauss-Kahn out of the picture because he was the socialist party candidate likely to defeat the

American puppet, Sarkozy, in the French presidential election. With Sarkozy, Washington finally has a French president who has abandoned all interest in an independent or semi-independent French foreign policy. Didn't I realize that if we lost Sarkozy, the French might revert to not going along with our invasions, as they refused to do when we had to get Saddam Hussein? With Sarkozy, the French are doing our bidding in Libya. Why in the world did I think Strauss-Kahn and some silly doctrine like the presumption of innocence were more important than French support for our wars?

Many left-wingers were just as indifferent to a legal principle that protects the innocent. They wanted Strauss-Kahn's blood, because he is a rich member of the establishment and as IMF director had made the poor in Greece, Ireland, and Spain pay for the mistakes of the rich. What did I mean, "presumption of innocence"? How could any member of the ruling establishment be innocent? One left-winger even wrote that I had "reverted to type," and that my babbling about presumption of innocence[35] proved that I was still a Reaganite defending the rich from the consequences of their crimes.[35]

Independent thought is not a concept with which very many Americans are familiar or comfortable. Most want to have their emotions stroked, to be told what they want to hear. They already know what they think. A writer's job is to validate it, and if the writer doesn't, he is, depending on the ideology of the reader, a misogynist, a pinko-liberal commie, or an operative for the fascist establishment. All will agree that he is a no good SOB.

As I wrote a while back, respect for truth has fallen and taken everything down with it.

WILL WASHINGTON FOMENT WAR BETWEEN CHINA AND INDIA?

June 5, 2011

What is Washington's solution for the rising power of China?

The answer might be to involve China in a nuclear war with India.

The staging of the fake death of bin Laden in a commando raid that violated Pakistan's sovereignty was sold to President Obama by the military/ security complex as a way to boost Obama's standing in the polls.

The raid succeeded in raising Obama's approval ratings. But another purpose was to target Pakistan and to show Pakistan that the US was contemplating invading Pakistan in order to make Pakistan pay for allegedly hiding bin Laden next door to Pakistan's military academy. The neocon, and increasingly the US military position, is that the Taliban can't be conquered unless NATO widens the war theater to Pakistan, where the Taliban allegedly has sanctuaries protected by the Pakistan government, which takes American money but doesn't do Washington's bidding.

Pakistan got the threat message and ran to China. On May 17 Pakistan's Prime Minister Yousuf Raza Gilani, as he departed for China, declared China to be Pakistan's "best and most trusted friend." China has built a port for Pakistan at Gwadar, which is close to the entrance of the Strait of Hormuz. The port might become a Chinese naval base on the Arabian Sea.

Raza Rumi reported in the *Pakistan Tribune* (June 4) that at a recent lecture at Pakistan's National Defense University, Husain Haqqani, Pakistan's ambassador to the US, asked the military officers whether the biggest threat to Pakistan came from within, from India, or from the US. A majority of the officers said that the US was the biggest threat to Pakistan.

China, concerned with India, the other Asian giant that is rising, is willing to ally with Pakistan. Moreover, China doesn't want Americans on its border, which is where they would be should Pakistan become another American battleground.

Therefore, China showed its displeasure with the US threat to Pakistan, and advised Washington to respect Pakistan's sovereignty, adding that any attack on Pakistan would be considered an attack on China

I do not think China's ultimatum was reported in the US press, but it was widely reported in India's press. India is concerned that China has stepped up to Pakistan's defense.

The Chinese ultimatum is important, because it is a WWI or WWII level of ultimatum. With this level of commitment of China to Pakistan, Washington will now seek a way to maneuver itself out of the confrontation and to substitute India.

The US has been fawning all over India, cultivating India in the most shameful ways, including the sacrifice of Americans' jobs. Recently, there have been massive US weapons sales to India, US-India military cooperation agreements, and joint military exercises.

Washington figures that the Indians, who were gullible for centuries about the British, will be gullible about the "shining city on the hill" that is "bringing freedom and democracy to the world" by smashing, killing, and destroying. Like the British and France's Sarkozy, Indian political leaders will find themselves doing Washington's will. By the time India and China realize that they have been maneuvered into mutual destruction by the Americans, it will be too late for either to back down.

With China and India eliminated, that only leaves Russia, which is already ringed by US missile bases and isolated from Europe by NATO, which now includes former constituent parts of the Soviet Empire. A large percentage of gullible Russian youth admires the US for its "freedom" (little do they know) and hates the "authoritarian" Russian state, which they regard as a continuation of the old Soviet state. These "internationalized Russians" will side with Washington, more of less forcing Moscow into surrender.

As the rest of the world, with the exception of parts of South America, is already part of the American Empire, Russia's surrender will let the US focus its military might on South America. Chavez will be overthrown, and if others do not fall into line, more examples will be made.

The only way the American Empire can be stopped is for China and Russia to realize their danger and to form an unbreakable alliance that reassures India, breaks off Germany from NATO and defends Iran.

Otherwise, the American Empire will prevail over the entire world. The US dollar will become the only currency, and therefore be spared exchange rate depreciation from debt monetization.

Gold and silver will become forbidden possessions, as will guns and a number of books, including the US Constitution.

CONSPIRACY
THEORY

June 20, 2011

In a June column, I concluded that "conspiracy theory" is a term applied to any fact, analysis, or truth that is politically, ideologically, or emotionally unacceptable. This column is about how common real conspiracies are. While every happening cannot be explained by a conspiracy, conspiracies are common everyday events. Therefore, it is paradoxical that "conspiracy theory" has become a synonym for "unbelievable."

Conspiracies are commonly used in order to advance agendas. In the July issue of *American Rifleman*, a National Rifle Association publication, the organization's executive vice president, Wayne Lapierre, reports on a congressional investigation led by Senator Charles Grassley and Representative Darrell Issa of a Bureau of Alcohol, Tobacco, Firearms, and Explosives (BATFE) and Department of Justice conspiracy to further gun control measures by smuggling guns across the border to Mexican criminals and blame it on American firearm sellers. Lapierre writes:

> Thanks to federal agents coming forth with evidence on the gun smuggling operation, this government sanctioned criminal conspiracy has been exposed . . . Leading an administration-wide cover up—marked by an arrogant dismissal of Congress' constitutional role—is Attorney General Eric Holder, who has blocked all efforts to get to the truth. His minions have directed federal employees with knowledge of the gun-running scam to refuse to cooperate with congressional investigators.

Many Americans will find this uncovered conspiracy hard to believe. The US Federal agency, BATFE, with the DOJ's participation, has been providing firearms to Mexico's drug cartels in order to create "evidence" to support the charge that US gun dealers are the source of weapons for Mexican drug gangs. The purpose of the government's conspiracy is to advance the gun control agenda.

Attorney General Eric Holder's stonewalling of the congressional investigation has resulted in Rep. Issa's warning to Holder: "We're not looking at the straw buyers, Mr. Attorney General. We're looking at you."

The most likely outcome will be that Grassley and Issa will have accidents or be framed on sex charges.

Conspiracies are also a huge part of economic life. For example, the Wall Street firm, Goldman Sachs, is known to have shorted financial instruments that it was simultaneously selling as sound investments to its customers. The current bailouts of EU countries' sovereign debt is a conspiracy to privatize the public domain.

Economic conspiracies are endless, and most succeed. NAFTA is a conspiracy against American labor, as are H-1B and L-1 work visas. Globalism is a conspiracy against First World jobs.

The sex charge against Dominique Strauss-Kahn could turn out to have been a conspiracy. According to *The New York Times*, the hotel maid has bank accounts in four states, and someone has been putting thousands of dollars into them.

Sometimes governments are willing to kill large numbers of their own citizens in order to advance an agenda. For example, Operation Northwoods was a plan for false flag terrorist events drafted by the US Joint Chiefs of Staff and signed by General Lyman Lemnitzer. It called for the CIA and other "black op" elements to shoot down Americans in the streets of Miami and Washington, D.C., to hijack or shoot down airliners, to attack and sink boats carrying Cuban refugees to the US, and to fabricate evidence that implicated Castro. The agenda of the Joint Chiefs and the CIA was to stir up American fear and hatred of Castro in order to support regime change in Cuba.

Before the knee-jerk reader cries "conspiracy theory," be apprised that the secret Operation Northwoods was made public on November 18, 1997, by the John F. Kennedy Assassination Records Review Board. When the plan was presented to President Kennedy in 1962, he rejected it and removed Lemnitzer as Chairman of the Joint Chiefs.

Wikipedia quotes extensively from the plan's menu of proposed false flag terrorist acts. Those who distrust Wikipedia can obtain a copy of the plan from the National Archives.

When I tell even highly educated people about Operation Northwoods, they react with disbelief—which goes to show that even US government-acknowledged conspiracies remain protected by public disbelief a half century after they were hatched and 14 years after being revealed by the government.

An example of a conspiracy that is proven, but not officially acknowledged, is Israel's attack on the *USS Liberty* in 1967. Captain Ward

Boston, one of the two US Navy legal officers ordered to cover up the attack, not investigate it, revealed the Johnson Administration's conspiracy, and that of every subsequent administration, to blame mistaken identity for what was an intentional attack. The unofficial Moorer Commission, led by Admiral Tom Moorer, former Chief of Naval Operations and Chairman of the Joint Chiefs of Staff, proved conclusively that the Israeli attack, which inflicted massive casualties on US servicemen, was an intentional attack. Yet, the US government will not acknowledge it, and few Americans even know about it.

Even the event Americans celebrate on July 4 was a conspiracy and was regarded as such by the British government and American colonials who remained loyal to King George. If we don't believe in conspiracies, why do we celebrate one on July 4?

WHO DOES THE
LAW SERVE?

June 27, 2011

When my book (with Lawrence Stratton), *The Tyranny of Good Intentions*, was published, progressives and the left-wing refused to believe that the rich suffer frame-ups from prosecutorial abuse. Their response was that law is controlled by the rich and functions in their service. Only the poor and minorities suffer at the hands of the law.

The political left knew that Michael Milken was guilty, because the rich "junk bond king" financed takeovers of corporations that threw workers out of jobs. Leftists accepted the Justice (*sic*) Department's fanciful claim that the Exxon Valdez oil spill was a criminal act, not an accident for which civil damages were the remedy. Leona Helmsley was guilty, because she was a rich bitch. So was Martha Stewart. The left-wing was firm: all rich white people in prison are guilty, and the only reason they are in prison is that they are so obviously guilty that the system couldn't let them off. In other words, they were so audacious in their crimes that the crimes couldn't be covered up.

The same mentality now dominates discussions of the Dominique Strauss-Kahn case. Strauss-Kahn, who was at the time of his highly publicized arrest the head of the International Monetary Fund and the expected winner of the next French presidential election, was arrested on sexual abuse and attempted rape charges on the word of an immigrant hotel maid in New York.

Whereas the police are required to respond to charges by questioning the accused, they are not supposed to make a public spectacle of him in order to create the impression that he is guilty before he is even charged. Yet DSK was arrested aboard an airliner as it was about to depart for France and portrayed by the police as a fleeing criminal. Photos were released of him in handcuffs and stripped of his business attire.

The judge refused bail to one of the West's most high profile persons on the basis of the prosecutor's statement that DSK would flee the country and hide out abroad. All of this quickly was passed to reporters, who obliged the prosecutors and police by portraying DSK as obviously guilty as he was apprehended fleeing from the country.

The police even planted the story that DSK was in such a hurry to flee that he left behind his cell phone and that that is how they found him. This was a bald-faced lie. The fact of the matter is that when DSK arrived at the airport, he discovered that he had left his cell phone and called the hotel, the scene of the alleged crime, to ask that it be retrieved and brought to him at the airport. When the police boarded his flight, he asked them, "Did you bring my cell phone." He had no idea the police were there to detain him for questioning.

DSK's treatment raises serious problems for the leftist myth that law serves the interests of the rich and powerful. If law was the preserve of the rich and powerful, DSK would never have been taken off a departing airliner and made a public spectacle on the basis of an immigrant hotel maid's accusation. The airliner would have been allowed to depart and the case would not have been pursued. If the maid's story was ever reported, the police would have dismissed it as the story of a hysterical person or a person out for money. In the unlikely case that the police were pressed by reporters, the police would say that DSK had left the country before they could find him and that they were arranging to question him in France. In the very least, DSK's detention would have been very discreet, and he would have been given the benefit of "innocent until proven guilty" and granted bail.

Clearly, in DSK's case, the law is not serving the rich and powerful. Moreover, there are powerful biases against him. Feminists "know" that DSK is guilty, because "all men are sexual predators." Progressives and leftists "know" that DSK is guilty, because "as a person of wealth and power, he is used to getting away with everything."

When it became known that the police had "found" DSK only because the alleged fleeing suspect telephoned the hotel and asked for his cell phone, leftists did not wonder why the police had painted DSK guilty with a false story. Instead, they explained the alleged criminal's revelation of his whereabouts on the basis of their myth that as one of the rich and powerful, he expected to be able to rape women at will with nothing ever done about it. Soon the story was that attempted rape was ordinary behavior on DSK's part. But leftists did not explain why this time the law failed to protect him from a hotel maid when it had protected him from higher placed women.

As readers know by now, I have little patience with those who let their emotions determine their analysis. Let's look further at this case. It is a known fact that Sarkozy's political operatives in France knew of Strauss-Kahn's arrest *before* it was announced by the New York police. French, but not American, newspapers have wondered how this could be.

Perhaps the hotel maid thought to call up Sarkozy's people and tell them.

Note also that the alleged victim has a very high-priced major league lawyer representing her that she not only does not need but also obviously cannot afford to pay. It is not up to the maid to prosecute the defendant. That job is done at public expense by a public prosecutor. The alleged victim has another high-priced lawyer in France whose job is to round up Strauss-Kahn victims among French women with the prospect of sharing in a settlement.

These facts mean one of two things: The "victim" is after money, not justice, and the lawyers are operating on contingency with shares in a settlement between DSK and whatever the collection of women turns out to be. Alternatively, Strauss-Kahn was set up, as he predicted that he would be, but there is no evidence other than a disheveled woman performing for the hotel security camera. Therefore, whoever is behind the set-up sent the fancy lawyer to the maid—certainly the emigrant maid would not have known how to find such a lawyer—with the instructions to drive the case toward settlement.

The public regards large financial settlements as evidence of guilt, and thus a settlement is all that is needed to terminate Strauss-Kahn's career. The left-wing would scream that money again had defeated justice. As DSK has already been convicted in the media, he no doubt would welcome a settlement rather than risk a trial by jurors prejudiced by the media.

A settlement, of course, has to be blamed on DSK, not on the maid or her attorneys. This is impossible to do, because if the maid was not after a settlement, she would not have two attorneys driving the case in that direction. How to pull this rabbit out of the hat?

If CounterPunch's accounts are correct, Harvard law professor Alan Dershowitz has stepped up to frame the story. If a crime actually occurred, a settlement between the two sides' lawyers would be obstruction of justice, itself a crime, and the lawyers know it. But the maid's attorneys know that the big money belongs to DSK's wife, not to DSK.

This rules out the maid getting much out of a civil suit for damages following a felony conviction of DSK. To get a settlement, the maid needs to get money from DSK's wife by agreeing not to testify, thus collapsing a trial. The path to a settlement, Dershowitz says, is for DSK's lawyers not to negotiate with the maid or the maid's lawyers, but with the maid's family as long as it is done outside of New York and her home country of Guinea.

Notice that in Dershowitz's explanation, it is DSK who initiates the settlement talks. Dershowitz says that the maid's lawyer "may want to see justice done, but ultimately, money is more important." If justice were the goal, the maid would not need a lawyer.

So who is using the law against whom? In the event of a settlement, the left-wing will say that DSK or his rich wife bought his way out of a crime. They will not consider the possibility that the law served an immigrant maid who bilked a wife out of millions of dollars and destroyed the reputation of a member of the establishment who was in the way of those more powerful than he.

The only way the left-wing's myth about law being the servant of the rich can be saved is by seeing the case as a set-up of DSK by someone who is richer and more powerful than he is. This someone could be the current president of France and the financial and political forces behind him, which includes the US government for which Sarkozy has been a reliable puppet.

A WORLD OVERWHELMED BY WESTERN HYPOCRISY

June 29, 2011

Western institutions have become caricatures of hypocrisy.

The International Monetary Fund and the European Central Bank (ECB) are violating their charters in order to bail out French, German, and Dutch private banks. The IMF is only empowered to make balance of payments loans, but is lending to the Greek government for prohibited budgetary reasons in order that the Greek government can pay the banks. The ECB is prohibited from bailing out member country governments, but is doing so anyway in order that the banks can be paid. The German parliament approved the bailout, which violates provisions of the European Treaty and Germany's own Basic Law. The case is in the German Constitutional Court, a fact unreported in the US media.

US President George W. Bush's designated lawyer ruled that the president has "unitary powers" that elevate him above statutory US law, treaties, and international law. According to this lawyer's legal decisions, the "unitary executive" can violate with impunity the Foreign Intelligence Surveillance Act, which prevents spying on Americans without warrants obtained from the FISA Court. Bush's man also ruled that Bush could violate with impunity the statutory US laws against torture as well as the Geneva Conventions. In other words, the fictional "unitary powers" make the president effectively a Caesar.

Constitutional protections such as habeas corpus, which prohibit government from holding people indefinitely without presenting charges and evidence to a court, and which prohibit government from denying detained people due process of law and access to an attorney, were thrown out the window by the US Department of Justice, and the federal courts went along with most of it.

As did Congress, "the people's representatives." Congress even enacted the Military Commissions Act of 2006, signed by the White House Brownshirt on October 17.

This act allows anyone alleged to be an "unlawful enemy combatant" to be sentenced to death on the basis of secret and hearsay evidence in a military court out of reach of US federal courts. The crazed Nazis in Congress who supported this total destruction of Anglo-American law masqueraded as "patriots in the war against terrorism."

The act designates anyone accused by the US, without evidence being presented, as being part of the Taliban, Al Qaeda, or "associated forces," to be an "unlawful enemy combatant," which strips the person of the protection of law.

The Taliban consists of indigenous Afghan peoples, who, prior to the US military intervention, were fighting to unify the country. The Taliban are Islamist, and the US government fears another Islamist government, like the one in Iran that was blowback following US intervention in Iran's internal affairs. The "freedom and democracy" Americans overthrew an elected Iranian leader and imposed a tyrant. American-Iranian relations have never recovered from the tyranny that Washington imposed on Iranians.

Washington is opposed to any government whose leaders cannot be purchased to perform as Washington's puppets. This is why George W. Bush's regime invaded Afghanistan, why Washington overthrew Saddam Hussein, and why Washington wants to overthrow governments in Libya, Syria, and Iran.

Barack Obama inherited the Afghan war, which has lasted longer than World War II with no victory in sight. Instead of keeping to his election promises and ending the fruitless war, Obama intensified it with a "surge."

The war is now ten years old, and the Taliban control more of the country than does the US and its NATO puppets. Frustrated by their failure, the Americans and their NATO puppets increasingly murder women, children, village elders, Afghan police, and aid workers.

A video taken by a US helicopter gunship, leaked to Wikileaks and released, shows American forces, as if they were playing video games, slaughtering civilians in Iraq, including camera men for a prominent news service, as they are walking down a peaceful street. A father with small children, who stopped to help the dying victims of American soldiers' fun and games, was also blown away, as were his children. The American voices on the video blame the children's demise on the father for bringing kids into a "war zone." It was no war zone, just a quiet city street with civilians walking along.

The video documents American crimes against humanity as powerfully as any evidence used against the Nazis in the aftermath of World War II at the Nuremberg Trials.

Perhaps the height of lawlessness was attained when the Obama regime announced that it had a list of American citizens who would be assassinated without due process of law.

One would think that if law any longer had any meaning in Western civilization, George W. Bush, Dick Cheney, indeed, the entire Bush/Cheney regime, as well as Tony Blair and Bush's other co-conspirators, would be standing before the International Criminal Court.

Yet it is Gaddafi for whom the International Criminal Court has issued arrest warrants. Western powers are using the International Criminal Court, which is supposed to serve justice, for self-interested reasons that are unjust.

What is Gaddafi's crime? His crime is that he is attempting to prevent regime change in Libya by a US-supported, and perhaps organized, armed uprising in Eastern Libya that is being used to evict China from its oil investments in Eastern Libya.

Libya is the first armed revolt in the so-called "Arab Spring." Reports have made it clear that there is nothing "democratic" about the revolt.

The West managed to push a "no-fly" resolution through its puppet organization, the United Nations. The resolution was limited to neutralizing Gaddafi's air force. However, Washington, and its French puppet, Sarkozy, quickly made an "expansive interpretation" of the UN resolution and turned it into authorization to become directly involved in the war.

Gaddafi has resisted the armed rebellion against the state of Libya, which is the normal response of a government to rebellion. The US would respond the same, as would the UK and France. But by trying to prevent his country from becoming another American puppet state, Gaddafi has been indicted. The International Criminal Court knows that it cannot indict the real perpetrators of crimes against humanity—Bush, Blair, Obama, and Sarkozy—but the court needs cases and so it accepts those victims that the West succeeds in demonizing.

In our times, everyone who resists or even criticizes the US is a criminal. For example, Washington considers Julian Assange and Bradley Manning to be criminals, because they made information available that exposed crimes committed by the US government. Anyone who even disagrees with Washington is considered to be a "threat," and Obama can have such "threats" assassinated or arrested as "terrorist suspects" or for "providing aid and comfort to terrorists." American conservatives and liberals, who once supported the US Constitution, are all in favor of shredding the Constitution in the interest of being "safe from terrorists." They even accept such intrusions as porno-scans and sexual groping in order to be "safe" on air flights.

The collapse of law is across the board. The Supreme Court decided that it is "free speech" for America to be ruled by corporations, not by law and certainly not by the people. On June 27, the US Supreme Court advanced the fascist state that the "conservative" court is creating with the ruling that Arizona cannot publicly fund election candidates in order to level the playing field currently unbalanced by corporate money. The "conservative" US Supreme Court considers public funding of candidates to be unconstitutional, but not the "free speech" funding by business interests who purchase the government in order to rule the country. The US Supreme Court has become a corporate functionary and legitimizes rule by corporations. Mussolini called the type of government that the US Supreme Court is imposing on the American people, fascism.

The Supreme Court also ruled on June 27 that California violated the US Constitution by banning the sale of violent video games to kids, despite evidence that the violent games trained the young to violent behavior. It is fine with the Supreme Court for soldiers, whose lives are on the line, to be prohibited under penalty of law from drinking beer before they are 21, but the idiot Court supports inculcating kids to be murderers, as long as it is in the interest of corporate profits, in the name of "free speech."

Amazing, isn't it, that a court so concerned with 'free speech" has not protected American war protesters from unconstitutional searches and arrests, or protected protesters from being attacked by police or herded into fenced-in areas distant from the object of protest.

As the second decade of the 21st century opens, those who oppose US hegemony and the evil that emanates from Washington risk being declared "terrorists." If they are American citizens, they can be assassinated. If they are foreign leaders, their country can be invaded. When captured, they can be executed, like Saddam Hussein, or sent off to the ICC, like the hapless Serbs, who tried to defend their country from being dismantled by the Americans.

Washington relies on fear to cover up its crimes. A majority of Americans now fear and hate Muslims, peoples about whom Americans know nothing but the racist propaganda which encourages Americans to believe that Muslims are hiding under their beds in order to murder them in their sleep.

The neoconservatives, of course, are the purveyors of this fear. The more fearful the sheeple, the more they seek safety in the neocon police state and the more they overlook Washington's crimes of aggression against Muslims.

Safety *uber alles*. That has become the motto of a once free and independent American people, who once were admired but today are despised.

In America lawlessness is now complete. Women can have abortions, but if they have stillbirths, they risk being arrested for murder.

Americans are such a terrified and abused people that a 95-year old woman dying from leukemia traveling to a last reunion with family members was forced to remove her adult diaper in order to clear airport security. Only a population totally cowed would permit such abuses of human dignity.

In a June 27 interview on National Public Radio, Ban Ki-moon,

Washington's South Korean puppet installed as the Secretary General of the United Nations, was unable to answer why the UN and the US tolerate the slaughter of unarmed civilians in Bahrain, but support the International Criminal Court's indictment of Gaddafi for defending Libya against armed rebellion. Gaddafi has killed far fewer people than the US, UK, or the Saudis in Bahrain. Indeed, NATO and the Americans have killed more Libyans than has Gaddafi. The difference is that the US has a naval base in Bahrain, but not in Libya.

There is nothing left of the American character. Only a people who have lost their soul could tolerate the evil that emanates from Washington.

PROSECUTORS BACK OFF FROM THEIR 'IRON-CLAD' CASE AGAINST STRAUSS-KAHN

July 1, 2011

The New York prosecutor has had to tell the judge that the police and prosecutors have lost confidence in their sexual assault case against former IMF chief Dominique Strauss-Kahn. The judge has released DSK from house arrest and returned his bail and bond money.

The prosecutors say that the immigrant hotel maid lied to the police about the incident and about other things, and the police have revealed that the "victim" discussed with an imprisoned man the possibility of turning the case into extortion. According to *The New York Times*, the maid's jailed confidant was among a number of people who had made multiple cash deposits totaling $100,000 to the maid's bank account. The police now suspect that the maid has connections to illegal drugs and money laundering.

The prosecutor says that he will continue to investigate the case. What that means is that the prosecutor, a politically ambitious Cy Vance, is hoping to extract a misdemeanor plea from DSK in order to rescue the prosecutor's own reputation from the fiasco of having been drawn into a plot against the person that French polls indicated was the public's choice to be the next president of France.. The prosecutor is sending DSK's legal team the message that the case is being kept open and could be reinstated unless DSK's attorneys secure DSK's permission to negotiate a deal on a minor charge, which essentially has no punishment, but saves the faces of the NY prosecutor and police.

We will probably never know whether the maid thought the scheme up on her own or whether it came from Sarkozy's operatives and their US allies. One indication that DSK's political enemies are implicated is the fact, made public by the French press, that Sarkozy's political team in France knew about DSK's arrest *before* the NY police announced it. This fact did not stop the NY prosecutor and police from painting DSK as guilty in numerous public statements and in unethical if not illegal leaks to reporters.

When police and prosecutors convict a suspect in the media before he is even charged, it typically means that there is no evidence against him and that demonization is serving as the substitute. Conviction is what is important to the system, not a determination of innocence or guilt.

On numerous Internet sites, I pointed out the problems with the case against DSK. For informing people of the obvious, I was denounced by the right-wing and the left-wing.

The right-wing gave me the finger for doubting the word and integrity of police and prosecutor. Didn't I know that these are the honorable guardians who protect the public from crime? How dare I question anything the police and prosecutor did or do. What was I, some kind of pinko-liberal-commie?

The left-wing also gave me the finger and said that I had revealed my real self as nothing but an apologist for the rich and powerful and for men who seduce women. How much was I paid for my service to the rich and powerful and seducers of innocent women?

The feminist left denounced me as a misogynist. Only a woman-hater could take the side of a rapist against his victim.

It is all so tiresome to endure the stupidity of people. Little wonder they are losing their liberty, their jobs and incomes, and their country and self-respect.

With DSK's reputation in tatters and DSK knocked out of the French presidential election and removed from the IMF, where he was beginning to raise questions about the establishment's use of the IMF to bail out rich bankers on the backs of poor peasants, the "justice system" has done its work. It is now safer for the authorities to release him than to risk a trial. The shrill bleating of the maid's legal team signifies their agony at having lost their share of the hoped-to-be extorted millions now that a monetary settlement would clearly indicate obstruction of justice and prison for them all.

Those few who actually care about justice, not only for DSK and everyman, but also for the Greek, Spanish, Irish, and Portuguese people, can find comfort in the fact that apparently DSK had come to New York in order to speak with Nobel economist Joe Stiglitz about a more humane and democratic way to resolve the sovereign debt crisis in Europe than the one imposed by the private creditor banks.

Obviously, anyone who would consult with Stiglitz is perceived by the rich and powerful as a threat to their interest.

However, this obvious fact has made no impression on the left-wing, which has issued its shrill cries that, once again, the money of the rich and powerful has prevailed over law and justice.

Update: The prosecutor announced that no evidence could be found to support a case against DSK and much evidence had been found to discredit his accuser and dropped all charges against DSK.

WILL STRAUSS-KAHN BE THE NEXT PRESIDENT OF FRANCE?

July 5, 2011

There's an old English ditty, "a young lady of Kent," that ends with these lines:

> "she knew what it meant,
> but she went."

Eight years after she went, Strauss-Kahn's French accuser says she didn't know what it meant. If what I have read about the charge of attempted rape now being brought against Strauss-Kahn in France is correct, eight years ago a young French woman agreed to meet Strauss-Kahn alone in an apartment that was not his address. She claims that, despite her protests, Strauss-Kahn persisted in sexually aggressive behavior. She construes, or perhaps misconstrues, his behavior as attempted rape.

If the woman's account is true, there is an innocent interpretation. By agreeing to the meeting, she sent a signal that she did not intend to send and which Strauss-Kahn interpreted, or misinterpreted, to mean that she was sexually available.

If this is the story, a French court would realize that, however frightening it was for the young woman, it was a misunderstanding and not an attempted rape. Strauss-Kahn would be guilty of boorish behavior, but this is not yet a crime.

French skepticism would explain why the charge lay dormant for eight years and came to life on the heels of the New York case, which has now fallen apart. The certainty with which the New York police, prosecutor, and American media initially treated Strauss-Kahn's guilt created credibility for the French woman's accusation. Certainly, the prospect of Strauss-Kahn's conviction on the New York charges would give a French lawyer more confidence in the French woman's story.

I offer this not as an excuse for Strauss-Kahn, who is much too horny for his own good, but as an innocent explanation of an event that also has non-innocent explanations.

For example, according to the French press, Strauss-Kahn predicted that his favorable standing in the election polls would result in Sarkozy, or the interests behind him, paying a woman one million euros in order to bring sex charges against him in order to knock him out of the presidential race.

We also know from press reports that the New York hotel maid had a French attorney who was assigned the task of bolstering her case for damages by finding some French victims of Strauss-Kahn. If the French case continues after the collapse of the New York one, Strauss-Kahn's attorneys will certainly investigate any contact between the hotel maid's attorneys and the French woman's attorneys.

We also know from the French press that Sarkozy's political operatives knew of Strauss-Kahn's arrest before the New York Police announced it. This introduces the element of conspiracy.

How will it end?

If the strength of the French case depends on the New York case, the French attorney will advise his client to drop the proceedings.

If the French case is perceived as one of extortion and not justice, the case will fall apart.

If the French public becomes convinced that conspiracy is involved, it will be electoral curtains for Sarkozy, and Strauss-Kahn will be the next president of France.

Update: The French case fell apart, also. Strauss-Kahn did not run for president of France, but the socialist party candidate defeated Washington's puppet, Sarkozy. Nevertheless the Western establishment with the complicity of the American left-wing and American feminists succeeded in terminating the political career of a man who stood for the people and not for the one percent.

THE ENEMY IS WASHINGTON

July 22, 2011

Recently, the bond rating agencies that gave junk derivatives triple-A ratings threatened to downgrade US Treasury bonds if the White House and Congress did not reach a deficit reduction deal and debt ceiling increase. The downgrade threat is not credible, and neither is the default threat. Both are make-believe crises that are being hyped in order to force cutbacks in Medicare, Medicaid, and Social Security.

If the rating agencies downgraded Treasuries, the company executives would be arrested for the fraudulent ratings that they gave to the junk that Wall Street peddled to the rest of the world. The companies would be destroyed and their ratings discredited. The US government will never default on its bonds, because unlike Greece, Spain, and Portugal, the US can print the money with which to redeem its bonds. Regardless of whether or not the debt ceiling is raised, the Federal Reserve will continue to purchase the Treasury's debt. If Goldman Sachs is too big to fail, then so is the US government.

There is no budget focus on the illegal wars and military occupations that the US government has underway in at least six countries or the 66-year-old US occupations of Japan and Germany, or the ring of military bases being constructed around Russia.

The total military/security budget is in the vicinity of $1.1-$1.2 trillion, or 70-75 per cent of the federal budget deficit.

In contrast, Social Security is solvent. Medicare expenditures are coming close to exceeding the 2.3 percent payroll tax that funds Medicare, but it is dishonest for politicians and pundits to blame the US budget deficit on "entitlement programs."

Entitlements are funded with a payroll tax. Wars are not funded. The criminal Bush regime lied to Americans and claimed that the Iraq war would only cost $70 billion at the most and would be paid for with Iraq oil revenues. When Bush's chief economic advisor, Larry Lindsay, said the Iraq invasion would cost $200 billion, Bush fired him. In fact, Lindsay was off by a factor of 20. Economic and budget experts have calculated that the Iraq and

Afghanistan wars have consumed $4,000 billion in out-of-pocket and already incurred future costs. In other words, the ongoing wars and occupations have already eaten up the $4 trillion by which Obama hopes to cut federal spending over the next ten years. Bomb now, pay later.

As taxing the mega-rich is not part of the solution, the focus is on continuing to collect the payroll tax while cutting the programs that it is earmarked to support. This would restore the surpluses in the Social Security and Medicare accounts that can be used to reduce the budget deficit.

Washington's priorities and those of its presstitutes could not be clearer. President Obama, like George W. Bush before him, both parties in Congress, the print and TV media, and National Public Radio have made it clear that war is a far more important priority than health care and old age pensions for Americans.

The American people and their wants and needs are not represented in Washington. Washington serves powerful interest groups, such as the military/security complex, Wall Street and the banksters, agribusiness, the oil companies, the insurance companies, pharmaceuticals, and the mining and timber industries. Washington endows these interests with excess profits by committing war crimes and terrorizing foreign populations with bombs, drones, and invasions, by deregulating the financial sector and bailing it out of its greed-driven mistakes after it has stolen Americans' pensions, homes, and jobs, by refusing to protect the land, air, water, oceans and wildlife from polluters and despoilers, and by constructing a health care system with the highest costs and highest profits in the world.

The way to reduce health care costs is to take out gobs of costs and profits with a single payer system. A private health care system can continue to operate alongside for those who can afford it.

The way to get the budget under control is to stop the gratuitous hegemonic wars, wars that will end in a nuclear confrontation.

The US economy is in a deepening recession from which recovery is not possible, because American middle class jobs in manufacturing and professional services have been off-shored and given to foreigners. US GDP, consumer purchasing power, and tax base have been handed over to China, India, and Indonesia in order that Wall Street, shareholders, and corporate CEOs can earn more.

When the goods and services produced offshore come back into America, they arrive as imports. The trade balance worsens, the US dollar declines further in exchange value, and prices rise for Americans, whose incomes are stagnant or falling.

This is economic destruction. It always occurs when an oligarchy seizes control of a government. The short-run profits of the powerful are maximized at the expense of the viability of the economy.

The US economy is driven by consumer demand, but with 22.3 percent unemployment—the real rate when discouraged workers who have given up on finding a job are included—stagnant and declining wages and salaries, and consumer debt burdens so high that consumers cannot borrow to spend, there is no consumer demand to drive the economy.

Washington's response to this dilemma is to increase the austerity! Cutting back Medicare, Medicaid, and Social Security, forcing down wages by destroying unions and off-shoring jobs (which results in a labor surplus and lower wages), and driving up the prices of food and energy by depreciating the dollar further erodes consumer purchasing power. The Federal Reserve can print money to rescue the crooked financial institutions, but it cannot rescue the American consumer.

As a final point, confront the fact that you are even lied to about "deficit reduction." Even if Obama gets his $4 trillion "deficit reduction" over the next decade, it does not mean that the current national debt will be $4 trillion less than it currently is. The "reduction" merely means that the growth in the national debt will be $4 trillion less than otherwise. Regardless of any "deficit reduction," the national debt ten years from now will be much higher than it presently is.

9/11 AFTER A DECADE: HAVE WE LEARNED ANYTHING?

August 24, 2011

In a few days it will be the tenth anniversary of September 11, 2001. How well has the US government's official account of the event held up over the decade?

Not very well. The chairman, vice chairman, and senior legal counsel of the 9/11 Commission wrote books partially disassociating themselves from the commission's report. They said that the Bush administration put obstacles in their path, that information was withheld from them, that President Bush agreed to testify only if he was chaperoned by Vice President Cheney and neither were put under oath, that Pentagon and FAA officials lied to the commission, and that the commission considered referring the false testimony for investigation for obstruction of justice.

In their book, *Without Precedent: The Inside Story of the 9/11 Commission*, the chairman and vice chairman, Thomas Kean and Lee Hamilton, wrote that the 9/11 Commission was "set up to fail." Senior counsel John Farmer, Jr. wrote that the US government made "a decision not to tell the truth about what happened," and that the NORAD "tapes told a radically different story from what had been told to us and the public." Kean said. "We to this day don't know why NORAD told us what they told us, it was just so far from the truth."

Most of the questions from the 9/11 families were not answered. Important witnesses were not called. The commission only heard from those who supported the government's account. The commission was a controlled political cover-up, not an investigation of events and evidence. Its membership consisted of former politicians. No knowledgeable experts were appointed to the commission.

One member of the 9/11 Commission, former Senator Max Cleland, responded to the constraints placed on the commission by the White House: "If this decision stands, I, as a member of the commission, cannot look any American in the eye, especially family members of victims, and say the commission had full access. This investigation is now compromised." Cleland resigned rather than have his integrity compromised.

To be clear, neither Cleland nor members of the commission suggested that 9/11 was an inside job to advance a war agenda. Nevertheless, neither Congress nor the media wondered, at least not out loud, why President Bush was unwilling to appear before the commission under oath or without Cheney, why Pentagon and FAA officials lied to the commission or, if the officials did not lie, why the commission believed they lied, or why the White House resisted for so long any kind of commission being formed, even one under its control.

One would think that if a handful of Arabs managed to outwit not merely the CIA and FBI but all 16 US intelligence agencies, all intelligence agencies of our allies including Mossad, the National Security Council, the State Department, NORAD, airport security four times on one morning, air traffic control, etc., the President, Congress, and the media would be demanding to know how such an improbable event could occur. Instead, the White House put up a wall of resistance to finding out, and Congress and the media showed little interest.

During the decade that has passed, numerous 9/11 Truth organizations have formed. There are Architects and Engineers for 9/11 Truth, Firefighters for 9/11 Truth, Pilots for 9/11 Truth, Scholars for 9/11 Truth, Remember Building 7.org, and a New York group which includes 9/11 families. These groups call for a real investigation.

David Ray Griffin has written 10 carefully researched books documenting problems in the government's account. Scientists have pointed out that the government has no explanation for the molten steel. NIST has been forced to admit that WTC 7 was in free fall for part of its descent, and a scientific team led by a professor of nano-chemistry at the University of Copenhagen has reported finding nano-thermite in the dust from the buildings.

Larry Silverstein, who had the lease on the World Trade Center buildings, said in a PBS broadcast that the decision was made "to pull" Building 7 late in the afternoon of 9/11. Chief fire marshals have said that no forensic investigation was made of the buildings' destruction and that the absence of investigation was a violation of law.

Some efforts have been made to explain away some of the evidence that is contrary to the official account, but most of the contrary evidence is simply ignored. The fact remains that the skepticism of a large number of knowledgeable experts has had no effect on the government's position other than a member of the Obama administration suggesting that the government infiltrate the 9/11 truth organizations in order to discredit them.

The practice has been to brand experts not convinced by the government's case as "conspiracy theorists." But of course the government's own theory is a conspiracy theory, an even less likely one once a person realizes the full implication of its intelligence and operational failures. The implied failures are extraordinarily large; yet, no one was ever held accountable.

Moreover, what do 1,500 architects and engineers have to gain from the prospect of being ridiculed as conspiracy theorists once they contest the official version? They certainly will never receive another government contract, and many surely lost business as a result of their "anti-American" stance. Their competitors must have made hay out of their "unpatriotic doubts." Indeed, my likely reward for reporting on how matters stand a decade after the event will be mail telling me that as I hate America so much, I should move to Cuba.

Scientists have even less incentive to express any doubts, which probably explains why there are not 1,500 Physicists for 9/11 Truth. Few physicists have careers independent of government grants or contracts. It was a high school physics teacher who forced NIST to abandon its account of Building 7's demise. Physicist Stephen Jones, who first reported finding evidence of explosives, had his tenure bought out by BYU, which no doubt found itself under government pressure.

Can we explain away contrary evidence as coincidences and mistakes and conclude that only the government got it all correct, the same government that got everything else wrong?

In fact, the government has not explained anything. The NIST report is merely a simulation of what might have caused the towers to fail if NIST's assumptions programmed into the computer model are correct. But NIST supplies no evidence that its assumptions are correct.

Building 7 was not mentioned in the 9/11 Commission Report, and many Americans are still unaware that three buildings came down on 9/11.

Let me be clear about my point. I am not saying that some black op group in the neoconservative Bush administration blew up the buildings in order to advance the neoconservative agenda of war in the Middle East. If there is evidence of a cover-up, it could be the government covering up its incompetence and not its complicity in the event. Even if there were definite proof of government complicity, it is uncertain that Americans could accept it. Architects, engineers, and scientists live in a fact-based community, but for most people facts are no match for emotions.

My point is how *uninquisitive* the executive branch, including the security agencies, Congress, the media, and much of the population are about the defining event of our time.

There is no doubt that 9/11 is the determinant event. It has led to a decade of ever expanding wars, to the shredding of the Constitution, and to a police state. On August 22 Justin Raimondo reported that he and his website,

Antiwar.com, are being monitored by the FBI's Electronic Communication Analysis Unit to determine if Antiwar.com is "a threat to National Security" working "on behalf of a foreign power."

Francis A. Boyle, an internationally known professor and attorney of international law, has reported that when he refused a joint FBI-CIA request to violate the attorney/client privilege and become an informant on his Arab-American clients, he was placed on the US government's terrorist watch list.

Boyle has been critical of the US government's approach to the Muslim world, but Raimondo has never raised, nor permitted any contributor to raise, any suspicion about US government complicity in 9/11. Raimondo merely opposes war, and that is enough for the FBI to conclude that he needs watching as a possible threat to national security.

The US government's account of 9/11 is the foundation of the open-ended wars that are exhausting America's resources and destroying its reputation, and it is the foundation of the domestic police state that ultimately will shut down all opposition to the wars. Americans are bound to the story of the 9/11 Muslim terrorist attack, because it is what justifies the slaughter of civilian populations in several Muslim countries, and a domestic police state as the only means of securing safety from terrorists, who already have morphed into "domestic extremists" such as environmentalists, animal rights groups, and antiwar activists.

Today Americans are unsafe, not because of terrorists and domestic extremists, but because they have lost their civil liberties and have no protection from unaccountable government power. One would think that how this came about would be worthy of public debate and congressional hearings.

IN AMERICA, THE RULE OF LAW IS VACATED

September 1, 2011

With bank fraudsters, torturers, and war criminals running free, the US Department of Justice (*sic*) has nothing better to do than to harass the famous Tennessee guitar manufacturer, Gibson,[36] arrest organic food producers in California[37] and send 12 abusive FBI agents armed with assault rifles to bust down yet another wrong door of yet another innocent family, leaving parents, children, and grandmother traumatized.[38]

What law did Gibson Guitar Corp break that caused federal agents to disrupt Gibson's plants in Nashville and Memphis, seize guitars, cause layoffs, and cost the company $3 million from disrupted operations?

No US law was broken. The feds claim that Gibson broke a law that is on the books in India.

India has not complained about Gibson or asked for the aid of the US government in enforcing its laws against Gibson. Instead, the feds have taken it upon themselves to both interpret and to enforce on US citizens the laws of India. The feds claim that Gibson's use of wood from India in its guitars is illegal, because the wood was not finished by Indian workers.

This must not be India's interpretation of the law as India allowed the unfinished wood to be exported. Perhaps the feds are trying to force more layoffs of US workers and their replacement by H-1B foreign workers. Perhaps Gibson can solve its problem by firing its Tennessee work force and hiring Indian citizens on H-1B work visas?

In Venice, California, feds spent a year dressed up as hippies purchasing raw goat milk and yogurt from Rawesome Foods and then, decked out in hemp anklets and reeking of patchouli, raided with guns drawn–always with guns drawn–the organic food shop. The owner's crime is that he supplied the normal everyday foods that I grew up with to customers who requested them. For this heinous act, James C. Stewart faces a 13 count indictment and is held on $123,000 bail.

How did raw milk become a "health threat?" Far more Americans have died from e-coli in fast food hamburgers and from salmonella in mass produced eggs and chicken. Like many of my generation, I was raised on raw milk. Mathis Dairy delivered it to the homes in Atlanta. Even decades later a person could purchase Mathis Dairy's raw milk in Atlanta's grocery stores. How did supplying an ordinary staple become a crime?

The FBI agents who broke down Gary Adams door in Bellevue, Pennsylvania, claim they were looking for a woman. Why does it take 12 heavily armed FBI agents to apprehend a woman? Are FBI agents that effete? If the feds have trouble getting the address right, how do we know they have the name and gender right?

I can remember when it only took one policeman to deliver a warrant and to arrest a person, and without gun drawn and without breaking down the door, tasering or shooting the suspect. It turns out that the FBI agents who broke into the Adams home not only were at the wrong address but also didn't even have a search warrant had they been at the correct address.

The practice of sending heavily armed teams into American homes has resulted in many senseless murders of US citizens. The practice must be halted and SWAT teams disbanded. SWAT teams have murdered far more innocents than they have dangerous criminals. Hostage situations are rare, and they are best handled without violence.

Jose Guerena, a US Marine who served two tours in Bush's Iraq War was murdered in his own home in front of his wife and two small children by a crazed SWAT team,[39] again in the wrong place, who shot him 60 times. When his wife told him that there were men sneaking around the house, he picked up his rifle and walked to the kitchen to see what was going on and was gunned down. The hysterical SWAT team fired 71 shots at him without cause. Brave, tough, macho cops out defending the public and murdering war heroes.

I have seen studies that show that police actually commit more acts of violence against the public than do criminals, which raises an interesting question: Are police a greater threat to the public than are criminals? On Yahoo I just searched "police brutality" and up came 4,840,000 results.

Meanwhile, the real master criminals, such as Dick Cheney, who, if tried for his actions at Nuremberg, would most definitely have been executed as a war criminal, run free. Cheney is all over TV hawking his memoirs. On August 29, interviewed by Jamie Gangel on NBC's Dateline, Cheney again proudly admitted that he authorized torture, secret prisons, and illegal wiretapping. These are crimes under US and international laws.

Cheney claims breaking laws against torture is "the right thing to do" if "we had a high-value detainee and that was the only way we can get him to talk."

Three questions immediately come to mind that no member of the presstitute media ever asks. The first is, why does Cheney think the office of

Vice President, President, or Attorney General has the power to "authorize" breaking a law? Our vaunted "rule of law" disappears if federal officials can authorize breaking laws.

The second is, what high-value detainees is Cheney talking about? Donald Rumsfeld declared the Guantanamo detainees to be "the most dangerous, best-trained, vicious killers on the face of the earth."[40] But the vast majority had to be released when it turned out, after years of their lives were spent in a torture prison, that the vast majority of the detainees were hapless innocents who were sold to the stupid Americans by warlords as "terrorists" for bounties. To save face, the US government has held on to a few detainees, but hasn't enough confidence in their alleged guilt to put them on trial in a court of law.

The third is why does Cheney think that he knows better than the accumulated documented evidence that torture doesn't produce truthful or useful information. If the person under torture is actually a terrorist, he knows that his tormentors don't know the answers that they are looking for and so he or she can tell the torturers whatever serves the tortured victim's purposes. If the person under torture is innocent, he has no idea what the answers are and seeks to discover what his torturer wants to hear so that he can tell his torturers what they want to hear.

As Glenn Greenwald makes clear,[41] Dick Cheney, who presided "over policies that left hundreds of thousands of innocent people dead from wars of aggression, constructed a worldwide torture regime, and spied on Americans without the warrants required by law" is now being feted and enriched thanks to "the protective shield of immunity bestowed upon him by the current administration."

Meanwhile Gibson Guitar faces prosecution because of the feds' off-the-wall interpretation of a law in India, and the owner of Rawesome has a 13-count indictment for supplying customers with a food staple that was a part of the normal diet from colonial times until recently.

In America we have the rule of law–only the law is not applied to banksters and members of the executive branch but, as Greenwald says, is only applied to "ordinary citizens and other nations' (unfriendly) rulers."

A country this utterly corrupt is certainly no "light unto the world."

THE LATEST ORCHESTRATED THREAT TO AMERICA: PAKISTAN AND "THE HAQQANI NETWORK"

September 26, 2011

Have you ever before heard of the Haqqanis? I didn't think so. Like Al Qaeda, about which no one had ever heard prior to 9/11, the "Haqqani Network" has popped up in time of need to justify America's next war— against Pakistan.

President Obama's claim that he had Al Qaeda leader Osama bin Laden exterminated deflated the threat from that long-serving bogyman. A terror organization that left its leader, unarmed and undefended, a sitting duck for assassination no longer seemed formidable. Time for a new, more threatening bogyman, the pursuit of which will keep the "war on terror" going.

America's new "worst enemy" is the Haqqanis. Moreover, unlike Al Qaeda, which was never tied to a country, the Haqqani Network, according to Admiral Mike Mullen, chairman of the US Joint Chiefs of Staff, is a "veritable arm" of the Pakistani government's intelligence service, ISI. Washington claims that the ISI ordered its Haqqani Network to attack the US Embassy in Kabul, Afghanistan, on September 13 along with the US military base in Wadak province.

Senator Lindsey Graham, a member of the Armed Services committee and one of the main Republican warmongers, declared that "all options are on the table" and gave the Pentagon his assurance that in Congress there was broad bipartisan support for a US military attack on Pakistan.

As Washington has been killing large numbers of Pakistani civilians with drones and has forced the Pakistani army to hunt for Al Qaeda throughout most of Pakistan, producing large numbers of dislocated Pakistanis in the process, Sen. Graham must have something larger in mind.

The Pakistani government thinks so, too. The Pakistani prime minister, Yousuf Raza Gilani, called his foreign minister home from talks in Washington and ordered an emergency meeting of the government to assess the prospect of an American invasion.

Meanwhile, Washington is rounding up additional reasons to add to the new threat from the Haqqanis to justify making war on Pakistan: Pakistan has nuclear weapons and is unstable and the nukes could fall into the wrong hands; the US can't win in Afghanistan until it has eliminated sanctuaries in Pakistan; blah-blah.

Washington has been trying to bully Pakistan into launching a military operation against its own people in North Waziristan. Pakistan has good reasons for resisting this demand. Washington's use of the new "Haqqani threat" as an invasion excuse could be Washington's way of overcoming Pakistan's resistance to attacking its North Waziristan province, or it could be, as some Pakistani political leaders say, and the Pakistani government fears, a "drama" created by Washington to justify a military assault on yet another Muslim country.

Over the years of its servitude as an American puppet, the Pakistan government has brought this on itself. Pakistanis let the US purchase the Pakistan government, train and equip its military, and establish CIA interface with Pakistani intelligence. A government so dependent on Washington could say little when Washington began violating its sovereignty, sending in drones and special forces teams to kill alleged Al Qaeda, but usually women, children, and farmers. Unable to subdue after a decade a small number of Taliban fighters in Afghanistan, Washington has placed the blame for its military failure on Pakistan, just as Washington blamed the long drawn-out war on the Iraqi people on Iran's alleged support for the Iraqi resistance to American occupation.

Some knowledgeable analysts' about whom you will never hear in the "mainstream media," say that the US military/security complex and their neoconservative whores are orchestrating World War III before Russia and China can get prepared. As a result of the communist oppression, a significant percentage of the Russian population is in the American orbit. These Russians trust Washington more than they trust Putin. The Chinese are too occupied dealing with the perils of rapid economic growth to prepare for war and are far behind the threat.

War, however, is the lifeblood of the military/security complex, and war is the chosen method of the neoconservatives for achieving their goal of American hegemony.

Pakistan borders China and former constituent parts of the Soviet Union in which the US now has military bases on Russia's borders. US war upon and occupation of Pakistan is likely to awaken the somnolent Russians and Chinese. As both possess nuclear ICBMs, the outcome of the military/ security complex's greed for profits and the neoconservatives' greed for empire could be the extinction of life on earth.

The patriots and super-patriots who fall in with the agendas of the military-security complex and the flag-waving neoconservatives are furthering the "end-times" outcome so fervently desired by the rapture evangelicals, who will waft up to heaven while the rest of us die on earth.

This is not President Reagan's hoped for outcome from ending the Cold War.

IS THE WAR ON TERROR A HOAX?

September 30, 2011

In the past decade, Washington has killed, maimed, dislocated, and made widows and orphans of millions of Muslims in six countries, all in the name of the "war on terror." Washington's attacks on the countries constitute naked aggression and impact primarily civilian populations and infrastructure and, thereby, constitute war crimes under law. Nazis were executed precisely for what Washington is doing today.

Moreover the wars and military attacks have cost American taxpayers in out-of-pocket and already-incurred future costs at least $4,000 billion dollars—one third of the accumulated public debt—resulting in a US deficit crisis that threatens the social safety net, the value of the US dollar and its reserve currency role, while enriching beyond all previous history the military/security complex and its apologists.

Perhaps the highest cost of Washington's "war on terror" has been paid by the US Constitution and civil liberties. Any US citizen that Washington accuses is deprived of all legal and constitutional rights. The Bush-Cheney-Obama regimes have overturned humanity's greatest achievement—the accountability of government to law.

If we look around for the terror that the police state and a decade of war has allegedly protected us from, the terror is hard to find. Except for 9/11 itself, assuming we accept the government's improbable conspiracy theory explanation, there have been no terror attacks on the US. Indeed, as RT pointed out on August 23, 2011,[42] an investigative program at the University of California discovered that the domestic "terror plots" hyped in the media were plotted by FBI agents.

FBI undercover agents now number 15,000, ten times their number during the protests against the Vietnam War when protesters were suspected of communist sympathies. As there apparently are no real terror plots for this huge workforce to uncover, the FBI justifies its budget, terror alerts, and invasive searches of American citizens by thinking up "terror plots" and finding some deranged individuals to ensnare. For example, the Washington DC Metro bombing plot, the New York City subway plot, and the plot to blow up the Sears Tower in Chicago were all FBI brainchilds organized and managed by FBI agents.

RT reports that only three plots might have been independent of the FBI, but as none of the three worked, they obviously were not the work of such a professional terror organization as Al Qaeda is purported to be. The Times Square car bomb didn't blow up, and apparently could not have.

The latest FBI sting ensnared a Boston man, Rezwan Ferdaus, who is accused of planning to attack the Pentagon and US Capitol with model airplanes packed with C-4 explosives.[43] US Attorney Carmen Ortiz assured Americans that they were never in danger, because the FBI's undercover agents were in control of the plot.

Ferdaus' FBI-organized plot to blow up the Pentagon and US Capitol with model airplanes has produced charges that he provided "material support to a terrorist organization" and plotted to destroy federal buildings—the most serious charge which carries 20 imprisoned years for each targeted building.

What is the terrorist organization that Ferdaus is serving? Surely not Al Qaeda, which allegedly outwitted all 16 US intelligence services, all intelligence services of America's NATO and Israeli allies, NORAD, the National Security Council, Air Traffic Control, Dick Cheney, and US airport security four times in one hour on the same morning. Such a highly capable terror organization would not be involved in such nonsense as a plot to blow up the Pentagon with a model airplane.

As an American who was in public service for a number of years and who has always stood up for the Constitution, a patriot's duty, I must hope that the question has already popped into readers' minds: Why are we expected to believe that a tiny model airplane is capable of blowing up the Pentagon when the purported 757 airliner loaded with jet fuel was incapable of doing the job, merely making a hole not big enough for an airliner?

When I observe the gullibility of my fellow citizens at the absurd "terror plots" that the US government manufactures, it causes me to realize that fear is the most powerful weapon any government has for advancing an undeclared agenda. If Ferdaus is brought to trial, no doubt a jury will convict him of a plot to blow up the Pentagon and US Capitol with model airplanes. Most likely he will be tortured or coerced into a plea bargain.

Apparently, Americans, or most of them, are so ruled by fear that they suffer no remorse from "their" government's murder and dislocation of millions of innocent people. In the American mind, one billion "towel-heads" have been reduced to terrorists who deserve to be exterminated. The US is on its way to a holocaust that makes the terrors Jews faced from National Socialism into a mere precursor.

Think about this: Are not you amazed that after a decade (2.5 times the length of WW II) of killing Muslims and destroying families and their prospects in six countries there are no real terrorist events in the US?

Think for a minute how easy terrorism would be in the US if there were any terrorists. Would an Al Qaeda terrorist from the organization that allegedly pulled off 9/11—the most humiliating defeat ever suffered by a Western power, much less "the world's only superpower"—still in the face of all the screening be trying to hijack an airliner or to blow one up?

Surely not, when there are so many totally soft targets. If America were really infected with a "terrorist threat," a terrorist could merely get in the massive lines waiting to clear airport "security" and set off his bomb. It would kill far more people than could be achieved by blowing up an airliner, and make it completely clear that "airport security" is unachievable.

It would be child's play for terrorists to blow up electric sub-stations as no one is there, nothing but a chain link fence. It would be easy for terrorists to blow up shopping centers. It would be easy for terrorists to dump boxes of roofing nails on congested streets and freeways during rush hours, tying up main transportation arteries for days.

Before, dear reader, you accuse me of giving terrorists ideas, do you really think that these kinds of ideas would not already have occurred to terrorists capable of pulling off 9/11?

But nothing happens. So the FBI arrests a guy for planning to blow up America with a model airplane. It is really depressing how many Americans will believe this.

Consider also that American neoconservatives, who have orchestrated the "war on terror," have no protection whatsoever and that the Secret Service protection of Bush and Cheney is minimal. If America really faced a terrorist threat, especially one so professional as to have brought off 9/11, every neoconservative along with Bush and Cheney could be assassinated within one hour on one morning or one evening.

The fact that neoconservatives such as Paul Wolfowitz, Donald Rumsfeld, Condi Rice, Richard Perle, Douglas Feith, John Bolton, William Kristol, Libby, Addington, et. al., live unprotected and free of fear is proof that America faces no terrorist threat.

Think now about the airliner shoe-bomb plot, the shampoo-bottled water plot, and the underwear-bomb plot. Experts, other than the whores hired by the US government, say that these plots are nonsensical. The "shoe bomb" and "underwear bomb" were colored fireworks powders incapable of blowing up a tin can. The liquid bomb, allegedly mixed up in an airliner toilet room, has been dismissed by experts as fantasy.

What is the purpose of these fake plots? And remember, all reports confirm that the "underwear bomber" was walked onto the airliner by an official, despite the fact that the "underwear bomber" had no passport. No investigation was ever conducted by the FBI, CIA, or anyone into why a passenger without a passport was allowed onto an international flight.

The purpose of these make-believe plots is to raise the fear level and to create the opportunity for former Homeland Security czar, Michael Chertoff, to make a fortune selling porno-scanners to the TSA.

The result of these hyped "terrorist plots" is that every American citizen, even those with high government positions and security clearances, cannot board a commercial airline flight without taking off his shoes, his jacket, his belt, submitting to a porno-scanner, or being sexually groped. Nothing could make it plainer that "airport security" cannot tell a Muslim terrorist from a gung-ho American patriot, a US Senator, a US Marine general, or a CIA operative.

If a passenger requires, for health or other reasons, quantities of liquids and creams beyond the limits imposed on toothpaste, shampoo, food, or medications, the passenger must obtain prior approval from TSA, which seldom works. One of America's finest moments is the case, documented on YouTube, of a dying woman in a wheelchair, who required special food, having her food thrown away by the gestapo TSA despite the written approval from the Transportation Safety Administration, her daughter arrested for protesting, and the dying woman in the wheelchair left alone in the airport.

This is America today. These assaults on innocent citizens are justified by the mindless right-wing as "protecting us against terrorism," a "threat" that all evidence shows is nonexistent.

No American is secure today. I am a former staff associate of the House Defense Appropriations subcommittee. I required high security clearances as I had access to information pertaining to all US weapons programs. As chief economist of the House Budget Committee I had information pertaining to the US military and security budgets. As Assistant Secretary of the US Treasury, I was provided every morning with the CIA's briefing of the President as well as with endless security information.

When I left the Treasury, President Reagan appointed me to a super-secret committee to investigate the CIA's assessment of Soviet capability. Afterwards I was a consultant to the Pentagon. I had every kind of security clearance.

Despite my record of highest security clearances and US government confidence in me including confirmation by the US Senate in a presidential appointment, the airline police cannot tell me from a terrorist.

If I were into model airplanes or attending anti-war demonstrations, there is little doubt I, too, would be arrested.

After my public service in the last quarter of the 20th century, I experienced, during the first decade of the 21st century, all of America's achievements, despite their blemishes, being erased. In their place was erected a monstrous desire for hegemony and highly concentrated wealth. Most of my friends and my fellow citizens in general are incapable of recognizing America's transformation into a warmonger police state that has the worst income distribution of any developed country.

It is extraordinary that so many Americans, citizens of the world's only superpower, actually believe that they are threatened by Muslim peoples who have no unity, no navy, no air force, no nuclear weapons, no missiles capable of reaching across the oceans.

Indeed, large percentages of these "threat populations," especially among the young, are enamored of the sexual freedom that exists in America. Even the Iranian dupes of the CIA-orchestrated "Green Revolution" have forgotten Washington's overthrow of their elected government in the 1950s. Despite America's decade-long abusive military actions against Muslim peoples, many Muslims still look to America for their salvation.

Many of their "leaders" are simply bought off with large sums of money.

With the "terrorist threat" and Al Qaeda deflated with President Obama's alleged assassination of its leader, Osama bin Laden, who was left unprotected and unarmed by his "world-wide terrorist organization," Washington has come up with a new bogyman—the Haqqanis.

According to John Glaser and anonymous CIA officials, US Joint Chiefs of Staff chairman Mike Mullen "exaggerated" the case against the Haqqani insurgent group when he claimed, setting up a US invasion of Pakistan, that the Haqqanis were an operating arm of the Pakistan government's secret service, the ISI. Adm. Mullen is now running from his "exaggeration," a euphemism for a lie. His aid, Captain John Kirby, said that Mullen's "accusations were designed to influence the Pakistanis to crack down on the Haqqani Network." In other words, the Pakistanis should kill more of their own people to save the Americans the trouble.

If you don't know what the Haqqani Network is, don't be surprised. You never heard of Al Qaeda prior to 9/11. The US government creates whatever new bogymen and incidents are necessary to further the neoconservative agenda of world hegemony and higher profits for the armaments industry.

For ten years, the "superpower" American population has been immobilized, terrified by the government's lies. While Americans sit sucking their thumbs in fear of non-existent "terrorists", millions of people in six countries have had their lives destroyed. As far as any evidence exists, the vast majority of Americans are unperturbed by the wanton murder of others in countries that they are incapable of locating on maps.

THE DAY
AMERICA DIED

October 2, 2011

September 30, 2011 was the day America was assassinated.

Some of us have watched this day approach and have warned of its coming, only to be greeted with boos and hisses from "patriots" who have come to regard the US Constitution as a device that coddles criminals and terrorists and gets in the way of the President who needs to act to keep us safe.

In our book, *The Tyranny of Good Intentions*,[44] Lawrence Stratton and I showed that long before 9/11 US law had ceased to be a shield of the people and had been turned into a weapon in the hands of the government. The event known as 9/11 was used to raise the executive branch above the law. As long as the president sanctions an illegal act, executive branch employees are no longer accountable to the law that prohibits the illegal act. On the president's authority, the executive branch can violate US laws against spying on Americans without warrants, indefinite detention, and torture and suffer no consequences.

Many expected President Obama to re-establish the accountability of government to law. Instead, he went further than Bush/Cheney and asserted the unconstitutional power not only to hold American citizens indefinitely in prison without bringing charges, but also to take their lives without convicting them in a court of law. Obama asserts that the US Constitution notwithstanding, he has the authority to assassinate US citizens, whom he deems to be a "threat," without due process of law.

In other words, any American citizen who is moved into the threat category has no rights and can be executed without trial or evidence.

On September 30 Obama used this asserted new power of the president and had two American citizens, Anwar al-Awlaki and Samir Khan, murdered. Khan was a wacky character associated with *Inspire Magazine* and does not readily come to mind as a serious threat.

Al-Awlaki was a moderate American Muslim cleric who served as an advisor to the US government after 9/11 on ways to counter Muslim extremism. Al-Awlaki was gradually radicalized by Washington's use of lies to justify military attacks on Muslim countries. He became a critic of the US government and told Muslims that they did not have to passively accept American aggression and had the right to resist and to fight back. As a result al-Awlaki was demonized and became a threat.

All that al-Awlaki did, as far as we know, was to give sermons critical of Washington's indiscriminate assaults on Muslim peoples. Washington's argument is that his sermons might have had an influence on some who are accused of attempting terrorist acts, thus making al-Awlaki responsible for the attempts.

Obama's assertion that al-Awlaki was some kind of high-level Al Qaeda operative is merely an assertion. Jason Ditz concluded that the reason al-Awlaki was murdered rather than brought to trial is that the US government had no real evidence that al-Awlaki was an Al Qaeda operative.[44]

Having murdered its critic, the Obama Regime is working hard to posthumously promote al-Awlaki to a leadership position in Al Qaeda.[45] The presstitutes and the worshippers of America's First Black President have fallen in line and regurgitated the assertions that al-Awlaki was a high-level dangerous Al Qaeda terrorist. If Al Qaeda sees value in al-Awlaki as a martyr, the organization will give credence to these claims. However, so far no one has provided any evidence. Keep in mind that all we know about al-Awlaki is what Washington claims and that the US has been at war for a decade based on false claims.

But what al-Awlaki did or might have done is beside the point. The US Constitution requires that even the worst murderer cannot be punished until he is convicted in a court of law. When the American Civil Liberties Union challenged in federal court Obama's assertion that he had the power to order assassinations of American citizens, the Obama Justice (*sic*) Department argued that Obama's decision to have Americans murdered was an executive power beyond the reach of the judiciary.

In a decision that sealed America's fate, federal district court judge, John Bates, ignored the Constitution's requirement that no person shall be deprived of life without due process of law and dismissed the case, saying that it was up to Congress to decide. Obama acted before an appeal could be heard, thus using Judge Bates' acquiescence to establish the power and advance the transformation of the president into a Caesar that began under George W. Bush.

Attorneys Glenn Greenwald and Jonathan Turley point out that al-Awlaki's assassination terminated the Constitution's restraint on the power of government.[46] Now the US government not only can seize a US citizen and confine him in prison for the rest of his life without ever presenting evidence and obtaining a conviction, but also can have him shot down in the street or blown up by a drone.

Before some readers write to declare that al-Awlaki's murder is no big deal because the US government has always had people murdered, keep in mind that CIA assassinations were of foreign opponents and were not publicly proclaimed events, much less was there a claim by the president to be above the law and have the right to do so. Indeed, such assassinations were denied, not claimed as legitimate actions of the President of the United States.

The Ohio National Guardsmen who shot Kent State students as they protested the US invasion of Cambodia in 1970 made no claim to be carrying out an executive branch decision. Eight of the guardsmen were indicted by a grand jury. The guardsmen entered a self-defense plea. Most Americans were angry at war protestors and blamed the students. The judiciary got the message, and the criminal case was eventually dismissed. The civil case (wrongful death and injury) was settled for $675,000 and a statement of regret by the defendants.

The point isn't that the government killed people. The point is that never prior to President Obama has a president asserted the power to murder citizens.

Over the last 20 years, the United States has had its own *Mein Kampf* transformation. Terry Eastland's book, *Energy in the Executive: The Case for the Strong Presidency*, presented ideas associated with the Federalist Society, an organization of Republican lawyers that works to reduce legislative and judicial restraints on executive power. Under the cover of wartime emergencies (the war on terror), the Bush/Cheney regime employed these arguments to free the president from accountability to law and to liberate Americans from their civil liberties. War and national security provided the opening for the asserted new powers, and a mixture of fear and desire for revenge for 9/11 led Congress, the judiciary, and the people to go along with the dangerous precedents.

As civilian and military leaders have been telling us for years, the war on terror is a 30-year project. After such time has passed, the presidency will have completed its transformation into Caesarism, and there will be no going back.

Indeed, as the neoconservative Project For a New American Century makes clear, the war on terror is only an opening for the neoconservative imperial ambition to establish US hegemony over the world.

As wars of aggression or imperial ambition are war crimes under international law, such wars require doctrines that elevate the leader above the law and the Geneva Conventions, as Bush was purported to have been elevated by his Justice (sic) Department with minimal judicial and legislative interference.

Illegal and unconstitutional actions also require a silencing of critics and punishment of those who reveal government crimes. Thus

Bradley Manning has been held for a year, mainly in solitary confinement under abusive conditions, without any charges being presented against him. A federal grand jury is at work concocting spy charges against Wikileaks' founder, Julian Assange. Another federal grand jury is at work concocting terrorist charges against antiwar activists.

"Terrorist" and "giving aid to terrorists" are increasingly elastic concepts. Homeland Security has declared that the vast federal police bureaucracy has shifted its focus from terrorists to "domestic extremists."

It is possible that al-Awlaki was assassinated because he was an effective critic of the US government. Police states do not originate fully fledged. Initially, they justify their illegal acts by demonizing their targets and in this way create the precedents for unaccountable power. Once the government equates critics with giving "aid and comfort" to terrorists, as they are doing with antiwar activists and Assange, or with terrorism itself, as Obama did with al-Awlaki, it will only be a short step to bringing accusations against Glenn Greenwald and the ACLU.

The Obama Regime, like the Bush/Cheney Regime, is a regime that does not want to be constrained by law. And neither will its successor. Those fighting to uphold the rule of law, humanity's greatest achievement, will find themselves lumped together with the regime's opponents and be treated as such.

This great danger that hovers over America is unrecognized by the majority of the people. When Obama announced before a military gathering his success in assassinating an American citizen, cheers erupted. The Obama regime and the media played the event as a repeat of the (claimed) killing of Osama bin Laden. Two "enemies of the people" have been triumphantly dispatched. That the President of the United States was proudly proclaiming to a cheering audience sworn to defend the Constitution that he was a murderer and that he had also terminated US citizens' protection under the US Constitution is extraordinary evidence that Americans are incapable of recognizing the threat to their liberty.

Emotionally, the people have accepted the new powers of the president. If the president can have American citizens assassinated, there is no big deal about torturing them. Amnesty International has sent out an alert that the US Senate is poised to pass legislation that would keep Guantanamo Prison open indefinitely and that Senator Kelly Ayotte (R-NH) might introduce a provision that would legalize "enhanced interrogation techniques," a euphemism for torture.

Instead of seeing the danger, most Americans will merely conclude that the government is getting tough on terrorists, and extend their approval. Smiling with satisfaction over the demise of their enemies, Americans are being led down the garden path to rule by government unrestrained by law and armed with the weapons of the medieval dungeon.

Americans have overwhelming evidence from news reports and YouTube videos of US police brutally abusing women, children, and the elderly, of brutal treatment and murder of prisoners not only in Abu Ghraib, Guantanamo, and secret CIA prisons abroad, but also in state and federal prisons in the US. Power over the defenseless attracts people of a brutal and evil disposition. And creates more of them.

A brutal disposition now infects the US military. The leaked video of US soldiers delighting, as their words and actions reveal, in their murder from the air of civilians and news service cameramen walking innocently along a city street in Iraq shows soldiers and officers devoid of humanity and military discipline. Excited by the thrill of murder, they repeated their crime when a father with two small children stopped to give aid to the wounded and they all were machine-gunned.

So many instances: the rape of a young girl and murder of her entire family; innocent civilians murdered and AK-47s placed by their side as "evidence" of insurgency; the enjoyment experienced not only by high school dropouts from torturing they-knew-not-who in Abu Ghraib and Guantanamo, but also by educated CIA operatives and Ph.D. psychologists. And no one was held accountable for these crimes except two lowly soldiers prominently featured in some of the torture photographs.

What do Americans think will be their fate now that the "war on terror" has destroyed the protection once afforded them by the US Constitution? If al-Awlaki really needed to be assassinated, why didn't President Obama protect American citizens from the precedent that their deaths too can be ordered without due process of law by first stripping al-Awlaki of his US citizenship? If the government can strip al-Awlaki of his life, it certainly can strip him of citizenship. The implication is hard to avoid that the executive branch desires to establish the precedent that it has the power to terminate citizens without due process of law.

Governments escape the accountability of law in stages. Washington understands that its justifications for its wars are contrived and indefensible. President Obama even went so far as to declare that the military assault that he authorized on Libya without consulting Congress was not a war, and, therefore, he could ignore the War Powers Resolution of 1973, a federal law intended to check the power of the President to commit the US to an armed conflict without the consent of Congress.

Americans are beginning to unwrap themselves from the flag. Some are beginning to grasp that initially they were led into Afghanistan for revenge for 9/11. From there they were led into Iraq for reasons that turned out to be false. They see more and more US military interventions: Libya, Yemen, Somalia, Pakistan and now calls for invasion of Pakistan and continued saber rattling for attacks on Syria, Lebanon, and Iran. The financial cost of a decade of the "war against terror" is starting to come home. Exploding annual federal budget deficits and national debt threaten Medicare and Social Security. Debt ceiling limits threaten government shut-downs.

War critics are beginning to have an audience. The government cannot begin its silencing of critics by bringing charges against US Representatives Ron Paul and Dennis Kucinich. It begins with antiwar protestors, who are elevated into "antiwar activists," perhaps a step below "domestic extremists." Washington begins with citizens who are demonized Muslim clerics radicalized by Washington's wars on Muslims. In this way, Washington establishes the precedent that war protestors give encouragement and, thus, aid, to terrorists. It establishes the precedent that those Americans deemed a threat are not protected by law. This is the slippery slope on which we now find ourselves.

Last year the Obama Regime tested the prospects of its strategy when Dennis Blair, Director of National Intelligence, announced that the government had a list of American citizens that it was going to assassinate abroad. This announcement, had it been made in earlier times by, for example, Richard Nixon or Ronald Reagan, would have produced a national uproar and calls for impeachment. However, Blair's announcement caused hardly a ripple. All that remained for the regime to do was to establish the policy by exercising it.

Readers ask me what they can do. Americans not only *feel* powerless, they *are* powerless. They have no systemic levers to do anything. The highly concentrated, corporate-owned, government-subservient print and TV media are useless and no longer capable of performing the historic role of protecting our rights and holding government accountable. Even many antiwar Internet sites shield the government from 9/11 skepticism, and most defend the government's "righteous intent" in its war on terror. To be acceptable, criticism has to be couched in words such as "it doesn't serve our interests."

Voting has no effect. President "Change" is worse than Bush/Cheney. As Jonathan Turley suggests, Obama is "the most disastrous president in our history." Ron Paul is the only presidential candidate who stands up for the Constitution, but the majority of Americans are too unconcerned with the Constitution to appreciate him.

To expect salvation from an election is delusional. All you can do, if you are young enough, is to leave the country. The only future for Americans is a nightmare

THE ROADS TO WAR AND ECONOMIC COLLAPSE

November 23, 2011

The day before the Thanksgiving holiday brought three extraordinary news items. One was the report on the Republican presidential campaign debate. One was the Russian President's statement about his country's response to Washington's missile bases surrounding his country. And one was the failure of a German government bond auction.

As the presstitute media will not inform us of what any of this means, let me try.

With the exception of Ron Paul, the only candidate in either party qualified to be the president of the US, the Republican candidates are even worse than Obama, a president who had the country behind him but sold out the American people to the special interests.

No newly elected president in memory, neither John F. Kennedy nor Ronald Reagan, had such an extraordinary response to his election as Barak Obama. A record-breaking number of people braved the cold to witness his swearing in ceremony. The mall was filled with Americans who could not see the ceremony except as televised on giant screens.

Obama had convinced the electorate that he would end the wars, stop the violation of law by the US government, end the regime of illegal torture, close the torture prison of Guantanamo, and attend to the real needs of the American people rather than stuff the pockets of the military/security complex with taxpayers' money.

Once in office, Obama renewed and extended the Bush/Cheney/ neoconservative wars.

He validated the Bush regime's assaults on the US Constitution. He left Wall Street in charge of US economic policy, he absolved the Bush regime of its crimes, and he assigned to the American people the financial cost necessary to preserve the economic welfare of the mega-rich.

One would think such a totally failed president would be easy to defeat. Given an historic opportunity, the Republican Party has put before the electorate the most amazingly stupid and vile collection of prospects, with the exception of Ron Paul who does not have the party's support, that Americans have ever seen.

In the November 22 presidential "debate," the candidates, with the exception of Ron Paul, revealed themselves as a collection of ignorant warmongers who support the police state. Gingrich and McCain said that Muslims "want to kill us all" and that "all of us will be in danger for the rest of our lives."

Bachmann said that the American puppet state, Pakistan, is "more than an existential threat." The moron Bachmann has no idea what is "more than an existential threat."

However, it sounded heavy, like an intellectual thing to say for the candidate who previously declared the long-defunct Soviet Union to be today's threat to the US.

Any sentient American who watched or read about the Republican presidential debate must wonder what there is to be thankful for as the national holiday approaches.

The Russian government, which prefers to use its resources for the economy rather than for the military, has decided that it has been taking too many risks in the name of peace. The day before Thanksgiving, Russian President Dmitry Medvedev said, in a televised address to the Russian people, that if Washington goes ahead with its planned missile bases surrounding Russia, Russia will respond with new nuclear missiles of its own, which will target the American bases and European capital cities.

The President of Russia said that the Russian government has asked Washington for legally binding guarantees that the American missile bases are not intended as a threat to Russia, but that Washington has refused to give such guarantees.

Medvedev's statement is perplexing. What does he mean *"if* Washington goes ahead?" The American missile and radar bases *are already in place*. Russia is already *surrounded*. Is Medvedev just now aware of what is already in place?

Russia's and China's slow response to Washington's aggression can only be understood in the context of the two countries' experience with communism. The sufferings of Russians and Chinese under communism was extreme, and the thinking part of those populations saw America as the ideal of political life. This delusion still controls the mentality of progressive thinkers in Russia and China. It might prove to be a disaster for Russia and China that these countries have citizens who are aligned with the US.

Belief in Washington's trustworthiness even pervades the Russian government, which apparently, according to Medvedev's statement, would be reassured by a "legally binding guarantee" from Washington. After the massive lies told by Washington in the 21st century—"weapons of mass destruction," "Al Qaeda connections," "Iranian nukes"—why would anyone put any credence in "a legally binding guarantee" from Washington? The guarantee would mean nothing. How could it be enforced? Such a guarantee would simply be another deceit in Washington's pursuit of world hegemony.

The day prior to Thanksgiving also brought another extraordinary development—the failure of a German government bond auction, an unparalleled event.

Why would Germany, the only member of the EU with financial rectitude, not be able to sell 35 per cent of its offerings of 10-year bonds? Germany has no debt problems, and its economy is expected by EU and US authorities to bear the lion's share of the bailout of the EU member countries that do lack financial rectitude.

I suspect that the answer to this question is that the failure of the German government's bond auction was orchestrated by the US, by EU authorities, especially the European Central Bank, and private banks in order to punish Germany for obstructing the purchase of EU member countries' sovereign debt by the European Central Bank.

The German government has been trying to defend the terms on which Germany gave up control over its own currency and joined the EU. By insisting on the legality of the agreements, Germany has been standing in the way of the ECB behaving like the US Federal Reserve and monetizing the debt of member governments.

From the beginning the EU was a conspiracy against Germany. If Germany remains in the EU, Germany will be destroyed. It will lose its political and economic sovereignty, and its economy will be bled on behalf of the fiscally irresponsible members of the EU.

If Germany had political leaders committed to Germany instead of to "Europe," Germany would exit the EU and NATO, bring back the Deutschmark, and form an economic partnership with Russia.

MISREADING
THE FIGHT OVER
MILITARY DETENTION

December 4, 2011

During an interview with RT on December 1, I said that the US Constitution had been shredded by the failure of the US Senate to protect American citizens from the detainee amendment to the Defense Authorization Bill sponsored by Republican John McCain and Democrat Carl Levin.

The amendment permits indefinite detention of US citizens by the US military. I also gave my opinion that the fact that all but two Republican members of the Senate had voted to strip American citizens of their constitutional protections and of the protection of the Posse Comitatus Act indicated that the Republican Party had degenerated into a Gestapo Party.

These conclusions are self-evident, and I stand by them.

However, I jumped to conclusions when I implied that the Obama regime opposes military detention on constitutional grounds.

Ray McGovern and Glenn Greenwald might have jumped to the same conclusions.

An article by Dahlia Lithwick in *Slate* reported that the entire Obama regime opposed the military detention provision in the McCain/Levin amendment. Lithwick wrote: "The secretary of defense, the director of national intelligence, the director of the FBI, the CIA director, and the head of the Justice Department's national security division have all said that the indefinite detention provisions in the bill are a bad idea. And the White House continues to say that the president will veto the bill if the detainee provisions are not removed."

I checked the URLs that Lithwick supplied. It is clear that the Obama regime objects to military detention, but Lithwick mistook this objection for constitutional scruples.

On further reflection I conclude that the Obama regime's objection to military detention is not rooted in concern for the constitutional rights of American citizens. The regime objects to military detention because *the implication of military detention is that detainees are prisoners of war.* As

Senate Armed Services Committee Chairman Carl Levin put it: Should somebody determined "to be a member of an enemy force who has come to this nation or is in this nation to attack us as a member of a foreign enemy, should that person be treated according to the laws of war? The answer is yes."

Detainees treated according to the laws of war have the protections of the Geneva Conventions. They cannot be tortured. The Obama regime opposes military detention, because detainees would have some rights. These rights would interfere with the regime's ability to send detainees to CIA torture prisons overseas. This is what the Obama regime means when it says that the requirement of military detention denies the regime "flexibility."

The Bush/Obama regimes have evaded the Geneva Conventions by declaring that detainees are not POWs, but "enemy combatants," "terrorists," or some other designation that removes all accountability from the US government for their treatment.

Requiring military detention of those captured would undo the accomplishment of the two regimes of removing POW status from detainees. A careful reading of the Obama regime's objections to military detention supports this conclusion.[47]

The November 17 letter to the Senate from the Executive Office of the President says that the Obama regime does not want the authority it has under the Authorization for Use of Military Force (AUMF), Public Law 107-40, to be codified. Codification is risky, the regime says. "After a decade of settled jurisprudence on detention authority, Congress must be careful not to open a whole new series of legal questions that will distract from our efforts to protect the country."

In other words, the regime is saying that under AUMF the executive branch has total discretion as to who it detains and how it treats detainees. Moreover, as the executive branch has total discretion, no one can find out what the executive branch is doing, who detainees are, or what is being done to them. Codification brings accountability, and the executive branch does not want accountability.

Those who see hope in Obama's threatened veto have jumped to conclusions if they think the veto is based on constitutional scruples.

WASHINGTON MOVES THE WORLD CLOSER TO WAR

January 16, 2012

Since my January 11 column[48] and the news alert posted on January 14,[49] more confirmation that Washington is moving the world toward a dangerous war has appeared. The Obama regime is using its Ministry of Propaganda, a.k.a., the American media, to spread the story that President Obama, Pentagon chief Panetta, and other high US officials are delivering strong warnings to Israel not to attack Iran.

For someone as familiar with Washington as I am, I recognize these reports for what they are. They are Br'er Rabbit telling Br'er Fox "please don't throw me in the briar patch."

If you don't know the Uncle Remus stories, you have missed a lot. Br'er Rabbit was born and raised in the briar patch.

What these "leaked" stories of Washington's warnings and protests to Israel are all about is to avoid Washington's responsibility for the war Washington has prepared. If the war gets out of hand, and if Russia and China intervene or nukes start flying, Washington wants the blame to rest on Israel, and Israel seems willing to accept the blame. Nikolai Patrushev, who heads Russia's Security Council, has apparently been deceived by Washington's manipulation of the media. According to the Interfax news agency, Patrushev condemned Israel for pushing the US towards war with Iran.

You get the picture. The helpless Americans. They are being bullied by Israel into acquiescing to a dangerous war. Otherwise, no more campaign contributions.

The facts are different. If Washington did not want war with Iran it would not have provided the necessary weapons to Israel. It would not have deployed thousands of US troops to Israel, with a view to putting American soldiers in the line of fire in an Iranian response to Israel's attack, thus "forcing" the US to enter the war. Washington would not have built a missile defense system for Israel and would not be conducting joint exercises with the Israeli military to make sure it works.

If Washington wants to stop Israel from starting a war, Washington would inform the Israeli government in no uncertain words that an Israeli strike on Iran means that the US will *not* veto the UN's denunciation of Israel and the sanctions that would be placed on Israel as a war criminal state. Washington would tell Israel that it is good-bye to the billions of dollars that the bilked American taxpayers, foreclosed from their homes by fraudulent mortgages and from jobs by offshoring, hand over by compulsion to Israel to support Israel's crimes against humanity.

If Washington did not want war with Iran, Washington would not have prepared for war by surrounding Iran with fleets and military bases, and Washington would not have prepared the public for war by demonizing Iran.

Washington's NATO puppets would not be an obstacle. "Great" Britain does as it is told, subservient and occupied Germany, bankrupt France, Italy occupied with US air bases with a government infiltrated by the CIA, bankrupt Spain and Greece will all, in hopes of an outpouring of US dollars and devoid of any dignity or honor, support the war that could end life on earth.

Only Russia and China can prevent the war.

Russia took the first step when the newly appointed Deputy Prime Minister for military affairs, Dmitry Rogozin told a press conference in Brussels that Russia would regard an attack on Iran as "a direct threat to our security."

Washington is counting on subverting Russia's opposition to Washington's next war. Washington can time the attack on Iran after the March elections in Russia. When Putin wins again as he will [and did], the treasonous Russian opposition parties, financed by the CIA, will unleash protests in the streets [as they did]. The subservient and corrupt Western media will denounce Putin for stealing the election [as they did]. The orchestrated protests in Russia could turn violent and discredit, if not prevent, any Russian response to the naked aggression against Iran.

For Rogozin's warning to be effective in preventing war, China needs to enter the fray. Washington is banking on China's caution. China deliberates and never rushes into anything. China's deliberation would serve Washington's war.

It is possible that the crazed neocon Washington government will have one more "victory" before Russia and China comprehend that they are next on the extermination list. As this date cannot be far off, life on earth might expire before the unpayable debts of the US and EU countries come due.

[Despite the late 2013 diplomatic initiative with Iran, US Representative Duncan Hunter, Jr. (R.CA) told C-SPAN on December 4, 2013, that it could still be necessary to set Iran "back a decade or two or three" by bombarding Iran "with tactical nuclear devices."]

DROWNING
IN HYPOCRISY

January 24, 2012

The US government is so full of self-righteousness that it has become a caricature of hypocrisy. Leon Panetta, a former congressman whom Obama appointed CIA director and now head of the Pentagon, just told the sailors on the *USS Enterprise*, an aircraft carrier, that the US is maintaining a fleet of 11 aircraft carriers in order to project sea power against Iran and to convince Iran that "it's better for them to try to deal with us through diplomacy."

If it requires 11 aircraft carriers to deal with Iran, how many will Panetta need to project power against Russia and China? But to get on with the main point, Iran has been trying "to deal with us through diplomacy." The response from Washington has been belligerent threats of military attack, unfounded and irresponsible accusations that Iran is making a nuclear weapon, sanctions and an oil embargo. Washington's accusations echo Israel's and are contradicted by Washington's own intelligence agencies and the International Atomic Energy Agency. Why doesn't Washington respond to Iran in a civilized manner with diplomacy? Really, which of the two countries is the greatest threat to peace?

Washington sends the FBI to raid the homes of peace activists and puts a grand jury to work to create a case against them for aiding a nebulous enemy by protesting Washington's wars. The Department of Homeland Security unleashes goon cop thugs to brutalize peaceful Occupy Wall Street demonstrators. Washington fabricates cases against Bradley Manning, Julian Assange, and Tarek Mehanna that negate the First Amendment by equating free speech with terrorism and spying. Chicago mayor and former Obama White House chief-of-staff, Rahm Israel Emanuel, pushes an ordinance that outlaws public protests in the City of Chicago. The list goes on. And in the midst of it all Secretary of State Hillary Clinton and other Washington hypocrites accuse Russia and China of stifling dissent.

Washington's grotesque hypocrisy goes unremarked by the American "media" and in the debates for the Republican presidential nomination. The corrupt Obama "Justice" Department turns a blind eye while goon cop thugs commit gratuitous violence against the citizens who pay the goon cop thugs' undeserved salaries.

But it is in the War Crimes Arena where Washington shows the greatest hypocrisy. The self-righteous bigots in Washington are forever rounding up heads of weak states whose countries were afflicted by civil wars and sending them off to be tried as war criminals. All the while Washington indiscriminately kills large numbers of civilians in six or more countries, dismissing its own war crimes as "collateral damage." Washington violates its own law and international law by torturing people.

On January 13, 2012, Carol Rosenberg of McClatchy Newspapers reported that Spanish judge Pablo Rafael Ruz Gutierrez re-launched an investigation into Washington's torture of prisoners in Guantanamo Prison.[50] The previous day British authorities opened an investigation into CIA renditions of kidnapped persons to Libya for torture.

Rosenberg reports that although the Obama regime has refused to investigate the obvious crimes of the Bush regime, and one might add its own obvious crimes, "other countries are still interested in determining whether Bush-era anti-terror practices violated international law."

There is no question that Bush/Cheney/Obama have trashed the US Constitution, US statutory law, and international law. But Washington, having overthrown justice, has established that might is right. No foreign government is going to send its forces into the US to drag the war criminals out and place them on trial.

International criminal tribunals are reserved for Washington's show trials. No foreign government is going to pay Washington several hundred millions of dollars to turn Bush, Cheney, Obama and their minions over to a tribunal in the way the US bought Milosevic from Serbia in order to create the necessary spectacle to justify Washington's naked aggression against Serbia.

No government can be perfect, because all governments are composed of humans, especially those humans most attracted by power and profit. Nevertheless, in my lifetime I have witnessed an extraordinary deterioration in the integrity of government in the United States. We have reached the point where nothing that our government says is believable. Not even the unemployment rate, the inflation rate, the GDP growth rate, much less Washington's reasons for its wars, its police state, and its foreign and domestic policies.

Washington has kept America at war for ten years while millions of Americans lost their jobs and their homes. War and a faltering economy have exploded the national debt, and a looming bankruptcy is being blamed on Social Security and Medicare.

The pursuit of war continues. On January 23 Washington's servile puppets—the EU member states—did Washington's bidding and imposed an oil embargo on Iran, despite the pleas of Greece, a member of the EU.

Greece's final ruin will come from the higher oil prices from the embargo, as the Greek government realizes.

The embargo is a reckless act. If the US navy tries to intercept oil tankers carrying Iranian oil, large scale war could break out. This, many believe, is Washington's aim.

It is easy for an embargo to become a blockade, which is an act of war. Remember how easily the UN Security Council's "no-fly zone" over Libya was turned by the US and its NATO puppets into a military attack on Libya's armed forces and population centers supportive of Gaddafi.

As the western "democracies" become increasingly lawless, the mask of law that imperialism wears is stripped away and with it the sheen of morality that has been used to cloak hegemonic ambitions. With Iran surrounded and with two of Washington's fleets in the Persian Gulf, another war of aggression seems inevitable.

Experts say that an attack on Iran by the US and NATO will disrupt the flow of oil that the world needs. The crazed drive for hegemony is so compelling that Washington and its EU puppets show no hesitation in putting their own struggling economies at risk of sharply rising energy costs.

War abroad and austerity at home is the policy that is being imposed on the western "democracies."

IS WESTERN DEMOCRACY REAL OR A FACADE?

February 14, 2012

The United States government and its NATO puppets have been killing Muslim men, women and children for a decade in the name of bringing them democracy. But is the West itself a democracy?

Skeptics point out that President George W. Bush was put in office by the Supreme Court and that a number of other elections have been decided by electronic voting machines that leave no paper trail. Others note that elected officials represent the special interests that fund their campaigns and not the voters. The bailout of the banks arranged by Bush's Treasury Secretary and former Goldman Sachs chairman, Henry Paulson, and Washington's failure to indict any banksters for the fraud that contributed to the financial crisis, are evidence in support of the view that the US government represents money and not the voters.

Recent events in Greece and Italy have created more skepticism of the West's claim to be democratic. Two elected European prime ministers, George Papandreou of Greece and Silvio Berlusconi of Italy, were forced to resign over the sovereign debt issue. Not even Berlusconi, a billionaire who continues to lead the largest Italian political party, could stand up to the pressure brought by private bankers and unelected European Union officials.

Papandreou lasted only 10 days after announcing, on October 31, 2011, that he would let the Greek voters decide in a referendum whether or not to accept the austerity being imposed on the Greek people from the outside. Austerity is the price charged by the EU for lending the Greek government the money to pay to the banks. In other words, the question was austerity or default. However, the question was decided without the participation of the Greek people.

Consequently, Greeks have taken to the streets. The conditions accompanying the latest tranche of the bailout have again brought large numbers of Greeks into the streets of Athens and other cities. Citizens are protesting a 20% cut both in the minimum wage and in pensions larger than

12,000 euros ($15,800) annually and more cuts in public sector jobs. Greek taxes were raised 2.3 billion euros last year and are scheduled to rise another 3.4 billion euros in 2013. The austerity is being imposed despite Greece's unemployment rate of 21% overall and 48% for those under the age of 25.

One interpretation is that the banks, which were careless in their loans to governments, are forcing the people to save the banks from the consequences of their bad decisions.

Another interpretation is that the European Union is using the sovereign debt crisis to extend its power and control over the individual member states of the EU.

Some say that the EU is using the banks for the EU's agenda, and others say the banks are using the EU for the banks' agenda.

Indeed, they may be using each other. Regardless, democracy is not part of the process.

Greece's appointed—not elected—prime minister is Lucas Papademos, He is a former governor of the Bank of Greece, a member of Rockefeller's Trilateral Commission, and former vice president of the European Central Bank. In other words, he is a banker appointed to represent the banks.

On February 12 the appointed prime minister, whose job is to deliver Greece to the banks or to Brussels, failed to see the irony in his statement that "violence has no place in a democracy." Neither did he see any irony in the fact that 40 elected representatives in the Greek parliament who rejected the bailout terms were expelled by the ruling coalition parties. Violence begets violence. Violence in the streets is a response to the economic violence being committed against the Greek people.

A democratic government devoid of democracy has also been formed in Italy. The appointed prime minister, Mario Monti, doesn't have to face an election until April 2013. Moreover, according to news reports, his "technocratic cabinet" does not include a single elected politician. The banks are taking no chances: Monti is both prime minister and minister of economics and finance.

Monti's background indicates that he represents both the EU and the banks. He is former European advisor to Goldman Sachs, European chairman of the Trilateral Commission, a member of the Bilderberg Group, a former EU Commissioner, and a founding member of the Spinelli Group, an organization launched in September 2010 to facilitate integration within the EU, that is, to advance central power over the member states.

There is little doubt that European governments, like Washington, have been financially improvident, living beyond their means and building up debt burdens on citizens. Something needed to be done. However, what is being done is extra-democratic. This is an indication that Western elites—the

Trilateral Commission, the Council on Foreign Relations, Bilderberg Group, the EU, transnational corporations, oversized banks, and the mega-rich—no longer believe in democracy. For these groups, democracy is merely a facade to cloak rule by the rich.

Perhaps future historians will conclude that democracy once served the interests of money in order to break free of the power of kings, aristocracy, and government predations, but as money established control over governments, democracy became a liability. Historians will speak of the transition from the divine right of kings to the divine right of money.

WASHINGTON'S INSOUCIANCE HAS NO RIVAL

February 15, 2012

Is Obama a hypocrite or merely insouciant? Or is he simply obediently reading the teleprompter?

According to news reports Obama's White House meeting on Valentine's Day with China's Vice President, Xi Jinping, provided an opportunity for Obama to raise "a sensitive human rights issue with the Chinese leader-in-waiting." The brave and forthright Obama didn't let etiquette or decorum get in his way. Afterwards, Obama declared that Washington would "continue to emphasize what we believe is the importance of realizing the aspirations and rights of all people."

Think about that for a minute. Washington is now in the second decade of murdering Muslim men, women, and children in six countries. Washington is so concerned with human rights that it drops bombs on schools, hospitals, weddings and funerals, all in order to uphold the human rights of Muslim people. You see, bombing liberates Muslim women from having to wear the burka and from male domination.

One hundred thousand, or one million, dead Iraqis, four million displaced Iraqis, a country with destroyed infrastructure, and entire cities, such as Fallujah, bombed and burnt with white phosphorus into cinders is the proper way to show concern for human rights.

Ditto for Afghanistan. And Libya.

In Pakistan, Yemen, and Somalia Washington's drones bring human rights to the people.

Abu Ghraib, Guantanamo, and secret CIA prison sites are other places to which Washington brings human rights. Obama, who has the power to murder American citizens without due process of law, is too powerless to close Guantanamo Prison.

He is powerless to prevent himself from supplying Israel with weapons with which to murder Palestinians and Lebanese citizens to whom Obama brings human rights by vetoing every UN resolution passed against Israel for its crimes against humanity.

Instead of following Washington's human rights lead, the evil Chinese invest in other countries, buy things from them, and sell them goods.

Has any foreign dignitary ever raised "a sensitive human rights issue" with Obama or his predecessor? How is the world so deranged that Washington can murder innocents for years on end and still profess to be the world's defender of human rights?

How many people has China bombed, droned, and sanctioned into non-existence in the 21st century?

Will Syria and Iran be the next victims of Washington's concern for human rights?

Nothing better illustrates the total unreality of life in the West than the fact that the entire Western world did not break out in riotous laughter over Obama's expression of his human rights concern over China's behavior.

Washington's concern with human rights does not extend as far as airport security where little girls and grandmothers are sexually groped. Antiwar activists have their homes invaded, their personal possessions carried off, and a grand jury is summoned to frame them up on some terrorist charge. US soldier Bradley Manning is held for two years in violation of the US Constitution while the human rights government concocts fabricated charges to punish him for revealing a US war crime. WikiLeaks' Julian Assange is harassed endlessly with the goal of bringing him into the human rights clutches of Washington. Critics of Washington's inhumane policies are monitored and spied upon.

Washington is the worst violator of human rights in our era, and Washington has only begun.

Who will liberate Americans from Washington's clutches?

SILENCING
THE CRITICS

February 20, 2012

In 2010 the FBI invaded the homes of peace activists in several states and seized personal possessions in what the FBI—the lead orchestrator of fake "terrorist plots"—called an investigation of "activities concerning the material support of terrorism."

Subpoenas were issued to compel antiwar protestors to testify before grand juries as prosecutors set about building their case that opposing Washington's wars of aggression constitutes giving aid and comfort to terrorists. The purpose of the raids and grand jury subpoenas was to chill the anti-war movement into inaction.

Last week in one fell swoop the last two remaining critics of Washington/Tel Aviv imperialism were removed from the mainstream media. Judge Napolitano's popular program, Freedom Watch, was cancelled by Fox TV, and Pat Buchanan was fired by MSNBC. Both pundits had wide followings and were appreciated for speaking frankly.

Many suspect that the Israel Lobby used its clout with TV advertisers to silence critics of the Israeli government's efforts to lead Washington to war with Iran. Regardless, the point before us is that the voice of the mainstream media is now uniform. Americans hear one voice, one message, and that message is propaganda. Dissent is tolerated only on such issues as whether employer-paid health benefits should pay for contraceptive devices. Constitutional rights have been replaced with rights to free condoms.

The western media demonizes those at whom Washington points a finger. The lies pour forth to justify Washington's naked aggression: the Taliban are conflated with Al Qaeda, Saddam Hussein has weapons of mass destruction, Gaddafi is a terrorist and, even worse, fortified his troops with Viagra in order to commit mass rape against Libyan women.

President Obama and members of Congress along with Tel Aviv continue to assert that Iran is making a nuclear weapon despite public contradiction by the US Secretary of Defense, Leon Panetta, and the CIA's National Intelligence Estimate. According to news reports, Pentagon chief Leon Panetta told members of the House of Representatives on February 16 that "Tehran has not made a decision to proceed with developing a nuclear weapon." However, in Washington facts don't count. Only the material interests of powerful interest groups matter.

At the moment the American Ministry of Truth is splitting its time between lying about Iran and lying about Syria. Recently, there were some explosions in far away Thailand, and the explosions were blamed on Iran. Last October the FBI announced that the bureau had uncovered an Iranian plot to pay a used car salesman to hire a Mexican drug gang to kill the Saudi Ambassador to the US. The White House con artist professed to believe the unbelievable plot and declared that he had "strong evidence," but no evidence was ever released. The purpose for announcing the non-existent plot was to justify Obama's sanctions, which amount to an embargo—an act of war—against Iran for developing nuclear energy.

As a signatory to the non-proliferation treaty, Iran has the right to develop nuclear energy. IAEA inspectors are permanently in Iran and report no diversion of nuclear material to a weapons program.

In other words, according to the reports of the International Atomic Energy Agency, the US National Intelligence Estimate, and the current Secretary of Defense, there is no evidence that Iran has nukes or is making nukes. Yet, Obama has placed illegal sanctions on Iran and continues to threaten Iran with military attack on the basis of an accusation that is contradicted by all known evidence.

How can such a thing happen? It can happen because there is no Helen Thomas, who also was eliminated by the Israel Lobby, to question, as a member of the White House press, President Obama as to why he placed war-like sanctions on Iran when his own CIA and his own Secretary of Defense, along with the IAEA, report that there is no basis for the sanctions.

The idea that the US is a democracy when it most definitely does not have a free watchdog press is laughable. But the media is not laughing. It is lying. Just like the government, every time the US mainstream media opens its mouth or writes one word, it is lying. Indeed, its corporate masters pay its employees to tell lies. That is their job. Tell the truth, and you are history, like Buchanan, Napolitano and Helen Thomas.

What the Ministry of Truth calls "peaceful protesters brutalized by Assad's military" are in fact rebels armed and financed by Washington. Washington has fomented a civil war. Washington claims its intention is to rescue the oppressed and abused Syrian people from Assad, just as Washington rescued the oppressed and abused Libyan people from Gaddafi. Today "liberated" Libya is a shell of its former self, terrorized by clashing militias. Thanks to Obama, another country has been destroyed.

Reports of atrocities committed against Syrian civilians by the military could be true, but the reports come from the rebels who desire

Western intervention to put them into power. Moreover, how would these civilian casualties differ from the ones inflicted on Bahraini civilians by the US supported Bahraini government, the military of which was fortified by Saudi Arabian troops? There is no outcry in the western press about Washington's blind eye to civilian atrocities committed by its puppet states.

How do the Syrian atrocities, if they are real, differ from Washington's atrocities in Afghanistan, Iraq, Pakistan, Yemen, Libya, Somalia, Abu Ghraib, Guantanamo prison, and secret CIA prison sites? Why is the American Ministry of Truth silent about these massive, unprecedented, violations of human rights?

Remember also the reports of Serbian atrocities in Kosovo that Washington and Germany used to justify NATO and US bombing of Serbian civilians, including the Chinese consulate, dismissed as another collateral damage. Now 13 years later, a prominent German TV program has revealed that the photographs that ignited the atrocity campaign were grossly misrepresented and were not photographs of atrocities committed by Serbs, but of Albanian separatists killed in a firefight between armed Albanians and Serbians. Serbian casualties were not shown.[51]

The problem that truth faces is that the western media continually lies. On the rare instances when the lies are corrected, it is always long after the event and, meantime, the crimes enabled by the media have been accomplished.

Washington set its puppet Arab League upon Syria in order to establish Syria's isolation among its own kind, the better to attack Syria. Assad forestalled Washington's set-up of Syria for destruction by calling a nationwide referendum on February 26 to establish a new constitution that would extend the prospect of rule beyond the Ba'athists (Assad's party).

One might think that, if Washington and its Ministry of Truth really wanted democracy in Syria, Washington would get behind this gesture of good will by the ruling party and endorse the referendum. But Washington does not want a democratic Syrian government. Washington wants a puppet state. Washington's response is that the dastardly Assad has outwitted Washington by taking steps toward Syrian democracy before Washington can obliterate Syria and install a puppet.

Here is Obama's response to Assad's move toward democracy: "It's actually quite laughable—it makes a mockery of the Syrian revolution," White House spokesman Jay Carney told reporters aboard Air Force One.

Obama, the neoconservatives, and the Israeli government are really pissed. If Washington and Israel can figure out how to get around Russia and China and overthrow Assad, Washington and Israel will put Assad on trial as a war criminal despite his proposing a democratic referendum.

Assad was an eye doctor in England until his father died, and he was called back to head the troubled government. Washington and Israel have demonized Assad for refusing to be their puppet. Another sore point is the Russian naval base at Tartus. Washington is desperate to evict the Russians from their only Mediterranean base in order to make the Mediterranean an American lake. Washington, inculcated with neocon visions of world empire, wants its own *mare nostrum.*

If the Soviet Union were still extant, Washington's designs on Tartus would be suicidal. However, Russia is politically and militarily weaker than the Soviet Union. Washington has infiltrated Russia with NGOs that work against Russia's interests and will disrupt the upcoming elections. Moreover, Washington-funded "color revolutions" have turned former constituent parts of the Soviet Union into Washington's puppet states. Shorn of communist ideology, Washington does not expect Russia to push the nuclear button. Thus, Russia is there for the taking, or so Washington thinks.

China is a more difficult problem. Washington's plan is to cut China off from independent sources of energy. China's oil investment in eastern Libya is the reason Gaddafi was overthrown, and oil is one of the main reasons that Washington has targeted Iran. China has large oil investments in Iran and gets 20% of its oil from Iran. Closing down Iran, or converting it into Washington's puppet state, closes down 20% of the Chinese economy.

Russia and China are slow learners. However, when Washington and its NATO puppets abused and violated the "no-fly" UN resolution concerning Libya by turning it into a tool purportedly legitimizing armed military aggression against Libya's armed forces, which had every right to put down a CIA sponsored rebellion, Russia and China finally got the message that Washington could not be trusted.

So when it came to Syria, Russia and China did not fall into Washington's trap. They vetoed the UN Security Council's set-up of Syria for military attack. Now Washington and Israel (it is not always clear which is the puppet and which is the puppet master) have to decide whether to proceed in the face of Russian and Chinese opposition.

The risks for Washington have multiplied. If Washington proceeds, the information that is conveyed to Russia and China is that they are next in line after Iran. Therefore, Russia and China, both being well-armed with nuclear weapons, are likely to put their foot down more firmly at the line drawn over Iran. If the crazed warmongers in Washington and Israel, with veins running strong with hubris and arrogance, again override Russian and Chinese opposition, the risk of a dangerous confrontation rises.

Why isn't the American media raising questions about these risks? Is it worth blowing up the world in order to stop Iran from having a nuclear energy program or even a nuclear weapon? Does Washington think China is unaware that Washington is taking aim at its energy supply? Does Washington think Russia is unaware that it is being encircled by hostile military bases?

Whose interests are being served by Washington's endless and multi-trillion dollar wars? Certainly not the interests of the 50 million Americans with no access to health care, nor the 1,500,000 American children who are homeless, living in cars, rundown motel rooms, tent cities, and the storm sewers under Las Vegas, while huge amounts of public funds are used to bail out banks and squandered in wars of hegemony.[52]

The US has no independent print and TV media. It has presstitutes who are paid for the lies that they tell. The US government in its pursuit of its immoral aims has attained the status of the most corrupt government in human history. Yet Obama speaks as if Washington is the font of human morality.

The US government does not represent Americans. It represents a few special interests and a foreign power. US citizens simply don't count, and certainly Afghans, Iraqis, Libyans, Iranians, Syrians, Somalis, Yemenis, and Pakistanis don't count. Washington regards truth, justice, and mercy as laughable values. Money, power, hegemony are all that count for Washington, the city upon the hill, the light unto nations, the example for the world.

WHY CAN'T AMERICANS HAVE DEMOCRACY?

March 2, 2012

Syria has a secular government as did Iraq prior to the American invasion. Secular governments are important in Arab lands in which there is division between Sunni and Shia. Secular governments keep the divided population from murdering one another.

When the American invasion, a war crime under the Nuremberg standard set by the US after WWII, overthrew the Saddam Hussein secular government, the Iraqi Sunnis and Shia went to war against one another. The civil war between Iraqis saved the American invasion. Nevertheless, enough Sunnis found time to fight the American occupiers of Iraq that the US was never able to occupy Bagdad, much less Iraq, no matter how violent and indiscriminate the US was in the application of force.

The consequence of the US invasion was not democracy and women's rights in Iraq, much less the destruction of weapons of mass destruction which did not exist as the weapons inspectors had made perfectly clear beforehand. The consequence was to transfer political power from Sunnis to Shias. The Shia version of Islam is the Iranian version. Thus, Washington's invasion transferred power in Iraq from a secular government to Shia allied with Iran.

Now Washington intends to repeat its folly in Syria. According to the American secretary of state, Hillary Clinton, Washington is even prepared to ally with Al Qaeda in order to overthrow Assad's government. Now that Washington itself has Al Qaeda connections, will the government in Washington be arrested under the anti-terrorism laws?

Washington's hostility toward Assad is hypocritical. On February 26, the Syrian government held a referendum on a new constitution for Syria that set term limits on future presidents and removed the political monopoly that the Ba'ath Party has enjoyed.

The Syrian voter turnout was 57.4%, matching the voter turnout for Obama in 2008. It was a higher voter turnout (despite the armed, western-supported rebellion in Syria) than in the nine US presidential elections from 1972 through 2004. The new Syrian constitution was approved by a vote of 89.4%.

But Washington denounced the democratic referendum and claims that the Syrian government must be overthrown in order to bring democracy to Syria.

Washington's allies in the region, unelected oil monarchies such as Saudi Arabia and Qatar, have issued statements that they are willing to supply weapons to the Islamist rebels in order to bring democracy—something they do not tolerate at home—to Syria.

For Washington "democracy" is a weapon of mass destruction. When Washington brings "democracy" to a country, it means the country's destruction, as in Libya and Iraq. It doesn't mean democracy. Libya is in chaos, a human rights nightmare without an effective government.

Washington installed Nouri al-Maliki as president of Iraq. He lost an election, but remained in power. He has declared his vice president to be a terrorist and ordered his arrest, and is using the state police to arrest Sunni politicians. Syria's Assad is more democratic than Iraq's Maliki.

For a decade Washington has misrepresented its wars of naked aggression as "bringing democracy and human rights to the Middle East." While supposedly doing so, Washington was destroying democracy in the US. Washington has resurrected medieval torture dungeons and self-incrimination. Washington has destroyed due process and habeas corpus. At Obama's request, Congress passed overwhelmingly a law that permits American subjects to be imprisoned indefinitely without a trial or presentation of evidence. Warrantless searches and spying, illegal and unconstitutional at the turn of the 21st century, are now routine.

Obama has even asserted the right, for which there is no law on the books, to murder any American anywhere if the executive branch decides, without presenting any evidence, that the person is a threat to the US government. Any American anywhere can be murdered on the basis of subjective opinion in the executive branch, which increasingly is the only branch of the US government. The other two "co-equal" branches have shriveled away under the "war on terror."

Why is Washington so determined to bring democracy to the Middle East (with the exception of Saudi Arabia, Bahrain, Qatar, and the Emirates), Africa, Iran, Afghanistan, Russia, and China, but is hostile to constitutional rights in America?

The rights that Americans gained from successful revolution against King George III in the 18th century have all been taken away by Bush/Obama in the 21st century. One might think that this would be a news story, but it isn't.

Don't expect the Ministry of Truth to say anything about it.

EMPIRES
THEN AND NOW

March 26, 2012

Great empires, such as the Roman and British, were extractive. The empires succeeded because the value of the resources and wealth extracted from conquered lands exceeded the cost of conquest and governance. The reason Rome did not extend its empire east into Germany was not the military prowess of Germanic tribes but Rome's calculation that the cost of conquest exceeded the value of extractable resources.

The Roman Empire failed because Romans exhausted manpower and resources in civil wars, fighting amongst themselves for power. The British Empire failed because the British exhausted themselves fighting Germany in two world wars.

In his book, *The Rule of Empires* (2010), Timothy H. Parsons replaces the myth of the civilizing empire with the truth of the extractive empire. He describes the successes of the Romans, the Umayyad Caliphate, the Spanish in Peru, Napoleon in Italy, and the British in India and Kenya in extracting resources. To lower the cost of governing Kenya, the British instigated tribal consciousness and invented tribal customs that worked to British advantage.

Parsons does not examine the American Empire, but in his introduction to the book he wonders whether America's empire is really an empire as the Americans don't seem to get any extractive benefits from it. After eight years of war and attempted occupation of Iraq, all Washington has for its efforts is several trillion dollars of additional debt and no Iraqi oil. After ten years of trillion dollar struggle against the Taliban in Afghanistan, Washington has nothing to show for it except possibly some part of the drug trade that can be used to fund covert CIA operations.

America's wars are very expensive. Bush and Obama have doubled the national debt, and the American people have no benefits from it. No riches, no bread and circuses flow to Americans from Washington's wars. So what is it all about?

The answer is that Washington's empire extracts resources from the American people for the benefit of the few powerful interest groups that rule

America. The military-security complex, Wall Street, and the Israel Lobby use the government to extract resources from Americans to serve their profits and power. The US Constitution has been extracted in the interests of the Security State, and Americans' incomes have been redirected to the pockets of the 1 percent. That is how the American Empire functions.

The New Empire is different. It happens without achieving conquest. The American military did not conquer Iraq and has been forced out politically by the puppet government that Washington established. There is no victory in Afghanistan, and after a decade the American military does not control the country.

In the New Empire success at war no longer matters. The extraction takes place *by being at war*. Huge sums of American taxpayers' money have flowed into the American armaments industries and huge amounts of power into Homeland Security. The American empire works by stripping *Americans* of wealth and liberty.

This is why the wars cannot end, or if one does end another starts. Remember when Obama came into office and was asked what the US mission was in Afghanistan? He replied that he did not know what the mission was and that the mission needed to be defined.

Obama never defined the mission. He renewed the Afghan war without telling us its purpose. Obama cannot tell Americans that the purpose of the war is to build the power and profit of the military/security complex at the expense of American citizens.

This truth doesn't mean that the objects of American military aggression have escaped without cost. Large numbers of Muslims have been bombed and murdered and their economies and infrastructure ruined, but not in order to extract resources from them.

It is ironic that under the New Empire the citizens of the empire are extracted of their wealth and liberty in order to extract lives from the targeted foreign populations. Just like the bombed and murdered Muslims, the American people are victims of the American empire.

WHAT IS OBAMACARE?

April 10, 2012

Growing up in the post-war era (after the Second World War), I never expected to live in the strange Kafkaesque world that exists today. The US government can assassinate any US citizen that the executive branch thinks could possibly be a "threat" to the US government, or throw the hapless citizen into a dungeon for the rest of his or her life without presenting any evidence to a court or obtaining a conviction of any crime, or send the "threat" to a puppet foreign state to be tortured until the "threat" confesses to a crime that never occurred or dies at the hands of "freedom and democracy" torturers while professing innocence.

It has never been revealed how a single citizen, or any number thereof, could possibly comprise a threat to a government that has a trillion plus dollars to spend each year on security and weapons, the world's largest navy and air force, 700 plus military bases across the world, large numbers of nuclear weapons, 16 intelligence agencies plus the intelligence agencies of its NATO puppet states and the intelligence service of Israel, and the NSA which records and stores every communication of every American citizen as well as citizens of America's allies and foreign leaders.

Nevertheless, air travelers are subjected to porno-scanning and sexual groping. Cars traveling on Interstate highways can expect to be stopped, with traffic backed up for miles, while Homeland Security and the federalized state or local police conduct searches.

I witnessed one such warrantless search on Easter Sunday. The south bound lanes of I-185 heading into Columbus, Georgia, were at a standstill while black SUV and police car lights flashed. US citizens were being treated by the "security" forces that they finance as if they were "terrorists" or "domestic extremists," another undefined class of Americans devoid of constitutional protections.

These events are Kafkaesque in themselves, but they are ever more so when one considers that these extraordinary violations of the US Constitution fail to be overturned in the Supreme Court. Apparently, American citizens lack standing to defend their civil liberties.

Yet, ObamaCare is before the US Supreme Court. The conservative majority might now utilize the "judicial activism" for which conservatives have criticized liberals. Hypocrisy should no longer surprise us. However, the fight over ObamaCare is not worth five cents.

It is extraordinary that "liberals," "progressives," "Democrats," whatever they are, are defending a "health program" that uses public monies to pay private insurance companies and that raises the cost of health care.

Americans have been brainwashed that "a single-payer system is unaffordable" because it is "socialized medicine." Despite this propaganda, accepted by many Americans, European countries manage to afford single-payer systems. Health care is not a stress, a trauma, an unaffordable expense for European populations. Among the Western Civilized Nations, only the richest, the US, has no universal health care.

The American health care system is the most expensive of all on earth. The reason for the extraordinary expense is the multiple of entities that must make profits. The private doctors must make profits. The private testing centers must make profits. The private specialists who receive the referrals from general practitioners must make profits. The private hospitals must make profits. The private insurance companies must make profits. The profits are a huge cost of health care.

On top of these profits come the costs of preventing and combating fraud. Because private insurance companies resist paying and Medicare pays a small fraction of the medical charges, private health care providers charge as much as they possibly can, knowing that the payments will be cut to the bone. But a billing mistake of even $300 can bankrupt a health care provider due to legal expenses accrued from defending him/her self from fraud accusations.

The beauty of a single-payer system is that it takes the profits out of the system. No one has to make profits. Wall Street cannot threaten insurance companies and private health care companies with being taken over because their profits are too low. No health-provider in a single-payer system has to worry about being displaced in a takeover organized by Wall Street because the profits are too low.

Because a single-payer system eliminates the profits that drive up the costs, Wall Street, Insurance companies, and "free market economists" hate a single-payer medical care system. They prefer a socialized "private" health care system in which public monies flow into private insurance companies.

To make the costs as high as possible, conservatives and the private insurance companies devised ObamaCare. The bill was written by conservative think tanks and the private insurance companies. What the ObamaCare bill does is to drive up the cost of private health insurance by imposing mandated coverage whether or not you need it and use taxes and penalties to subsidize the high ObamaCare medical premiums for those who cannot afford them.

The real purpose of ObamaCare is to guarantee billions of dollars in profits to private insurance companies.

It remains to be seen whether such a ridiculous health care scheme, nowhere extant on earth except in Romney's Massachusetts, will provide health care or just private profits.

WASHINGTON LEADS THE WORLD INTO LAWLESSNESS

April 12, 2012

The US government pretends to live under the rule of law, to respect human rights, and to provide freedom and democracy to citizens. Washington's pretense and the stark reality are diametrically opposed.

Now Washington is forcing as much of the world as it can to overthrow international treaties and international law. Washington has issued a ukase that its word alone is international law. Any country (except those who receive Washington's dispensation) that engages in trade with Iran or purchases Iran's oil will be sanctioned by the US. These countries will be cut off from US markets, and their banking systems will not be able to use banks that process international payments. In other words, Washington's "sanctions against Iran" apply not to Iran but to countries that defy Washington and meet their energy needs with Iranian oil.

According to the *Christian Science Monitor*, so far Washington has granted special privileges to Japan and 10 European Union countries to continue purchasing Iranian oil. Requiring countries to shutdown their economies in order to comply with Washington's vendetta against Iran, a vendetta that has been ongoing ever since the Iranians overthrew the Washington-installed puppet, the Shah of Iran, more than three decades ago, was more than Washington could get away with. Washington has permitted Japan to keep importing between 78-85% of its normal oil imports from Iran.

Washington's dispensations, however, are arbitrary. Dispensations have not been granted to China, India, Turkey, and South Korea. India and China are the largest importers of Iranian oil, and Turkey and South Korea are among the top ten importers. Before looking at possible unintended consequences of Washington's vendetta against Iran, what is Washington's case against Iran?

Frankly, Washington has no case. It is the hoax of "weapons of mass destruction" all over again. Iran, unlike Israel, signed the non-proliferation treaty. All countries that sign the treaty have the right to nuclear energy.

Washington claims that Iran is violating the treaty by developing a nuclear weapon. There is no evidence whatsoever for Washington's assertion. Washington's own 16 intelligence agencies are unanimous that Iran has had no nuclear weapons program since 2003. Moreover, the International Atomic Energy Agency's weapons inspectors are in Iran and have reported consistently that there is no diversion of nuclear material from the energy program to a weapons program.

On the rare occasion when Washington is reminded of the facts, Washington makes a different case. Washington asserts that Iran's rights under the non-proliferation treaty notwithstanding, Iran cannot have a nuclear energy program, because Iran would then have learned enough to be able at some future time to make a bomb. The world's hegemon has unilaterally decided that the possibility that Iran might one day decide to make a nuke is too great a risk to take. It is better, Washington says, to drive up the oil price, disrupt the world economy, violate international law, and risk a major war than to have to worry that a future Iranian government will make a nuclear weapon. This is the Jeremy Bentham tyrannical approach to law that was repudiated by the Anglo-American legal system.

It is difficult to characterize Washington's position as one of good judgment.

Moreover, Washington has never explained why the possibility of an Iranian nuke is such a huge risk. Why is this risk so much greater than the risk associated with Soviet nukes or with the nukes of the US, Russia, China, Israel, Pakistan, India, and North Korea today? Iran is a relatively small country. It does not have Washington's world hegemonic ambitions. Unlike Washington, Iran is not at war with a half dozen countries. Why is Washington destroying America's reputation as a country that respects law and risking a major war and economic dislocation over some possible future development, the probability of which is unknown?

There is no good answer to this question. Lacking evidence for a case against Iran, Washington and Israel have substituted demonization. A lie has been fabricated that the current president of Iran [no longer in office] intends to wipe Israel off the face of the earth.

This lie has succeeded as propaganda even though numerous language experts have proven that the intention attributed to the Iranian president by American-Israeli propaganda is a gross mistranslation of what the president of Iran said. Once again, for Washington and its presstitutes, facts do not count. The agenda is all that counts, and any lie will be used to advance it.

Washington's sanctions could end up biting Washington harder than they bite Iran. What will Washington do if India, China, Turkey and South Korea do not succumb to Washington's threats?

According to recent news reports, India and China are not inclined to inconvenience themselves and harm their economic development in order to support Washington's vendetta against Iran. Having watched China's rapid rise and having observed North Korea's immunity to American attack, South Korea might be wondering how much longer it intends to remain Washington's puppet state. Turkey, where the civilian and somewhat Islamist government has managed to become independent of the US- controlled Turkish military, appears to be slowly coming to the realization that Washington and NATO have Turkey in a "service role" in which Turkey is Washington's agent against its own kind. The Turkish government appears to be reassessing the benefits of being Washington's pawn.

What Turkey and South Korea have to decide is basically whether their countries will be independent countries or be subsumed within Washington's empire. The success of the American-Israeli assault on Iran's independence depends on India and China.

If India and China give the bird to Washington, what can Washington do? Absolutely nothing. What if Washington, drowning in its gigantic hubris, announced sanctions against India and China?

Wal-Mart's shelves would be empty, and America's largest retailer would be hammering on the White House door.

Apple Computer and innumerable powerful US corporations, which have offshored their production for the American market to China, would see their profits evaporate. Together with their Wall Street allies, these powerful corporations would assault the flunky in the White House with more force than the Red Army. The Chinese trade surplus would cease to flow into US Treasury debt. The offshored-to-India back office operations of banks, credit card companies, and customer service departments of utilities throughout the US would cease to function.

In America, chaos would reign. Such are the rewards to the Empire of globalism.

Obama and the neoconservative and Israeli warmongers who urge him on to more wars do not understand that the US is no longer an independent country. America is owned by offshoring corporations and the foreign countries in which the corporations have located their production for US markets. Sanctions on China and India (and South Korea) mean sanctions on US corporations. Sanctions on Turkey mean sanctions on a NATO ally.

Do China, India, South Korea and Turkey realize that they hold the winning cards? Do they understand that they can give the bird to the American Empire, or are they brainwashed like Europe and the rest of the world that the powerful Americans cannot be resisted?

Will China and India exercise their power over the US, or will the two countries fudge the issue and adopt a pose that saves face for Washington while they continue to purchase Iranian oil?

The answer to this question is: how much will Washington pay China and India in secret concessions for their pretense that China and India acknowledge Washington's dictatorial powers over the world?

Without concession to China and India, Washington is likely to be ignored while it watches its power evaporate. A country that cannot produce industrial and manufactured goods, but can only print debt instruments and money is not a powerful country. The American empire can continue to strut around until the proverbial boy says: "The Emperor has no clothes".

Update: China is responding to the sanctions by taking advantage of the drop in demand for Iranian oil to negotiate lower prices for its purchases. The result of Washington's sanctions on Iran is to lower the cost of energy for China and to raise it for everyone else.

HOW LIBERTY
WAS LOST

April 24, 2012

When did things begin going wrong in America?

"From the beginning," answer some. English colonists, themselves under the thumb of a king, exterminated American Indians and stole their lands, as did late 18th and 19th century Americans. Over the course of three centuries, the native inhabitants of America were dispossessed, just as Israelis have been driving Palestinians off their lands since 1948.

Demonization always plays a role. The Indians were savages and the Palestinians are terrorists. Any country that can control the explanation can get away with evil.

I agree that there is a lot of evil in every country and civilization. In the struggle between good and evil, religion has at times been on the side of evil. However, the notion of moral progress cannot so easily be thrown out.

Consider, for example, slavery. In the 1800s, slavery still existed in countries that proclaimed equal rights. Even free women did not have equal rights. Today no Western country would openly tolerate the ownership of humans or the transfer of a woman's property upon her marriage to her husband.

It is true that Western governments have ownership rights in the labor of their citizens through the income tax. This remains as a mitigated form of serfdom. So far, however, no government has claimed the right of ownership over the person himself. A large part of a citizen's income and wealth can be seized, but the person himself cannot be seized and sold to another.

Sometimes I hear from readers that my efforts are pointless, that elites are always dominant and that the only solution is to find one's way into the small, connected clique of elites either through marriage or service to their interests.

This might sound like cynical advice, but it is not devoid of some truth. Indeed, it is the way Washington and New York work, and increasingly the way the entire country operates.

Washington serves powerful private interests, not the public interest. University faculties in their research increasingly serve private interests and decreasingly serve truth. In the US the media is no longer a voice and protection for the people. It is becoming increasingly impossible in America to get a good job without being connected to the system that serves the elites.

The problem I have with this "give up" attitude is that over the course of my life, and more broadly over the course of the 20th century, many positive changes occurred through reforms. It is impossible to have reforms without good will, so even the elites who accepted reforms that limited their powers were part of the moral progress.

Labor unions became a countervailing power to corporate management and Wall Street.

Working conditions were reformed. Civil rights were extended. People excluded by the system were brought into it. Anyone who grew up in the 20th century can add his own examples.

Progress was slow—unduly so from a reformer's standpoint—and mistakes were made. Nevertheless, whether done properly or improperly there was a commitment to the expansion of civil liberty.

This commitment ended suddenly on September 11, 2001. In 11 years the Bush/Obama Regime repealed 800 years of human achievements that established law as a shield of the people and, instead, converted law into a weapon in the hands of the government. Today Americans and citizens of other countries can, on the will of the US executive branch alone, be confined to torture dungeons for the duration of their lives with no due process or evidence presented to any court, or they can be shot down in the streets or exterminated by drone missiles.

The power that the US government asserts over its subjects and also over the citizens of other countries is unlimited. Lenin described unlimited power as power "resting directly on force, not limited by anything, not restricted by any laws, nor any absolute rules."

Washington claims that it is the government of the indispensable country representing the exceptional people and thereby has the right to impose its will and "justice" on the rest of the world and that resistance to Washington constitutes terrorism to be exterminated by any possible means.

Thus, the American neoconservatives speak of nuking Iran for insisting on its independence from American hegemony and exercising its rights to nuclear energy under the non-proliferation treaty to which Iran is a signatory.

In other words, Washington's will trumps international treaties that have the force of law, treaties which Washington itself imposed on the world. According to the neoconservatives and Washington, Iran is not protected by the legal contract that Iran made with Washington when Iran signed the non-proliferation treaty.

Iran finds itself seen by the forces of evil that dominate Washington, D.C. as just another 17th or 18th century American Indian tribe to be deprived of its rights and exterminated.

The vast majority of "superpower" Americans plugged into the Matrix, where they are happy with the disinformation pumped into their brains by Washington and its presstitute media, would demur rather than face my facts.

This raises the question: how does one become unplugged and unplug others from the Matrix? Readers have asked, and I do not have a complete answer.

It seems to happen in a number of ways. Being fired and forced to train your H-1B foreign replacement who works for lower pay, being convicted of a crime that you did not commit, having your children stolen from you by Child Protective Services because bruises from sports activities were alleged to be signs of child abuse, having your home stolen from you because a mortgage based on fraud was given the force of law, being laid off by "free market capitalism" as your age advanced and the premium of your employer-provided medical insurance increased, being harassed by Homeland Security on your re-entry to the US because you are a non-embedded journalist who reports truthfully on US behavior abroad. There are many instances of Americans being jolted into reality by the "freedom and democracy" scales falling away from their eyes.

It is possible that becoming unplugged from the Matrix is a gradual lifelong experience for the few who pay attention. The longer they live, the more they notice that reality contradicts the government's and media's explanations. The few who can remember important stuff after watching reality shows and their favorite sports teams and fantasy movies gradually realize that there is no "new economy" to take the place of the manufacturing economy that was given away to foreign countries. Once unemployed from their "dirty fingernail jobs," they learn that there is no "new economy" to employ them.

Still seething from the loss of the Vietnam War and angry at war protesters, some flag-waving patriots are slowly realizing the consequences of criminalizing dissent and the exercise of First Amendment rights. "You are with us or against us" is taking on threatening instead of reassuring connotations, implying that anyone who opens his or her mouth in any dissent is thereby transformed into an "enemy of the state."

More Americans, but far from enough, are coming to the realization that the extermination of the Branch Davidians at Waco in 1993 was a test run to confirm that the public and Congress would accept the murder of civilians who had been demonized with false charges of child abuse and gun-running.

The next test was the Oklahoma City Bombing in 1995. Whose explanation would prevail: the government's or that of experts? Air Force General Partin, a top expert on explosives, proved conclusively in a heavily documented report given to every member of Congress that the Murrah Federal Office Building blew up from the inside out, not from the outside in from the fertilizer car bomb. But General Partin's facts lost out to the government's propaganda and to Congress' avoidance of cognitive dissonance.

Once the "national security" government learned that its pronouncements and those of the presstitute media carried more weight than the facts presented by experts, conspiracies such as the earlier abandoned Operation Northwoods could be put into play. A 9/11 became possible.

The Pentagon, CIA, and military/security complex were desperate for a new enemy to replace the "Soviet threat," which had ceased to exist. The military/security complex and its servants in Congress were determined to replace the profits made from the Cold War and to preserve and increase the powers accumulated in the Pentagon and CIA. The only possible replacement for the Soviet threat was "Muslim terrorists." Thus, the creation of the "Al Qaeda threat" and the bizarre conflation of this new threat with secular Arab governments such as Iraq's and Syria's, which were the real targets of Islamists.

Despite the evidence provided by experts that secular Arab governments, such as Saddam Hussein's, were allies against revolutionary Islam, US government propaganda linked the secular Iraqi government with Iraq's Islamist enemies.

Once Washington confirmed that the American public was both too ignorant and too inattentive to pay any attention to events that would alter their lives and jeopardize their existence, everything else followed: the PATRIOT Act, the suspension of the Constitution and destruction of civil liberty, Homeland Security which has quickly extended its gestapo reach from airports to train stations, bus terminals, highway road blocks,[53] and to locking down 100 square miles of Boston and its suburbs in a search for one 19 year old wounded kid, the criminalization of dissent, the equating of critics of the government with supporters of terrorism, the home invasions of antiwar protesters and their arraignment before a grand jury, the prosecution of whistleblowers who reveal government crimes, and the equating of journalism organizations such as WikiLeaks with spies. The list goes on.

The collapse not only of truth but also of interest in truth both in the US and in its puppet states is a major challenge to my view that truth and good will are powers that can prevail over evil. It is possible that my perception that moral progress has occurred in various periods of Western civilization is mistaken and that reforms were granted in order to lull populations to new evils being perpetrated.

But I think not. Reason is an important part of human existence. Some are capable of it. Imagination and creativity can escape chains. Good can withstand evil. The extraordinary film, The Matrix, affirmed that people could be unplugged. I believe that even Americans can be unplugged. If I give up this belief, I will cease writing.

TRIALS WITHOUT CRIMES OR EVIDENCE

April 25, 2012

Andy Worthington is a superb reporter who has specialized in providing the facts of the US government's illegal abuse of "detainees," against whom no evidence exists.[54] In an effort to create evidence, the US government has illegally resorted to torture. Torture produces false confessions, plea bargains, and false testimony against others in order to escape further torture.

For these reasons, in Anglo-American law self-incrimination secured through torture has been impermissible as evidence for centuries. So also has the withholding of evidence from the accused and his attorney. Secret evidence cannot be confronted. Secret evidence is distrusted as made-up in order to convict the innocent. The evidence is secret because it cannot stand the light of day.

The US government relies on secret evidence in its cases against alleged terrorists, claiming that national security would be threatened if the evidence were revealed. This is abject nonsense. It is an absurd claim that presenting evidence against a terrorist jeopardizes the national security of the United States.

To the contrary, *not* presenting evidence jeopardizes the security of each and every one of us. Once the government can convict defendants on the basis of secret evidence, even the concept of a fair trial will disappear. Fair trials are already history, but the concept lingers.

Secret evidence destroys the concept of a fair trial. It eliminates justice and the rule of law. Secret evidence means anyone can be convicted of anything. As in Kafka's *The Trial*, people will cease to know the crimes for which they are being tried and convicted.

This extraordinary development in Anglo-American law, a development demanded by the unaccountable Bush/Obama Regime, has not led to impeachment proceedings; nor has it caused an uproar from Congress, the federal courts, the presstitute media, law schools, constitutional scholars, and bar associations.

Having bought the government's 9/11 conspiracy theory, Americans just want someone to pay. They don't care who as long as someone pays. To accommodate this desire, the government has produced some "high value detainees" with Arab or Muslim names.

But instead of bringing these alleged malefactors to trial and presenting evidence against them, the government has kept them in torture dungeons for years trying to create, through the application of pain and psychological breakdown, guilt by self-incrimination in order to fabricate a case against them.

The government has been unsuccessful and has nothing that it can bring to a real court. So the Bush/Obama Regime created and recreated "military tribunals" to lend "national security" credence to the absolute need that non-existent evidence be kept secret.

Andy Worthington in his numerous reports does a good job in providing the history of the detainees and their treatment. He deserves our commendation and support. But what I want to do is to ask some questions, not of Worthington, but about the idea that the US is under terrorist threat.

By this September, 9/11 will be eleven years ago. Yet despite the War on Terror, the loss of Americans' privacy and civil liberties, an expenditure of trillions of dollars on numerous wars, violations of US and international laws against torture, and so forth, no one has been held accountable. Neither the perpetrators nor those whom the perpetrators outwitted, assuming that they are different people, have been held accountable. Going on 11 years and no trials of villains or chastisement of negligent public officials. This is remarkable.

The government's account of 9/11 implies massive failure of all US security and intelligence agencies along with those of our NATO puppets and Israel's Mossad. The government's official line also implies the failure of the National Security Council, NORAD and the US Air Force, Air Traffic Control, Airport Security four times in one hour on the same morning. It implies the failure of the President, the Vice President, the National Security Adviser, the Secretary of Defense.

Many on the left and also libertarians find this apparent failure of the centralized and oppressive government so hopeful that they cling to the official "government failure" explanation of 9/11. However, such massive failure is simply unbelievable. How in the world could the US have survived the Cold War with the Soviets if the US government were so totally incompetent?

This just doesn't smell right. Total failure and no accountability. Despite allegedly being caught off guard by the 9/11 attacks, the FBI was soon able to identify the 19 hijackers despite the fact that apparently none of the alleged hijackers' names are on the passenger lists of the airliners that they allegedly hijacked.

How did 19 passengers get on airplanes in the US without being on the passenger lists?

I do not personally know if the alleged hijackers were on the four airliners. Moreover, defenders of the official 9/11 story claim that the passenger lists released to the public were "victims lists," not passenger lists, because the names of the hijackers were withheld and only released some four years later after 9/11 researchers had had years in which to confuse victims lists with passenger lists. This seems an odd explanation. Why encourage public misinformation for years by withholding the passenger lists and issuing victims lists in their place? It cannot have been to keep the hijackers' names a secret as the FBI released a list of the hijackers several days after 9/11. Even more puzzling, if the hijackers' names were on the airline passenger lists, why did it take the FBI several days to confirm the names and numbers of hijackers?

Researchers have found contradictions in the FBI's accounts of the passenger lists with the FBI adding and subtracting names from its various lists and some names being misspelled, indicating possibly that the FBI doesn't really know who the person is. The authenticity of the passenger lists that were finally released in 2005 is contested, and the list apparently was not presented as evidence by the FBI in the Moussaoui trial in 2006. David Ray Griffin has extensively researched the 9/11 story. In one of his books, *9/11 Ten Years Later*, Griffin writes: "Although the FBI claimed that it had received flight manifests from the airlines by the morning of 9/11, the 'manifests' that appeared in 2005 had names that were not known to the FBI until a day or more after 9/11. These 2005 'manifests,' therefore, could not have been the original manifests for the four 9/11 flights."

The airlines themselves have not been forthcoming. We are left with the mystery of why simple and straightforward evidence, such as a list of passengers, was withheld for years and mired in secrecy and controversy.

We have the additional problem that the BBC and subsequently other news organizations established that 6 or 7 of the alleged hijackers on the FBI's list are alive and well, and have never been part of any terrorist plot.

These points are not even a beginning of the voluminous reasons that the government's 9/11 story looks very thin.

But the American public, being thoroughly plugged into the Matrix, is not suspicious of the government's thin story. Instead, they are suspicious of the facts and of those experts who are suspicious of the government's story. Architects, engineers, scientists, first responders, pilots, and former public officials who raise objections to the official story are written off as conspiracy theorists. Why does an ignorant American public think it knows more than experts? Why do Americans believe a government that told them the intentional lie that Saddam Hussein had weapons of mass destruction despite the fact that the weapons inspectors reported to President Bush that Hussein had no such weapons? And now we see the same thing all over again with the alleged, but non-existent, Iranian nukes.

As Frantz Fanon wrote, the power of cognitive dissonance is extreme. It keeps people comfortable and safe from threatening information. Most Americans find the government's lies preferable to the truth. They don't want to be unplugged from the Matrix. The truth is too uncomfortable for emotionally and mentally weak Americans.

Worthington focuses on the harm being done to detainees. They have been abused for much of their lives. Their innocence or guilt cannot be established because the evidence is compromised by torture, self-incrimination, and coerced testimony against others. They stand convicted by the government's accusation alone. These are real wrongs, and Worthington is correct to emphasize them.

In contrast, my focus is on the harm to America, on the harm to truth and truth's power, on the harm to the rule of law and accountability to the people of the government and its agencies, on the harm to the moral fabric of the US government and to liberty in the United States.

As the adage goes, a fish rots from the head. As the government rots, so does the United States of America.

BREWING A CONFLICT WITH CHINA

April 30, 2012

Washington has pressured the Philippines, whose government it owns, into conducting joint military exercises in the South China Sea. Washington's excuse is that China has territorial disputes with the Philippines, Indonesia, and other countries concerning island and sea rights in the South China Sea. Washington asserts that China's territorial disputes with the likes of Indonesia and the Philippines are a matter of United States' national interests.

Washington has not made it clear what Washington's stake is in the disputes. The reason Washington cannot identify why China's disputes with the Philippines and Indonesia are threats to the United States is that there is no reason. Nevertheless, the undefined "threat" has become the reason Washington needs more naval bases in the Philippines and South Korea.

What this is all about is provoking a long-term cold war conflict with China that will keep profits and power flowing into Washington's military-security complex. Large profits flow to armaments companies. A portion of the profits reflow into campaign contributions to "the people's representatives" in DC and to presidential candidates who openly sell out their country to private interests.

Washington is going to construct new naval bases in the Philippines and on the environmentally protected Jeju Island belonging to South Korea. Washington will waste tax revenues, or print more money, in order to build the unnecessary fleets to occupy these bases. Washington is acquiring bases in Australia for US Marines to protect Australia from China, despite the lack of Chinese threats against Australia. Bush and Obama are the leading models of the "people's president" who sell out the people, at home and abroad, to private interests.

Why is Washington ramping up a new cold war?

The answer begins with President Eisenhower's warning to the American people in his last public address about the military/industrial complex in 1961. I won't quote the warning as it is available online. Eisenhower pointed out to Americans that unlike previous wars after which the US demilitarized, after World War II the Cold War with the Soviet Union kept the power and profits flowing into the military/industrial complex, now known as the military/security complex. President Eisenhower said that the flow of power and profit into the military/industrial complex was a threat to the economic wellbeing and liberty of the American people.

No one paid any attention, and the military/security complex was glad to be rid of the five-star general war hero president when his second term expired. Thanks to the hype about the "Soviet threat," the military/security complex faced an unlimited horizon of mounting profits and power as Americans sacrificed their future to the interests of those who protected Americans from the Soviet threat.

The good times rolled for the armaments companies and security agencies for almost three decades until Reagan and Gorbachev reached agreement and ended the Cold War. When the Soviet Union subsequently collapsed, the future outlook for the power and profit of the US military/security complex was bleak. The one percent was about to lose its fortunes and the secret government was about to lose its power.

The military/security complex went to work to revive the need for a massive "defense" and "security" budget. Among their willing tools were the neoconservatives, with their French Jacobin ideology and Israeli loyalties. The neocons defined America as the "indispensable people." Such extraordinary people as Americans must establish hegemony over the world as the sole remaining superpower. As most neoconservatives are allied with Israel, the Muslim Middle East became the target of opportunity.

Muslims are sufficiently different from Westerners that Muslims are easy to demonize. The demonization began in the neoconservative publications. Once Dick Cheney had the George W. Bush regime staffed with neoconservatives, the next step was to create "threats" to Americans out of verbiage about the Taliban's responsibility for 9/11 and about "Iraqi weapons of mass destruction," including verbal images from Bush's National Security Advisor of "mushroom clouds" over US cities.

No one in the US government or the "free" US media or the media of the US puppet states in England, Europe, Japan, Taiwan, Canada, Australia and South Korea was struck by Washington's proposition that "the world's sole superpower" was threatened by the likes of Iraq and Iran, neither of which had any offensive military capability or any modern weapons, according to the unequivocal reports of the weapons inspectors.

What kind of "superpower" is threatened by Iraq and Iran? Certainly, not a real one.

No one seemed to notice that the alleged 9/11 hijackers were Saudi Arabians, not Afghans or Iraqis, yet it was Afghanistan and Iraq that were labeled "terrorist threats." Saudi Arabia and Bahrain, which do terrorize their subjects, are safe from having America bring them democracy, because they are Washington's puppets, not independent countries.

As fear of nonentities swept over the population of "the world's sole superpower," the demands for war against "America's enemies"—"you are with us or against us"—swept through the country. "Support the troops" plastic ribbons appeared on American cars. Americans went into a frenzy. The "towel heads" were after us, and we had to fight for our lives or be murdered in our beds, shopping centers, and airliner seats.

It was all a hoax to replace the Soviet threat with the Muslim threat.

The problem that developed with the "Muslim threat" is that in order to keep the profits and power flowing into the military/security complex, the promised six-week war in Iraq had to be extended into 8 years. The war in Afghanistan against a few thousand lightly armed Taliban has persisted for more than a decade, longer than the attempted Red Army occupation of Afghanistan.

In other words, the problem with hot wars is that the need *not* to win them in order to keep them going (Korea, Vietnam, Iraq, Afghanistan are all long-term wars never won) in order that the profits and power continue to flow to the military/security complex demoralizes the US military and creates the worldwide impression that the "world's sole superpower" cannot even defeat a few thousand insurgents armed with AK-47s, much less a real army.

In Iraq and Afghanistan more US soldiers have died from demoralization and suicides than from combat. In Iraq, the US was humiliated by having to end the war by putting the Sunni insurgents on the US military payroll and paying them to stop killing US troops. In Korea the US was stopped by an army of a backward third world country that lived on rice. What would happen today if the US "superpower's" militarily confronted China, a country with an economy on which the US is dependent, about equal in size to the US economy, operating on its home territory? The only chance the evil in Washington would have to win would be by nuclear war, which would mean the destruction of the entire world by Washington's hubris.

Fortunately, profits are more important to Washington than ending life on earth. Therefore, in the absence of miscalculation and accident, war with China probably will be avoided, just as it was avoided with the Soviet Union. However, China will be presented by Washington and its prostitute media, especially *The New York Times*, *Washington Post*, and Murdoch's collection of whores, as the rising threat to America. The media story will shift the importance of America's allies from Europe to countries bordering the South China Sea. American taxpayers' money, or newly printed money, will flow into the "new alliance against China."

China's rise is a great boon to the US military/security complex, which governs America in which there is a pretense of "freedom and democracy." China is the profitable replacement for the "Soviet threat." As the days go by, the presstitute media will create in the feeble minds of Americans "The CHINA Threat."

Soon whatever little remains of the US living standards will be sacrificed to Washington's confrontation with China, along with the seizure of our pensions and personal savings in order to deter "the China threat."

If only Americans could be moved to think. Then they might have some prospect of holding on to their incomes, remaining wealth, and liberty. Unfortunately, Americans are so thoroughly plugged into the Matrix that they seem to be doomed, incapable of thought, reason, or ability to comprehend the facts that the rest of world sees clearly.

Can reality be brought to the American people? Perhaps a miracle will occur. Stay tuned.

DOES THE WEST
HAVE A FUTURE?

May 10, 2012

Living in America is becoming very difficult for anyone with a moral conscience, a sense of justice, or a lick of intelligence. Consider:

We have had a second fake underwear bomb plot, a much more fantastic one than the first hoax. The second underwear bomber was a CIA operative or informant allegedly recruited by Al Qaeda, an organization that US authorities have recently claimed to be defeated, in disarray, and no longer significant.

This defeated and insignificant organization, which lacks any science and technology labs, has invented an "invisible bomb" that is not detected by the porno-scanners. A "senior law enforcement source" told *The New York Times* that "the scary part" is that "if they buil[t] one, they probably built more."

Secretary of State Hillary Clinton declared that "the plot itself indicates that the terrorists keep trying to devise more and more perverse and terrible ways to kill innocent people." Hillary said this while headlines proclaimed that the US continues to murder women and children with high-tech drones in Afghanistan, Pakistan, Yemen, and Africa. The foiled fake plot, Hillary alleged, serves as "a reminder as to why we have to remain vigilant at home and abroad in protecting our nation and in protecting friendly nations and peoples like India and others."

FBI Director Robert Mueller told Congress that the fake plot proves the need for warrantless surveillance in order to detect—what, fake plots? In Congress Republican Pete King and Democrat Charles Ruppersberger denounced the media for revealing that the plot was a CIA operation, claiming that the truth threatened the war effort and soldiers' lives.

Even alternative news media initially fell for this fake plot. Apparently, no one stops to wonder how Al Qaeda, which has become so disorganized and helpless that it is on the run and purportedly left its revered leader, Osama bin Laden, in a Pakistani village alone and unguarded to be murdered by US Navy Seals, could catch the CIA off guard with an "undetectable" bomb, to use the description provided by Senate Intelligence Committee chairman Dianne Feinstein, who was briefed on the device by US intelligence personnel.

Notice that the Secretary of State has committed the bankrupt US and its unraveling social safety net to the protection of "India and others" from terrorists. But the real significance of this latest hoax is to introduce into the fearful American public the idea of an undetectable underwear bomb.

What does this bring to mind? Anyone of my generation or any science fiction aficionado immediately thinks of Robert Heinlein's *The Puppet Masters*.

Written in 1951 but set in our time, the book depicts Earth as invaded by small creatures that attach to the human body and take over the person. The humans become the puppets of their masters. Large areas of America succumb to the invaders before the morons in Washington understand that the invasion is real and not a conspiracy theory.

On clothed humans, the creatures cannot be detected, and the edict goes out that anyone clothed is a suspect. Everyone must go about naked. Women are not even allowed to carry purses in their hands, because the creature can be in the purse.

Does this mean, if the CIA, the news sources, and Dianne Feinstein's briefers are correct, that if defeated Al Qaeda has come up with an "undetectable" bomb, we will have to pass through airport security naked?

If so, how will this be possible? If each airline passenger must go through a personal screening by disrobing in a room, how long will it take to clear "airport security"? I doubt there is any place in North or South America that the traveler couldn't drive there faster. Or perhaps this is an answer to depression level US unemployment. Millions of unemployed Americans will be hired to view naked people before they board airliners.

As the Transportation Safety Administration division of Homeland Security has taken its intrusions, unchallenged, into train, bus, and highway travel, are we faced with the total collapse of the clothing industry? Stay tuned.

A couple of years ago a noted philosopher wrote an article in which he suggested that Americans live in an artificial or virtual reality. Another noted philosopher said that he thought there was a 25% chance that this first philosopher was right. I am convinced that he is right. Americans live in the Matrix. Nothing that they know or think that they know is correct.

For example, our non-truth-telling "leaders" continually declare that "Israel is the only democracy in the Middle East." This myth is one of the many reasons rolled out to justify American taxpayers' declining incomes being taxed to provide the Israeli government with the means to murder Palestinians and steal their country.

Israeli democracy a myth, you say? Yes, a myth. According to news reports compiled and reported by Antiwar.com (May 8), the September 4 Israeli elections have been cancelled, because the "opposition leader Shaul Mofaz is joining the government."

Mofaz sold out his party for personal power, a typical politician's behavior.

Mofaz's treachery produced protests from his followers, but, according to news reports, "Israeli police were quick to crack down on the protest, terming it 'illegal' and arresting a number of journalists."

Ah, "Israel is the only democracy in the Middle East."

In truth Israel is a fascist state, one that has been in violation of international law and Christian morality during the entirety of its existence. Yet, in America Israel is a hallowed icon. Like Bush, Cheney, and Obama, millions of American "christians" worship Israel and believe it is "God's calling" for Americans to die for Israel in places like Iraq.

If you believe in murdering your opponents rather than negotiating with them, dispossessing the powerless, creating a fictional world based on lies and paying the corporate media to uphold them, you are part of what the rest of the world perceives as "The West."

Let me back off from being too hard on The West. The French and Greek peoples have shown in the recent elections that they are unplugging from the Matrix and understand that their elites are serving up the 99% as the sacrificial lambs for the mistakes of the 1% mega-rich, who compete with one another in terms of how many billions of dollars or euros, how many yachts, collections of exotic cars, and exotic *Playboy* and *Penthouse* centerfolds they have as personal possessions.

The central banks of the West—the US Federal Reserve, the European Central Bank, and the Bank of England—are totally committed to the prosperity of the mega-rich. No one else counts. Marx and Lenin never had the kind of target that exists today. Yet, the left wing is today so feeble and brainwashed that it does not exist as even a minor countervailing power. The American left wing has even accepted the absurd official account of 9/11 and of Osama bin Laden's murder in Pakistan by Navy Seals. A movement so devoid of mental and emotional strength is useless. It might as well not exist.

People without valid information have no rock to stand on, and that is where the hapless Western peoples are, today. The new tyranny is arising in the West, not in Russia and China. The danger to humanity is in the nuclear button briefcase in the Oval Office and in the brainwashed and militant American population, the most disinformed and gullible people on earth.

THE CASE OF THE MISSING TERRORISTS

May 14, 2012

If there were any real terrorists, Jose Rodriguez would be dead. Who is Jose Rodriguez? He is the criminal who ran the CIA torture program. Most of his victims were not terrorists or even insurgents. Most were hapless individuals kidnapped by warlords and sold to the Americans as "terrorists" for the bounty paid.

If Rodriguez's identity was previously a secret, it is no more. He has been on CBS "60 Minutes" taking credit for torturing Muslims and using the information allegedly gained to kill leaders of Al Qaeda. If terrorists were really the problem that Homeland Security, the FBI and CIA claim, Rodriguez's name would be a struck through item on the terrorists' hit list. He would be in his grave.

So, also, would John Yoo, who wrote the Justice (*sic*) Department memos giving the green light to torture, despite US and International laws prohibiting it. Apparently, Yoo, a professor at the University of California, Berkeley School of Law (Boalt Hall), was ignorant of US and international law. And so was the US Department of Justice. Yoo's legal ignorance did not prevent him from being a tenured professor of law at Berkeley.

Notice that Rodriguez, "The Torturer of the Muslims," doesn't have to hide. He can go on national television, reveal his identity, and revel in his success in torturing and murdering Muslims. Rodriguez has no Secret Service protection. But he appears to have to fear of being an easy mark for assassination by terrorists so capable as to have, allegedly, pulled off 9/11.

Another easy mark for assassination would be former Secretary of Defense Donald Rumsfeld, who staffed up the Pentagon with neoconservative warmongers such as Paul Wolfowitz and Douglas Feith, who in turn concocted the false information used to justify the invasions of Iraq and Afghanistan. Rumsfeld himself declared members of Al Qaeda to be the most vicious and dangerous killers on earth. Yet Rumsfeld, Wolfowitz, Feith, Richard Perle, together with neoconservative media propagandists, such as William Kristol and Max Boot, have been walking around safe for years unmolested by terrorists seeking revenge or bringing retribution to those responsible for as many as 1,000,000 Muslim deaths.

Condi Rice, Colin Powell, who delivered the Speech of Lies to the UN inaugurating the invasion of Iraq, and Dick Cheney, whose minimal Secret Service protection could not withstand a determined assassination attempt, also enjoy lives unmolested by terrorists.

Remember the deck of cards that the Bush regime had with Iraqi faces? If terrorists had a similar deck, all of those named above would be "high value targets." Yet, there has not been a single attempt on any one of them.

Strange, isn't it, that none of the above is faced with a terrorist threat? Yet, the tough, macho Navy Seals who allegedly killed Osama bin Laden must have their identity kept hidden so that they don't become terrorist targets. These American supermen, highly trained killers themselves, purportedly don't dare show their faces, but Rodriguez, Rumsfeld, and Condi Rice can walk around unmolested. Indeed, the Seals' lives are so endangered that President Obama gave up the enormous public relations political benefit of a White House ceremony with the heroic Navy Seals. Very strange behavior for a politician. A couple of weeks after the alleged bin Laden killing, the Seals unit, or most of it, was wiped out in a helicopter crash in Afghanistan.

If you were a Muslim terrorist seeking retribution for Washington's crimes, would you try to smuggle a bomb aboard an airliner in your underwear or shoe in order to blow up people whose only responsibility for Washington's war against Muslims is that they fell for Washington's propaganda? If you wanted to blow up the innocent, wouldn't you instead place your bomb in the middle of the mass of humanity waiting to clear airport security and take out TSA personnel along with passengers? Terrorists could coordinate their attacks, hitting a number of large airports across the US at the same minute. This would be real terror. Moreover, it would present TSA with an insoluble problem: how can people be screened before they are screened?

Or coordinated attacks on shopping malls and sports events?

Why should terrorists, if they exist, bother to kill people when it is easy to cause mayhem without having to kill them? There are a large number of unguarded electric power substations. Entire regions of the country could be shut down. The simplest disruptive act would be to release large quantities of roofing nails in the midst of rush hour traffic in Boston, New York, Washington DC, Atlanta, Dallas, Chicago, Los Angeles, San Francisco. You get the picture: thousands and thousands of cars disabled with flat tires blocking the main arteries for days.

Before some reader accuses me of giving terrorists ideas, ask yourself if you really think people so clever as to have allegedly planned and carried out 9/11 couldn't think of such simple tactics as these, plots that could be carried out without having to circumvent security or kill innocent people? My point isn't what terrorists, if they exist, should do. The point is that the absence of easy-to-do acts of terrorism suggests that the terrorist threat is more hype than reality. Yet, we have an expensive, intrusive security apparatus that seems to have no real function except to exercise power over American citizens.

In place of real terrorists carrying out easily achievable plots, we have dysfunctional "terrorist" plots dreamed up by FBI and CIA agents, who then recruit some hapless or demented dupes, bribing them with money and heroic images of themselves, and supplying them with the plan of action and fake explosives. These are called "sting operations," but they are not. They are orchestrations by our own security agencies that produce fake terrorist plots that are then "foiled" by the security agencies that hatched the plots. Washington's announcement is always: "The public was never in danger." Some terrorist plot! We have never been endangered by one, but the airports have been on orange alert for 11.5 years.

The federal judiciary and brainwashed juries actually treat these concocted plots as real threats to American security despite the government's announcements that the public was never in danger.

The announcements of the "foiled" plots keep the brainwashed public docile and amenable to intrusive searches, warrantless spying, the growth of an unaccountable police state, and endless wars.

The "War on Terror" is a hoax, one that has been successfully used to destroy the US Constitution and to complete the transformation of law from a shield of the people into a weapon in the hands of the state. By destroying habeas corpus, due process, and the presumption of innocence, the "War on Terror" has destroyed our security.

WASHINGTON'S HYPOCRISIES

May 26, 2012

The US government is the second worst human rights abuser on the planet and the sole enabler of the worst—Israel. But this doesn't hamper Washington from pointing the finger elsewhere.

The US State Department's "human rights report" focuses its ire on Iran and Syria, two countries whose real sin is their independence from Washington, and on the bogyman- in-the-making–China, the country selected for the role of Washington's new Cold War enemy.

Hillary Clinton, another in a long line of unqualified Secretaries of State, informed "governments around the world: we are watching, and we are holding you accountable," only we are not holding ourselves accountable or Washington's allies like Bahrain, Saudi Arabia, Israel, and the NATO puppets.

Hillary also made it "clear to citizens and activists everywhere: You are not alone. We are standing with you," only not with protesters at the Chicago NATO summit or with the Occupy Wall Street protesters, or anywhere else in the US where there are protests..

The State Department stands with the protesters funded by the US in the countries whose governments the US wishes to overthrow. Protesters in the US stand alone as do the occupied Palestinians who apparently have no human rights to their homes, lands, olive groves, or lives.

Here are some arrest numbers for a few recent US protests. The *New York Daily News* reports that as of November 17, 2011, 1,300 Occupy Wall Street protesters were arrested in New York City alone.[55] Fox News reported (October 2, 2011) that 700 protesters were arrested on the Brooklyn Bridge.[56] At the NATO summit in Chicago last week, 90 protesters were arrested (*Chicago Journal*).[57]

In the US some protesters are being officially categorized as "domestic extremists" or "domestic terrorists," a new threat category that Homeland Security announced is now the focus of its attention, displacing Muslim terrorists as the number one threat to the US. In September 2010, federal police raided the homes of peace activists in Chicago and Minneapolis. The FBI is trying to concoct a case against them by claiming that the peace activists donated money to the Popular Front for the Liberation of Palestine. As demanded by Israel, the US government has designated the PFLP as a terrorist group.

In Chicago last week, among the many arrested NATO protesters with whom the State Department does not stand are three young white Americans arrested for "domestic terrorism" in what Dave Lindorff reports was "a warrantless house invasion reminiscent of what US military forces are doing on a daily [and nightly] basis in Afghanistan."[58] If the US government, which stands with protesters everywhere except in America, Bahrain, Saudi Arabia, Yemen and Palestine, can make this into a terrorism case, the three Americans can be convicted on the basis of secret evidence or simply be incarcerated for the rest of their lives without a trial.

Meanwhile the three American "domestic terrorists" are being held in solitary confinement. Like many of the NATO protesters, they came from out of town. Brian Church, 20 years old, came from Fort Lauderdale, Florida. Jared Chase, 27, came from Keene, New Hampshire. Brent Betterly, 24, came from Oakland Park, Florida. Charged with providing material support for terrorism, the judge set their bail at $1.5 million each.

These three are not charged with actually throwing a Molotov cocktail at a person or thing. They are charged with coming to Chicago with the idea of doing so. Somehow the 16 federal intelligence agencies plus those of our NATO puppets and Israel were unable to discover the 9/11 plot in the making, but the Chicago police knew in advance why two guys from Florida and one from New Hampshire came to Chicago. The domestic terrorism cases turn out to be police concoctions that are foiled before they happen, so we have many terrorists but no actual terrorist acts.

Two other young Americans are being framed by their Human Rights Government. Sebastian Senakiewicz, 24, of Chicago is charged with "falsely making a terrorist threat," whatever that means. His bail was set at $750,000. Mark Neiweem, 28, of Chicago is charged with "solicitation for explosives or incendiary devices." His bail is set at $500,000.

This is human rights in America. But the State Department's human rights report never examines the US. It is a political document aimed at Washington's chosen enemies.

Meanwhile, Human Rights America continues to violate the national sovereignty of Pakistan, Yemen, and Afghanistan by sending in drones, bombs, special forces and in Afghanistan, 150,000 US soldiers to murder people, usually women, children and village elders. Weddings, funerals, children's soccer games, schools and farmers' houses are also favorite targets for Washington's attacks. On May 25 the *Pakistani Daily Times* reported that Pakistani Foreign Office spokesman Moazzam Ali Khan strongly condemned the drone attacks: "We regard them as a violation of our territorial integrity. They are in contravention of international law. They are illegal, counterproductive and totally unacceptable."[59]

The US reportedly funnels money to the Iranian terrorist group, MEK, declared terrorists by no less than the US State Department. But it is OK as long as MEK is terrorizing Iran. Washington stands with MEK's protests delivered via bombs and the assassin's bullet. After all, we have to bring freedom and democracy to Iran, and violence is Washington's preferred way to achieve this goal.

Washington is desperate to overthrow the Syrian government in order to get rid of the Russian naval base. On May 15 the *Washington Post* reported that Washington is coordinating the flow of arms to Syrian rebels. Washington's justification for interfering in Syria's internal affairs is human rights charges against the Syrian government. However, a UN report finds that the rebels are no more respectful of human rights than the Syrian government.[60] The rebels torture and murder prisoners and kidnap civilians wealthy enough to bring a ransom.

NATO, guided by Washington, violated the UN resolution declaring a no-fly zone over Libya. NATO, in blatant violation of the UN resolution, provided the air attack on the Libyan government that enabled the CIA-supported "rebels" to overthrow Gaddafi, killing many Libyan civilians in the process.

Under the Nuremberg standard (principle VI.a.i),[61] it is a war crime to launch a war of aggression, which is what Washington and its NATO puppets launched against Libya, but no sweat, Washington brought Libya freedom and democracy.

Assassinating foreign opponents is the West's preferred diplomacy. The British were at ease with it, and Washington picked up the practice. In his 2010 book, *The Decline and Fall of the British Empire*, Cambridge University historian Piers Brendon, the Keeper of the Churchill Archives, reports from the documents he has at hand, that in the build up to the "Suez Crisis" in 1956, British Prime Minister Anthony Eden told Foreign Office minister Anthony Nutting, "I want him [Nasser, Egypt's leader] murdered."

Brendon goes on to report: "Doubtless at the Prime Minister's behest, the Secret Intelligence Service did hatch plots to assassinate Nasser and to topple his government. Its agents, who proposed to pour nerve gas into Nasser's office through the ventilation system, were by no means discreet." The secret agents talked too much, and the scheme never came to fruition.

Last week in Malaysia a war crimes tribunal found George W. Bush, Dick Cheney, Donald Rumsfeld and their legal advisers, Alberto Gonzales, David Addington, William Haynes II, Jay Bybee, and John Choon Yoo guilty of war crimes.

But don't expect Washington to take any notice. The war crimes convictions are merely a "political statement."

CAN THE WORLD SURVIVE WASHINGTON'S HUBRIS?

June 28, 2012

When President Reagan nominated me as Assistant Secretary of the Treasury for Economic Policy, he told me that we had to restore the US economy, to rescue it from stagflation, in order to bring the full weight of a powerful economy to bear on the Soviet leadership in order to convince them to negotiate the end of the cold war. Reagan said that there was no reason to live any longer under the threat of nuclear war.

The Reagan administration achieved both goals, only to see these accomplishments discarded by successor administrations. It was Reagan's own vice president and successor, George Herbert Walker Bush, who first violated the Reagan-Gorbachev understandings by incorporating former constituent parts of the Soviet Empire into NATO and taking Western military bases to the Russian frontier.

The process of surrounding Russia with military bases continued unabated through successor US administrations with various "color revolutions" financed by the US National Endowment for Democracy, regarded by many as a front for the CIA. Washington even attempted to install a Washington-controlled government in Ukraine and did succeed in this effort in former Soviet Georgia, the birthplace of Joseph Stalin. The President of Georgia, a country located between the Black Sea and the Caspian Sea, is a Washington puppet. Recently, he announced that former Soviet Georgia is on schedule to become a NATO member in 2014.

Those old enough to remember know that NATO, the North Atlantic Treaty Organization, was an alliance between Western Europe and the US against the threat of the Red Army overrunning Western Europe. The North Atlantic is a long, long way from the Black and Caspian Seas. What is the purpose of Georgia being a NATO member except to give Washington a military base on the Russian underbelly?

The evidence is simply overwhelming that Washington—both parties—has Russia and China targeted. Whether the purpose is to destroy both countries or merely to render them unable to oppose Washington's world hegemony is unclear at this time. Regardless of the purpose, nuclear war is the likely outcome as Washington's growing arrogance and hubris carry its provocations to an extreme

The presstitute American press pretends that an evil Syrian government is murdering innocent citizens who only want democracy and that if the UN won't intervene militarily, the US must in order to save human rights. Russia and China are vilified by US functionaries for opposing any pretext for a NATO invasion of Syria.

The facts, of course, are different from those presented by the presstitute American media and members of the US government. The Syrian "rebels" are well armed with military weapons. The "rebels" are battling the Syrian army. The rebels massacre civilians and report to their media whores in the West that the deed was done by the Syrian government, and the Western presstitutes spread the propaganda.

Someone is arming the "rebels" as obviously the weapons can't be purchased in local Syrian markets. Most intelligent people believe the weapons are coming from the US or from US surrogates.

So, Washington has started a civil war in Syria, as it did in Libya, but this time the gullible Russians and Chinese have caught on and have refused to permit a UN resolution like the one the West exploited against Gaddafi.

To get around this roadblock, fish out an ancient Phantom fighter jet from the 1960s Vietnam War era and have Turkey fly it into Syria. The Syrians will shoot it down, and then Turkey can appeal to its NATO allies to come to its aid against Syria. Denied the UN option, Washington can invoke its obligation under the NATO treaty, and go to war in defense of a NATO member against a demonized Syria. (Washington tried it, but it didn't work.)

The neoconservative lie behind Washington's wars of hegemony is that the US is bringing democracy to the invaded and bombed countries. To paraphrase Mao, "democracy comes out of the barrel of a gun." However, the Arab Spring has come up short on democracy, as have Iraq and Afghanistan, two countries "liberated" by US democratic invasions.

What the US is bringing is civil wars and the breakup of countries, as President Bill Clinton's regime achieved in former Yugoslavia. The more countries can be torn into pieces and dissolved into rival factions, the more powerful is Washington.

Russia's Putin understands that Russia itself is threatened not only by Washington's funding of the "Russian opposition," but also by the strife among Muslims unleashed by Washington's wars against secular Muslim states, such as Iraq and Syria. This discord spreads into Russia itself and presents Russia with problems such as Chechen terrorism.

When a secular state is overthrown, the Islamist factions contend for power. The internal strife renders the countries impotent. As I wrote previously, the West always prevails in the Middle East because the Islamist factions hate one another more than they hate their Western conquerors. Thus, when Washington destroys secular, non-Islamist governments as in Iraq and now targeted in Syria, the Islamists emerge and battle one another for supremacy. This suits Washington and Israel as these states cease to be coherent opponents.

Russia is vulnerable, because Putin is demonized by Washington and the US media and because Putin's Russian opposition is financed by Washington and serves US, not Russian, interests. The turmoil that Washington is unleashing in Muslim states leaks back to Russia's Muslim populations.

It has proved to be more difficult for Washington to interfere in China's internal affairs, although discord has been sowed in some provinces. Several years from now, the Chinese economy is expected to exceed in size the US economy, with an Asian power displacing a Western one as the world's most powerful economy.

Washington is deeply disturbed by this prospect. In the thrall and under the control of Wall Street and other special interest business groups, Washington is unable to rescue the US economy from its decline. The short-run gambling profits of Wall Street, the war profits of the military/security complex, and the profits from offshoring the production of goods and services for US markets have far more representation in Washington than the wellbeing of US citizens. As the US economy sinks, the Chinese economy rises.

Washington's response is to militarize the Pacific. The US Secretary of State has declared the South China Sea to be an area of American national interest. The US is wooing the Philippine government, playing the China threat card, and working on getting the US Navy invited back to its former base at Subic Bay. Recently there were joint US/Philippines military/naval exercises against the "China threat."

The US Navy is reallocating fleets to the Pacific Ocean and constructing a new naval base on a South Korean island. US Marines are now based in Australia and are being reallocated from Japan to other Asian countries. The Chinese are not stupid. They understand that Washington is attempting to corral China.

For a country incapable of occupying Iraq after 8 years and incapable of occupying Afghanistan after 11 years, to simultaneously take on two nuclear powers is an act of insanity. The hubris in Washington, fed daily by the crazed neocons, despite extraordinary failure in Iraq and Afghanistan, has now targeted formidable powers—Russia and China. The world has never in its entire history witnessed such idiocy. The psychopaths, sociopaths, and morons who prevail in Washington are leading the world to destruction.

The government in Washington, regardless whether Democrat or Republican, regardless of the outcome of the next election, is the greatest threat to life on earth that has ever existed.

Moreover, the only financing the Washington criminals have is the printing press.Will the US economy complete its collapse before the war criminals in Washington can destroy the world?

CAN AMERICANS ESCAPE THE DECEPTION?

July 4, 2012

Hot Air Day is upon us. On July 4 hot air will spew forth all over the country as dignitaries deliver homilies to our "freedom and democracy" and praise "our brave troops" who are protecting our freedom by "killing them over there before they come over here."

Not a single one of these speeches will contain one word of truth. No speaker will lament the death of the US Constitution or urge his audience to action to restore the only document that protects their liberty. No speaker will acknowledge that in the 21st century the Bush/Obama Regime, with the complicity of the Department of Justice, federal courts, Congress, presstitute media, law schools, bar associations, and an insouciant public, have murdered the Constitution in the name of the "war on terror."

As in medieval times, American citizens can be thrown into dungeons and never accounted for. No evidence or charges need be presented to a court. No trial is required, and no conviction.

As in tyrannies, US citizens can be executed at the sole discretion of the despot in the Oval Office, who sits there drawing up lists of people to be murdered.

Protestors exercising their constitutionally guaranteed rights to freedom of speech and freedom of association are attacked by armed police, beaten, tasered, tear-gassed, pepper sprayed, and arrested.

Whistleblowers who report the government's crimes are prosecuted despite the statute that protects them.

US soldier Bradley Manning, who allegedly gave Wikileaks the documents revealing US war crimes, including the video of US soldiers in a helicopter gunship enjoying themselves murdering civilians walking along the street as if the soldiers were playing a video game, has been arrested and held in conditions of torture while the government tries to invent a case against him.

According to the US Military Code, US soldiers are required to make war crimes known. However, the law on the books provided no protection to Bradley Manning, and conservative Republicans whom I know are foaming at the mouth for Manning to be executed for letting out the truth. The truth, what is mere truth compared to the "exceptionalism of the great American people"? America has carte blanche to do whatever it wishes to the unexceptional peoples. Manning deserves to die, they say, because he took the side of the oppressed and not the side of the American oppressors.

After the Swedish prosecutorial office dropped the case against Wikileaks' Julian Assange, ruling that the charges of rape had no foundation, another prosecutor, many believe at the urging of the US government, demanded Assange be extradited from England in order to be questioned. Normally, extradition only applies to those who have been charged with a crime and for whom a warrant has been issued, which is most certainly not the case with Assange. But, of course, if Washington wants Assange, Washington will be sure every law is broken or bent until they get him. The Swedish puppet will do the exceptional country's will and be paid well for its service.

Peace activists in several states had their homes invaded by FBI, computers and personal records taken, and a grand jury was convened in an attempt to indict them for supporting terrorism by their protests of Washington's illegal wars, wars that are war crimes under the Nuremberg standard established by the US government itself.

None of this will be mentioned in July 4 patriotic speeches. The inebriated masses will be wrapped in the flag and return home full of the hubris that despises lesser foreigners, such as Muslims, Arabs, Chinese, and the French.

And no dignitary will mention that those that "we are killing over there" are mainly women, children, village elders, and aid workers. The US troops seem to specialize in soft targets like weddings, funerals, kids' soccer games, farm houses, and schools.

Recently Washington reduced the "collateral damage" count by declaring every murdered male of military age to have been a Taliban fighter or terrorist. Obviously, Washington has no way of knowing whether they were or not, but Washington's declaration is intended as a green light to murder Afghan males of military age.

Currently, Washington has wars underway, or occupations, or is violating the sovereignty of countries with drones and/or troops in seven Muslim countries, and is arming rebels in Syria. All of this is being done without the constitutionally-required authorization by Congress, allegedly the people's representatives. What a joke! In short, in "freedom and democracy" America, the people have no voice and no rights and no representatives. Yet, this huge deficit of democracy and liberty will pass unmentioned by July 4th orators.

The crimes against humanity, the dismantling of the US Constitution and the lawlessness both domestic and international that define 21st century America are the results of September 11, 2001.

Washington's account of 9/11 is the wildest conspiracy theory known to mankind. The absurdity of Washington's account is as follows: A few Saudi Arabians without any government's backing or that of any intelligence service outwitted not only the CIA and the FBI but all 16 US intelligence agencies, even the Defense Intelligence Agency and the National Security Agency which spies on the entire world, together with the intelligence agencies of all of Washington's NATO allies and Israel's Mossad, which has infiltrated every radical Muslim group.

These humble Saudis of no known distinction or powers also simultaneously outwitted the National Security Council, NORAD, the Pentagon, Air Traffic Control, and caused Airport Security to fail four times in one hour on the same morning.

In other words, every part of America's defenses failed at the same moment.

Think about that for a minute. If such a thing had actually happened, the President, Vice President, Congress, and media would have been demanding to know how such universal failure of every aspect of the national security state was possible. An investigation would have started immediately, not over a year later as a result of pressure from 9/11 families who could not be bought off with monetary payments. Such complete and total failure of every aspect of US security would mean that Americans were not safe one single minute during the 40-year stand-off with the Soviet Union. At any moment the Soviets could have utterly destroyed the US and we would never have known what hit us.

In a real investigation, the 9/11 evidence would not have been illegally destroyed, and the investigation would have been conducted by experts, not by government agencies assigned a cover-up and by political hacks. The NIST report is abject nonsense. It explains nothing. It is a fabricated computer simulation. The co-chairmen and legal counsel of the 9/11 Commission later wrote books in which they stated that information was withheld from the commission, the military lied to the commission, and the commission "was set up to fail." Yet, these astounding admissions by the leaders of the 9/11 Commission had no impact on Congress, the presstitute media, or the public. All heads were in the sand. Please, whatever you do, don't make us emotional weaklings face the facts.

More than one hundred firefighters, police, first responders, and building maintenance personnel report hearing and experiencing scores of explosions in the twin towers, including powerful explosions in the sub-basements prior to the airliners hitting the towers.

Distinguished scientists, authors of many peer-reviewed scientific papers, report finding both reacted and unreacted nano-thermite in the dust from the towers, tested it for its explosive and high-heat producing ability, and reported the unequivocal results.

Seventeen hundred architects and engineers have testified in a petition to Congress that the three World Trade Center buildings were not brought down by fire and airplanes and have demanded a real scientific investigation of the cause of the buildings' destruction.

Yet, we are left with the paradox that scientific opinion based on careful examination of the remaining evidence has been designated by the ignorant and unwashed as a "conspiracy theory," while Washington's absurd conspiracy theory stands as the truth of the event.

Architects and Engineers for 9/11 Truth headed by high-rise architect Richard Gage has driven the final nail in the coffin of Washington's concocted conspiracy theory with its new film: "9/11: Explosive Evidence—Experts Speak Out," and they do speak out. Scores of top level demolition experts and experts on the design, engineering, and construction of high rise steel structures provide the scientific, architectural, and engineering reasons that the three World Trade Center buildings came down only with the assistance of explosives that were placed and timed to remove the powerful structural support and permit the sudden collapse of the buildings. As the buildings were engineered and constructed according to known and tested principles that absolutely prevent rapid collapse, fire and structural damage that two of the three skyscrapers suffered from airliners could not possibly have caused the sudden disintegration of the three buildings.

I saw the film in Atlanta on July 2. Atlanta was a stop on the 32-city premier of the film. The film was shown at the 7 Stages Theater on Euclid Avenue, the former Euclid Theater to which 65 years ago we kids used to ride our bikes to see Tarzan battle giant reptiles and ride elephants to victory over evil black tribesmen or evil white hunters, or to watch Randolph Scott bring justice with his six-shooter to a town ruled by black hats, or to witness the brave American soldiers liberate Europe from the Nazis. We never dreamed that we, residents of the "land of the free" would be menaced by a gestapo police state.

America's descent into a gestapo police state could be arrested, perhaps, if Americans were not so ignorant of science or were capable of even realizing that what they see with their own eyes when they watch videos of the twin towers' destruction is buildings blowing up, not buildings falling down from structural damage. Building 7's destruction is the total and complete picture of controlled demolition.

At the end of the powerful film, psychologists explain why the majority of a population lacks the mental and emotional strength to confront highly disturbing facts. A government that so thoroughly spies on its population as Washington does obviously knows its population's profile and sees nothing but weakness and fear that can be manipulated.

What fact is more disturbing than the likely fact that 9/11 was a false flag event designed to provide the neoconservatives with their "new Pearl Harbor" in order to launch Washington's Wars of Hegemony in the Middle East, and from there to Iran and to the nuclear powers: Russia and China, which are being encircled, as Iran has been, with US military bases?

What we are experiencing is a replay of the French Revolution, this time on a world stage. Napoleon, the inheritor of the French Revolution, conquered Europe several times in the effort to expand the New Order in France to all of Europe. The French Revolution was the first claim of a New World Order, but at that time the world was Europe.

Washington's "wars of liberation" are wars of world hegemony and wars of massive profits for the military/security complex. The combination of power and money that are the motives for Washington's concocted wars are hidden motives, wrapped in the flag, patriotic sentiments, and fear of dark-skinned demonized Muslims.

Can Architects and Engineers for 9/11 truth or any truth break through and liberate Americans from the artificial reality created by government liars and a corrupt presstitute media, or are Americans doomed to expire in the Matrix that has been created for them?

Perhaps the hope is that the economy will collapse under the would-be hegemons, and people who will not fight for principles and their liberty will fight for their economic survival.

WAR
ON ALL FRONTS

July 16, 2012

The Russian government has finally caught on that its political opposition is being financed by the US taxpayer-funded National Endowment for Democracy and other CIA/State Department fronts in an attempt to subvert it and install an American puppet state in the geographically largest country on earth, the one country with a nuclear arsenal sufficient to deter Washington's aggression.

Just as earlier this year Egypt expelled hundreds of people associated with foreign-funded "non-governmental organizations" (NGOs) for "instilling dissent and meddling in domestic policies," the Russian Duma (parliament) has just passed a law that Putin is expected to sign that requires political organizations that receive foreign funding to register as foreign agents. The law is based on the US law requiring the registration of foreign agents.

Much of the Russian political opposition consists of foreign-paid agents, and once the law passes leading elements of the Russian political opposition will have to sign in with the Russian Ministry of Justice as foreign agents of Washington. The Itar-Tass News Agency reported on July 3 that there are about 1,000 organizations in Russia that are funded from abroad and engaged in political activity. Try to imagine the outcry if the Russians were funding 1,000 organizations in the US engaged in an effort to turn America into a Russian puppet state. (In the US the Russians would find a lot of competition from Israel.)

The Washington-funded Russian political opposition masquerades behind "human rights" and says it works to "open Russia." What the disloyal and treasonous Washington-funded Russian "political opposition" means by "open Russia" is to open Russia for brainwashing by Western propaganda, to open Russia to economic plunder by the West, and to open Russia to having its domestic and foreign policies determined by Washington.

"Non-governmental organizations" are very governmental. They have played pivotal roles in both financing and running the various "color revolutions" that have established American puppet states in former constituent parts of the Soviet Empire. NGOs have been called "coup d'etat machines," and they have served Washington well in this role. They are currently working in Venezuela against Chavez.

Of course, Washington is infuriated that its plans for achieving hegemony over a country too dangerous to attack militarily have been derailed by Russia's awakening, after two decades, to the threat of being politically subverted by Washington-financed NGOs. While Washington requires foreign-funded organizations to register as foreign agents (unless they are Israeli funded), this fact doesn't stop Washington from denouncing the new Russian law as "anti-democratic," "police state," blah-blah. Caught red-handed in subversion, Washington calls Putin names. The pity is that most of the brainwashed West will fall for Washington's lies, and we will hear more about "gangster state Russia."

China is also in Washington's crosshairs. China's rapid rise as an economic power is perceived in Washington as a dire threat. China must be contained. Obama's US Trade Representative has been secretly negotiating for the last 2 or 3 years a Trans Pacific Partnership, whose purpose is to derail China's natural economic leadership in its own sphere of influence and replace it with Washington's leadership.

Washington is also pushing to form new military alliances in Asia and to establish new military bases in the Philippines, South Korea, Thailand, Vietnam, Australia, New Zealand, and elsewhere.

Washington quickly inserted itself into Chinese disputes with Vietnam and with the Philippines. Washington aligned with its former Vietnamese enemy in its dispute with China over the resource rich Paracel and Spratly islands and with the Philippines in its dispute with China over the resource rich Scarborough Shoal.

Thus, like England's interference in the dispute between Poland and National Socialist Germany over the return to Germany of German territories that were given to Poland as World War I booty, Washington sets the stage for war.

China has been cooperative with Washington, because the offshoring of the US economy to China has been an important component in China's unprecedented high rate of economic development. American capitalists got their short-run profits, and China got the capital and technology to build an economy that in another few years will have surpassed the sinking US economy. Jobs offshoring, mistaken for free trade by free market economists, has built China and destroyed America.

Washington's growing interference in Chinese affairs has convinced China's government that military countermeasures are required to neutralize Washington's announced intentions to build its military presence in China's sphere of influence. Washington's view is that only Washington, no one else, has a sphere of influence, and Washington's sphere of influence is the entire world.

On July 14 China's official news agency, Xinhua, said that Washington was interfering in Chinese affairs and making China's disputes with Vietnam and the Philippines impossible to resolve.

It looks as if an over-confident US government is determined to have a three-front war: Syria, Lebanon, and Iran in the Middle East, China in the Far East, and Russia in Europe. This would appear to be an ambitious agenda for a government whose military was unable to occupy Iraq after nine years or to defeat the lightly-armed Taliban after eleven years, and whose economy and those of its NATO puppets is in trouble and decline with corresponding rising internal unrest and loss of confidence in political leadership.[62]

SYRIA: WASHINGTON'S LATEST WAR CRIME

July 26, 2012

One wonders what Syrians are thinking, as "rebels" vowing to "free Syria" take the country down the same road to destruction as "rebels" in Libya. Libya, under Gaddafi a well run country whose oil revenues were shared with the Libyan people instead of being monopolized by a princely class as in Saudi Arabia, now has no government and is in disarray, with contending factions vying for power.

Just as no one knew who the Libyan "rebels" were, with elements of Al Qaeda reportedly among them, no one knows who the Syrian "rebels" are, or indeed if they are even rebels. Some "rebels" appear to be bandit groups who seize the opportunity to loot and to rape and set themselves up as the governments of villages and towns. Others appear to be Al Qaeda.

The fact that the "rebels" are armed is an indication of interference from outside. There have been reports that Washington has ordered its Saudi and Bahraini puppet governments to supply the "rebels" with military weaponry. Some suspect that the explosion that killed the Syrian Defense Minister and the head of the government's crisis operations was not the work of a suicide bomber but the work of a US drone or missile, reminiscent of Washington's failed attempts to murder Saddam Hussein. Regardless, Washington depicted the terror attack as a success, declaring that it showed the rebels were gaining "real momentum" and called on the Syrian government to respond to the attack by resigning.

The following is from a leaked intelligence document describing a previous Western terrorist intervention in Syria just in case any reader is so naive as to think that "our government would never do that."

> In order to facilitate the action of liberative forces ...
> a special effort should be made to eliminate certain key
> individuals. ...[to] be accomplished early in the course of
> the uprising and intervention, ...

Once a political decision has been reached to proceed with internal disturbances in Syria, CIA is prepared, and SIS (MI6) will attempt to mount minor sabotage and coup de main incidents within Syria, working through contacts with individuals.

… Incidents should not be concentrated in Damascus …

Further: a "necessary degree of fear ... frontier incidents and (staged) border clashes", would "provide a pretext for intervention... the CIA and SIS [MI6] should use … capabilities in both psychological and action fields to augment tension." (Joint US-UK leaked Intelligence Document, London and Washington, 1957) (globalreasearch.ca)

Obama has not said why his government is so desperate to overthrow the Syrian government. The current president was an eye doctor in London who was brought back to Syria to replace his father, who had passed away, as president of the country. Washington masks its real motives with high-sounding humanitarian rhetoric, but they are nonetheless transparent.

One motive is to get rid of the Russian naval base in Syria, thus depriving Russia of its only Mediterranean base.

A second motive is to eliminate Syria as a source of arms and support to Hizbullah in order that Israel can succeed in its attempts to occupy southern Lebanon and acquire its water resources. Hizbullah's fighters have twice defeated the Israeli military's attempts to invade and to occupy southern Lebanon.

A third motive is to destroy the unity of Syria with sectarian conflict, as Washington destroyed Libya and Iraq, and facilitate Syria's warring factions' dismemberment of the country, thus removing another obstacle to Washington's hegemony.

Syria, a secular Arab state, like Iraq was, is ruled by a political party composed of Alawis, more or less Shia Muslims. The Alawis comprise about 12% of the Syrian population and are regarded as heretics by the Sunni Muslims who comprise about 74% of the Syrian population. Thus the orchestrated "uprising" appeals to many Sunnis who see the opportunity to take over. (In Iraq it was a Sunni minority that ruled a Shia majority, and in Syria it is the opposite.)

The divisions among Arabs make Arabs vulnerable to Western interference and rule. The Sunni-Shia split makes it impossible for an Arab country to unite against an invader or for one Arab country to come to the aid of another. In 1990 the Shia Syrian government lined up with the US against the Sunni Iraq government in the First Iraq War. Neither Lawrence of Arabia, Nasser, nor Gaddafi succeeded in creating an Arab consciousness.

Washington's violent overthrow of other governments is always cloaked in moralistic verbiage. First the target is demonized, and then Washington's naked aggression is described as "bringing freedom and democracy," "overthrowing a brutal dictator," "protecting women's rights." Any assortment of cant words and phrases seems to work.

Hillary Clinton has been especially strident in advocating the overthrow of the Syrian government. The silly woman even issued threats to Russia and China for daring to block Washington's attempt to use a UN resolution as cover for invading Syria. Washington misrepresents the Syrian government's resistance to being overthrown as a government conducting terror against its own people. But Washington had no condemnation for the terror attack, whether its own or that of a suicide bomber, that killed high-level Syrian government officials. Washington's double standard prompted the Russian Foreign Minister, Sergey Lavrov, to accuse Washington of having "a sinister position."

Indeed, Washington does. But what is surprising about Washington's sinister position after Iraq, Afghanistan, Libya, Somalia, Yemen, and Pakistan? Undoubtedly, after Syria is overthrown, Washington will move on to Iran. Russia itself is already being surrounded by US missile bases, and the Russian government has a disloyal and traitorous political opposition financed by American money. China is confronting a rapid buildup of US air, naval, and troop bases in the Pacific. How long before China's government has a disloyal opposition financed by Washington?

The hegemon is on the march, but what short-sighted Syrian Sunnis see is a chance to overthrow the Alawite Shia. The Syrian Sunnis will ally with Washington despite the fact that Washington overthrew the Iraqi Sunnis. Few Arabs, it seems, mind being puppets of a foreign regime that hands out billions of dollars and helps them to triumph over their fellow Muslims.

Washington loosely refers to Syrian President Assad as a "dictator" or "brutal dictator," but obviously if Assad is a dictator he is not very effective in that role. Normally, dictators don't permit an opposition to rise, much less arm itself. It would be more accurate to say that the ruling party is authoritarian, but the ruling party has introduced elements of democracy with the new constitution.

As Iraq has proved, Arab governments have to be authoritarian if their Sunni and Shia populations are not to be constantly engaged in civil war. Both Bush and Obama claim that Washington brought "freedom and democracy" to Iraq. However, the ongoing violence in Iraq is as intense or more intense than under the American occupation. Here are the reports for the last three days:

July 23: "A wave of bomb attacks and shootings in Baghdad and north of the capital has killed at least 107 people. At least 216 were wounded."

July 24: "A second day of intensified attacks left at least 145 Iraqis killed and 379 more wounded."

July 25: "Attacks continue across Iraq: 17 killed, 60 wounded."

This is what Washington did for Iraq. Far from bringing "freedom and democracy," Washington brought endless mayhem and death. And this is precisely what Washington is in the process of bringing to Syria.

THE NEOCONSERVATIVE WAR CRIMINALS IN OUR MIDST

August 1, 2012

The State Department has an office that hunts German war criminals. Bureaucracies being what they are, the office will exist into next century when any surviving German prison guards will be 200 years old. From time to time the State Department claims to have found a lowly German soldier who was assigned as a prison camp guard. The ancient personage, who had lived in the US for the past 50 or 60 years without doing harm to anyone, is then merciless persecuted, usually on the basis of hearsay. I have never understood what the State Department thinks the alleged prison guard was supposed to have done—freed the prisoners, resign his position?—when Prussian aristocrats, high-ranking German Army generals and Field Marshall and national hero Erwin Rommel were murdered for trying to overthrow Hitler.

What the State Department needs is an office that rounds up American war criminals.

They are in abundance and not hard to find. Indeed, recently 56 of them made themselves public by signing a letter to President Obama demanding that he send in the US Army to complete the destruction of Syria and its people that Washington has begun.

At the Nuremberg Trials of the defeated Germans after World War II, the US government established the principle that naked aggression—the American way in Afghanistan, Iraq, Libya, Somalia, Pakistan, and Yemen—is a war crime. Therefore, there is a very strong precedent for the State Department to round up those neoconservatives who are fomenting more war crimes.

But don't expect it to happen. Today, war criminals run the State Department and the entire US Government. They are elected to the presidency, the House, and the Senate, and appointed to the federal courts as judges. American soldiers, such as Bradley Manning, who behave as the State Department expects German soldiers to have behaved, are not honored, but are thrown into dungeons and tortured while a court martial case is concocted against them.

Hypocrisy is Washington's hallmark, and all but the most delusional are now accustomed to their rulers speaking one way and behaving in the opposite. It is now part of the American character to regard ourselves as members of the "virtuous nation," "the indispensable people," while our rulers commit war crimes around the globe.

Whereas we have all been made complicit in war crimes by "our" government, it still behooves us to know who are the active war criminals in our midst who have burdened us with our war criminal reputation.

You can learn the identity of many of those who are driving the world into World War Three, while their policies result in the murder of large numbers of Arabs and Muslims in Syria, Afghanistan, Libya, Somalia, Pakistan, Yemen, Iraq, and Lebanon, by perusing the signatures to the contrived letter to Obama from the neoconsevatives calling on Obama to invade Syria in order to "rescue" the Syrian people from their government.

According to the letter signed by 56 neoconservatives, only the Syrian government is responsible for deaths in Syria. The Washington sponsored and armed "rebels" are merely protecting the Syrian people from the Assad government. According to the letter signers, the only way the Syrian people can be saved is if Washington overthrows the Syrian government and installs a puppet state attentive to the needs of Israel and Washington.

Among the 56 signatures are a few names from the Syrian National Congress, believed to be a CIA front, and a few names from dupes among the goyim. The rest of the signatures are those of Jewish neoconservatives tightly allied with Israel, some of whom are apparently dual-Israeli citizens who participate in the formation of US foreign policy. The names on this list comprise a concentration of evil, whose purpose is to bring Armageddon to the Syrian people through war that could bring Armageddon to the world.

The letter to Obama is part of the propaganda operation to demonize the Syrian government with lies in order to get rid of a government that supports Hizbollah, the Muslim organization in Lebanon which has twice driven the vaunted but cowardly Israeli army out of Lebanon, thus preventing the Israeli government from achieving its aim of stealing the water resources of southern Lebanon.

Not a single sentence in the letter is correct. Listen to this one for example: "The Assad regime poses a grave threat to national security interests of the United States." What utter total absurdity, and the morons who signed the letter pretend to be "security experts."

How do we evaluate these 56 people who have no shame whatsoever and lie to the President of the United States, putting in writing for all the world to see the most absurd and obvious false things in order to advance their personal agenda at the expense not merely of the lives of Syrians but, by leading to wider war, of life on earth?

These same neocon architects of Armageddon are also working against Iran, Russia, the former Soviet central Asian countries, Ukraine, Belarus, and China. It seems that they can't wait to start a nuclear war.

You can find the names of some of humanity's worst enemies here: http://www.informationclearinghouse.info/article32021.htm

THE NEXT ELECTION: HIGH STAKE OUTCOMES BASED ON NON-ISSUES

August 11, 2012

The election of the next puppet president of the "world's only superpower" is about two and one-half months off, and what are the campaign issues? There aren't any worthy of the name.

Romney won't release his tax returns, despite the fact that release is a customary and expected act. Either the non-release is a strategy to suck in Democrats to make the election issue allegations that Romney is another mega-rich guy who doesn't pay taxes, only to have the issue collapse with a late release that shows enormous taxes paid, or Romney's tax returns, as a candidate who advocates lower taxes for the rich, don't bear scrutiny.

What are Romney's issues? The candidate says that his first act will be to repeal ObamaCare, a program that Romney himself first enacted as governor of Massachusetts. This will cost Romney political contributions from the insurance industry, which is thankful for the 50 million new private insurance policies that ObamaCare, crafted not by Obama but by the private insurance companies, provides at public expense. It is not to the insurance industry's benefit to have a single payer system like other western countries.

Romney's other issue is to blame Obama for America's unemployment caused by the offshoring of the US economy by Republican corporate CEOs. In order to enhance their compensation packages, the Republican CEOs sent millions of America's best jobs to India, China and elsewhere. The lower cost of labor in these offshore sites means much higher earnings, which drives up share prices for shareholders and drives up performance bonuses for management, while wrecking US employment, GDP growth and tax base and driving up the deficit in the balance of payments.

America's main economic problem–the relocation of the US economy offshore—is not a campaign issue. Therefore, the US economy's main problem will remain unaddressed.[63]

The real issues can nowhere be found in the campaigns or in the media. There is no mention of the Bush/Obama destruction of the US Constitution and its legal protections of citizens from arbitrary government power. Due process no longer exists for anyone whom the executive branch suspects of being connected in any way to Washington's chosen enemies. US citizens can be thrown into dungeons for life on suspicion alone without any evidence ever being presented to a court, and they can be executed any place on earth, along with whoever happens to be with them at the time, on suspicion alone.

Last May federal district court judge Katherine Forrest ruled that indefinite detention of US citizens is unconstitutional and issued an injunction against the Obama regime using this police state measure in the National Defense Authorization Act (NDAA). The Obama regime gave the federal judge the finger. During the week of August 6-10 the Justice (*sic*) Department's Brownshirt lawyers refused to tell Judge Forrest if the Obama regime is complying with the injunction. The position of the Obama regime is: "We are above the law and do not answer to federal courts." One would think that Romney would be all over this, but he isn't because he wants the power himself.

The Obama police state will shop around and find a federal appeals court dominated by Republican Brownshirt judges and get Judge Forrest's ruling overturned. All those Republican federal judges we had to have to save us from liberal Democrats will now complete our deliverance to a total police state where all power rests in an unaccountable executive branch. This is what the Republican Federalist Society has wanted for years, and they are on the verge of obtaining it.

That the United States has degenerated into a police state in the short period of eleven years should be the campaign issue. Who would ever have thought such a thing possible. Yet, there is no mention of the destruction of the rule of law in the name of a hoax "war on terror."

The Bush regime created the propaganda that "they (Muslims) hate us for our freedom and democracy," but how can Muslims hate us for what does not exist? The arbitrary unaccountable power asserted by the executive branch is totally incompatible with freedom and democracy. Yet, neither Obama nor Romney makes this an issue. And neither does the media.

There is no war on terror. There is war on countries that are not Washington's puppet states. Unaccountable Washington is currently slaughtering thousands of Muslims in a variety of countries and is preparing Syria as its next holocaust. Washington, taking advantage of the splits between Sunnis and Shia and between Islamists and secular Muslims, has organized a rebellion in Syria in order to overthrow a government that is not a puppet of Washington and Israel.

Among the foreigners streaming into Syria to overthrow the secular state in which Sunni and Shia Arabs have lived peacefully, are the Islamist extremists that Washington has squandered $6 trillion fighting for 11 years.

The extremists are on Washington's side. They want the secular Syrian government overthrown, because it is not an Islamic government.

This suits Washington's policy, so now the taxes extracted from hard-pressed Americans are flowing to the Islamists that Americans have been fighting.

Speaking before the Council on Foreign Relations on August 8, Obama's national security aid, John Brennan, defended the diversion of American taxpayers' money to the outside forces Washington has organized, financed and provided with military weapons to overthrow the government of Syria. John Brennan said, with a straight face, that the Obama administration is careful that the financial and military aid does not go to the rebels affiliated with Al Qaeda. Brennan has to make this claim, because the Obama regime, being in cahoots with Al Qaeda, is in violation of its own NDAA and is subject to arrest and indefinite detention.

Does anyone believe that Washington, determined to overthrow the Syrian government, is refusing to arm the most effective part of the fighting force that is involved? Is there anyone so naive not to know that military aid to "rebels" is fungible?

Having suffered damage to its superpower reputation by being fought to a standoff by a few thousand Al Qaeda in Iraq and Afghanistan, Washington learned that the trick was to employ Al Qaeda not as an enemy but as an ally.

The test case was in Libya, where the US-Al Qaeda alliance worked to overthrow the Libyan government. The advantage for Washington is that Libya is now beset by warring factions and is no longer a country that could get in Washington's way.

Libya is the roadmap for Syria.

Syria made its mistake when it thought it could appease Washington by taking Washington's side in the first war against Iraq, confirming for Washington that Arabs are incapable of sticking together and thus are an easy mark to be overthrown.

If Syria falls, Washington will have destroyed yet another nation. But this is not a part of the presidential debate. Both candidates agree that Washington should prevail in establishing a puppet state in Syria. Even Amnesty International has been suborned and lends its influence to the demonization of the Syrian government. Only the US is moral, indispensable, virtuous, humane, a light upon mankind. By definition, any opponent chosen by Washington is debauched, evil, sinful, a country that suppresses dissent and tortures its opponents, something Washington would never do, being, of course, the "light unto the world."

Unlike the 1957 plot by British Prime Minister Harold Macmillan and US President Dwight Eisenhower to foment an "uprising" in Syria and assassinate the Syrian leadership[64] the Obama administration cloaks its intervention in humanitarian language, as do the rebels while they murder and execute civilians who support the Assad government. The presstitute western media describes the mayhem and murder as "humanitarian intervention," and the brainwashed western public reposes in its moral superiority.

After Syria is destroyed, the last independent country in the region is Iran. Iran has also been weakened, not by Washington's embargo, an act of war in itself, but by Washington's financing of the "Green Revolution." Iran now has a fifth column within itself.

Iran, the second oldest country after China, is now surrounded by 40 or more US military bases and is confronted by four US fleets in its own Persian Gulf.

There are a large number of nominal Muslims interested only in money and power who are working with Washington to overthrow the Syrian and Iranian governments.

If Iran falls, with both Russia and China surrounded by US missiles and military bases, the world as we know it will enter its final stage. Will Russia and China, having sacrificed all their buffers without a fight, surrender and be content to be ruled by puppet governments, or will they resist?

Don't expect the packaged political campaign of the next couple of months to deal with any significant issue. Americans are oblivious to their fate, and so apparently is the rest of the world.

The selection of the next president of the US will depend on one thing alone—which of the two candidates financed by the ruling private oligarchy has the most effective propaganda.

Whether you vote Republican or Democrat, the oligarchs will win.

IS WASHINGTON DEAF TO RUSSIAN WARNINGS?

August 16, 2012

The morons who rule the American sheeple are not only dumb and blind, they are deaf as well. The ears of the American "superpower" only work when the Israeli prime minister, the crazed Netanyahu, speaks. Then Washington hears everything and rushes to comply.

Israel is a tiny insignificant state, created by the careless British and the stupid Americans. It has no power except what its American protector provides. Yet, despite Israel's insignificance, it rules Washington.

When a resolution introduced by the Israel Lobby is delivered to Congress, it passes unanimously. If Israel wants war, Israel usually gets its wish. When Israel commits war crimes against Palestinians and Lebanon and is damned by the hundred plus UN resolutions passed against Israel's criminal actions, the US bails Israel out of trouble with its veto.

The power that tiny Israel exercises over the "world's only superpower" is unique in history. Millions of "christians" bow down to this power, reinforcing it, moved by the exhortations of their "christian" ministers.

Netanyahu lusts for war against Iran. He strikes out against all who oppose his war lust. Recently, he called Israel's top generals "pussies" for warning against a war with Iran. He regards former Israeli prime ministers and former heads of the Israeli intelligence service as traitors for opposing his determination to attack Iran. He has denounced America's servile president Obama and America's top military leader for being "soft on Iran." The latest poll in Israel shows that a solid majority of the Israelis are opposed to an Israeli attack on Iran. But Netanyahu is uninterested in the opinion of Israeli citizens. He has Washington watching his back, so he is war mad. It is a mystery why Israelis put Netanyahu in public office instead of in an insane asylum.

Netanyahu is not alone. He has the American neoconservatives in his corner. The American neoconservatives are as crazed as Netanyahu. They believe in nuclear war and are itching to nuke some Muslim country and then get on to nuking Russia and China. It is amazing that no more than two or three dozen people have the fate of the entire world in their hands.

The Democratic Party is helpless before them.

The Republican Party is their vehicle.

The Russians, watching Netanyahu push Washington toward dangerous confrontations, keep raising their voices about the danger of nuclear war.

On May 17 Russian Prime Minister Dmitry Medvedev warned the West against launching "hasty wars," which could result "although I do not want to scare anyone" in "the use of a nuclear weapon."

On November 30 of last year the Chief of the General Staff of the Armed Forces of Russia warned of nuclear war with NATO. General Nikolai Makarov said that NATO's eastward expansion meant that the risk of Russia coming into conflict with NATO had "risen sharply." General Makarov said, "I do not rule out local and regional armed conflicts developing into a large-scale war, including using nuclear weapons."

Here is Russian president Medvedev (currently the prime minister) describing the steps toward nuclear war that Russia has taken pushed by the crazed warmongers in Washington wallowing in their insane hubris with regard to the American missile bases on Russia's borders:

> I have made the following decisions. First, I am instructing the Defense Ministry to immediately put the missile attack early warning radar station in Kaliningrad on combat alert. Second, protective cover of Russia's strategic nuclear weapons will be reinforced as a priority measure under the program to develop our air and space defenses. Third, the new strategic ballistic missiles commissioned by the Strategic Missile Forces and the Navy will be equipped with advanced missile defense penetration systems and new highly-effective warheads. Fourth, I have instructed the Armed Forces to draw up measures for disabling missile defense system data and guidance systems. These measures will be adequate, effective, and low-cost. Fifth, if the above measures prove insufficient, the Russian Federation will deploy modern offensive weapon systems in the west and south of the country, ensuring our ability to take out any part of the US missile defense system in Europe. One step in this process will be to deploy Iskander missiles in Kaliningrad Region. Other measures to counter the European missile defense system will be drawn up and implemented as necessary. Furthermore, if the situation continues to develop not to Russia's favor, we reserve the right to discontinue further disarmament and arms control measures.

Russian president Vladimir Putin has said, as politely as possible, that the US seeks to enslave the world, that the US seeks vassals, not allies, that the US seeks to rule the world and that the US is a parasite on the world economy. It would be difficult for an informed person to take exception with Putin's statements.

Putin told the politicians in Washington and Western and Eastern European capitals that surrounding Russia with anti-ballistic missiles "raises the specter of nuclear war in Europe." Putin said that the Russian response is to point nuclear armed cruise missiles, which cannot be intercepted by anti-ballistic missiles, at the US missile bases and at European capitals. The American move, Putin said, "could trigger nuclear war."

Putin has been trying to wake up the American puppet states in Europe at least since February 13, 2007. At the 43rd Munich Conference on Security Policy, Putin said that the unipolar world that Washington was striving to achieve under its banner, "is a world in which there is one master, one sovereign. And at the end of the day this is pernicious not only for all those within this system, but also for the sovereign itself because it destroys itself from within."

That has certainly happened to the US which now has a police state as thorough-going as Nazi Germany. And even better armed.[65]

Putin went on to tell his European audience that in Russia, "we are constantly being taught about democracy. But for some reason those who teach us do not want to learn themselves." Instead, Putin said, "we are seeing a greater and greater disdain for the basic principles of international law. And independent legal norms are, as a matter of fact, coming increasingly closer to one state's legal system. One state and, of course, first and foremost the United States, has overstepped its national borders in every way. This is visible in the economic, political, cultural and educational policies it imposes on other nations. Well, who likes this? Who is happy about this?"

People are not happy, Putin said, because they don't feel safe. Not to feel safe "is extremely dangerous. It results in the fact that no one feels safe. I want to emphasize this—no one feels safe!" The result, Putin said, is "an arms race."

Putin politely unbraided the Italian defense minister, a person owned by Washington, for suggesting that NATO or the EU could take the place of the UN in justifying the use of force against sovereign countries. Putin took exception to the idea that Washington could use its puppet organization or its puppet states to legitimize an act of US aggression. Putin stated flatly: "The use of force can only be considered legitimate if the decision is sanctioned by the UN."

Putin went on to discuss the forked tongue of Washington. Reagan and Gorbachev had firm agreements, but Reagan's successors put "frontline forces on our borders. . . . The stones and concrete blocks of the Berlin Wall have long been distributed as souvenirs. But we should not forget that the fall of the Berlin Wall was possible thanks to a historic choice—one that was also made by our people, the people of Russia—a choice in favor of democracy, freedom, openness and a sincere partnership with all the members of the big European family. And now they are trying to impose new dividing lines and walls on us—these walls may be virtual but they are nevertheless dividing ones that cut through our continent. And is it possible that we will once again require many years and decades, as well as several generations of politicians, to disassemble and dismantle these new walls."

Putin's speech shows that he has Washington's number. Washington is The Great Pretender, pretending to respect human rights while it slaughters Muslims in seven countries on the basis of lies and fabricated intelligence. The American people, "the indispensable people," support this murderous policy. Washington uses the status of the dollar as reserve currency to exclude countries that do not do Washington's bidding from the international clearing system.

Awash in hubris like Napoleon and Hitler before they marched off into Russia, Washington has turned a deaf ear to Putin during the entirety of the 21st century. Speaking on May 10, 2006, Putin said: "We are aware of what is gong on in the world. Comrade wolf [the US] knows whom to eat, he eats without listening, and he's clearly not going to listen to anyone."

"Where," Putin asked, is Washington's "pathos about protecting human rights and democracy when it comes to the need to pursue its own interests?" For Washington, "everything is allowed, there are no restrictions whatsoever."

China also has caught on. Now the hubris that drives Washington toward world hegemony confronts two massive nuclear powers. Will the criminal gang in Washington drive the world to nuclear extinction?

Washington, thinking that it owns the world, has imposed more unilateral sanctions on Iran without any basis in any recognized law. The imposed sanctions are nothing but Washington's assertion that its might is right.

The Russian Foreign Ministry said that Washington could stick its sanctions up its ass. "We consider efforts to impose internal American legislation on the entire world completely unacceptable."

Washington will do what it can to assassinate Putin and effect regime change through the Russian "opposition" that Washington funds. Failing that, Washington's pursuit of world hegemony has run up against a brick wall. If the sociopaths in Washington with their hubris-inflated egos don't back off, that mushroom cloud they have been warning about will indeed blossom over Washington.

CORREA STANDS UP TO THE JACKBOOTED BRITISH GESTAPO

August 16, 2012

A coward dies many deaths; a brave man dies but once.

The once proud British government, now reduced to Washington's servile whore, put on its Gestapo Jackboots and declared that if the Ecuadorean Embassy in London did not hand over WikiLeaks' Julian Assange, British storm troopers would invade the embassy with military force and drag Assange out. Ecuador stood its ground. "We want to be very clear, we are not a British colony," declared Ecuador's Foreign Minister. Far from being intimidated the President of Ecuador, Rafael Correa, replied to the threat by granting Assange political asylum.[66]

The British government had no shame in announcing that it would violate the Vienna Convention and assault the Ecuadorean Embassy, just as the Islamic students in the 1979 Khomeini Revolution in Iran took over the US Embassy and held the diplomatic staff captive. Pushed by their Washington overlords, the Brits have resorted to the tactics of a pariah state. Maybe we should be worried about British nuclear weapons.

Let's be clear, Assange is not a fugitive from justice. He has not been charged with any crime in any country. He has not raped any women. There are no indictments pending in any court, and as no charges have been brought against him, there is no validity to the Swedish extradition request. It is not normal for people to be extradited for questioning, especially when, as in Assange's case, he expressed his complete cooperation with being questioned a second time by Swedish officials in London.

What is this all about? First, according to news reports, Assange was picked up by two celebrity-hunting Swedish women who took him home to their beds. Later for reasons unknown, one complained that he had not used a condom, and the other complained that she had offered one helping, but he had taken two. A Swedish prosecutor looked into the case, found that there was nothing to it, and dismissed the case.

Assange left for England. Then another Swedish prosecutor, a woman, claiming what authority I do not know, reopened the case and issued an extradition order for Assange. This is such an unusual procedure that it worked its way through the entire British court system to the Supreme Court and then back to the Supreme Court on appeal. In the end British "justice" did what the Washington overlord ordered and came down on the side of the strange extradition request.

Assange, realizing that the Swedish government was going to turn him over to Washington to be held in indefinite detention, tortured, and framed as a spy, sought protection from the Ecuadorean Embassy in London. As corrupt as the British are, the UK government was unwilling to release Assange directly to Washington. By turning him over to Sweden, the British could feel that their hands were clean.

Sweden, formerly an honorable country like Canada once was where American war resisters could seek asylum, has been suborned and brought under Washington's thumb. Recently, Swedish diplomats were expelled from Belarus where they seem to have been involved in helping Washington orchestrate a "color revolution" as Washington keeps attempting to extend its bases and puppet states deeper into traditional Russia.

The entire world, including Washington's servile puppet states, understands that once Assange is in Swedish hands, Washington will deliver an extradition order, with which Sweden, unlike the British, would comply. Ecuador too understands this. The Foreign Minister Ricardo Patino announced that Ecuador granted Assange asylum because "there are indications to presume that there could be political persecution." In the US, Patino acknowledged, Assange would not get a fair trial and could face the death penalty in a trumped up case.

The US Puppet State of Great Britain announced that Assange would not be permitted to leave Britain. So much for the British government's defense of law and human rights. If the British do not invade the Ecuadorean Embassy and drag Assange out dead or in chains, the British position is that Assange will live out his life inside the London Embassy of Ecuador. According to *The New York Times*, Assange's asylum leaves him "with protection from arrest only on Ecuadorean territory (which includes the embassy). To leave the embassy for Ecuador, he would need cooperation that Britain has said it will not offer." When it comes to Washington's money or behaving honorably in accordance with international law, the British government comes down on the side of money.

The Anglo-American world, which pretends to be the moral face of humanity, has now revealed for all to see that under the mask is the face of the Gestapo.

AMERICA'S FUTURE IS DEATH

August 20, 2012

*"The day we see truth and do not speak
is the day we begin to die."*
Martin Luther King

Conspiracy theories have now blossomed into what the smug presstitute media calls a "conspiracy culture." According to the presstitutes, Americans have to find some explanation for their own frustrations and failings, so Americans shift the blame to the Bilderbergers, the Rothschilds, the New World Order and so forth and so on.

Readers will not be surprised that I disagree with the presstitutes. Indeed, the conspiracy culture is the product of the presstitute media's failure to investigate and to report truthfully. I am certain that the Western media is worse than the Soviet media was. The Soviet media devised ways for helping the public to read between the lines, whereas the Western media is so proud to be confidants of the government that they deliver the propaganda without any clues to the readers that it is propaganda.

Americans have been fed lies by "their" government and the government's presstitute media for so long that it is not surprising that Americans increasingly believe that there is a conspiracy operating against them. Millions of Americans have been evicted from their jobs, careers, and homes while the crooks who stole from them run free and bankroll the presidential candidates. The world as millions of Americans knew it has come to an end, and no one has been held accountable. The explanation that Americans get from the media is that it is their own fault. They bought houses they shouldn't have bought, and they didn't train for the right jobs. It is not unreasonable for Americans to conclude that a conspiracy is operating against them.

Any American citizen accustomed to travel America's "wide open spaces" prior to 9/11 must be astonished by the sudden rise of the intrusive Homeland Security, a gestapo-sounding name if there ever was one. Porno-scans and genital feel-ups have spread from airports to bus and train stations and to the public highways, despite the absence of terrorist events. Even some of the gullible flag-waving conservatives are beginning to wonder about all the security. The reports that the Department of Homeland Security has ordered 750 million rounds of people-killing ammunition are puzzling even to those conservatives who have been taking vicarious pleasure in the slaughter of "towelheads."

Why does the Department of Homeland Security need enough ammunition to shoot every American 2.5 times? Why is Homeland Security equipping itself with full-body armor? Why is Homeland Security acquiring new laser technology that can "instantly know everything about you from 164 feet away?"[67] A new army manual for "Civil Disturbance Operations" describes how the military is to be used domestically within the US to put down protests, not just confiscating firearms but killing citizens.[68]

The police state that is being constructed in "freedom and democracy" America is without parallel in history. When the only terrorists are dupes organized by the FBI, it is clear that the purpose of the police state is not to protect Americans from Muslim terrorists. The purpose of the police state is to terrorize US citizens.

It is not only Homeland Security that is being militarized. The government reported that a further large ammunition order was made by the National Weather Service, later updated to have been the Fisheries Office. If you are surprised at this, why has the Social Security Administration ordered 174,000 rounds of hollow-point bullets?

Lists of Homeland Security's ammunition orders are available online. Clearly, it is not ammunition for target practice. It is ammunition for killing people: hollow-point bullets for the military rifle, the M-16. Match grade bullets for .308 sniper rifles. 12 gauge shotgun buckshot and slug ammunition. Hollow-point bullets for .357 magnum and .40 caliber pistols.

As there have been no terrorist attacks in the US since the 9/11 attack (itself suspect by experts), except for those organized by the FBI, this massive purchase of firepower is obviously not to protect Americans from Muslim terrorists. So what is it for?

Perhaps this film, "Gray State", explains what is in store for the American people who trusted "their" government. War protestors and critics of the government are being redefined as "domestic extremists" who can be arrested for aiding and abetting the enemies of the United States. If Americans wake up to the fact that they are being dispossessed economically, politically, and socially, while Washington is leading them into World War III, and take to the streets in protest, they will encounter extreme military force.

The liberal-left is even more delusional than the flag-waving conservatives. No matter what the government does, conservatives will come down on the government's side. This is because conservatives confuse patriotism with support for the government, not with defense of the Constitution, a suspect document that coddles criminals, terrorists, and war protesters who cause America to lose wars. The liberal-left regards Obama with his half-black origin as a member of the oppressed class, personages endowed by the liberal-left with higher morality. The liberal-left continues to regard Obama as the redeemer even as Obama sits in the Oval Office approving lists of American citizens to be executed without due process of law. Not even Naomi Wolf can wake up the liberal-left.

Do not expect Congress or the presstitutes to do anything about the rapid concentration of power in the police state that Bush and Obama have created. Do not expect to be rescued by federal courts. Even if some judges are inclined to defend the Constitution from its domestic enemy, the courts are powerless if the executive branch does not respect the rule of law. Currently, the executive branch is ignoring a federal judge's injunction against the indefinite detention of US citizens. The Department of Justice (*sic*) lawyers will not even answer the judge's questions.[69]

A gullible population is helpless if government decides to enslave the people. It is child's play for government to discredit a people's natural leaders and those who provide the people with accurate information. Most Americans have a very small knowledge base and very large ideological preconceptions. Consequently, they cannot tell fiction from fact.

Consider the case of Julian Assange. When the US government, angry that WikiLeaks had published leaked documents that revealed the mendacity and deceit of Washington, first struck out at Assange, support for Assange was almost universal. Then Washington put out the story on the Internet that Assange was an intelligence agent working for the CIA or the even more hateful Mossad. Both leftwing and rightwing Internet sites fell for the obvious lie. Here we have gullibility on the level with those who believed Stalin's charge that Nikolai Bukharin was a capitalist agent.

It was like Dominique Strauss-Kahn all over again. Falsely accused of sexually assaulting a New York hotel maid, the Director of the International Monetary Fund, chased on two continents by celebrity-hunting women, was knocked out of the race for the French presidency and had to resign his IMF position. The New York police, trained by decades of feminist propaganda to regard every sex charge brought by a woman as the absolute truth, looked foolish and incompetent when clear evidence emerged that the charge was fabricated in order to extract money from Strauss-Kahn and possibly in order to knock him out of contention for the French presidency.

Many websites and normally reliable commentators were taken in by the false stories. The Washington hegemons and their presstitute media have been even more successful in fooling Americans about terrorist attacks, Osama bin Laden, the Taliban, Afghanistan, Iraq, Libya, Somalia, Yemen,

Pakistan, Syria, and Iran. What is astonishing is the fact that there have not been any attacks on America, despite the enormous provocations Washington has provided by murdering as many as one million Muslims, destroying three Muslim countries, conducting military operations against seven Muslim countries and preparing an attack on an eighth—Iran.

The President of Russia, whose thermo-nuclear ballistic missiles can remove the US from the face of the earth, stated for all the world to hear that Washington has the entire world in fear of its hegemonic drive. "No one feels safe," said Putin. And certainly not the Russians with American missile bases on their borders and a Washington-funded disloyal and traitorous political "opposition" which serves as Washington's fifth column inside Russia.

America, Putin acknowledged, wants to rule the world. But Washington is not going to rule Russia and China. If the current White House flunky keeps his promise[70] to Israeli Prime Minister Netanyahu that the US will attack Iran next June if Iran does not close down its nuclear energy program (a non-weapons program permitted to Iran as a signatory of the Nuclear Non-proliferation Treaty), the White House will have opened the door to World War III. In such a war the US would not be immune from attack as it was in WW I and WW II. This time America could disappear in nuclear holocaust. If any of the world survives, people will be thankful for Washington's removal from the scene.

Death is what "your" government in Washington, both Republicans and Democrats, are bringing you. Both parties are driven by the neoconservatives who believe that American hegemony over the world is worth nuclear war to accomplish. If these dangerous ideologues continue to prevail, life on earth has a very short-run prospect.

Update: Major General Jerry Curry reports that the DHS and Social Security Administration ammunition orders total almost two billion rounds.[71] US police are now full-fledged Gestapo, the enemy of the people.

PUSSY RIOT, THE UNFORTUNATE DUPES OF AMERICAN HEGEMONY

August 22, 2012

My heart goes out to the three Russian women who comprise the Russian rock band, Pussy Riot. They were brutally deceived and used by the Washington-financed NGOs that have infiltrated Russia. Pussy Riot was sent on a mission that was clearly illegal under statutory law.

You have to admire and to appreciate the spunk of the women. But you have to bemoan their gullibility. Washington needed a popular issue with which to demonize the Russian government for standing up to Washington's intention to destroy Syria, just as it had destroyed Iraq, Afghanistan, and Libya, and as it intends to destroy Lebanon and Iran.

By intentionally offending religious worshipers—which would be a hate crime in the US and its European, Canadian, and British puppet states—the women violated a statutory Russian law.

Prior to the women's trial, Russian President Putin expressed his opinion that the women should not be harshly punished. Taking the cue from Putin, the judge gave the women, deceived and betrayed by the American-financed NGOs, two years instead of seven years.

The women were not waterboarded, raped, or forced to sign false confessions, all well-established practices of American "justice."

The chances were good that after six months Putin would see that the women are released. But, of course, that would not serve the propaganda of the American Empire. The instructions to the Washington-financed fifth column in Russia will be to make any government leniency for Pussy Riot impossible.

Washington-organized protests, riots, property damage, assaults on state and religious images by Washington's Russian dupes can make it impossible for Putin to stand up to national opinion and commute the sentences of the Pussy Riot women.

Distrust of the Russian government and dissension within Russia are what Washington wants. As Washington continues to murder vast numbers of people around the globe, it will point its finger at the fate of Pussy Riot. The western bought-and-paid-for presstitute media will focus on Russia's evil, not on the evil of Washington, London, and the EU puppet states who are slaughtering Muslims by the bucketful.

The disparity between human rights in the west and in the east is astonishing. When a Chinese trouble-maker sought protection from Washington, the Chinese "authoritarian" government allowed the person to leave for America. But when Julian Assange, who, unlike the presstitute western media, actually provides truthful information for the western peoples, was granted political asylum by Ecuador, Great Britain, bowing to the country's American master, refused the obligatory free passage from the UK.

The UK government, unlike the Chinese government, doesn't mind violating international law, because it will be paid buckets of money by Washington for being a pariah state.

As Karl Marx said, money turns everything into a commodity that can be bought and sold: government, honor, morality, the writing of history, legality. Nothing is immune to purchase. This development of capitalism has reached the highest stage in the US and its puppet states, the governments of which sell out the interest of their peoples in order to please Washington and be made rich, like Tony Blair, who has garnered $35 million. Sending their citizens to fight for Washington's empire in distant parts of the world is the service for which the utterly corrupt European politicians are paid. Despite the wondrous entity known as European Democracy, the European and British peoples are unable to do anything about their misuse in Washington's interest. This is a new form of slavery. If a country is an American ally, its people are American slaves.

The international attention focused on Pussy Riot, an obscure rock group which apparently has no recordings on the market, demonstrates the complicity of the Western media in US propaganda. Pussy Riot is not the Beatles of the 1960s. I doubt that most of the young people demonstrating in favor of Pussy Riot had ever before heard of the group or have any understanding of how they are being manipulated.

There are so many more important issues on which media attention should be focused. There is Bradley Manning's illegal detention and torture by the US government. Manning has already been in prison without trial for longer than Pussy Riot's sentence!

What is Manning's "crime." No one knows. Washington accuses him of doing his duty under the US Military Code and revealing the war crime of the "thrill killing" of civilians by US military personnel and of releasing documents to WikiLeaks revealing the mendacity of the US government. In other words, Manning is a hero, and so off he is dragged to the torture chamber.

WikiLeaks Julian Assange, accused of posting on the Internet the leaked documents, is confined to the Ecuadorean embassy in London. The British "human rights" regime refuses to abide by international law and allow Assange, who has been granted political asylum by Ecuador, safe passage. Everyone familiar with international law knows that asylum takes precedence over the other legal claims, especially specious ones.

Washington has armed and financed outsiders to destroy Syria and to break the country up into warring factions. Instead of protesting this heinous act by Washington, the world protests the Syrian government for resisting its overthrow by Washington. I don't think that even George Orwell imagined that the peoples of the world were this utterly stupid.

In "freedom and democracy" America, President Obama refuses to obey a federal court order to cease and desist from violating the clear, unambiguous Constitutional rights of US citizens. Instead, the President of the United States defies the court's order and continues to hold US citizens in indefinite detention, and there is no movement to impeach this tyrant. To the contrary, America is presented as the example of democracy to the world.

Where are the protests?

Update: President Putin, realizing that these women were duped into breaking the law by Washington-funded NGOs, pardoned them after serving a little over one year of their sentence.

A CULTURE OF
DELUSION

September 27, 2012

A writer's greatest disappointments are readers who have knee-jerk responses. Not all readers, of course. Some readers are thoughtful and supportive. Others express thanks for opening their eyes. But the majority are happy when a writer tells them what they want to hear and are unhappy when he writes what they don't want to hear.

For the left-wing, Ronald Reagan is the great bogeyman. Those on the left don't understand supply-side economics as a macroeconomic innovation that cured stagflation by utilizing the impact of fiscal policy on aggregate supply. Instead, they see "trickle-down economics" and tax cuts for the rich. Leftists don't understand that the Reagan administration intervened in Grenada and Nicaragua in order to signal to the Soviets that there would be no more Soviet expansion or client states and that it was time to negotiate the end of the Cold War. Instead, leftists see in Reagan the origin of rule by the one percent and the neoconservatives' wars for US hegemony.

In 1981 curtailing inflation meant collapsing nominal GNP and tax revenues. The result would be budget deficits—anathema to Republicans—during the period of readjustment. Ending the Cold War meant curtailing the military/security complex and raised the specter in conservative circles of "the anti-Christ" Gorbachev deceiving Reagan and taking over the world.

In pursuing his two main goals, Reagan was up against his own constituency and relied on rhetoric to keep his constituency on board with his agenda. The left wing heard the rhetoric but failed to comprehend the agenda.

When I explain these facts, easily and abundantly documented, some of leftish persuasion send in condescending and insulting emails telling me that they look forward to the day that I stop lying about Reagan and tell the truth about Reagan like I do about everything else.

"Knee-jerk liberal" is a favorite term of conservatives. But conservatives can be just as knee-jerk. When I object to Washington's wars, the mistreatment of detainees and the suspension of civil liberties, some on the right tell me that if I hate America so much I should move to Cuba.

Many Republicans cannot get their minds around the fact that if civil liberties are subject to the government's arbitrary discretion, then civil liberties do not exist. The flag-waving element of the population is prone to confuse loyalty to the country with loyalty to the government, unless, of course, there's a Democrat in the White House.

Rationally, it makes no sense for readers to think that a writer who would lie to them about one thing would tell them the truth about another. But as long as they hear what they want to hear, it is the truth. If they don't want to hear it, it is a lie.

Both left and right also confuse explanations with justifications.

When a writer writes about the perils that we as a society face and the implications, it is very discouraging for the writer to know that many readers will not listen unless it is what they want to hear. This discouragement is precisely what every truth-teller faces, which is why there are so few of them.

This is one reason I stopped writing a couple of years ago. I found that solid facts and sound analysis could not penetrate brainwashed and closed minds seeking vindication to keep the mind locked tightly against unsettling truths. Americans want to have their beliefs vindicated more than they want the truth. The success of print and TV pundits is based on allying with a prominent point of view or interest group and serving it. Those served make the writer or talking head successful. I never thought much of that kind of success.

But success as a whore is about the only kind of success that can occur in Washington or in the media these days. Those who refuse to prostitute themselves arouse pity and denunciation, not admiration. A couple of years ago an acquaintance from a university in the northeast called me to say he had recently had lunch with some of my former associates in Washington. When he inquired about me, he said the response was, "Poor Craig, if he hadn't turned critic, he would be worth tens of millions of dollars like us."

I replied that my former associates were undoubtedly correct. My acquaintance said that he hadn't realized that he was having lunch with a bunch of prostitutes.

The incentive to speak the truth and the reward for doing so are very weak. And not just for a writer, but also for academics and experts who can make far more money by lying than by telling the truth. How else would we have got GMOs, jobs offshoring, the "unitary executive," and a deregulated financial system? It is a very lucrative career to testify as an expert in civil lawsuits. It is part of America's romance with the lie that experts purchased by the opposing sides in a lawsuit battle it out as gladiators seeking the jury's thumbs-up.

And look at Congress. The two members of the House who stood up for the Constitution and truth in government will soon be gone. Ron Paul is stepping down, and Dennis Kucinich was redistricted out of his seat. Crossover Republican voters and the Israel Lobby unseated Cynthia McKinney from the House of Representatives in 2002. Independent voices are simply not tolerated in Congress.

As for the Senate, these thoughtful personages recently voted 90-1 to declare war on Iran, as the sole dissenter, Rand Paul, pointed out. The Senate is very much aware, although only a few will publicly admit it, that the US has been totally frustrated and held to a standoff, if not a defeat, in Afghanistan and is unable to subdue the Taliban. Despite this, the Senate wants a war with Iran, a war which could easily turn out to be even less successful. Obviously, the Senate not only lies to the public but also to itself.

Last week the Pentagon chief, Panetta, told China that the new US naval, air, and troop bases surrounding China are not directed at China. What else could be the purpose of the new bases? Washington is so accustomed to lying and to being believed that Panetta might actually think China will believe his completely transparent lie. Panetta has confused China with the American people: tell them what they want to hear, and they will believe it.

Americans live in a matrix of lies. They seldom encounter a truthful statement. There is no evidence that the majority of Americans can any longer tell the difference between the truth and a lie. Americans fell for all of these lies and more: Saddam Hussein has weapons of mass destruction and Al Qaeda connections. Saddam Hussein's troops seized Kuwaiti babies from incubators and threw them on the floor. Gaddafi fed his troops Viagra to help them rape Libyan women. Iran has a nuclear weapons program. Change—yes we can! The US is "the indispensable country." America is broke because of food stamps and Social Security, not because of wars, bankster bailouts, and a failing economy. Russia is America's number one enemy. China is America's number one enemy. Iran is a terrorist state. Jobs offshoring is free trade and good for the US economy. Israel is America's most loyal ally. The US missile shield surrounding Russia is not directed at Russia. The South China Sea is an area of US national interest. Financial markets are self-regulating.

The list is endless. Lies dominate every policy discussion, every political decision. The most successful people in America are liars.

The endless lies have created a culture of delusion. And this is why America is lost. The beliefs of many Americans, perhaps a majority, are comprised of lies. These beliefs have become emotional crutches, and Americans will fight to defend the lies that they believe. The inability of Americans to accept facts that are contrary to their beliefs is the reason the country is leaderless and will remain so. Unless the scales fall from their eyes, Americans are doomed.

AMERICA'S MORAL DEGENERACY

October 10, 2012

On May 31, 2010, the Israeli right-wing government sent armed military troops to illegally board in international waters the aid ships of the Gaza Freedom Flotilla organized by the Free Gaza Movement and the Turkish Foundation for Human Rights and Freedoms and Humanitarian Relief. The Israelis murdered 8 Turkish citizens and one US citizen in cold blood. Many others were wounded by the forces of "the only democracy in the Middle East."

Despite the murder of its citizen, Washington immediately took the side of the crazed Israeli government. The Turks had a different response. The prime minister of Turkey, Erdogan, said that the next aid ships would be protected by the Turkish navy. But Washington got hold of its puppet and shut him up. Once upon a time, the Turks were a fierce people. Today they are Washington's puppets.

This past week has indicated as much. The Turkish government is permitting the Islamists from outside Syria, organized by the CIA and Israel, to attack Syria from Turkish territory. On several occasions a mortar shell has, according to news reports if you believe them, fallen just inside the Turkey border. The Turkish military has used it as an excuse to launch artillery barrages into Syria.

People who with good cause no longer believe the US and western media or the US and western governments think that the mortar shells were fired by US or Israeli operatives, or by the "rebels" they support, in order to give Turkey the excuse to start a NATO war with Syria. A UN sanctioned NATO invasion or air strikes, as in Libya, has been blocked by the Russians and Chinese. But if Syria and Turkey get into a war, NATO must come to the aid of its NATO member, Turkey.

Once again we see that Muslims are easily dominated and slaughtered by Western countries, because Muslim countries are incapable of supporting one another. Instead of supporting one another, Muslim governments accept payoffs to support instead the Christian/Zionist forces of the Western bloc.

Washington knows this, which is one reason why Washington began its assertion of world hegemony in the Muslim Middle East.

In the West, the Ministry of Propaganda continues to talk about the "Syrian revolt." There is no revolt. What has happened is that the US and Israel have equipped with weapons and sent into Syria Islamists who wish to overthrow the secular Syrian government. Washington knows that if the Syrian government can be destroyed, the country will dissolve into warring factions like Iraq and Libya.

America's European and Japanese puppet states are, of course, part of Washington's operation. There will be no complaints from them. But why is the rest of the world content for Washington to interfere in the sovereign affairs of nations to the point of invading, sending in drones and assassination teams, and murdering vast numbers of citizens in seven countries?

Does this acquiescence mean that the world has accepted Washington's claim that it is the indispensable country with the right to rule the world?

Why, for example, do Russia and Venezuela permit the US government to fund their political opposition?

The one party American state has no political opposition. But imagine if it did. Would Washington tolerate the funding of its opposition by Russia or Venezuela? Obviously not. Those running against America with foreign money would be arrested and imprisoned, but not in Venezuela or Russia, countries where, apparently, treason is legal.

On October 8, Hugo Chavez defeated his American-financed opponent, Henrique Capriles, 54% to 44%.

This would be an amazing margin of victory in a US presidential election. However, in his previous reelection Chavez won by 27%. Obviously, Washington's money and the propaganda activities of the US-financed nongovernmental organizations succeeded in swaying Venezuelans and reducing Chavez's margin of victory to 10%. Washington's interference is a massive barrier to leadership in other countries. Fully 44% of the Venezuelan people were too brainwashed or too stupid to vote for their own country's candidate and voted instead for Washington's candidate.

It is extraordinary that 44% of the Venezuelan voters voted to become an American puppet state, like Turkey, England, France, Germany, Italy, Spain, Ireland, Portugal, Slovakia, the Czech Republic, Poland, the Baltics, Scandinavia, Canada, Japan, South Korea, Australia, Mexico, Belgium, Taiwan, Colombia, Pakistan, Yemen. Probably, I have left out a few.

As a high government official once told me, "Empire costs us a great deal of money."

Washington has to pay its puppets to represent Washington instead of their own peoples.

Washington in its hubris forgets that its rule is purchased and not loved.

Washington's puppets have sold their integrity and that of their countries for filthy lucre. When the money runs out, so does the empire.

By then the American people will be as corrupted as the foreign "leaders." In his review of *The United States and Torture*, edited by Marjorie Cohn (New York University Press, 2011) in the Fall 2012 *Independent Review*, Anthony Gregory writes:

> In Reagan's America, a common theme in Cold War Rhetoric was that the Soviets tortured people and detained them without cause, extracted phony confessions through cruel violence, and did the unspeakable to detainees who were helpless against the full, heartless weight of the Communist state. As much as any other evil, torture differentiated the bad guys, the Commies, from the good guys, the American people and their government. However imperfect the U.S. system might be, it had civilized standards that the enemy rejected.

By 2005, a year after torture photos from Abu Ghraib were leaked, polls of Americans showed that 38% had succumbed to the propaganda that torture was justified in some circumstances. After four more years of neoconservative advocacy of torture, an Associated Press poll reported in 2009 that 52% of Americans approved of torture. We can only hope that those who approve it will be the ones who experience it.

Torture apparently was an instrument of US Cold War policy. Torture was taught to Latin American militaries by the US School of the Americas, which operated in Panama and subsequently at Fort Benning, Georgia. However, this was a clandestine operation. It awaited the neoconservative Bush regime for US Department of Justice (sic) attorneys, graduates of the best law schools, to write legal memos justifying torture despite US statutory and international laws prohibiting torture, and for both the president and vice president of the United States to openly acknowledge and justify torture. Some of the criminals who wrote these memos are now teaching in prestigious law schools. One was appointed to the federal judiciary and sits as a judge sentencing others for their offenses.

We can conclude with Anthony Gregory that it is not only foreign political regimes that are corrupted by Washington's evil, but also Americans themselves. "Nothing better demonstrates the moral degeneracy of American political culture than the U.S. torture state."

Washington still masquerades as the one wearing the white hat, and most of the leadership of the rest of the world is paid to go along with the masquerade.

THE SPECIAL INTERESTS WON AGAIN

November 7, 2012

The election that was supposed to be too close to call turned out not to be so close after all. In my opinion, Obama won for two reasons: (1) Obama is non-threatening and inclusive, whereas Romney exuded an "us vs. them" impression that many found threatening, and (2) the election was not close enough for the electronic voting machines to steal.

As readers know, I don't think that either candidate is a good choice or that either offers a choice. Washington is controlled by powerful interest groups, not by elections. What the two parties fight over is not alternative political visions and different legislative agendas, but which party gets to be the whore for Wall Street, the military-security complex, Israel Lobby, agribusiness, and energy, mining, and timber interests.

Being the whore is important, because whores are rewarded for the services that they render. To win the White House or a presidential appointment is a career-making event as it makes a person sought after by rich and powerful interest groups. In Congress the majority party can provide more services and is thus more valuable than the minority party. One of our recent presidents who was not rich ended up with $36 million shortly after leaving office, as did former UK prime minister Tony Blair, who served Washington far better than he served his own country.

Wars are profitable for the military/security complex. Israel rewards its servants and punishes its enemies. Staffing environmental regulatory agencies with energy, mining, and timber executives is regarded by those interests as very friendly behavior.

Many Americans understand this and do not bother to vote as they know that whichever candidate or party wins, the interest groups prevail. Ronald Reagan was the last president who stood up to interest groups, or, rather, to some of them. Wall Street did not want his tax rate reductions, as Wall Street thought the result would be higher inflation and interest rates and the ruination of their stock and bond portfolios. The military/security complex did not want Reagan negotiating with Gorbachev to end the Cold War.

What is curious is that voters don't understand how politics really works. They get carried away with the political rhetoric and do not see the hypocrisy that is staring them in the face. Proud patriotic macho American men voted for Romney who went to Israel and, swearing allegiance to his liege lord, groveled at the feet of Netanyahu. Obama plays on the heart strings of his supporters by relating a story of a child with leukemia now protected by ObamaCare, while he continues to murder thousands of children and their parents with drones and other military actions in seven countries. Obama was able to elicit cheers from supporters as he described the onward and upward path of America toward greater moral accomplishments, while his actual record is that of a tyrant who codified into law the destruction of the US Constitution and the civil liberties of the American people.

The election was about nothing except who gets to serve the interest groups. The wars were not an issue in the election. Washington's provoking of Iran, Russia, and China by surrounding them with military bases was not an issue. The unconstitutional powers asserted by the executive branch to detain citizens indefinitely without due process and to assassinate them on suspicion alone were not an issue in the election. The sacrifice of the natural environment to timber, mining, and energy interests was not an issue, except to promise more sacrifice of the environment to short-term profits. Out of one side of the mouth came the nonsense promise of restoring the middle class while from the other side of the mouth issued defenses of the offshoring of their jobs and careers as free trade.

The inability to acknowledge and to debate real issues is a threat not only to the United States but also to the entire world. Washington's reckless pursuit of hegemony driven by an insane neoconservative ideology is leading to military confrontation with Russia and China. Eleven years of gratuitous wars with more on the way and an economic policy that protects financial institutions from their mistakes have burdened the US with massive budget deficits that are being monetized. The US dollar's loss of the reserve currency role and hyperinflation are plausible consequences of disastrous economic policy.

How is it possible that "the world's only superpower" can hold a presidential election without any discussion of these very real and serious problems being part of it? How can anyone be excited or made hopeful about such an outcome?

OBDURATE WASHINGTON

December 11, 2012

With its power declining, Washington was no longer able to keep Russia out of the World Trade Organization. Congress showed its spite over its impotence by hooking the normalizing of trade with Russia to what is called the "Magnitsky rule."[72]

Sergei Magnitsky was a Russian attorney who represented a British investment firm accused of tax evasion and fraud in Russia. Apparently, the UK firm supplied information to the media alleging government misconduct and participation in corruption inside state-owned Russian companies.

Magnitsky represented the accused UK firm. He claimed that the firm had not committed fraud but had been a victim of fraud. In turn, Magnitsky was arrested. He developed serious illnesses in prison for which he apparently received inadequate medical care.

Whether he died of untreated illnesses, we cannot know. But the US Congress, acting on the unsubstantiated allegation that Magnitsky was tortured and murdered, attached to the trade normalization bill a provision that requires the US government to release a list of Russian government officials believed or imagined to have been involved with the violation of Magnitsky's human rights and to freeze the assets of these members of the Russian government and to deny them visas to travel to the US. Considering Washington's belief that its law is the universal law of humankind, Washington probably intends for every country to enforce its edict or be sanctioned in turn.

The Russian government finds the "Magnitsky rule" amusing. Here is the Russian government accused, without any evidence, of ONE torture and death, while Washington has such a large number of torture deaths from Abu Ghraib to Gitmo to the secret CIA torture centers to endless drone attacks on kids' soccer games, weddings, funerals, medical clinics, schools, farm houses and aid workers. The evidence is completely clear that Washington has tortured a number of individuals to death and into false confessions and blown to pieces thousands of innocents known as "collateral damage." No one but Washington and its servants denies this. But one alleged Russian offense against human rights brings forth an act of the US Congress, all in a huff about the violation of a Russian lawyer's human rights.

A number of rulers in human history have been this arrogant. But has a democracy ever been? Athens perhaps, but Sparta taught Athens a lesson.

What do the members of Congress think is the response of the rest of the world to Washington's utter hypocrisy? How can Washington pass a law punishing Russian government officials for allegedly doing once what we know for an absolute fact Washington does every day?

The holier-than-thou presence that Washington presents to the world is so phony and shopworn that Washington is becoming not only despised but a laughing stock. Peoples cease to fear the "superpower" when they laugh at its folly, hypocrisy and utter stupidity.

Certainly, the Russians are not afraid. The Russian Prime Minister, Dmitry Medvedev, responded to the Washington morons as follows: "It is inadmissible when one country tries to dictate its will to another." The Magnitsky rule will bring forth a "symmetrical and asymmetrical reaction from Russia." The Russian Duma seems intent that this be the case.[73]

Washington is like the drunk in a bar who picks a fight with a bruiser. Washington is full of itself, but Russia and China are not going to put up with a financially busted and militarily overstretched popinjay.

ATTACK ON SOVEREIGNTY

January 15, 2013

Those concerned about "The New World Order" speak as if the United States is coming under the control of an outside conspiratorial force. In fact, it is the US that is the New World Order. That is what the American unipolar world, about which China, Russia, and Iran complain, is all about.

Washington has demonstrated that it has no respect for its own laws and Constitution, much less any respect for international law and the law and sovereignty of other countries. All that counts is Washington's will as the pursuit of hegemony moves Washington closer to becoming a world dictator.

The examples are so numerous someone should compile them into a book. During the Reagan administration the long established bank secrecy laws of Switzerland had to bend to Washington's will. The Clinton administration attacked Serbia, murdered civilians and sent Serbia's president to be tried as a war criminal for defending his country. The US government engages in widespread spying on Europeans' emails and telephone calls that is unrelated to terrorism. Julian Assange is confined to the Ecuadoran embassy in London, because Washington won't permit the British government to honor his grant of political asylum. Washington refuses to comply with a writ of habeas corpus from a British court to turn over Yunus Rahmatullah, whose detention a British Court of Appeals has ruled to be unlawful. Washington imposes sanctions on other countries and enforces them by cutting sovereign nations that do not comply out of the international payments system.

Last week the Obama regime warned the British government that it was a violation of US interests for the UK to pull out of the European Union or reduce its ties to the EU in any way.

In other words, the sovereignty of Great Britain is not a choice to be made by the British government or people. The decision is made by Washington in keeping with Washington's interest.

The British are so accustomed to being Washington's colony that Deputy Prime Minister Nick Clegg and a group of UK business executives quickly lined up with Washington.

This leaves Great Britain in a quandary. The British economy, once a manufacturing powerhouse, has been reduced to the City of London, Britain's equivalent to Wall Street. London, like New York, is a world financial center; there are none in Europe. Without its financial status, there wouldn't be much left of the UK. It is because of the City's financial importance that the UK, alone of the major EU member states, kept the British pound as its currency and did not join the euro. Because the UK has its own currency and central bank, it was spared the sovereign debt crisis that has plagued other EU member states. The Bank of England, like the Federal Reserve in the US, was able to bail out its own banks, whereas other EU states sharing a common currency could not create money. The European Central Bank is prohibited by its charter (at Germany's insistence) from bailing out member states.

The quandary for the UK is that the solution to the sovereign debt crisis toward which the EU is moving is to strip the member governments of their fiscal sovereignty. For the individual countries, the spending, taxing and, thereby, deficit or surplus positions of the member countries' budgets will be set by EU central authority. This would mean the end of national sovereignty for European countries.

For Britain to remain an EU member while retaining its own currency and central bank would mean special status for Great Britain. The UK would be the only significant member of the EU that remained a sovereign country. What are the chances that the UK will be permitted such exceptional status? Is this acceptable to Germany and France?

If the British are to fold themselves into Europe, they will have to give up their currency, central bank, their law, and their economic status as a world financial center and accept governance by the EU bureaucracy. The British will have to give up being somebody and become nobody.

It would, however, free the UK from being Washington's puppet unless the EU itself is Washington's puppet.

According to reports, sometime this year Scotland, a constituent part of the UK, is to vote on leaving the UK and becoming an independent country. How ironic that as the UK debates its dismemberment the country itself faces being merged into a multi-national state.

THE INSTITUTIONALIZATION OF TYRANNY

January 18, 2013

Republicans and conservative Americans are still fighting Big Government in its welfare state form. Apparently, they have never heard of the militarized police state form of Big Government, or if they have, they are comfortable with it and have no objection.

Republicans, including those in the House and Senate, are content for big government to initiate wars without a declaration of war or even Congressional assent, and use drones to murder citizens of countries with which Washington is not at war. Many Republicans do not mind that federal "security" agencies spy on American citizens without warrants and record every email, Internet site visited, Facebook posting, cell phone call, and credit card purchase. Republicans in Congress even voted to fund the massive structure in Utah in which this information is stored.

But heaven forbid that big government should do anything for a poor person.Republicans have been fighting Social Security ever since President Franklin D. Roosevelt signed it into law in the 1930s, and they have been fighting Medicare ever since President Lyndon Johnson signed it into law in 1965 as part of the Great Society initiatives.

Conservatives accuse liberals of the "institutionalization of compassion." Writing in the February, 2013, issue of *Chronicles*, John C. Seiler, Jr. damns Johnson's Great Society as "a major force in turning a country that still enjoyed a modicum of republican liberty into the centralized, bureaucratized, degenerate, and bankrupt state we endure today."

It doesn't occur to conservatives that in Europe democracy, liberty, welfare, rich people, and national health services all coexist, but that somehow American liberty is so fragile that it is overturned by a limited health program only available to the elderly.

Neither does it occur to conservative Republicans that it is far better to institutionalize compassion than to institutionalize tyranny.

The institutionalization of tyranny is the achievement of the Bush/Obama regimes of the 21st century. This, and not the Great Society, is the decisive break from the American tradition. The Bush Republicans demolished almost all of the constitutional protections of liberty erected by the Founding Fathers. The Obama Democrats codified Bush's dismantling of the Constitution and removed the protection afforded to citizens from being murdered by the government without due process. One decade was time enough for two presidents to make Americans the least free people of any developed country, indeed, perhaps of any country. In what other country or countries has the chief executive officer secured the legal right to murder citizens without due process?

It turns one's stomach to listen to conservatives bemoan the destruction of liberty by compassion while they institutionalize torture, indefinite detention in violation of habeas corpus, murder of citizens on suspicion and unproven accusation alone, complete and total violation of privacy, interference with the right to travel by unaccountable "no-fly" lists and highway check points, the brutalization by police of citizens and those exercising their right to protest, frame-ups of critics, and narrow the bounds of free speech.

In America today only the executive branch of the federal government has any privacy. The privacy is institutional, not personal—witness the fate of CIA director Petraeus. While the executive branch destroys the privacy of everyone else, it insists on its own privilege of privacy. National security is invoked to shield the executive branch from its criminal actions. Federal prosecutors actually conduct trials in which the evidence against defendants is classified and withheld from defendants' attorneys. Attorneys such as Lynne Stewart have been imprisoned for not following orders from federal prosecutors to violate the attorney-client privilege.

Conservatives accept the monstrous police state that has been erected, because they think it makes them safe from "Muslim terrorism." They haven't the wits to see that they are now open to terrorism by the government.

Consider, for example, the case of Bradley Manning. He is accused of leaking confidential information that reveals US government war crimes despite the fact that it is the responsibility of every soldier to reveal war crimes. Virtually every one of Manning's constitutional rights has been violated by the US government. He has been tortured. In an effort to coerce Manning into admitting trumped-up charges and implicating WikiLeaks' Julian Assange, Manning had his right to a speedy trial violated by nearly three years of pre-trial custody and repeated trial delays by government prosecutors. And now the judge, Col. Denise Lind, who comes across as a member of the prosecution rather than an impartial judge, has ruled that Manning cannot use as evidence the government's own reports that the leaked information did not harm national security. Lind has also thrown out the legal principle of *mens rea* by ruling that Manning's motive for leaking information about US war crimes cannot be presented as evidence in his trial.[74] *Mens rea* says that a crime requires criminal intent. By discarding this legal principle, Lind has prevented Manning from showing that his motive was to do his duty under the military code and reveal evidence of war crimes. This allows prosecutors to turn a dutiful act into the crime of aiding the enemy by revealing classified information.

Of course, nothing that Manning allegedly revealed helped the enemy in any way as the enemy, having suffered the war crimes, was already aware of them.

Obama Democrats are no more disturbed than conservative Republicans that a dutiful American soldier is being prosecuted because he has a moral conscience. In Manning's trial, the government's definition of victory has nothing whatsoever to do with justice prevailing. For Washington, victory means stamping out moral conscience and protecting a corrupt government from public exposure of its war crimes.

IN AMERICA LAW NO LONGER EXISTS

January 31, 2013

In the 21st century Americans have experienced an extraordinary collapse in the rule of law and in their constitutional protections. Today American citizens, once a free people protected by law, can be legally assassinated and detained in prison indefinitely without any evidence being presented to a court of their guilt, and they can be sentenced to prison on the basis of secret testimony by anonymous witnesses not subject to cross examination. The US "justice system" has been transformed by the Bush/Obama regime into the "justice system" of Gestapo Germany and Stalinist Russia. There is no difference.

In an article available at the Washington Report on Middle East Affairs, Stephen Downs, formerly Chief Attorney with the New York State Commission on Judicial Conduct and Kathy Manley, a criminal defense attorney and member of the New York Civil Liberties Union, report on how the US government destroyed a charity, the Holy Land Foundation, which provided money for feeding the poor and for building schools and hospitals in Palestine.[75]

The charity, aware of the perils of being based in the US and doing anything for Palestinians, relied on the US State Department and the US Department of Justice (*sic*) for guidance on where to send humanitarian aid. The charity sent its aid to the same aid committees in Palestine that the US Agency for International Development and the UN used to distribute aid to the Palestinians.

In the first trial of the Holy Land Foundation, the US government admitted that none of the charity's donations had gone to terrorist organizations, and the federal prosecutors failed to achieve a conviction. So the prosecutors tried the charity again.

In the second trial, the judge permitted the prosecutors to call an "anonymous expert" to tell the jury that some of the committees used by USAID and the UN and approved by the US Department of State were controlled by Hamas, the elected government of Palestine that Israel requires the US government to brand as "terrorist."

As Downs and Manley point out, an "anonymous expert" cannot "be challenged because he is unknown." There cannot be a cross examination. The "expert" could be anyone—someone paid to lie to the jury, a Zionist who believes all help to Palestinians comprises "aid to terrorists," or a member of Mossad, the Israeli intelligence service that has thoroughly infiltrated the US according to US intelligence experts.

Injustices are everywhere, the authors admit, so why is this important to you? The answer is that the due process clause of the US Constitution requires that criminal laws give fair notice as to what conduct is prohibited. According to Downs and Manley, the Holy Land Foundation followed the US State Department's list of designated terrorist organizations and avoided all contact with organizations on the list, but were indicted and convicted regardless. *This tells us that federal prosecutors are viciously corrupt and that jurors are so inept and propagandized that they are useless to defendants.*

The US Supreme Court refused to review this most blatant case of wrongful conviction. By so doing, the US Supreme Court established that the court, like the US House of Representatives, the US Senate, and the executive branch, is not only a servant of the police state but also a servant of Israel and supports the destruction of the Palestinians by designating aid to Palestine as an act of terrorism.

What this means for you is that your involvement in legal transactions or associations can be declared ex post facto by secret witnesses to be criminal involvements. The criminality of your past behavior can now be established, according to Downs and Manley, by "anonymous experts," mouthpieces for the government prosecutors who cannot "be confronted or cross-examined within the meaning of the 6th Amendment."

Downs and Manley write: "The implications are enormous. The government can now criminalize political, religious and social ideology and speech. Donating to peace groups, participating in protests, attending church, mosque or synagogue, entertaining friends, and posting material on the Internet, for example, could later be found to be illegal because of 'associations,' manufactured by anonymous experts, which in some way allegedly support designated terrorist organizations one has never heard of."

The authors could have added that if the government wants to get you, all it has to do is to declare that someone or some organization somewhere in your past was connected in a vague undefined way with terrorism. The government's assertion suffices. No proof is needed. The brainwashed jury will not protect you.

Be prepared in the next year or two for all criticism of "our freedom and democracy" government to be shut down. In America, truth is about to be exterminated.

OBAMA'S EXPANDING KILL LIST

February 11, 2013

Prosecutors always expand laws far beyond their intent. Attorneys in civil cases do the same. For example, the 1970 Racketeer Influenced and Corrupt Organizations Act was passed in order to make it easier for the government to convict members of the Mafia. However, the law, despite its intent, was quickly expanded by prosecutors and attorneys and used in cases against pro-life activists, Catholic bishops, corporations accused of hiring illegal immigrants, and in divorce cases. "Junk bond king" Michael Milken, a person with no ties to organized crime, was threatened with indictment under the RICO Act. Prosecutors have found that the asset freeze provision in the Act is a convenient way to prevent a defendant from being able to pay attorneys and, therefore, makes it easier for prosecutors to coerce innocent defendants into a guilty plea.

We are now witnessing the expansion of Obama's Kill List. The list began under the Bush regime as a rationale for murdering suspect citizens of countries with which the US was not at war. The Obama regime expanded the scope of the list to include the execution, without due process of law, of US citizens accused, without evidence presented in court, of association with terrorism. The list quickly expanded to include the American teen-age son of a cleric accused of preaching jihad against the West. The son's "association" with terrorism apparently was his blood relationship to his father.

As Glenn Greenwald recently wrote, the power of government to imprison and to murder its citizens without due process of law is the certain mark of dictatorship. Dictatorship is government unconstrained by law. On February 10 the *Wall Street Journal* revealed that the Obama dictatorship now intends to expand the Kill List to include those accused of acting against foreign governments. Mokhtar Belmokhtar, an "Algerian militant" accused of planning the January attack on an Algerian natural gas facility, has been chosen as the threat that is being used to expand Obama's Kill List to include participants in the internal disputes and civil wars of all other countries.

If the Obama regime is on the side of the government, as in Algeria, it will kill the rebels opposing the government. If the Obama regime is on the side of the rebels, as in Libya, it will kill the government's leaders. Whether Washington would dare to send a drone to murder Putin and the president of China remains to be seen. But don't be surprised if Washington has targeted the president of Iran.

The elasticity of the Kill List and its easy expansion makes it certain that Washington will be involved in extra-judicial executions of those "associated with terrorism" over much of the world. Americans themselves should be alarmed, because the term "association with terrorism" is very elastic. Federal prosecutors have interpreted the term to include charitable contributions to Palestinians.

The next time former US Representative Cynthia McKinney gets on an aid ship to Palestine, will Washington give the green light to Israel to kill her as a terrorist agent for her association with aid to Gaza, ruled by the "terrorist organization," Hamas?

Already a year or two ago, the director of Homeland Security said that the federal police agency's focus had shifted from terrorists to "domestic extremists," another elastic and undefined term. A domestic extremist will be all who disagree with Washington. They also are headed for the Kill List.

Where is the government going with this? Is the most likely outcome down the road that everyone disliked or distrusted by those who have the power to add to the Kill List will find themselves on the list? The government can expand the Kill List beyond the original intent as easily as the RICO Act was expanded beyond its original intent.

As the Founding Fathers knew and the American people have forgotten, no one is safe in a dictatorship.

Clearly, the American public lacks sufficient comprehension to remain a free people. All indications are that the large majority of Americans fear alleged terrorists in distant lands more than they fear their government's acquisition of dictatorial powers over them—powers that allow government to place itself above the law and to be unaccountable to law. This is despite the fact that 99.999% of all Americans will never, ever, experience any terrorism except that of their own government.

According to a recent poll of registered American voters, 75% approve of Washington's assassination of foreign citizens abroad based on suspicion that they might be terrorists, despite the fact that the vast majority of the Gitmo detainees, declared by the US government to be the most dangerous men on earth, turned out to be totally innocent. Only 13% of registered voters disapprove of the extra-judicial murders carried out by Washington against foreign citizens, whether based on wrong intelligence, hearsay, or actual deeds.[76]

Registered voters have a different view of the extra-judicial murder of US citizens. In what the rest of the world will see as further evidence of American double-standards, 48% believe it is illegal for Washington to murder US citizens without due process of law. However, 24% agree with the Obama regime that it is permissible for the government to murder its own citizens on accusation alone without trial and conviction of a capital crime. As *The Onion* put it, "24% of citizens were unequivocally in favor of being obliterated at any point, for any reason, in a massive airstrike."[77]

Are we to be reassured or alarmed that 24% of registered voters believe that the terrorist threat is so great that suspicion alone without evidence, trial, and conviction is sufficient for Washington to terminate US citizens? Should we not be disturbed that a quarter of registered voters, despite overwhelming evidence that Washington's wars are based on conscious lies—"weapons of mass destruction," "Al Qaeda connections"—are still prepared to believe the government's claim that the person it just murdered was a terrorist? Why are so many Americans willing to believe a proven liar?

If we add up all the costs of the "war on terror," it is obvious that the costs are many magnitudes greater than the terror threat that the war is alleged to contain. If terrorists were really a threat to Americans, shopping centers and electric substations would be blowing up constantly. Airport security would be a sham, because terrorists would set off the bombs in the crowded lines waiting to clear security. Traffic would be continually tied up from roofing nails dispensed on all main roads in cities across the country for each rush hour. Water supplies would be poisoned. Police stations would be bombed and police officers routinely terminated on the streets. Instead, nothing has happened despite Washington's killing and displacement of huge numbers of Muslims in seven or eight countries over the past 11 years.

The cost of the "war on terror" is not merely the multi-trillion dollar financial bill documented by Joseph Stiglitz and Linda Bilmes. The cost of Washington's wars is the main reason for the large national debt, the threat of which politicians are using to destroy the social safety net. This is a huge cost for a pointless war that pleases Israel and enriches the armament companies but does nothing for Americans.

The financial cost is huge, but how important is this cost compared to another cost—the domestic police state supported by a significant percentage of the population and a majority in Congress and the media? Is the war on terror worth the evisceration of the US Constitution? A war that costs us the Constitution means our total defeat.The cost in human life has been enormous. Millions of Muslims have been killed, wounded, orphaned, and displaced, and entire countries have been destroyed as socio-political entities. Washington has Iraq locked in sectarian murder. Libya has no government, just warring factions, and now Syria is in the process of being disintegrated. The prospects for people's lives in these countries have been ruined for years to come.

The cost in American lives has also been high. More than 400,000 American lives have been adversely affected by 11 years of pointless war. The deaths of 6,656 US troops, the 50,000 wounded, the 1,700 life-changing limb amputations, and the suicides[78] are just the tip of the iceberg. Since the Bush-Obama wars began, 129,731 US troops have been diagnosed with post-traumatic stress disorder. And now we learn from a new Congressional Research Service report that more than a quarter million of US troops have experienced Traumatic Brain Injury. Based on current diagnostic capability, three-fourths of the cases are classified as mild.[79]

These lost, ruined and impaired lives affect also the lives of many others—spouses, children, parents, siblings, and those disheartened by their government's pointless wars who have to care for the damaged. There are many Americans who have been collaterally damaged by Washington's pointless wars.

Will Americans wake up in time? I wish I could answer "yes," but I regret that Americans are an insouciant people. They are unaware. Americans are more concerned with sports events, sales, and which celebrities are sleeping together than they are with their liberty. Washington can create a police state, because there are insufficient citizens with the intelligence, education, and awareness to stop it.

Congress has accepted the police state. It has given up too much of its power to the executive branch and is too beholden to the special interests that benefit from the police state to do anything about it. Congress is even content for the CIA or the Pentagon, perhaps both, to murder by robot innocent people on the Benthamite presumption that at some future time they might commit a terrorist act. Some US Senators want a cloak of legality for the murders and suggest a secret court to rubber-stamp Obama's Kill List. CIA nominee director John Brennan reportedly objected to a secret court on the grounds that not all drone murders are retaliation; some victims are murdered for what some executive branch official thinks they might do at some future time, and without evidence the court would have nothing objective to go by.[80]

The federal judiciary has proven to be almost as impotent. Federal judges did not ask federal prosecutors why, in violation of the whistleblower protection laws, they were prosecuting National Security Agency senior executive Thomas Drake for blowing the whistle on the NSA's illegal spying on US citizens instead of the officials who broke the law and committed felonies. Judges did not ask why CIA agent John Kiriakou was prosecuted for blowing the whistle on the torture program instead of those who committed crimes by authorizing and committing torture.[81]

The innocent and the truth-tellers were prosecuted. The criminals and the liars were not. The federal judges went along with the Justice (*sic*) Department's prosecutions of those who obeyed the law and did their duty and non-prosecution of criminals who clearly without any doubt violated the law, trampled upon the US Constitution, and committed felonies.

In a police state it is always the innocent who are the most heavily punished. In his history, *The Gulag Archipelago*, Alexander Solzhenitsyn explains that in the prison camps, the Soviet equivalent to Guantanamo and the CIA's secret torture prisons, common criminals such as murderers, rapists, and robbers had a privileged position compared to the political prisoners who mistakenly thought that the Soviet Constitution meant something. It will be the same in America.

The destruction of truth and the law in the US is the legacy of 9/11. Both conservatives and the left-wing have bought into the government's preposterous story that a few Saudi Arabians, unsupported by any government or intelligence agency, outwitted every institution of the National Security State and inflicted the most humiliating blow against a superpower in human history. They buy into this story despite unequivocal evidence that WTC building 7 came down at free fall speed, an event that can only occur as a result of controlled demolition.

But evidence and expert testimony no longer have authority in the US, which now has its own form of Lysenkoism.

Lysenko was a quack Soviet scientist, a charlatan who successfully persecuted Soviet geneticists for "setting themselves against Marxism" by not having a Marxist theory of genetics. Soviet geneticists were arrested and executed for being "against the people." Even the world famous Soviet geneticist, Nikolai Vavilov, was arrested and died in prison.

Americans don't know any more about physics and structural architecture and engineering than the Soviet population and Stalin knew about genetics. Today "Lysenkoism" is used as a metaphor to denote the corruption of science in behalf of a social, political, or ideological purpose.

Lysenko used lies to gain power, just as Ponzi scheme operators use lies to gain wealth. Power is an Aphrodisiac, and everyone in Washington wants it. All indications are that they have it.

Liberty is disappearing before our eyes. The government's reaction to *Hedges v. Obama* indicates that the NDAA may already be holding US citizens in indefinite detention.[82]

Expect no help from "progressives," who believe in Obama more than they believe in liberty. The *Guardian* article by Glen Greenwald is scathing.[83]

WHEN LEFT AND RIGHT FIGHT, POWER WINS

February 14, 2013

My experience with the American left and right leads to the conclusion that the left sees private power as the source of oppression and government as the countervailing and rectifying power, while the right sees government as the source of oppression and a free and unregulated private sector as the countervailing and rectifying power. Both are concerned with restraining the power to oppress, but they take opposite positions on the source of the oppressive power and remedy.

The right is correct that government power is the problem, and the left is correct that private power is the problem. Therefore, locating power within the government or private sectors cannot reduce, constrain, or minimize it.

How does the Obama Regime, billed as progressive, differ from the tax-cut, deregulation Bush/Cheney Regime? Both are complicit in the maximization of executive branch power and in the minimization of citizens' civil liberties and, thus, of the people's power. Did the progressive Obama reverse the right-wing Bush's destruction of habeas corpus and due process? No. Obama further minimized the people's power. Bush could throw us in prison for life without proof of cause. Obama can execute us without proof of cause. They do this in the name of protecting us from terrorism, but not from their terrorism.

Those Americans who have no experience with, or knowledge of, tyranny believe that only terrorists will experience the unchecked power of the state. They will believe this until it happens to them, or their children, or their friends.

The view of human nature held by the right and the left depends on where those humans are located. For the right (and for libertarians) human nature expressed through the private sector is good and serves the public, but when in the government sector it is evil and oppressive. For the left, it is the opposite. As the same people go back and forth from one sector to the other, one marvels at the presumable transformations of their characters and morality. A good man becomes evil, and an evil man becomes good, depending on the location of his activities.

One of my professors, James M. Buchanan, who won a Nobel Prize, pointed out that people are just as self-serving whether they are in the private sector or in government. The problem is how to constrain government and private power to the best extent possible.

Our Founding Fathers' solution was to minimize the power of government and to rely on contending factions among private interests to prevent the rise of an oligarchy. In the event that contending private interests failed, the oligarchy that seized the government would not have much public power to exercise.

The Founding Fathers' design more or less worked except for interludes of civil war and economic crisis until the Cold War built up the power of government and the deregulation of the Clinton and Bush presidencies built up the power of private interests. It all came together with the accumulation of new, dictatorial powers in the executive branch in the name of protecting us from terrorists and with deregulation's creation of powerful corporations "too big to fail."

Now we have a government whose elected members are beholden to a private oligarchy, consisting of the military/security complex, Wall Street and the financial sector, the Israel Lobby, agribusiness, pharmaceuticals, and the energy, mining, and timber businesses, with the power to shut down people's protests at their exploitation by robber barons and government alike.

Vast amounts of government debt have been added to taxpayers' burdens in order to fight wars that only benefit the military/security complex and the Israel Lobby. More vast amounts have been added in order to force taxpayers to cover the reckless gambling bets of the financial sector. Taxpayers are denied interest on their savings in order to protect the balance sheets of a corrupt financial sector. Legitimate protestors are brutalized by police and equated by Homeland Security with "domestic extremists," defined by Homeland Security as in close relation to terrorists.

Today Americans are not safe from government or private power and suffer at the hands of both.

What can be done? From within, probably very little. The right blames the left, and the left blames the right. The two sides are locked in ideological combat while power grows in both the private and public sectors, but not the benevolent power that the two ideologies presuppose. Instead, a two-headed power monster has risen.

If the power that has been established over the American people is to be shattered, it will come from outside. The Federal Reserve's continuing monetization of the enormous debt that Washington is generating can destroy the dollar's exchange value, sending up interest rates, collapsing the bond, stock, and real estate markets, and sinking the economy into deep depression at a time in history when Americans have exhausted their savings and are deeply in debt with high levels of joblessness and homelessness. The rise in import prices from a drop in the dollar's exchange value would make survival an issue for a large percentage of the population.

Overnight the US could transition from superpower to third world penitent begging for a rescue program.

Who would grant it? The Russians encircled by US military bases and whose internal serenity is disrupted by inflows of American money to dissident groups in an effort to destabilize the Russian State? The Chinese, whose government is routinely denounced by a hypocritical Washington for human rights abuses while Washington surrounds China with newly constructed military bases and new deployments of troops and naval vessels? South America, a long-suffering victim of Washington's oppression? Europe, exhausted by conflicts and by Washington's organizing them as puppet states and using them as mercenaries in Washington's wars for hegemony?

No country, except perhaps the bought-and-paid-for puppets of Britain, Canada, Australia, and Japan, would come to Washington's aid.

In the ensuing collapse, the power of Washington and the power of the private robber barons would evaporate. Americans would suffer, but they would be rid of the power that has been established over them and that has changed them from a free people to exploited serfs.

This is, perhaps, an optimistic conclusion, but those relatively few Americans who are aware need some hope. This is the best that I can do.

HUGO CHAVEZ

On March 5, 2013, Hugo Chavez, President of Venezuela and world leader against imperialism, died. Washington imperialists and their media and think tank whores expressed gleeful sighs of relief as did the brainwashed US population. An "enemy of America" was gone.

Chavez was not an enemy of America. He was an enemy of Washington's hegemony over other countries, an enemy of Washington's alliance with elite ruling cliques who steal from the people they grind down and deny sustenance. He was an enemy of Washington's injustice, of Washington's foreign policy based on lies and military aggression, bombs and invasions.

Washington is not America. Washington is Satan's home town.

Chavez was a friend of truth and justice, and this made him unpopular throughout the Western World where every political leader regards truth and justice as dire threats.Chavez was a world leader. Unlike US politicians, Chavez was respected throughout the non-western world. He was awarded honorary doctorates from China, Russia, Brazil, and other countries, but not from Harvard, Yale, Cambridge, and Oxford.

Chavez was a miracle. He was a miracle, because he did not sell out to the United States and the Venezuelan elites. Had he sold out, Chavez would have become very rich from oil revenues, like the Saudi Royal Family, and he would have been honored by the United States in the way that Washington honors all its puppets: with visits to the White House. He could have become a dictator for life as long as he served Washington.

Each of Washington's puppets, from Asia to Europe and the Middle East, anxiously awaits the invitation that demonstrates Washington's appreciation of his or her servitude to the global imperialist power that still occupies Japan and Germany 68 years after World War II and South Korea 60 years after the end of the Korean War, and has placed troops and military bases in a large number of other "sovereign" countries.

It would have been politically easy for Chavez to sell out. All he had to do was to continue populist rhetoric, promote his allies in the army, throw more benefits to the underclass than its members had ever previously experienced, and divide the rest of the oil revenues with the corrupt Venezuelan elites.

But Chavez was a real person, like Rafael Correa, the three-term elected president of Ecuador, who stood up to the United States and granted political asylum to the persecuted Julian Assange, and Evo Morales, the first indigenous president of Bolivia since the Spanish conquest. The majority of Venezuelans understood that Chavez was a real person. They elected him to four terms as president and would have continued electing him as long as he lived. What Washington hates most is a real person who cannot be bought.

The more the corrupt western politicians and media whores demonized Chavez, the more Venezuelans loved him. They understood completely that anyone damned by Washington was God's gift to the world.

It is costly to stand up to Washington. All who are bold enough to do so are demonized. They risk assassination and being overthrown in a CIA-organized coup, as Chavez was in 2002. When CIA-instructed Venezuelan elites sprung their coup and kidnapped Chavez, the coup was defeated by the Venezuelan people who took to the streets and by elements of the military before Chavez could be murdered by the CIA-controlled Venezuelan elites. These escaped with their own venal lives only because, unlike them, Chavez was a humanitarian. The Venezuelan people rose in instantaneous and massive public defense of Chavez and put the lie to the Bush White House claim that Chavez was a dictator.

Showing its sordid corruption, *The New York Times* took the side of the undemocratic coup by a handful of elitists against the democratically elected Chavez, and declared that Chavez's removal by a small group of rich elites and CIA operatives meant that "Venezuelan democracy is no longer threatened by a would-be dictator."

The lies and demonization continue with Chavez's death. He will never be forgiven for standing up for justice. Neither will Correa and Morales, both of whom are no doubt on Washington's assassination lists.

CounterPunch, Fairness & Accuracy in Reporting, and other commentators have collected examples of the venom-spewing obituaries that the western presstitutes have written for Chavez, essentially celebrations that death has silenced the bravest voice on earth.[84]

Perhaps the most absurd of all was Associated Press business reporter Pamela Sampson's judgment that Chavez wasted Venezuela's oil wealth on "social programs including state-run food markets, cash benefits for poor families, free health clinics and education programs," a poor use of money that could have been used to build sky scrapers such as "the world's tallest building in Dubai and branches of the Louvre and Guggenheim museums in Abu Dhabi."[85]

Among the tens of millions of Washington's victims in the world—the people of Afghanistan, Iraq, Libya, Sudan, Pakistan, Yemen, Somalia, Syria, Palestine, Lebanon, Mali, with Iran, Russia, China, and South America

waiting in the wings for sanctions, destabilization, conquest or re-conquest—
Chavez's September 20, 2006 speech at the UN General Assembly during the
George W. Bush regime will stand forever as the greatest speech of the early
21st century.

Chavez beards the lion, or rather Satan, in his own den:

> Yesterday, the devil himself stood right here, at this
> podium, speaking as if he owned the world. You can still
> smell the sulfur...
>
> We should call a psychiatrist to analyze yesterday's
> statement made by the president of the United States. As the
> spokesman of imperialism, he came to share his nostrums,
> to try to preserve the current pattern of domination,
> exploitation and pillage of the peoples of the world. An
> Alfred Hitchcock movie could use it as a scenario. I would
> even propose a title: 'the Devil's Recipe.'

The UN General Assembly had never heard such words, not even in
the days when the militarily powerful Soviet Union was present. Faces broke
out in smiles of approval, but no one dared to clap. Too much US money for
the home country was at stake. [A reader pointed out that although Chavez's
speech was not interrupted with clapping, he received a healthy round of
applause at the end.]

The US and UK delegations fled the scene, like vampires confronted
with garlic and the Cross or werewolves confronted with silver bullets.

Chavez spoke about the false democracy of elites that is imposed
on others by force, by "weapons and bombs." Chavez asked, "What type of
democracy do you impose with Marines and bombs?"

Wherever George W. Bush looks, Chavez said,

> he sees extremists. And you, my brother—he looks at your
> color, and he says, oh, there's an extremist. Evo Morales,
> the worthy president of Bolivia, looks like an extremist to
> him. The imperialists see extremists everywhere. It is not
> that we are extremists. It is that the world is waking up. It
> is waking up all over and people are standing up.

In two short sentences totaling 20 words, Chavez defined for all
times early 21st century Washington:

> *The imperium is afraid of truth, is afraid of independent
> voices. It calls us extremists, but they are the extremists.*

Throughout South America and the non-western world, Chavez's death is being blamed on Washington. South Americans are aware of the US congressional hearings in the 1970s when the Church Committee brought to light the various CIA schemes to poison Fidel Castro.

The official document presented to President John F. Kennedy by the US Joint Chiefs of Staff, known as the Northwoods Project, is known to the world and is available online. The Northwoods project proposed a false flag attack on American citizens in order to blame Cuba and create public and world acceptance for US-imposed regime change in Cuba. President Kennedy rejected the proposal as inconsistent with morality and accountable government.[86]

The belief has already hardened in South America that Washington with its hideous technologies of death infected Chavez with cancer in order to remove him as an obstacle to Washington's hegemony over South America.

This belief will never die: Chavez, the greatest South American since Simon Bolivar, was murdered by Washington. True or false, the belief is set in stone. As Washington and globalism destroy more countries, the lives of elites become more precarious.

President Franklin Delano Roosevelt understood that security for the rich required economic security for the underclasses. Roosevelt established in the US a weak form of social democracy that European politicians had already understood was necessary for social cohesion and political and economic stability.

The Clinton, Bush, and Obama regimes set about undermining the stability that Roosevelt provided, as Thatcher, Major, Blair, and the current prime minister of the UK undermined the social agreement between classes in the UK. Politicians in Canada, Australia, and New Zealand also made the mistake of handing power over to private elites at the expense of social and economic stability.

Gerald Celente predicts that the elites will not survive the hatred and anger that they are bringing upon themselves. I suspect that he is correct. The American middle class is being destroyed. The working class has become a proletariat, and the social welfare system is being destroyed in order to reduce the budget deficit caused by the loss of tax revenues to jobs offshoring and the expense of wars, overseas military bases, and financial bailouts. The American people are being compelled to suffer in order that elites can continue with their agendas.

The US elites know what is coming. That is why they created a Nazi-style Ministry of the Interior known as Homeland Security, armed with enough ammunition to kill every American five times and with tanks to neutralize the Second Amendment rights of Americans.[87]

Pistols and rifles are useless against tanks, as the Branch Davidians found out in Waco, Texas. The protection of a small handful of elites from the Americans they are oppressing is also the reason the police are being militarized, brought under Washington's control and armed with drones that can assassinate the real leaders of the American people who will be, not in the legislative, executive, or judicial chambers, but in the streets.[88]

Internment camps in the US appear to be real and not a conspiracy theory, as indicated by excerpts from the leaked February 2010 Department of Defense document FM 3-39.40 entitled "Interment and Resettlement Options".[89]

The threat that the US government poses to its own citizens was recognized on March 7, 2013, by two US Senators, Ted Cruz (R-TX) and Rand Paul (R-KY), who introduced a bill to prevent the US government from murdering its own citizens: "The Federal Government may not use a drone to kill a citizen of the United States who is located in the United States" unless the person "poses an imminent threat of death or serious bodily injury to another individual. Nothing in this section shall be construed to suggest that the Constitution would otherwise allow the killing of a citizen of the United States in the United States without due process of law."

The "indispensable people" with their presidents Bush and Obama have begun the 21st century with death and violence. That is their only legacy.

The death and violence that Washington has unleashed will come back to Washington and to the corrupt political elites everywhere. As Gerald Celente says, the first great war of the 21st century has begun.

IRAQ
AFTER TEN YEARS

March 18, 2013

March 19, 2013. Ten years ago today the Bush regime invaded Iraq. It is known that the justification for the invasion was a packet of lies orchestrated by the neoconservative Bush regime in order to deceive the United Nations and the American people. The US Secretary of State at that time, General Colin Powell, has expressed his regrets that he was used by the Bush regime to deceive the United Nations with fake intelligence that the Bush and Blair regimes knew to be fake. But the despicable presstitute media has not apologized to the American people for serving the corrupt Bush regime as its Ministry of Propaganda and Lies.

It is difficult to discern which is the most despicable, the corrupt Bush regime, the presstitutes that enabled it, or the corrupt Obama regime that refuses to prosecute the Bush regime for its unambiguous war crimes, crimes against the US Constitution, crimes against US statutory law, and crimes against humanity.

In his book, *Cultures of War*,[90] the distinguished historian John W. Dower observes that the concrete acts of war unleashed by the Japanese in the 20th century and by the Bush imperial presidency in the 21st century

> invite comparative analysis of outright war crimes like torture and other transgressions. Imperial Japan's black deeds have left an indelible stain on the nation's honor and good name, and it remains to be seen how lasting the damage to America's reputation will be. In this regard, the Bush administration's war planners are fortunate in having been able to evade formal and serious investigation remotely comparable to what the Allied powers pursued vis-a-vis Japan and Germany after World War II.

Dower quotes Arthur Schlesinger Jr.:

"The president [Bush] has adopted a policy of 'anticipatory self-defense' that is alarmingly similar to the policy that imperial Japan employed at Pearl Harbor on a date which, as an earlier American president said it would, lives in infamy. Franklin D. Roosevelt was right, but today it is we Americans who live in infamy."

Americans have paid an enormous sum of money for the shame of living in infamy. Joseph Stiglitz and Linda Bilmes calculated that the Iraq war cost US taxpayers $3,000 billion dollars. This estimate might turn out to be optimistic. The latest study concludes that the war could end up costing US taxpayers twice as much.[91]

In order to pay for the profits that have flowed into the pockets of the US military-security complex and from there into political contributions, Americans are in danger of losing Social Security, Medicare, and the social cohesiveness that the social welfare system provides.

The human cost to Iraq of America's infamy is extraordinary: 4.5 million displaced Iraqis, as many as 1 million dead civilians leaving widows and orphans, a professional class that has departed the country, an infrastructure in ruins, and social cohesion destroyed by the Sunni-Shia conflict that was ignited by Washington's destruction of the Saddam Hussein government.

The notion that the United States government brought freedom and democracy to Iraq is little more than a sick joke. What the Washington war criminals brought was death and the destruction of a country.

The US population, for the most part, seems quite at ease with the gratuitous destruction of Iraq and all that it entails: children without parents, wives without husbands, birth defects from "depleted" uranium, unsafe water—a country without hope mired in sectarian violence. Washington's puppet state governments in the UK, Europe, the Middle East and Japan seem equally pleased with the victory—over what? What threat did the victory defeat? There was no threat. Weapons of mass destruction was a propaganda hoax. Mushroom clouds over American cities was fantasy propaganda. How ignorant do populations have to be to fall for such totally transparent propaganda? Is there no intelligence anywhere in the Western world?

At a recent conference the neoconservatives responsible for the deaths and ruined lives of millions and for the trillions of dollars that their wars piled onto US national debt were unrepentant and full of self-justification. While Washington looks abroad for evil to slay, evil is concentrated in Washington itself.[92]

The American war criminals walk about unmolested. They are paid large sums of money to make speeches about how Americans are bringing freedom and democracy to the world by invading, bombing and murdering people. No war crimes tribunal has issued arrest warrants. The US Department of State, which is still hunting for Nazi war criminals, has not kidnapped the American ones and sent them to be tried at The Hague. The Americans who suffered are the 4,801 troops who lost their lives, the thousands of troops who lost limbs and suffer from other permanent wounds, the tens of thousands who suffer from post-traumatic stress and from the remorse of killing innocent people, the families and friends of the American troops, and the broken marriages and single-parent children that have resulted from the stress of war.

Other Americans have suffered on the home front. Those whose moral conscience propelled them to protest the war were beaten and abused by police, investigated and harassed by the FBI, and put on no-fly lists. Some might actually be prosecuted. The United States has reached the point where any citizen who has a moral conscience is an enemy of the state. The persecution of Bradley Manning demonstrates this truth.

A case could be made that the historians' comparison of the Bush regime with Japanese war criminals doesn't go far enough. By this October 7, Washington will have been killing people, mainly women, children, and village elders, in Afghanistan for 12 years. No one knows why America has brought such destruction to the Afghan people. First the Soviets; then the Americans. What is the difference? When Obama came into the presidency, he admitted that no one knew what the US military mission was in Afghanistan. We still don't know. The best guess is profits for the US armaments industry, power for the Homeland Security industry, and a police state for the insouciant US population.

Washington has left Libya in ruins and internal conflict. There is no government, but it is not libertarian nirvana.

The incessant illegal drone attacks on Pakistani civilians is radicalizing elements of Pakistan and provoking civil war against the Pakistani government, which is owned by Washington and permits Washington's murder of its citizens in exchange for Washington's money payments to the political elites who have sold out their country.

Washington has destabilized Syria and destroyed the peace that the Assad family had imposed on the Islamic sects. Syria seems fated to be reduced to ruins and permanent violence like Libya and Iraq.

Washington is at work killing people in Yemen.

As the video released to WikiLeaks by Bradley Manning shows, some US troops don't care who they kill—journalists and civilians walking peacefully along a street, a father and his children who stop to help the wounded. As long as someone is killed, it doesn't matter who.

Killing is winning.

The US invaded Somalia, has its French puppets militarily involved in Mali, and perhaps has Sudan in its crosshairs for drones and missiles.

Iran and Lebanon are designated as the next victims of Washington's aggression.

Washington protects Israeli aggression against the West Bank, Gaza, and Lebanon from UN censure and from embargoes. Washington has arrested and imprisoned people who have sent aid to the Palestinian children. Gaza, declares Washington which regards itself as the only fount of truth, is ruled by Hamas, a terrorist organization. Thus any aid to Gaza is aid to terrorism. Aide to starving and ill Palestinian children is support for terrorism. This is the logic of an inhumane war criminal state.

What is this aggression against Muslims about?

The Soviet Union collapsed and Washington needed a new enemy to keep the US military/security complex in power and profits. The neoconservatives, who totally dominated the Bush regime and might yet dominate the Obama regime, declared Muslims in the Middle East to be the enemy. Against this make-believe "enemy," the US launched wars of aggression that, according to the US imposed Nuremberg standard that was applied to the defeated WWII Germans, are war crimes.

Although the British and French started World War II by declaring war on Germany, it was Germans, defeated by the Red Army, who were tried by Washington as war criminals for starting a war. A number of serious historians have reached the conclusion that America's war crimes, with the fire-bombings of the civilian populations of Dresden and Tokyo and the gratuitous nuclear attacks on the civilian populations of Hiroshima and Nagasaki, are of the same cloth as the war crimes of Hitler and the Japanese.

The difference is that the winners paint the defeated in the blackest tones and themselves in high moral tones. Honest historians know that there is not much difference between US WWII war crimes and those of the Japanese and Germans. But the US was on the winning side.

By its gratuitous murder of Muslims in seven or eight countries, Washington has ignited a Muslim response: bitter hatred of the United States. This response is termed "terrorism" by Washington and the war against terrorism serves as a source of endless profits for the military complex and for a police state to "protect" Americans from terrorism, but not from the terrorism of their own government.

The bulk of the American population is too misinformed to catch on, and the few who do understand and are attempting to warn others will be silenced. The 21st century will be one of the worst centuries in human history. All over the Western world, liberty is dying.

WHAT IS THE GOVERNMENT'S AGENDA?

June 11, 2013

It has been public information for a decade that the US government secretly, illegally, and unconstitutionally spies on its citizens. Congress and the federal courts have done nothing about this extreme violation of the US Constitution and statutory law, and the insouciant US public seems unperturbed.

In 2004 a whistleblower informed *The New York Times* that the National Security Agency (NSA) was violating the Foreign Intelligence Surveillance Act (FISA) by ignoring the FISA court and spying on Americans without obtaining the necessary warrants. *The New York Times* put the interests of the US government ahead of those of the American public and sat on the story for one year until George W. Bush was safely reelected.

By the time *The New York Times* published the story of the illegal spying one year later, the law-breaking government had had time to mitigate the offense with ex-post-facto law or executive orders and explain away its law-breaking as being in the country's interest.

Last year William Binney, who was in charge of NSA's global digital data gathering program, revealed that the NSA had everyone in the US under total surveillance, that every email, Internet site visited and phone call is captured and stored. In 2012, Binney received the Callaway Award for Civic Courage, an annual award given to those who champion constitutional rights at risk to their professional and personal lives.

There have been a number of whistleblowers. For example, in 2006 Mark Klein revealed that AT&T had a secret room in its San Francisco office that NSA used to collect Internet and phone-call data from US citizens who were under no suspicion.[93]

The presstitute media handled these stories in ways that protected the government's lawlessness from scrutiny and public outrage. The usual spin was that the public needs to be safe from terrorists, and safety is what the government is providing.

The latest whistleblower, Edward Snowden, has sought refuge in Hong Kong, which has a better record of protecting free speech than the US government. Snowden did not trust any US news source and took the story to Glenn Greenwald.

There is no longer any doubt whatsoever that the US government is lawless, that it regards the US Constitution as a scrap of paper, that it does not believe Americans have any rights other than those that the government tolerates at any point in time, and that the government has no fear of being held accountable by the weak US Congress, the sycophantic federal courts, a controlled media, and an insouciant public.

Binney and Snowden have described in precisely accurate detail the extreme danger arising from the government's surveillance of the population. No one is exempt, not the Director of the CIA, US Army Generals, Senators and Representatives, not even the president himself. Anyone with access to a computer and the Internet can find interviews with Binney and Snowden and become acquainted with why you do have very much indeed to fear whether or not you are doing anything wrong.

James Clapper, the lying Director of National Intelligence condemned Snowden as "reprehensible" for insisting that in a democracy the public should know what the government is doing. Clapper insisted that secretly spying on every ordinary American was essential in order to "protect our nation."[94]

Clapper is "offended" that Americans now know that the NSA is spying on the ordinary life of every American. Clapper wants Snowden to be severely punished for his "reckless disclosure" that the US government is totally violating the privacy that the US Constitution guarantees to every US citizen.

President Obama, allegedly educated in constitutional law, justified Clapper's program of spying on every communication of every American citizen as a necessary violation of Americans' civil liberties that "protects your civil liberties." Contrast the lack of veracity of the President of the United States with the truthfulness of Snowden, who correctly stated that the NSA spying is an "existential threat to democracy."

The presstitutes are busy at work defending Clapper and Obama. On June 9, CNN rolled out former CIA case officer Bob Baer to implant into the public's mind that Snowden, far from trying to preserve US civil liberties, might be a Chinese spy and that Snowden's revelations might be indicative of a Chinese espionage case.

Demonization is the US government's technique for discrediting Bradley Manning for complying with the US Military Code and reporting war crimes and for persecuting Julian Assange of Wikileaks for reporting leaked information about the US government's crimes. Demonization and false charges will be the government's weapon against Snowden.

If Washington and its presstitutes can convince Americans that courageous people, who are trying to inform Americans that their historic rights are disappearing as America evolves into a police state, are instead espionage agents of foreign powers, America can continue to be subverted by its own government.

This brings us to the crux of the matter. What is the purpose of the spying program?

Even if an American believes the official stories of 9/11 and the Boston Marathon Bombing, these are the only two terrorist acts in the US that resulted in the loss of human life in 12 years. Far more people are killed in traffic accidents and from bad diets. Why should the Constitution and civil liberty be deep-sixed because of two alleged terrorist acts in 12 years?

What is astounding is the absence of terrorist attacks. Washington is in the second decade of invading and destroying Muslim governments and countries. Civilian casualties in Iraq, Afghanistan, and Libya are extremely high, and in those countries that Washington has not yet invaded, such as Pakistan, Yemen, and Syria, civilians are being murdered by Washington's drones and proxies on the ground.

It is extraordinary that Washington's brutal 12-year assault on Muslim lives in six countries has not resulted in at least one dozen real, not fake FBI orchestrated, terrorist attacks in the US every day.

How can something as rare as terrorism justify the destruction of the US Constitution and US civil liberty? How safe is any American when their government regards every citizen as a potential suspect who has no rights?

Why is there no discussion of this in American public life? Watch the presstitutes turn Snowden's revelations into an account of his disaffection and motives, and away from the existential threat to democracy and civil liberty.

What is the government's real agenda? Clearly, "the war on terror" is a front for an undeclared agenda. In "freedom and democracy" America, citizens have no idea what their government's motives are in fomenting endless wars and a gestapo police state. The only information Americans have comes from whistleblowers, whom Obama ruthlessly prosecutes. The presstitutes quickly discredit the information and demonize the whistleblowers.

Germans in the Third Reich and Soviet citizens in the Stalin era had a better idea of their governments' agendas than do "freedom and democracy" Americans today.

In America there is no democracy that holds government accountable. There is only a brainwashed people who are chaff in the wind.

WASHINGTON
IS WAR-CRAZY

June 17, 2013

In the 21st century the two hundred year-old propaganda that the American people control their government has been completely shattered. Both the Bush and Obama regimes have made it unmistakably clear that the American people don't even influence, much less control, the government. As far as Washington is concerned, the American people are not in the loop.

Polls demonstrate that 65% of the US population opposes US intervention in Syria. Despite this clear indication of the people's will, the Obama regime is ramping up a propaganda case for more arming of Washington's mercenaries sent to overthrow the secular Syrian government and for a "no-fly zone" over Syria, which, if Libya is the precedent, means US or NATO aircraft attacking the Syrian army on the ground, thus serving as the air force of Washington's imported mercenaries, euphemistically called "the Syrian rebels."

Washington declared some time ago that the "red line" that would bring Syria under Washington's military attack was the Assad government's use of chemical weapons of mass destruction against Washington's mercenaries. Once this announcement was made, everyone with a brain immediately knew that Washington would fabricate false intelligence that Assad had used chemical weapons, just as Washington presented to the United Nations via Secretary of State Colin Powell the intentional lie that Saddam Hussein had dangerous weapons of mass destruction. Remember National Security Advisor Condi Rice's image of a "mushroom cloud over American cities?" Propagandistic lies were Washington's orders of the day.

And they still are. Now Washington has fabricated the false intelligence, and president Obama has announced it with a straight face, that Syria's Assad has used sarin gas on several occasions and that between 100 and 150 "of his own people," a euphemism for the US supplied foreign mercenaries, have been killed by the weapon of mass destruction.

Think about that for a minute. As unfortunate as is any death from war, is 100-150 deaths "mass destruction?" According to low-ball estimates, the US-sponsored foreign mercenary invasion of Syria has cost 93,000 lives, of which 150 deaths amounts to 0.0016 or sixteen hundredths of one percent.

In other words, 92,850 of the deaths did not cross the "red line." But 150 did, allegedly.

Yes, I know. Washington's position makes no sense. But when has it ever made any sense?

Let's stretch our minds just a tiny bit farther. Assad knows about Washington's "red line." It has been repeated over and over in order to create in the minds of the distracted American public that there is a real, valid reason for attacking Syria. Why would Assad use the proscribed weapons of mass destruction in order to kill a measly 100-150 mercenaries when his army is mopping up the US mercenaries without the use of gas and when Assad knows that the use of gas brings in the US military against him?   ·

As the Russian government made clear, Washington's accusation is not believable. No informed person could possibly believe it. No doubt, many Americans wearing patriotism on their sleeves will fall for Washington's latest lie, but no one else in the world will. Even Washington's NATO puppets calling for attacking Syria know that the justification for the attack is a lie. For the NATO puppets, Washington's money overwhelms integrity, for which the rewards are low.

The Russians certainly know that Washington is lying. The Russian Foreign Minister Lavrov said: "The [Assad] government, as the opposition is saying openly, is enjoying military success on the ground. The [Assad] regime isn't driven to the wall. What sense is there for the regime to use chemical arms—especially in such small amounts."

Lavrov is a relatively civilized person in the role of Russia's main diplomat. However, other Russian officials can be more pointed in their dismissal of Washington's latest blatant lies. Yury Ushakov, an aide to Russian President Putin said: "The Americans tried to present us with information on the use of chemical weapons by the [Assad] regime, but frankly we thought that it was not convincing. We wouldn't like to invoke references to [the infamous lies of] Secretary of State Powell [at the UN alleging Iraqi WMD], but the facts don't look convincing in our eyes." Aleksey Pushkov, the chairman of the Russian Duma's Foreign Affairs Committee, cut to the chase. "The data about Assad's use of chemical weapons is fabricated by the same facility that made up the lies about Saddam Hussein's weapons of mass destruction. Obama is walking George W. Bush's path."

Here in America no one will ever hear straight talk like this from the US presstitutes.

Orwellian double-speak is now the language of the United States government. Secretary of State John Kerry condemned Assad for harming "peace talks" while the US arms its Syrian mercenaries.

Washington's double-speak is now obvious to the world. Not only Assad, but also the Russians, Chinese, Iranians, and every US puppet state which includes all of NATO and Japan, are fully aware that Washington is again lying through its teeth. The Russians, Chinese, and Iranians are trying to avoid confrontation with Washington, as war with modern nuclear weapons would destroy all life on planet earth. What is striking is that despite 24/7 brainwashing by the presstitutes, a large majority of the American population opposes Obama's war on Syria.

This is good news. It means more Americans are developing the ability to think independently of the lies Washington feeds to them.

What the neocon nazis, the Bush/Obama regime, and the presstitute media have made clear is that Washington is going to push its agenda of world hegemony to the point of starting World War III, which, of course, means the end of life on earth.

Russia and China, either one of which can destroy the United States, have learned that the US government is a liar and cannot be trusted. The Libyan "no-fly" policy to which Russia and China agreed turned out to be a NATO air attack on the Libyan army so that the CIA-sponsored mercenaries could prevail.

Russia and China, having learned their lesson, are protesting Washington's assault on Syria that Washington pretends is a "civil war." If Syria falls, Russia and China know that Iran is next.

Iran is Russia's underbelly, and for China Iran is 20% of its energy imports. Both Russian and Chinese governments know that after Iran falls, they are next. There is no other explanation for Washington surrounding Russia with missile bases and surrounding China with naval and air bases.

Both Russia and China are now preparing for the war that they see as inevitable. Washington's crazed, demented drive for world hegemony is bringing unsuspecting Americans up against two countries with hydrogen bombs whose combined population is five times the US population. In such a conflict everyone dies.

Considering the crazed government ruling in Washington, if human life exists in 2020, it will be a miracle. All the worry about future Medicare and Social Security deficits is meaningless. There will be no one here to collect the benefits.

STASI IN THE
WHITE HOUSE

June 21, 2013

On June 19, 2013, US President Obama, hoping to raise himself above the developing National Security Agency (NSA) spy scandals, sought to associate himself with two iconic speeches made at the Brandenburg Gate in Berlin.[95]

Fifty years ago, President John F. Kennedy pledged: "Ich bin ein Berliner". In 1987, President Ronald Reagan challenged: "Mr. Gorbachev, tear down this wall."

Obama's speech was delivered to a relatively small, specially selected audience of invitees. Even so, Obama spoke from behind bullet proof glass.

Obama's speech will go down in history as the most hypocritical of all time. Little wonder that the audience was there by invitation only. A real audience would have hooted Obama out of Berlin.

Perhaps the most hypocritical of all of Obama's statements was his proposal that the US and Russia reduce their nuclear weapons by one-third. The entire world, and certainly the Russians, saw through this ploy. The US is currently surrounding Russia with anti-ballistic missiles on Russia's borders and hopes to leverage this advantage by talking Russia into reducing its weapons, thereby making it easier for Washington to target them. Obama's proposal is clearly intended to weaken Russia's nuclear deterrent and ability to resist US hegemony.

Obama spoke lofty words of peace, while beating the drums of war in Syria and Iran and establishing new military bases in the Pacific Ocean with which to confront China.

This is the same Obama who promised to close the Guantanamo Torture Prison, but did not; the same Obama who promised to tell us the purpose for Washington's decade-long war in Afghanistan, but did not; the same Obama who promised to end the wars, but started new ones; the same Obama who said he stood for the US Constitution, but shredded it; the same Obama who refused to hold the Bush regime accountable for its crimes against law and humanity; the same Obama who unleashed drones against civilian populations in Afghanistan, Pakistan, and Yemen; the same Obama who claimed and exercised power to murder US citizens without due process and who continues the Bush regime's unconstitutional practice of violating habeas corpus and detaining US citizens indefinitely; the same Obama who promised transparency but runs the most secretive government in US history.

The tyrant's speech of spectacular hypocrisy elicited from the invited audience applause on 36 occasions. Like so many others, Germans proved themselves willing to be used for Washington's propaganda purposes.

Here was Obama, who consistently lies, speaking of "eternal truth."

Here was Obama, who enabled Wall Street to rob the American and European peoples and who destroyed Americans' civil liberties and the lives of vast numbers of Iraqis, Afghans, Yemenis, Libyans, Pakistanis, Syrians, and others, speaking of "the yearnings of justice." An Obama who equates demands for justice with "terrorism."

Here was Obama, who has constructed an international spy network and a domestic police state, speaking of "the yearnings for freedom."

Here was Obama, president of a country that has initiated wars or military action against six countries since 2001 and has three more Muslim countries—Syria, Lebanon, and Iran—in its crosshairs and perhaps several more in Africa, speaking of "the yearnings of peace that burns in the human heart," but clearly not in his own.

Obama has taken hypocrisy to new heights. He has destroyed US civil liberties guaranteed by the Constitution. In place of a government accountable to law, he has turned law into a weapon in the hands of the government. He has suborned a free press and prosecutes whistleblowers who reveal his government's crimes. He makes no objection when American police brutalize peacefully protesting citizens. His government intercepts and stores in National Security Agency computers every communication of every American and also the private communications of Europeans and Canadians, including the communications of the members of the governments, the better to blackmail those with secrets. Obama sends in drones or assassins to murder people in countries with which the US is not at war, and his victims on most occasions turn out to be women, children, farmers, and village elders. Obama kept Bradley Manning in solitary confinement for nearly a year assaulting his human dignity in an effort to break him and obtain a false confession. In defiance of the US Constitution, Obama denied Manning a trial for three years. On Obama's instructions, London denies Julian Assange free passage to his political asylum in Ecuador, turning him into a modern-day Cardinal Mindszenty. This is the Obama who asked at the orchestrated event at the Brandenburg Gate: "Will we live free or in chains? Under governments that uphold our universal rights, or regimes that suppress them? In open societies that respect the sanctity of the individual and our free will, or in closed societies that suffocate the soul?"

When the Berlin Wall came down, the Stasi Spy State that suffocates the soul moved to Washington.

A NEW BEGINNING WITHOUT WASHINGTON'S SANCTIMONIOUS MASK

June 25, 2013

It is hard to understand the fuss that Washington and its media whores are making over Edward Snowden. We have known for a long time that the National Security Agency (NSA) has been spying for years without warrants on the communications of Americans and people throughout the world. Photographs of the massive NSA building in Utah built for the purpose of storing the intercepted communications of the world have been published many times.

It is not clear to an ordinary person what Snowden has revealed that William Binney and other whistleblowers have not already revealed. Perhaps the difference is that Snowden has provided documents that prove it, thereby negating Washington's ability to deny the facts with its usual lies.

Whatever the reason for Washington's blather, it certainly is not doing the US government any good. Far more interesting than Snowden's revelations is the decision by governments of other countries to protect a truth-teller from the Stasi in Washington.

Hong Kong kept Snowden's whereabouts secret so that an American black-op strike or a drone could not be sent to murder him. Hong Kong told Washington that its extradition papers for Snowden were not in order and permitted Snowden to leave for Moscow.

The Chinese government did not interfere with Snowden's departure.

The Russian government says it has no objection to Snowden having a connecting flight in Moscow en route to Ecuador.

Ecuador's Foreign Minister Ricardo Patino responded to Washington's threats with a statement that the Ecuadorian government puts human rights above Washington's interests. Foreign Minister Patino said that Snowden served humanity by revealing that the Washington Stasi was violating the rights of "every citizen in the world." Snowden merely betrayed "some elites that are in power in a certain country," whereas Washington betrayed the entire world.

With Hong Kong, China, Russia, Ecuador, and Cuba refusing to obey the Stasi's orders, Washington is flailing around making a total fool of itself and its media prostitutes.

Secretary of State John Kerry has been issuing warnings hand over fist. He has threatened Russia, China, Ecuador, and every country that aids and abets Snowden's escape from the Washington Stasi. Those who don't do Washington's bidding, Kerry declared, will suffer adverse impacts on their relationship with the US.

What a stupid thing for Kerry to say. Here is a guy who once was for peace but who has been turned into an asset for the NSA. Try to realize the extraordinary arrogance and hubris in Kerry's threat that China, Russia, and other countries will suffer bad relations with the US. Kerry is saying that America doesn't have to care whether "the indispensable people" have bad relations with other countries, but those countries have to be concerned if they have bad relations with the "indispensable country." What an arrogant posture for the US government to present to the world.

Here we have a US Secretary of State lost in delusion along with the rest of Washington. A country that is bankrupt, a country that has allowed its corporations to destroy its economy by moving the best jobs offshore, a country whose currency is in the hands of the printing press, a country that after eleven years of combat has been unable to defeat a few thousand lightly armed Taliban is now threatening Russia and China. God save us from the utter fools who comprise our government.

The world is enjoying Washington's humiliation at the hands of Hong Kong. A mere city state gave Washington the bird. In its official statement, Hong Kong shifted the focus from Snowden to his message and asked the US government to explain its illegal hacking of Hong Kong's information systems.

China's state newspaper, *The People's Daily*, wrote: "The United States has gone from a model of human rights to an eavesdropper on personal privacy, the manipulator of the centralized power over the international internet, and the mad invader of other countries' networks. . . The world will remember Edward Snowden. It was his fearlessness that tore off Washington's sanctimonious mask."

China's *Global Times*, a subsidiary of *The People's Daily*, accused Washington of attacking "a young idealist who has exposed the sinister scandals of the US government." Instead of apologizing "Washington is showing off its muscle by attempting to control the whole situation."

China's official Xinhua news agency reported that Snowden's revelations had placed "Washington in a really awkward situation. They demonstrate that the United States, which has long been trying to play innocent as a victim of cyber attacks, has turned out to be the biggest villain in our age."

The Russian Foreign Minister Sergei Lavrov made it clear that Russia's sympathy is with Snowden, not with the American Stasi state. Human rights ombudsman Vladimir Lukin said that it was unrealistic to expect the Russian government to violate law to seize a transit passenger who had not entered Russia and was not on Russian soil. RT's Gayane Chichakyan reported that Washington is doing everything it can to shift attention away from Snowden's revelations that "show that the US has lied and has been doing the same as they accuse China of doing."

Ecuador says the traitor is Washington, not Snowden.

The stuck pig squeals from the NSA director—"Edward Snowden has caused irreversible damage to US"—are matched by the obliging squeals from members of the House and Senate, themselves victims of the NSA spying, as was the Director of the CIA who was forced to resign because of a love affair. The NSA is in position to blackmail everyone in the House and Senate, in the White House itself, in all the corporations, the universities, the media, every organization at home and abroad, who has anything to hide. You can tell who is being blackmailed by the intensity of the squeals, such as those of Dianne Feinstein (D, CA) and Mike Rogers (R, MI). With any luck, a patriot will leak what the NSA has on Feinstein and Rogers, neither of whom could possibly scrape any lower before the NSA.

The subservience of the White House and Congress to the NSA makes a person wonder who is running the government.

Let's quit calling the NSA the National Security Agency. Clearly, the NSA is a threat to the security of every person in the entire world. Let's call the NSA what it really is–the National Stasi Agency, the largest Gestapo in human history. You can take for granted that every media whore, every government prostitute, every ignorant flag-waver who declares Snowden to be a traitor is either brainwashed or blackmailed. They are the protectors of NSA tyranny. They are our enemies.

The world has been growing increasingly sick of Washington for a long time. The bullying, the constant stream of lies, the gratuitous wars and destruction have destroyed the image hyped by Washington of the US as the "indispensable people" who are a "light unto the world." The world sees the US as a plague upon the world.

Following Snowden's revelations, Germany's most important magazine, *Der Spiegel,* had the headline: "Obama's Soft Totalitarianism: Europe Must Protect Itself From America." The first sentence of the article asks: "Is Barack Obama a friend? Revelations about his government's vast spying program call that into doubt. The European Union must protect the Continent from America's reach for omnipotence."

Der Spiegel continues: "We are being watched. All the time and everywhere. And it is the Americans who are doing the watching. On Tuesday, the head of the largest and most all-encompassing surveillance system ever invented is coming for a visit. If Barack Obama is our friend then we really don't need to be terribly worried about our enemies."

There is little doubt that German Interior Minister Hans Peter Friedrich has lost his secrets to NSA spies. Friedrich rushed to NSA's defense, declaring: "that's not how you treat friends." As *Der Spiegel* made clear, the minister was not referring "to the fact that our trans-Atlantic friends were spying on us. Rather, he meant the criticism of that spying. Friedrich's reaction is only paradoxical on the surface and can be explained by looking at geopolitical realities. The US is, for the time being, the only global power—and as such it is the only truly sovereign state in existence. All others are dependent—either as enemies or allies. And because most prefer to be allies, politicians—Germany's included—prefer to grin and bear it."

It is extraordinary that the most important publication in Germany has acknowledged that the German government is Washington's puppet state. *Der Spiegel* says:

> German citizens should be able to expect that their government will protect them from spying by foreign governments. But the German interior minister says instead: 'We are grateful for the excellent cooperation with US secret services.' Friedrich didn't even try to cover up his own incompetence on the surveillance issue. 'Everything we know about it, we have learned from the media,' he said. The head of the country's domestic intelligence agency, Hans-Georg Maassen, was not any more enlightened. 'I didn't know anything about it,' he said. And Justice Minister Sabine Leutheusser-Schnarrenberger was also apparently in the dark. 'These reports are extremely unsettling,' she said. With all due respect: These are the people who are supposed to be protecting our rights? If it wasn't so frightening, it would be absurd.

For those naive Americans who say, "I'm not doing anything wrong, I don't care if they spy," *Der Spiegel* writes that a *"monitored human being is not a free one."* We have reached the point where we "free Americans" have to learn from our German puppets that we are not free.

You can read it for yourself at *Der Spiegel*.[96]

Present day Germany is a new country, flushed of its past by war and defeat. Russia is also a new country that has emerged from the ashes of an unrealistic ideology. Hope always resides with those countries that have most experienced evil in government. If Germany were to throw off its American overlord and depart NATO, American power in Europe would collapse. If Germany and Russia were to unite in defense of truth and human rights, Europe and the world would have a new beginning.

A new beginning is desperately needed. Chris Floyd explains precisely what is going on, which is something you will never hear from the presstitutes. Read it while you still can, at Globalresearch.ca.[97]

There would be hope if Americans could throw off their brainwashing, follow the lead of Debra Sweet and others, and stand up for Edward Snowden and against the Stasi State.[98]

WASHINGTON IS DRIVING THE WORLD TO THE FINAL WAR

June 28, 2013

"V For Vendetta," a film that portrays evil in a futuristic England as a proxy for the evil that exists today in America, ends with the defeat of evil.

But this is a movie in which the hero has super powers. If you have not seen this film, you should watch it. It might wake you up and give you courage. The film shows that, at least among some filmmakers, the desire for liberty still exists.

Whether the desire for liberty exists in America remains to be seen. If Americans can overcome their gullibility, their lifelong brainwashing, their propensity to believe every lie that "their" government tells them, and if Americans can escape the Matrix in which they live, they can reestablish the morality, justice, peace, freedom, and liberty that "their" government has taken from them. It is not impossible for Americans to again stand with uplifted heads. They only have to recognize that "their" government is the enemy of truth, justice, human rights and life itself.

Can mere ordinary Americans triumph over the evil that is "their" government without the aid of a superhero? If ideas are strong enough and Americans can comprehend them, good can prevail over the evil that is concentrated in Washington. What stands between the American people and their comprehension of evil is their gullibility.

If Washington's evil is not defeated, our future is a boot stamping on the human face forever.

If you, an American, living in superpower America, lack the courage to stand up to the evil that is "your" government, perhaps the courage of Edward Snowden, Bradley Manning, Julian Assange, and tiny Ecuador will give you heart.

A US senator from New Jersey, Robert Menendez, the Democratic chairman of the Senate Foreign Relations Committee, told the Ecuadoran government that he would block the import of vegetables and flowers from Ecuador if Ecuador gives asylum to Edward Snowden. The cost to Ecuador would be one billion dollars in lost revenues.

Menendez's statement—"Our government will not reward countries for bad behavior"—is ironic. It equates bad behavior with protecting a truth-teller and good behavior with betraying a truth-teller. Menendez's statement is also a lie. The US government *only* rewards bad behavior. The US government consistently rewards those who conspire against the elected governments of their own countries, setting them up as dictators when Washington overthrows the elected governments.

Menendez's threat did not work, but the senator did succeed in delivering yet another humiliating blow to Washington's prestige. The Ecuadoran President, Rafael Correa, beat Menendez to the punch and cancelled the trade pact with the US on the grounds that the pact was a threat to the sovereignty of Ecuador and to moral principles, and was being used by Washington to blackmail Ecuador. "Ecuador doesn't accept pressure or threats from anyone," added Communications Secretary Fernando Alvarado who then offered Washington foreign aid to provide human rights training to combat torture, illegal executions and attacks on peoples' privacy.

Exposed violating the privacy of the entire world and prevented by its hubris from acknowledging its illegal behavior and apologizing, Washington has so mishandled the Snowden affair that it has done far more damage to itself than occurred from Snowden's revelations. Washington has proven conclusively that it has no respect for anyone's human rights, that it has no respect for any country's sovereignty, that it has no respect for any moral principles, especially those it most often mouths, and that it relies on coercion and violence alone. The rest of the world now knows who its enemy is.

Washington's presstitutes, by helping Washington demonize Snowden, Glenn Greenwald, Manning, Assange, and Ecuador, have once again demonstrated to the world that the US media is devoid of integrity and that nothing it reports can be believed. The US print and TV media and NPR comprise a ministry of propaganda for Washington's immoral agendas.

On June 24, the Stasi State's favorite whore, the *Washington Post*, denounced three times democratically-elected Rafael Correa as "the autocratic leader of tiny, impoverished Ecuador," without realizing that the editorial not only demonstrated the *Washington Post*'s lack of any ethics whatsoever but also showed the entire world that if "tiny, impoverished Ecuador" can stand up to Washington's threats, so can the rest of the world.

President Correa replied that the *Washington Post* "managed to focus attention on Snowden and on the 'wicked' countries that support him, making us forget the terrible things against the US people and the whole world that he denounced." Correa added that Washington's "world order isn't only unjust, it's immoral."

The reason Washington hates Correa has nothing to do with Snowden. That Ecuador is considering asylum for Snowden is just an excuse.

Correa is hated, because in the second year of his first term he repudiated the $3 billion dollar foreign debt that corrupt and despotic prior regimes had been paid to contract with international finance. Correa's default threat forced the international financial gangsters to write down the debt by 60 percent.

Washington also hates Correa because he has been successful in reducing the high rates of poverty in Ecuador, thus building public support that makes it difficult for Washington to overthrow him from within.

Yet another reason Washington hates Correa is because he took steps against the multinational oil companies' exploitation of Ecuador's oil resources and limited the amount of offshore deposits in the country's banks in order to block Washington's ability to destabilize Ecuador's financial system.

Washington also hates Correa for refusing to renew Washington's lease of the air base in Manta.

Essentially, Correa has fought to take control of Ecuador's government, media and national resources out of Washington's hands and the hands of the small rich elite allied with Washington. It is a David vs. Goliath story.

In other words, Correa, like Venezuela's Chavez, is the rare foreign leader who represents the interests of his own country instead of Washington's interest.

Washington uses the various corrupt NGOs and the puppet government in Colombia as weapons against Correa and the Ecuadoran government. Many believe that it is only a matter of time before Washington succeeds in assassinating Correa.

American patriots, who feel that they should be on "their" government's side regardless of the facts, would do well to remember what true patriotism is. For Americans, patriotism has always meant allegiance to the Constitution, not to the government. The oath is to defend the Constitution against enemies domestic and foreign. The Bush and Obama regimes have proven themselves to be the Constitution's worst enemies. It is not possible for a true patriot to support a government that destroys the Constitution. Without its Constitution, the US would not be the US. It would be some different political entity. Our country is not the Obama regime, the Bush regime, or some other transitory administration. Our country is the Constitution. The Constitution is our country.

Beyond obligations to one's own country, all humans have a responsibility to human life itself. Washington's puppet states, such as the NATO countries, Japan and Colombia, by providing cover and support for Washington's aggression, are enabling Washington to drive the world into World War III.

The temptation of Washington's lucre easily overwhelms weak characters such as Tony Blair and David Cameron. But the governments of

NATO countries and other accommodating states are not only selling out their own peoples by supporting Washington's wars of aggression, they are selling out humanity. Washington's hubris and arrogance grow as Washington destroys country after country. Sooner or later Russia and China, will realize that they themselves are targets and will draw firmer lines which Washington must not cross. Arrogance will prevent Washington from acknowledging the lines, and the final war will be launched.

Washington's hegemonic impulse is driving the world to destruction. The peoples of the world should realize this and force their governments to stop enabling Washington's aggression.

HAS WASHINGTON'S ARROGANCE UNDONE ITS EMPIRE?

July 1, 2013

No one likes a bully, and Washington's NATO puppets have been bullied for six decades. British prime ministers, German chancellors, and French presidents have to salute and say "yes sir."

They all hate it, but they love Washington's money; so they prostitute themselves and their countries for Washington's money. Even a person of Winston Churchill's stature had to suck up to Washington in order to get his bills and his country's bills paid.

But what the bought European leaders are finding is that Washington doesn't pay enough for the prostitution required. One year out of office Tony Blair was worth $35 million dollars. But that's not enough to get Blair on the waiting list for $50 million 200 foot yachts, to have a chalet in Gstaad, $50 million penthouses in Paris and New York, and a private plane to fly between them, or to wear a $736,000 Franck Muller watch on his wrist, sign his name with a $700,000 Mont Blanc jewel-encrusted pen, and drink $10,000 "martinis on a rock" (gin or vodka poured over a diamond) at New York's Algonquin Hotel.

In a world in which every member of the *Forbes* Four Hundred is a billionaire plus or multi-billionaire, $35,000,000 just doesn't cut it. In 2006 the manager of one hedge fund was paid $1,700,000,000 for one year's thieving. Another 25 were paid $575,000,000 for their skills in front-running trades. $35 million is probably the annual budget for their household servants.

The British seem content in their role as Washington's favorite lackey, but France and Germany have not enjoyed that role. France's last real leader, General de Gaulle, would have nothing to do with it and refused to join NATO. Germany, dismembered with East Germany occupied by the Soviets, had no choice. Germans' gratitude to President Reagan for their unification resulted in re-unified Germany falling under Washington's hegemony.

However, if news reports from Berlin are true, Germany has had enough. The catalyst was Edward Snowden's revelations that Washington spies on everyone including its allies, both Germany and the EU in particular. Moreover, Washington uses Britain as the Trojan Horse within the EU as a backup spy in case NSA misses something.

According to news reports, the German, French, and EU governments are upset to find out that their extreme subservience to Washington has not protected them and their citizens from being spied upon. Here they are, fighting Washington's wars in far distant Afghanistan, the fate of which is completely unrelated to their own, and what does Washington do but embarrass them by spying on the personal lives of their citizens.

Who does the Merkel government represent, Germans are asking, Germans or the NSA? Why does the Merkel government kowtow to Washington? The next question will be: "What do Washington's spies have on Merkel?"

With the German government put on the spot by Washington's betrayal, news headlines are: "Germany Ready to Charge UK and US Intelligence Over Bugging Operations."

Little wonder Washington and its media whores hate Edward Snowden. "A spokesman for the [German] Federal Prosecutor said the office was preparing to bring charges against" the UK and US intelligence services. In light of the Snowden affair, it will be wonderful if Germany issues arrest warrants, and Washington and London refuse to extradite their NSA and UK spy operatives who have violated every law and every trust.

The German Justice Minister, Sabine Leutheusser-Schnarrenburger, demanded an "immediate explanation" why Washington was applying to Germany policies "reminiscent of the actions against enemies during the Cold War."

The president of France has said that France will not again cooperate with Washington on any issue until France receives "full assurances" that Washington will cease spying on France.

The president of the European Parliament, Martin Schulz, and the EU Commissioner for Justice, Viviane Reding, demand Washington's answer to Snowden's revelations that Washington has betrayed its own allies.

The question that must be asked is: do any of these protests from politicians who are almost certain to be on Washington's payroll mean anything, or are they just make-believe protests to quiet the domestic European populations who have been betrayed by their elected leaders? Why would the French president and the German justice minister think any reassurance from Washington meant anything? When in human memory has Washington told the truth about anything? When has Washington's reassurance meant anything?

The Tonkin Gulf? Iraqi weapons of mass destruction? Iranian nukes? Assad's sarin gas attack? FBI orchestrated "terror attacks"? It is a proven fact that the US government lies every time it opens its mouth. Compared to Washington, Stalin, Hitler, Tojo, and Pol Pot were truthful.

Washington's reply to Europe's demands for explanation is: "We will discuss these issues bilaterally with EU member states," but "we are not going to comment publicly on specific alleged intelligence activities."

You know what that means. Bilateral means that Washington is going to talk with each EU country separately, using the information NSA has obtained to blackmail each complainant into silence. Whereas the EU together could stand up to Washington, separately the countries can be browbeaten and offered more money or threats that illicit love affairs will be revealed to shut them up. Washington is betting on its power to intimidate individual countries with the threat of isolation and being cut off from money. If the EU countries agree to the secret bilateral explanations from Washington, the affair will end and the spying on Europe will continue while Washington and the EU politicians deny that the spying continues.

By now the entire world must know that Washington is not merely lawless, but also totally out of control, reveling in arrogance and hubris, driven by desires for hegemony over the entire world. Washington is so paranoid and distrustful that it doesn't even trust its own citizens or the European puppet governments that it has bought and paid for.

Washington is the only government that has ever used nuclear weapons, and it used them against a defeated government that was trying to surrender. Today the craziness in Washington is much worse. Decision-making councils are full of crazed neoconservative warmongers, such as National Security Advisor Susan Rice, a threat to humanity. Washington think tanks and media are over-represented by neoconservatives such as William Kristol who wants to know "what good are nuclear weapons if you can't use them?"

The sleazy European politicians and media who took Washington's money provided for their own economic security, but they betrayed the security of the entire world. By enabling Washington's hegemony, they unleashed Washington's arrogance. This arrogance now threatens not merely the independence of every country but life on earth.

Instead of meeting alone with Washington, the European countries should stand together. After all, supposedly there is an EU. If there is an EU, Washington should meet with the EU, not with its constituent parts individually, no one of which can stand up to Washington's intimidation and bribes.

If thermo-nuclear war is to be avoided and life is to continue on earth, Europe must disband NATO. The North Atlantic Treaty Organization was formed in the aftermath of World War II. Its purpose was to prevent the powerful Red Army, which defeated Nazi Germany, from overrunning all of Western Europe.

The Soviet Union collapsed in 1991, twenty-two years ago. Yet, NATO still exists. Moreover, against President Reagan's intentions, NATO has grown. NATO now includes former constituent parts of the Soviet Empire, such as Eastern Europe, and might soon include former constituent parts of the Soviet Union itself, such as Georgia, the government of which is bought and paid for by Washington. The NGOs that Washington funds might even deliver Ukraine into Washington's fold.

Egged on by Washington, Georgia initiated a war with present day Russia, which superior Russian forces quickly ended. In the opinion of many, the Russian government showed far too much tolerance for its defeated enemy, which is being rearmed by Washington and encouraged into new military adventures. Washington is working to make Georgia, located in Asia between the Black and Caspian seas, a member of the North Atlantic Treaty Organization. NATO membership would make Georgia a treaty protectorate of Washington and its NATO puppets. Washington thinks that this elevation of Georgia would result in Russia acquiescing to Georgian aggression in order to avoid war with the US and NATO.

China, also, has been amazingly abused by Washington, and instead of replying in kind, has taken it in stride. This magnanimity on the part of the Chinese has been misinterpreted by Washington as fear. The fear that Washington imagines is causing China to quake in its boots has encouraged Washington to surround China with new naval, air, and troop bases. The fact that however numerous are Washington's bases in the Pacific and South China Sea, Washington itself is an ICBM away has not registered on those who rule America. Overwhelmed by its hubris, Washington threatens all life on earth.

LAWLESSNESS
IS THE NEW NORMAL

July 5, 2013

In various articles and in my latest book, *The Failure of Laissez Faire Capitalism and Economic Dissolution of the West*, I have pointed out that the European sovereign debt crisis is being used to terminate the sovereignty of the countries that are members of the EU. There is no doubt that this is true, but the sovereignty of the EU member states is only nominal. Although the individual countries still retain some sovereignty in relation to the EU government, they are all under Washington's thumb, as demonstrated by the recent illegal and hostile action taken on Washington's orders by France, Italy, Spain, Portugal, and Austria against the airliner carrying Bolivia's President Evo Morales.

Flying back to Bolivia from Moscow, Morales' plane was denied overflight and refueling permission by Washington's French, Italian, Spanish, and Portuguese puppets and had to land in Austria, where the presidential plane was searched for Edward Snowden. It was a power play by Washington to kidnap Snowden from Bolivia's presidential airliner in defiance of international law and to teach upstart reformers like Morales that independence from Washington's orders is not permitted.

The European puppet states went along with this extraordinary breach of diplomacy and international law despite the fact that each of the countries is incensed that Washington is spying on their governments, diplomats, and citizens. Their thanks to Snowden, whose revelations made them aware that Washington was recording their every communication, was to try to help Washington capture Snowden.

This tells us how much morality, honor, integrity there is left in Western civilization: Zero.

Snowden informed the countries of the world that their communications have no independence or privacy from Washington's eyes and ears. Washington's hubris and arrogance are shocking. Yet, no country has been willing to stand up to Washington and to give Snowden asylum. Ecuador's Correa was intimidated and slapped down by Washington and withdrew his offer to Snowden. For China and Russia, Washington's favorite targets for human rights demonization, giving Snowden asylum would have been a propaganda triumph, but neither country wanted the confrontations that Washington's reprisals would have caused, although Russia might conditionally and gradually grant Snowden asylum.

In short, the governments of the countries on earth want Washington's money and good graces more than they want truth and integrity or even their independence.

Washington's sordid interventions against Snowden and Morales give the world another chance to hold Washington accountable before Washington's hubris and arrogance force the world into a choice between accepting its hegemony and World War III. The countries, split among themselves and grasping for money and favor, are, instead, permitting Washington to establish that whatever it does is legitimate. Washington's diktat, however lawless, is being established as the new normal.

The South American governments are unlikely to stand together against Washington's affront. A few of the countries are led by reformers who represent the people instead of the rich elites allied with Washington, but most prefer calm relations with Washington and domestic elites. South Americans assume that Washington will succeed in overthrowing the reformers as it has in the past.

In Europe headlines are that "NSA surveillance threatens the EU free trade deal" and "Merkel demands explanations." The protests are the necessary public posturing of puppets and will be regarded as such by Washington. The French government says the trade talks should be temporarily suspended "for a couple of weeks to avoid any controversy." However, the German government says, "We want this free trade agreement and we want to start the talks now." In other words, what Merkel describes as "unacceptable Cold War-style behavior" is acceptable as long as Germany gets the free trade agreement.

The lust for Washington's money blinds Europe to the real consequences of the free trade deal. What the deal will do is to fold Europe's economies into Washington's economic hegemony. The deal is designed to draw Europe away from trade with Russia, just as the Trans-Pacific Partnership is designed to draw Asian countries away from China and fold them into US-structured relationships. These deals have little to do with free trade and everything to do with US hegemony.

These "free trade" deals will commit the European and Asian "partners" to support the dollar. Indeed, it is possible that the dollar will supplant the euro and Asian currencies and become the monetary unit of the "partners." In this way Washington can institutionalize the dollar and protect it from the consequences of the printing press that is being used to boost the solvency of banks too big to fail and to finance never-ending federal budget deficits.

PUTIN DRESSES DOWN THE GANG OF 8

July 10, 2013

Below is a translation from As-Safir, *a Lebanese newspaper, July 6, 2013, by Arabic-English translator Eric Mueller. As the translator was not present at the Group of Eight meeting, he cannot vouch for the accuracy of the report, only for the accuracy of the translation. The report by Dawud Rimal does reflect Putin's no-nonsense manner of speaking. The report from* As-Safir *contrasts with the US coverage.*

Diplomatic sources:
Putin tells G8 "You want Asad to resign. Look at the leaders you've made in the Middle East."
by Dawud Rimal (translation by Eric Mueller)
As-Safir newspaper, No 12522, Saturday, 6 July 2013.
http://www.assafir.com/Article.aspx?ArticleId=654&EditionId=2506&ChannelId=60427

Beirut: A diplomatic source has reported that the West has been discussing for some time the issue of the escalating role of Islamists in Lebanon and the Arab countries. The source reports that this discussion might wind up concluding that there is a need to rein in the role of the Islamists. It is along this line of thinking that the West has been encouraging the Lebanese regular army since the 'Abra Battle. [A two-day battle between Lebanese regular army forces and the gang of a Sunni Salafi Shaykh Ahmad al-Asir 'Abra near the southern Lebanese city of Sidon in late June 2013. Translator's note.]

The diplomatic source reports that the changes underway in Egypt were expected by the Western countries and that the leaders of the G8 discussed the matter of Islamists coming to power in a number of Arab countries, including Egypt, in their recent meeting in Northern Ireland. [The Group of Eight or "G8" (Britain, Canada, France, Germany, Italy, Japan, the USA, and Russia) met in Lough Erne, Northern Ireland, on 17-18 June 2013. Translator's note.]

The diplomatic source reports that during that G8 meeting, Russian President Putin delivered a long intervention on that subject.

The prominent European diplomatic source reports that in his statement, the Russian President addressed the leaders participating in the G8 meeting, saying:

> You want President Bashar al-Asad to step down? Look at the leaders you've made in the Middle East in the course of what you have dubbed the "Arab Spring." Now the peoples of the region are rejecting those leaders. The revolution against Muhammad Mursi in Egypt continues and anybody who knows the character of Egyptian society is aware of the fact that it is a deeply rooted secular society of varied cultures and civilizations with a history of advanced political activity. It will never accept attempts to impose things upon it by force. As to Receb Tayyib Erdoğan [in Turkey], the street is moving against him and his star is beginning to wane. In Tunisia the Muslim Brotherhood-Salafi rule that you formed there is no longer stable and the fate of Tunisia won't be very far from the army seizing power, because Europe will never accept chaos on its borders and Tunisia is an entry way to Europe." [Putin said this before the Chairman of the Joint Chiefs of Staff of Tunisia resigned to declare his candidacy for president of the republic. Note by as-Safir.]

Putin went on: "You have spread anarchy in Libya after Mu'ammar al-Qadhdhafi. Nobody can put together an authority capable of working to rebuild the state there. Yemen after the departure of 'Ali 'Abdallah Salih lacks stability in government and there is no peace in the streets. Military and security unrest continues to prevail in all the regions of the country. As to the Persian Gulf, the whole area from Bahrain to the rest of the states there is sitting atop a volcano," Putin said.

The diplomatic source reported the Russian President as saying: "You want Russia to abandon Asad and his regime and go along with an Opposition whose leaders don't know anything except issuing *fatwas* declaring people heretics, and whose members—who come from a bunch of different countries and have multiple orientations—don't know anything except how to slaughter people and eat human flesh. You use double standards and approach the crisis in Syria using summer and winter styles under one roof. You lie to your own peoples so as to further your interests. This is none of our business. But it is impermissible for you to lie to us and to the countries and peoples of the world, because the international stage is no longer yours alone. Your ability to monopolize it the way you did two decades ago is now gone for good."

Putin continued: "In Syria all of you are standing on the side of the forces that for the last 10 years you have claimed to be fighting against under the rubric of 'fighting terror.' Now today you are with them, helping them to take power across the region. You declare that you're going to arm them and work to facilitate sending their fighters to Syria to bring it down, weaken it, and break it up." Putin asked, "In God's name what kind of democracy are you talking about? You want a democratic regime in Syria to take the place of the Asad regime, but are Turkey and the countries you're allied with in the region blessed with democracy?"

Putin addressed US President Obama specifically, saying: "Your country sent its army to Afghanistan in the year 2001 on the excuse that you are fighting the Taliban and the al-Qaʻidah Organization and other fundamentalist terrorists whom your government accused of carrying out the 11 September attacks on New York and Washington. And here you are today making an alliance with them in Syria. And you and your allies are declaring your desire to send them weapons. And here you have Qatar in which you [the US] have your biggest base in the region and in the territory of that country the Taliban are opening a representative office."

Putin turned to the President of France [François

Hollande] to ask, "How can you send your army to Mali to fight fundamentalist terrorists on the one hand, while on the other you are making an alliance with them and supporting them in Syria, and you want to send them heavy weapons to fight the regime there?"

British Prime Minister David Cameron came in for some of Putin's sharpest remarks, when the Russian President told him: "You are loudly demanding that the terrorists in Syria be armed and yet these are the same people two of whom slaughtered a British soldier on a street in London in broad daylight in front of passersby, not caring about your state or your authority. And they have also committed a similar crime against a French soldier in the streets of Paris."

The diplomatic report indicates that the leaders gathered at the summit were surprised then when German Chancellor Angela Merkel supported every word that Putin said in his address. She declared her rejection of any solution in Syria other than a peaceful one, saying "because the military solution will lead Syria and the whole region into the unknown." She strongly opposed arming the Syrian Opposition, "so that these weapons don't get into the hands of the terrorists who plan to use them in attacks against cities in the European Union." She also indicated that she did not want to see some of her European partners getting involved in military and political adventures that would only serve to further deepen their financial and economic deficits, "because Germany is no longer able to serve as a financial and economic rescue line for those countries in order to help cover up their mistakes."

COUP D'ÉTAT

July 13, 2013

The American people have suffered a coup d'etat, but they are hesitant to acknowledge it. The policies of the regime ruling in Washington today lack constitutional and legal legitimacy. Americans are ruled by usurpers who claim that the executive branch is above the law and that the US Constitution is a mere "scrap of paper."

A government that contravenes the American Constitution is therefore an illegitimate government. The oath of allegiance requires defense of the Constitution "against all enemies, foreign and domestic." As the Founding Fathers made clear, the main enemy of the Constitution is the government itself. Power does not like to be bound and tied down and constantly works to free itself from constraints.

The policies of the post-911 regimes in Washington and the legal regimen they have introduced to support them reflect their usurpation of power. The Obama Regime, like the Bush/Cheney Regime, has no legitimacy. Americans are oppressed by a government ruling, not according to law and the Constitution, but by lies and naked force. Those in government see the US Constitution as a "chain that binds our hands."

The South African apartheid regime was more legitimate than the regime in Washington. Even the apartheid Israeli regime in Palestine is more legitimate. The Taliban are more legitimate. Muammar Gaddafi and Saddam Hussein were more legitimate.

The only constitutional protection that the Bush/Obama regime has left standing is the Second Amendment, a meaningless amendment considering the disparity in arms between Washington and what is permitted to the citizenry. No citizen standing with a rifle can protect himself and his family from one of the Department of Homeland Security's 2,700 tanks, or from a drone, or from a heavily armed SWAT force in body armor.

Like serfs in the dark ages, American citizens can be picked up on the authority of some unknown person in the executive branch and thrown in a dungeon, subjected to torture, without any evidence ever being presented to a court or any information provided to the person's relatives of his/her whereabouts. Or they can be placed on a list without explanation that curtails their right to travel by air. Every communication of every American, except

359

face-to-face conversation in non-bugged environments, is intercepted and recorded by the National Stasi Agency from which phrases can be strung together to produce a "domestic extremist."

If throwing an American citizen into a dungeon is too much trouble, the citizen can simply be blown up with a hellfire missile launched from a drone. No explanation is necessary.

For the Obama tyrant, the exterminated human being was just a name on a list.

The president of the United States has declared that he possesses these constitutionally forbidden rights, and his regime has used them to oppress and murder US citizens. The president's claim that his will is higher than law and the Constitution is public knowledge. Yet, there is no demand for the usurper's impeachment. Congress is supine. The serfs are obedient.

The people who helped transform a democratically accountable president into a Caesar include John Yoo, who was rewarded for his treason by being accepted as a law professor at the University of California, Berkeley, School of Law (Boalt Hall). Yoo's colleague in treason, Jay Scott Bybee, was rewarded by being appointed a federal judge on the US Court of Appeals for the Ninth Circuit. We now have a Berkeley law professor teaching, and a federal circuit judge ruling, that the executive branch is above the law.

The executive branch coup against America has succeeded. The question is: will it stand? Today, the executive branch consists of liars, criminals, and traitors. The evil on earth seems concentrated in Washington.

Washington's response to Edward Snowden's evidence that Washington, in total contravention of law both domestic and international, is spying on the entire world has demonstrated to every country that Washington places the pleasure of revenge above law and human rights.

On Washington's orders, its European puppet states refused overflight permission to the Bolivian presidential airliner carrying President Morales and forced the airliner to land in Austria and be searched. Washington thought that Edward Snowden might be aboard the airliner. Capturing Snowden was more important to Washington than respect for international law and diplomatic immunity.

How long before Washington orders its UK puppet to send in a SWAT team to drag Julian Assange from the Ecuadoran embassy in London and hand him over to the CIA for waterboarding?

On July 12 Snowden met in the Moscow airport with human rights organizations from around the world. He stated that the illegal exercise of power by Washington prevents him from traveling to any of the three Latin American countries who have offered him asylum. Therefore, Snowden said that he accepted Russian President Putin's conditions and requested asylum in Russia.

Insouciant Americans and the young unaware of the past don't know what this means. During my professional life it was Soviet Russia that persecuted truth tellers, while America gave them asylum and tried to protect them. Today it is Washington that persecutes those who speak the truth, and it is Russia that protects them.

The American public has not, this time, fallen for Washington's lie that Snowden is a traitor. The polls show that a majority of Americans see Snowden as a whistleblower.

It is not the US that is damaged by Snowden's revelations. It is the criminal elements in the US government that have pulled off a coup against democracy, the Constitution, and the American people who are damaged. It is the criminals who have seized power, not the American people, who are demanding Snowden's scalp.

Department of Homeland Security boss Janet Napolitano, recently rewarded for her service to tyranny by being appointed Chancellor of the of the University of California system, said that Homeland Security had shifted its focus from Muslim terrorists to "domestic extremists," an elastic and undefined term that can be applied to anyone.

If Americans acquiesce to the coup d'état, they will have placed themselves firmly in the grip of tyranny.

ROLE REVERSAL: HOW THE US BECAME THE USSR

July 23, 2013

I spent the summer of 1961 behind the Iron Curtain. I was part of the US-USSR student exchange program. It was the second year of the program that operated under auspices of the US Department of State. Our return to the West via train through East Germany was interrupted by the construction of the Berlin Wall. We were sent back to Poland. The East German rail tracks were occupied with Soviet troop and tank trains as the Red Army concentrated in East Germany to face down any Western interference.

Fortunately, in those days there were no neoconservatives. Washington had not grown the hubris it so well displays in the 21st century. The wall was built and war was avoided. The wall backfired on the Soviets. Both JFK and Ronald Reagan used it to good propaganda effect.

In those days America stood for freedom, and the Soviet Union for oppression. Much of this impression was created by Western propaganda, but there was some semblance to the truth in the image. The communists had a Julian Assange and an Edward Snowden of their own. His name was Cardinal Jozef Mindszenty, the leader of the Hungarian Catholic Church.

Mindszenty opposed tyranny. For his efforts he was imprisoned by the Nazis. Communists also regarded him as an undesirable, and he was tortured and given a life sentence in 1949.

Freed by the short-lived Hungarian Revolution in 1956, Mindszenty reached the American Embassy in Budapest and was granted political asylum by Washington. However, the communists would not give him the free passage that asylum presumes, and Mindszenty lived in the US Embassy for 15 years, 79% of his remaining life.

In the 21st century roles have reversed. Today it is Washington that is enamored of tyranny. On Washington's orders, the UK will not permit Julian Assange free passage to Ecuador, where he has been granted asylum. Like Cardinal Mindszenty, Assange is stuck in the Ecuadoran Embassy in London.

Washington will not permit its European vassal states to allow overflights of airliners carrying Edward Snowden to any of the countries that have offered Snowden asylum. Snowden is stuck in the Moscow airport.

In Washington politicians of both parties demand that Snowden be captured and executed. Politicians demand that Russia be punished for not violating international law, seizing Snowden, and turning him over to Washington to be tortured and executed, despite the fact that Washington has no extradition treaty with Russia.

Snowden did United States citizens a great service. He told us that despite constitutional prohibition, Washington had implemented a universal spy system intercepting every communication of every American and much of the rest of the world. Special facilities are built in which to store these communications.

In other words, Snowden did what Americans are supposed to do—disclose government crimes against the Constitution and against citizens. Without a free press there is nothing but the government's lies. In order to protect its lies from exposure, Washington intends to silence all truth tellers.

The Obama Regime is the most oppressive regime ever in its prosecution of whistleblowers. Whistleblowers are protected by law, but the Obama Regime insists that whistleblowers are not really whistleblowers. Instead, the Obama Regime defines whistleblowers as spies, traitors, and foreign agents. Congress, the media, and the faux judiciary echo the executive branch propaganda that whistleblowers are a threat to America. It is not the government that is violating and raping the US Constitution that is a threat. It is the whistleblowers who inform us of the rape who are the threat.

The Obama Regime has destroyed press freedom. A lackey federal appeals court has ruled that *New York Times* reporter James Risen must testify in the trial of a CIA officer charged with providing Risen with information about CIA plots against Iran. The ruling of this court destroys confidentiality and is intended to end all leaks of the government's crimes to media.

What Americans have learned in the 21st century is that the US government lies about everything and routinely breaks the law. Without whistleblowers, Americans will remain in the dark as "their" government enserfs them, destroying every liberty, and impoverishes them with endless wars for Washington and Wall Street's hegemony.

Snowden harmed no one except the liars and traitors in the US government. Contrast Washington's animosity against Snowden with Bush's commutation of the sentence given to Dick Cheney aide, Libby, who took the fall for his boss for blowing the cover, a felony, of a covert CIA operative in retaliation for her spouse's exposure of fake "yellow cake" uranium charges against Saddam Hussein.

Whatever serves the tiny clique that rules America is legal; whatever exposes the criminals is illegal. That's all there is to it.

THE TWO FAUX DEMOCRACIES THREATEN LIFE ON EARTH

July 24, 2013

Amitai Etzioni has raised an important question: "Who authorized preparations for war with China?"[99] Etzioni says that the war plan is not the sort of contingency plan that might be on hand for an improbable event. Etzioni also reports that the Pentagon's war plan was not ordered by, and has not been reviewed by, US civilian authorities. We are confronted with a neoconized US military out of control endangering Americans and the rest of the world.

Etzioni is correct that this is a momentous decision made by a neoconized military. China is obviously aware that Washington is preparing for war with it. If the *Yale Journal* knows it, China knows it. If the Chinese government is realistic, the government is aware that Washington is planning a pre-emptive nuclear attack against it. No other kind of war makes any sense from Washington's standpoint. The "superpower" was never able to occupy Baghdad, and after 11 years of war has been defeated in Afghanistan by a few thousand lightly armed Taliban. It would be curtains for Washington to get into a conventional war with China.

When China was a primitive third world country, it fought the US military to a stalemate in Korea. Today China has the world's second largest economy and is rapidly overtaking the failing US economy destroyed by jobs offshoring, bankster fraud, and corporate and congressional treason.

The Pentagon's war plan for China is called "AirSea Battle." The plan describes itself as "interoperable air and naval forces that can execute networked, integrated attacks-in-depth to disrupt, destroy, and defeat enemy anti-access area denial capabilities."

Yes, what does that mean? It means many billions of dollars more profits for the military/security complex while the 99 percent are ground under the boot. It is also clear that the plan given expression in this nonsensical jargon cannot defeat a Chinese army. But this kind of saber-rattling can lead to war, and if the Washington war criminals get another war going, the only way Washington can prevail in this one is with nuclear weapons. The radiation alone will kill Americans as well.

Nuclear war is on Washington's agenda. The rise of the Neocon Nazis has negated the nuclear disarmament agreements that Reagan and Gorbachev made. The extraordinary, mainly truthful 2012 book, *The Untold History of the United States* by Oliver Stone and Peter Kuznick, describes the post-Reagan breakout of preemptive nuclear attack as Washington's first option.

During the Cold War nuclear weapons had a defensive purpose. The purpose was to prevent nuclear war by the US and USSR each having sufficient retaliatory power to ensure "mutually assured destruction." MAD, as it was known, meant that nuclear weapons had no offensive advantage for either side.

The Soviet collapse and China's focus on its economy instead of its military have resulted in Washington's advantage in nuclear weaponry that, according to two US Dr. Strangelove characters, Keir Lieber and Daryl Press, gives Washington first-strike capability. Lieber and Press write that the "precipitous decline of Russia's arsenal, and the glacial pace of modernization of China's nuclear forces," have created a situation in which neither Russia nor China could retaliate to Washington's first strike.

The Pentagon's "AirSea Battle" and Lieber and Press' article in *Foreign Affairs* have informed China and Russia that Washington is contemplating pre-emptive nuclear attack on both countries. To ensure Russia's inability to retaliate, Washington is placing anti-ballistic missiles on Russia's borders in violation of the US-USSR agreement.

Because the American press is a corrupt government propaganda ministry, the American people have no idea that neoconized Washington is planning nuclear war. Americans are no more aware of this than they are of former President Jimmy Carter's recent statement, reported only in Germany, that the United States no longer has a functioning democracy.

The possibility that the United States would initiate nuclear war was given reality eleven years ago when President George W. Bush, at the urging of Dick Cheney and the neocons that dominated his regime, signed off on the 2002 Nuclear Posture Review.

This neocon document, signed off on by America's most moronic president, resulted in consternation and condemnation from the rest of the world and launched a new arms race. Russian President Putin immediately announced that Russia would spend all necessary sums to maintain Russia's retaliatory nuclear capability. The Chinese displayed their prowess by knocking a satellite out of space with a missile. The mayor of Hiroshima, recipient city of a vast American war crime, stated: "The nuclear Non-Proliferation

Treaty, the central international agreement guiding the elimination of nuclear weapons, is on the verge of collapse. The chief cause is US nuclear policy that, by openly declaring the possibility of a pre-emptive nuclear first strike and calling for resumed research into mini-nukes and other so-called 'useable nuclear weapons,' appears to worship nuclear weapons as God."

Polls from all over the world consistently show that Israel and the US are regarded as the two greatest threats to peace and to life on earth. Yet, these two utterly lawless governments prance around pretending to be the "world's greatest democracies." Neither government accepts any accountability whatsoever to international law, to human rights, to the Geneva Conventions, or to their own statutory law. The US and Israel are rogue governments, throwbacks to the Hitler and Stalin era.

The post World War II wars originate in Washington and Israel. No other country has imperial expansionary ambitions. The Chinese government has not seized Taiwan, which China could do at will. The Russian government has not seized former constituent parts of Russia, such as Georgia, which, provoked by Washington to launch an attack, was instantly overwhelmed by the Russian Army. Putin could have hung Washington's Georgian puppet and reincorporated Georgia into Russia, where it resided for several centuries and where many believe it belongs.

For the past 68 years, most military aggression can be sourced to the US and Israel. Yet, these two originators of wars pretend to be the victims of aggression. It is Israel that has a nuclear arsenal that is illegal, unacknowledged, and unaccountable. It is Washington that has drafted a war plan based on nuclear first strike. The rest of the world is correct to view these two rogue unaccountable governments as direct threats to life on earth.

AMERICA
DISCREDITED

August 1, 2013

As Washington loses its grip on the world, defied by Venezuela, Bolivia, Ecuador, and now Russia, the US government resorts to public temper tantrums. The constant demonstration of childishness on the part of the White House and Congress embarrasses every American.

Washington's latest outburst of infantile behavior is a response to the Russian Immigration Service granting US whistleblower Edward Snowden asylum in Russia for one year while his request for permanent asylum is considered. Washington, having turned the US into a lawless state, no longer has any conception of what legal procedure is. Law is whatever serves Washington. As Washington sees it, law is only the juridical expression of Washington's will. Any person or country that interferes with Washington's will is behaving unlawfully.

Because Obama, like Bush before him, routinely disobeys US law and the US Constitution, the White House actually thinks that Russian President Putin should disobey Russian and international law, overturn the Russian Immigration Service's asylum decision, and hand over Snowden to Washington.

Washington expected Russia to hand over Snowden simply because Washington demanded it. Like a two-year old, Washington cannot conceive that its demands don't take precedence over international law and the internal legal procedures of other countries. How dare Russia stand up for its own law against "the indispensable nation."

The current White House spokesman, who is so unimpressive that I cannot remember his/her name/gender, declared that Obama might punish Putin by not going to visit him in Moscow next month. I doubt Putin cares whether Obama shows up.

Obama's term of office is close to an end, but Putin, unless the CIA assassinates him, will be there for another decade. Moreover, every Russian leader has learned that a US president's word means nothing. Clinton, the two Bushes and the current WH liar violated every agreement that Reagan made with Gorbachev. Why would the president of Russia, a nation ruled by law, want to meet with a tyrant?

Not to be outdone by the WH in childish behavior, members of the House and Senate added their two-bits to America's embarrassment. Congressional shills "reacted furiously," according to news reports, and warned "of serious repercussions in US-Russian relations." Here we have another extraordinary demonstration of Washington's hubris. Only Russia has to worry about repercussions in the relationship. Washington doesn't have to worry. His Imperial Majesty will simply deny Putin an audience.

Congress seems unaware of its schizophrenia. On the one hand Congress is outraged about the National Stasi Agency's illegal and unconstitutional spying—especially on Congress—and is attempting to defund the Stasi Agency's surveillance program. The amendment to the military spending bill by Justin Amash, a Republican from Michigan, almost passed. The amendment was barely defeated by votes purchased by the spy industry.

On the other hand, despite its outrage over being spied upon, Congress wants the scalp of the brave hero, Edward Snowden, who informed them that they were being spied upon. Here we have a demonstration of the historical stupidity of government—shoot the messenger.

Only a few right-wing crazies believe that universal surveillance of every American is necessary to US security. The National Stasi Agency will fight hard and blackmail every member of the House and Senate, but the blackmail itself will lead to the National Stasi Agency's wings being clipped, or so we can hope. If it is not done soon, the Stasi Agency will have time to organize a false flag event that will terrify the sheeple and bring an end to the attempts to rein in the rogue agency.

The United States is on the verge of economic collapse. The alleged "superpower," a bankrupt entity, was unable after 8 years of efforts to occupy Iraq and had to give up. After 11 years the "superpower" has been defeated in Afghanistan by a few thousand lightly armed Taliban, and is now running for cover with its tail between its legs.

Washington compensates for its military impotence by committing war crimes against civilians. The US military is a great killer of women, children, village elders, and aid workers. All the mighty "superpower" can do is to lob missiles shot from pilotless drones into farm houses, mud huts, schools, and medical centers.

The schizophrenic denizens of Washington have made Americans a hated people. Those with the foresight to escape from the growing tyranny also know that wherever they might seek refuge, they will be seen as vermin from the most hated nation, subjected to being scapegoated as spies and evil influences, and at risk of being decimated in reprisals against Washington's latest atrocity.

Washington has destroyed the prospects of Americans both at home and abroad.

BRADLEY MANNING VERDICT CONVICTS WASHINGTON

August 1, 2013

Bradley Manning's conviction is more conclusive evidence that the US government is illegitimate. Manning's "trial" was equivalent to Joseph Stalin's "trial" of Nikolai Bukharin. It did not take place in a real court with a real jury. The military officer who served as a "judge" was not impartial. Manning was convicted for obeying the US Military Code and doing his sworn duty to report war crimes. There is no difference between Manning's "conviction" and the "conviction" of Bukharin as a capitalist spy. Both trials were political trials.

The absurdity and injustice of these two convictions tells you all you need to know about the governments behind the convictions. The governments are tyrannical. Imagine the US government accusing Manning of aiding the enemy when the US government itself is supporting Al Qaeda's attempt to overthrow the Syrian government! And Bloomberg reports that Al Qaeda backers in Afghanistan are receiving US military contracts![100]

Americans are a gullible people. They do not understand that the "justice system" is corrupted. Prosecutors and judges have no interest in innocence or guilt. For them conviction alone is the mark of career success. The more people a prosecutor can put in prison, the more successful his career. The more judges bend justice to serve the success of the government's case, the greater the probability of promotion to higher judicial office. American "justice" has degenerated. Willingness to corrupt the law has become the highest qualification for appointment to a judgeship or as a US Attorney.

If Manning had been permitted a real trial, possibly jurors might have weighed the evidence. Did Manning obey the Military Code or disobey it? Did Manning serve the public interest or harm it? But, of course, nothing relevant was part of the trial. In American courts today, exculpatory evidence is not allowed into the courtroom.

If a poor person steals a loaf of bread, the government can turn the case into an act of terrorist sabotage. That's more or less what the government did to Bradley Manning.

WASHINGTON'S DRIVE FOR HEGEMONY IS A DRIVE TO WAR

August 8, 2013

It was five years ago that the president of Georgia, Mikheil Saakashvilli, who was installed in power by the Washington supported "Rose Revolution," launched a military invasion of South Ossetia, a break-away province under its own government. The Georgian attack killed Russian peace-keeping troops and numerous Ossetians.

The Russian military response overwhelmed the US trained and equipped Georgian army to the embarrassment of Saakashvilli and his Washington sponsors.

Washington began the training and equipping of the Georgian military in 2002, and continues to conduct joint military exercises with Georgia. In March and April of this year the US again conducted joint military exercises with Georgia. Washington is pushing to have Georgia admitted as a member of NATO.

Most analysts regard it as unlikely that Saakashvilli on his own would violate the peace agreement and attack Russian troops. Certainly Saakashvilli would have cleared the aggression with his Washington sponsor.

Saakashvilli's attempt to recover the territories was an opportunity for Washington to test Russia. Washington saw the attack as a way of embarrassing the Russian government and as a way of testing Russia's response and military in action. If Russia did not respond, the government would be embarrassed by its failure to protect its interests and the lives of those Russia regards as citizens. If Russia did respond, Russia could be denounced, as it was by President George Bush, as a bully that invaded a "democratic country" with a Washington-installed president. Especially interesting to Washington was the ability to observe the Russian military's tactics and operational capabilities.

North Ossetia is part of Russia. South Ossetia extends into Georgia. In 1801 Ossetia and Georgia became part of Russia and subsequently were part of the Soviet Union. Under Russian law former Soviet citizens have the right to be Russian citizens. Russia permitted Georgia to become independent, but South Ossetia and Abkhazia broke away from Georgia in the 1990s.

If Washington succeeds in installing Georgia into NATO, then an attempt by Georgia to recover what it regards as lost territories would escalate the conflict. An attack by Georgia would comprise an attack by the US and NATO against Russia. Despite the risk to Europe of being pulled into a war with Russia, this month the chief of Denmark's Home Guard was in Georgia on Washington's mission, discussing cooperation between the defense ministries of Denmark and Georgia on regional security issues.

Georgia lies to the East of the Black Sea. What "regional security issues" does Georgia have with Denmark and the North Atlantic Treaty Organization? NATO was established to defend Western Europe against Soviet attack.

Finland and Sweden remained neutral during the Cold War, but both are now being recruited by NATO. NATO lost its purpose with the collapse of the Soviet Union. Yet, it has been greatly expanded and now includes former constituent parts of the Soviet Empire. NATO has become a cover for US military aggression and supplies troops for Washington's wars. Georgia's troops are fighting for Washington in Afghanistan and fought for Washington in Iraq.

Washington kept NATO alive and made it into a mercenary army that serves Washington's world empire.

In a provocation to both Russia and China, the US is currently conducting military exercises in Mongolia. Troops from Korea and Tajikistan, formerly part of the Soviet Union, are also participating. Washington calls such operations "building interoperability between peacekeeping nations." Obviously, foreign military forces are being incorporated into the Empire's army.

Are Americans aware that Washington is conducting military exercises all over the world, is surrounding Russia and China with military bases, and now has an Africa Command? Have Congress and the American people signed off on *Amerika Uber Alles*?

HUMANITY IS DROWNING IN WASHINGTON'S CRIMINALITY

August 13, 2013

Americans will soon be locked into an unaccountable police state unless US Representatives and Senators find the courage to ask questions and to sanction the executive branch officials who break the law, violate the Constitution, withhold information from Congress, and give false information about their crimes against law, the Constitution, the American people and those in Afghanistan, Pakistan, Yemen, Iraq, Libya, Syria, Somalia, Guantanamo, and elsewhere. Congress needs to use the impeachment power that the Constitution provides and cease being subservient to the lawless executive branch. The US faces no threat that justifies the lawlessness and abuse of police powers that characterize the executive branch in the 21st century.

Impeachment is the most important power of Congress. Impeachment is what protects the citizens, the Constitution, and the other branches of government from abuse by the executive branch. If the power to remove abusive executive branch officials is not used, the power ceases to exist. An unused power is like a dead letter law. Its authority disappears. By acquiescing to executive branch lawlessness, Congress has allowed the executive branch to place itself above law and to escape accountability for its violations of law and the Constitution.

National Intelligence Director James R. Clapper blatantly lied to Congress and remains in office. Keith B. Alexander, Director of the National Security Agency, has also misled Congress, and he remains in office. Attorney General Holder avoids telling Congress the truth on just about every subject, and he also remains in office. The same can be said for President Obama, one of the great deceivers of our time, who is so adverse to truth that truth seldom finds its way out of his mouth.

If an American citizen lies to a federal investigator, even if not under oath, the citizen can be arrested, prosecuted, and sent to prison. Yet, these same federal personnel can lie to Congress, to courts and juries, and to citizens with impunity. Whatever the American political system is, it has nothing whatsoever to do with accountable government. In America no one is accountable but citizens, who are accountable not only to law but also to unaccountable charges for which no evidence is required.

Congress has the power to impeach any presidential appointee as well as the president. In the 1970s Congress was going to impeach President Richard Nixon simply because he lied about when he learned of the Watergate burglary. To avoid impeachment, Nixon resigned. In the 1990s, the House impeached President Bill Clinton for lying about his sexual affair with a White House intern. The Senate failed to convict, no doubt as many had sexual affairs of their own and didn't want to be held accountable themselves.

In the 1970s when I was on the Senate staff, corporate lobbyists would send attractive women to seduce Senators so that the interest groups could blackmail the Senators to do their bidding. Don't be surprised if the NSA has adopted this corporate practice.

The improprieties of Nixon and Clinton were minor, indeed of little consequence, when compared to the crimes of George W. Bush and Obama, their vice presidents, and the bulk of their presidential appointees. Yet, impeachment is "off the table," as Nancy Pelosi infamously declared.[101] Why do Californian voters send a person to Congress who refuses to protect them from an unaccountable executive branch? Who does Nancy Pelosi serve? Certainly not the people of California. Most certainly not the US Constitution. Pelosi is in total violation of her oath of office. Will Californians re-elect her yet again? Little wonder America is failing.

The question demanding to be asked is: What is the purpose of the domestic surveillance of all Americans? This is surveillance out of all proportion to the alleged terrorist threat. The US Constitution is being ignored and domestic law violated. Why? Does the US government have an undeclared agenda for which the "terrorist threat" is a cover?

What is this agenda? Whose agenda is more important than protecting the US Constitution and ensuring the accountability of government to law? No citizen is secure unless government is accountable to the Constitution and to law. It is an absurd idea that any American is more threatened by terrorism than by unaccountable government that can execute them, torture them, and throw them into prison for life without due process or any accountability whatsoever. Under Bush/Obama, the US has returned to the unaccountable power of caesars, czars, and autocrats.

In the famous play, "A Man for All Seasons," Sir Thomas More, Chancellor of England, asks: So, you would have me to cut down the law in order to chase after devils? And what will we do, with the law cut down, when the devil turns on us?

This is the most important legal question ever asked, and it is seldom asked today, not in our law schools, not by our bar associations, and most certainly not by the Justice (*sic*) Department or US Attorneys.

American conservatives regard civil liberties as mere excuses for liberal judges to coddle criminals and terrorists. Never expect a conservative Republican, or more than two or three of them, to defend your civil liberty. Republicans simply do not believe in civil liberty. Democrats cannot conceive that Obama—the first black president in office, a member of an oppressed minority—would not defend civil liberty. This combination of disinterest and denial is why the US has become a police state.

Civil liberty has few friends in government, the political parties, law schools, bar associations, or the federal judiciary. Consequently, no citizen is secure. Recently, a housewife researched online for pressure cookers looking for the best deal. Her husband was searching for a backpack. The result was that a fully armed SWAT team appeared at the door demanding to search the premises and to have questions answered.[102]

I am always amazed when someone says: "I haven't done anything wrong. I have nothing to fear." If you have nothing to fear from the government, why do you think that the Founding Fathers put the protections in the Constitution that Bush and Obama have stripped out? Unlike the Founding Fathers who designed our government to protect the citizens, the American sheeple trust the government to their own demise.

Glenn Greenwald recently explained how the mass of data that is being accumulated on every American is being mined for any signs of *non-terrorist-related* criminal behavior.[103] As such warrantless searches are illegal evidence in a criminal trial, the authorities disguise the illegal way in which the evidence is obtained in order to secure conviction based on illegally obtained evidence.

In other words, the use of the surveillance justified by the "war on terror" has already spread into prosecutions of ordinary criminals where it has corrupted legal safeguards and the integrity, if any, of the criminal court system, prosecutors and judges.

This is just one of the many ways in which you have much to fear, whether you think you are doing anything wrong or not. You can be framed for crimes based on inferences drawn from your Internet activity and jokes with friends on social media. Jurors made paranoid by the "terrorist threat" will convict you.

We should be very suspicious of the motive behind the universal spying on US citizens. The authorities are aware that the terrorist threat does not justify the unconstitutional and illegal spying. There have been hardly any real terrorist events in the US, which is why the FBI has to find clueless people around whom to organize an FBI orchestrated plot in order to keep the "terrorist threat" alive in the public's mind. At last count, there have been 150 "sting operations" in which the FBI recruits people, who are out of touch with reality, to engage in a well-paid FBI designed plot. Once the dupes agree, they are arrested as terrorists and the plot revealed, always with the accompanying statement that the public was never in any danger as the FBI was in control.

When 99 percent of all terrorism is organized by the FBI, why do we need NSA spying on every communication of every American and people in the rest of the world?

Terrorism seldom comes from outside. The source almost always is the government in power. The Czarist secret police set off bombs in order to blame and arrest labor agitators. The Nazis burned down the Reichstag in order to decimate the communists and assume unaccountable power in the name of "public safety." An alleged terrorist threat is a way of using fear to block popular objection to the exercise of arbitrary government power.

In order to be "safe from terrorists," the US population, with few objections, has accepted the demise of their civil liberties, such as habeas corpus, which reaches back centuries to the Magna Carta as a constraint on government power. How, then, are they safe from their government? Americans today are in the same position as the English prior to the Great Charter of 1215. They are no longer protected by law and the Constitution from government tyranny.

If citizens allow the government to take away the Constitution, they might be safe from foreign terrorists, but they are no longer safe from their government.

Who do you think has more power over you, foreign terrorists or "your" government?

Washington defines all resistance to its imperialism and tyranny as "terrorism." Thus, Americans who defend the environment, who defend wildlife, who defend civil liberties and human rights, who protest Washington's wars and robbery of the people in behalf of special interests, all become "domestic extremists," the term Homeland Security has substituted for "terrorist." Those who are out of step with Washington and the powerful private interests that exploit us, other peoples, and the earth for their profits and power fall into the wrong side of Bush's black and white division of the world: "you are for us or against us."

In the United States independent thought is on the verge of being criminalized as are constitutionally guaranteed protests and the freedom of the press.[104] The constitutional principle of freedom of speech is being redefined as treason, as aiding an undefined enemy, and as seeking to overthrow the government by casting aspersions on its motives and revealing its secret misdeeds. The power-mad inhabitants of Washington have brought the US so close to Gestapo Germany and Stalinist Russia that it is sometimes difficult to see the difference.

The neoconservatives have declared that Americans are the "exceptional" and "indispensable people." Yet, the civil liberties of Americans have declined the more "exceptional" and "indispensable" that Americans become. We are now so exceptional and indispensable that we no longer have any rights.

And neither does the rest of the world. Neoconservatism has created a dangerous new American nationalism. Neoconservatives have given Washington a monopoly on right and endowed its military aggressions with a morality that supersedes the Geneva Conventions and human rights. Washington, justified by its "exceptionalism," has the right to attack populations in countries with which Washington is not at war, such as Pakistan and Yemen. Washington is using the cover of its "exceptionalism" to murder people in many countries.[105]

How does the "indispensable, exceptional nation" have a diplomatic policy? How can a neoconized State Department be based on anything except coercion? It can't. That is why Washington produces nothing but war and threats of war.

Washington's threat—"We are going to bomb you into the Stone age" if you don't do what we want and agree to what we require—resounds around the world. "We are going to impose sanctions," Washington's euphemism for embargoes, "and starve your women and children to death, permit no medical supplies, ban you from the international payments system unless you relent and consent to being our puppet, and ban you from posting your news broadcasts on the Internet."

This is the face that Washington presents to the world: the hard, mean face of a tyrant.

Washington's power will survive a bit longer, because there are still politicians in Europe, the Middle East, Africa, Asia, Latin America and in Canada, Australia, New Zealand, and the NGOs in Russia, who are paid off by the almighty dollar. In exchange for Washington's money, they endorse Washington's immorality and murderous destruction of law and life.

But the dollar is being destroyed by Quantitative Easing, and the domestic US economy is being destroyed by jobs offshoring.[106]

Rome was powerful until the Germans ceased to believe it. Then the rotten edifice collapsed. Washington faces sooner or later the same fate. An inhumane, illegal, unconstitutional regime based on violence alone, devoid of all morality and all human compassion, is not acceptable to China, Russia, India, Iran, and Brazil, or to readers of this column.

The evil that is Washington cannot last forever. The criminals might destroy the world in nuclear war, but the lawlessness and lack of humanity in Washington, which murders more people as I write, is no longer acceptable to the rest of the world, not even to its European puppet states, despite their leaders being on Washington's payroll.

Gorbachev is correct. The collapse of the Soviet Union was a debacle for the entire world. It transformed the US from the "city upon the hill," the "beacon for humanity," into an aggressive militarist state. Consequently, America has become despised by everyone who has a moral conscience and a sense of justice.

GANGSTER STATE US/UK

August 21, 2013

On July 23 I wrote about how the US reversed roles with the USSR and became the tyrant that terrifies the world. We have now had further confirmation of that fact. It comes from two extraordinary actions by Washington's British puppet state.

David Miranda, the Brazilian partner of Glenn Greenwald, who is reporting on the illegal and unconstitutional spying by the National Stasi Agency, was seized, no doubt on Washington's orders, by the puppet British government from the international transit zone of a London airport. Miranda had not entered the UK, but he was seized by UK authorities.[107] Washington's UK puppets simply kidnapped him, threatened him for nine hours, and stole his computer, phones, and all his electronic equipment. As a smug US official told the media, "the purpose was to send a message."

You might remember that Edward Snowden was stuck for some weeks in the international transit zone of the Moscow airport. The Obama tyrant repeatedly browbeat Russia's President Putin to violate the law and kidnap Snowden. Unlike the once proud and law-abiding British, Putin refused to place Washington's desires above law and human rights.

The second extraordinary violation occurred almost simultaneously with UK authorities appearing at the *Guardian* newspaper and illegally destroying the hard drives on the newspaper's computers with the vain intention of preventing the newspaper from reporting further Snowden revelations of US/UK high criminality.

It is fashionable in the US and UK governments and among their sycophants to speak of "gangster state Russia." But we all know who the gangsters are. The worst criminals of our time are the US and UK governments. Both are devoid of all integrity, all honor, all mercy, all humanity. Many members of both governments would have made perfect functionaries in Stalinist Russia or Nazi Germany.

This is extraordinary. It was the English who originated liberty. True, in 1215 it was the freedom of the barons' rights from the king's infringement, not the freedom of the commoner. But once the principle was established it spread into the entire society. By 1680 the legal revolution was complete. The king and the government were subject to law. The king and his government were no longer the law and above the law.

In the 13 colonies the Englishmen who populated them inherited this English achievement. When King George's government refused the colonies the Rights of Englishmen, the colonists revolted, and the United States was born.

The descendants of these colonists now live in an America where their Constitutional protections have been overthrown by a tyrannical government that claims it is above the law. This raw fact has not stopped the US government or its puppets from continuing to cloak the war crime of military aggression in the faux language of "bringing freedom and democracy." If the Obama and Cameron governments were in the dock at Nuremberg, the entirety of both governments would be convicted.

The question is: are there sufficient brainwashed people in both countries to sustain the US/UK myth that "freedom and democracy" can be attained via war crimes?

There is no shortage of brainwashed Americans who love to be told that they are "indispensable" and "exceptional," and therefore entitled to work their will on the world. It is difficult to discern in these clueless Americans much hope for the revival of liberty. But there is some indication that the British, who did not inherit liberty but had to fight for it for five centuries, might be more determined.

The British Home Affairs Committee, chaired by Keith Vaz, is demanding an explanation from Obama's lap dog, the British prime minister. Also, Britain's watchman over anti-terrorism enforcement, David Anderson, is demanding that the UK Home Office and police explain the illegal use of anti-terrorism laws against Miranda, who is not a terrorist or connected to terrorism in any way.

Brazil's foreign minister has joined the fray, demanding that London explain why the UK violated its own law and abused a Brazilian citizen.

Of course, everyone knows that Washington forced its UK puppet to violate law in order to serve Washington. One wonders if the British will ever decide that they would be better off as a sovereign country.

The White House denied involvement in Miranda's kidnapping, but refused to condemn the illegal action of its puppet.

As for the UK's destruction of press freedom, the White House supports that, too. It is already happening here.

Meanwhile, get accustomed to the police state.

SYRIA: ANOTHER WESTERN WAR CRIME IN THE MAKING

August 26, 2013

UPDATE August 29, 2013: *The British Parliament has rejected British military intervention in Syria. The US puppet, Cameron, who serves as Prime Minister was forced to admit that he had no evidence that Assad had used chemical weapons, and Parliament said, no evidence, no war. It is unlikely the French will go along without the British, so this leaves Obama all alone with Israel. If Washington goes ahead with the strike, Obama will be branded with the War Criminal moniker.*

This decisive action by Parliament shames the cowardly US Congress.[108]

The war criminals in Washington and other Western capitals are determined to maintain their lie that the Syrian government used chemical weapons. Having failed in efforts to intimidate the UN chemical inspectors in Syria, Washington has demanded that UN Secretary General Ban Ki-moon withdraw the chemical weapons inspectors before they can assess the evidence and make their report. The UN Secretary General stood up to the Washington war criminals and rejected their demand. As with Iraq, Washington's decision to commit aggression against Syria is not based on any facts.[109]

The US and UK governments have revealed none of the "conclusive evidence" they claim to have that the Syrian government used chemical weapons. Listening to their voices, observing their body language, and looking into their eyes, it is completely obvious that John Kerry and his British and German puppets are lying through their teeth. This is a far more shameful situation than the massive lies that former Secretary of State Colin Powell told the UN about Iraqi weapons of mass destruction. Colin Powell claims that he was deceived by the White House and did not know that he was lying. Kerry and the British, French, and German puppets know full well that they are lying.

The face that the West presents to the world is the brazen face of a liar.

Washington and its British and French puppet governments are poised to yet again reveal their criminality. The image of the West as War Criminal is not a propaganda image created by the West's enemies, but the portrait that the West has painted of itself.

The UK *Independent* reports that over this past weekend Obama, Cameron, and Hollande agreed to launch cruise missile attacks against the Syrian government within two weeks despite the lack of any authorization from the UN and despite the absence of any evidence in behalf of Washington's claim that the Syrian government has used chemical weapons against the Washington-backed "rebels", largely US supported external forces, seeking to overthrow the Syrian government.

Indeed, one reason for the rush to war is to prevent the UN inspection that Washington knows would disprove its claim and possibly implicate Washington in the false flag attack by the "rebels," who murdered children while Washington pinned the blame on the Syrian government.

Another reason for the rush to war is that Cameron, the UK prime minister, wants to get the war going before the British parliament can block him for providing cover for Obama's war crimes the way that Tony Blair provided cover for George W. Bush, for which Blair was duly rewarded. What does Cameron care about Syrian lives when he can leave office into the waiting arms of a $50 million fortune.[110]

The Syrian government, knowing that it is not responsible for the chemical weapons incident, has agreed for the UN to send in chemical inspectors to determine the substance used and the method of delivery. However, Washington has declared that it is "too late" for UN inspectors and accepts the self-serving claim of the al Qaeda affiliated "rebels" that the Syrian government attacked civilians with chemical weapons.[111]

The UN chemical inspectors who arrived on the scene were fired upon by snipers in "rebel" held territory in an attempt to prevent them from doing their work, and forced off site, although a later report from RT says the inspectors have returned to the site to conduct their inspection.[112]

The corrupt British government has declared that Syria can be attacked without UN authorization, just as Serbia and Libya were militarily attacked without UN authorization. In other words, the Western democracies have already established precedents for violating international law. "International law? What international law!" The West knows only one rule: Might is Right. As long as the West has the Might, the West has the Right.

In a response to the news report that the US, UK, and France are preparing to attack Syria, the Russian Foreign Minister, Lavrov, said that such unilateral action is a "severe violation of international law," and that the violation was not only a legal one but also an ethical and moral violation. Lavrov referred to the lies and deception used by the West to justify its grave violations of international law in military attacks on Serbia, Iraq, and Libya and how the US government had used preemptive moves to undermine every hope for peaceful settlements in Iraq, Libya, and Syria.

Once again Washington has attempted to preempt any hope of peaceful settlement. By announcing the forthcoming attack, the US destroyed any incentive for the "rebels" to participate in the peace talks with the Syrian government. On the verge of these talks taking place, the "rebels" now have no incentive to participate as the West's military is coming to their aid.

In his press conference Lavrov spoke of how the ruling parties in the US, UK, and France stir up emotions among poorly informed people that, once aroused, have to be satisfied by war. This, of course, is the way the US manipulated the public in order to attack Afghanistan and Iraq. But the American public is tired of the wars, the goal of which is never made clear, and has grown suspicious of the government's justifications for more wars.

A Reuters/Ipsos poll finds that "Americans strongly oppose U.S. intervention in Syria's civil war and believe Washington should stay out of the conflict even if reports that Syria's government used deadly chemicals to attack civilians are confirmed."[113] However, Obama could not care less that only 9 percent of the public supports his warmongering. As former president Jimmy Carter recently stated, "America has no functioning democracy."[114] It has a police state in which the executive branch has placed itself above all law and the Constitution.

This police state is now going to commit yet another Nazi-style war crime of unprovoked aggression. At Nuremberg the Nazis were sentenced to death for precisely the identical actions being committed by Obama, Cameron, and Hollande. The West is banking on might, not right, to keep it out of the criminal dock.

The US, UK, and French governments have not explained why it matters whether people in the wars initiated by the West are killed by chemical agents rather than explosives made of depleted uranium or any other weapon. It was obvious from the beginning that Obama was setting up the Syrian government for attack. Obama demonized chemical weapons–but not nuclear "bunker busters" that the US might use on Iran. Then Obama drew a red line, saying that the use of chemical weapons by the Syrians was such a great crime that the West would be obliged to attack Syria. Washington's UK puppets, William Hague and Cameron, have just repeated this nonsensical claim.[115] The final step in the frame-up was to orchestrate a chemical incident and blame the Syrian government.

What is the West's real agenda? This is the unasked and unanswered question. Clearly, the US, UK, and French governments, which have displayed continuously their support for dictatorial regimes that serve their purposes, are not the least disturbed by dictatorships per se. They brand Assad a dictator as a means of demonizing him for the ill-informed Western masses. But Washington, UK, and France support any number of dictatorial regimes, such as the ones in Bahrain, Saudi Arabia, and now the military dictatorship in Egypt that is ruthlessly killing Egyptians without any Western government speaking of invading Egypt for "killing its own people."

Clearly also, the intended Western attack on Syria has nothing whatsoever to do with bringing "freedom and democracy" to Syria any more than freedom and democracy were reasons for the attacks on Iraq and Libya, neither of which gained any "freedom and democracy."

The Western attack on Syria is unrelated to human rights, justice or any of the high sounding causes with which the West cloaks its criminality.

The Western media, and least of all the American presstitutes, never ask Obama, Cameron, or Hollande what the real agenda is. It is difficult to believe than any reporter is sufficiently stupid or gullible to believe that the agenda is bringing "freedom and democracy" to Syria or punishing Assad for allegedly using chemical weapons against murderous thugs trying to overthrow the Syrian government.

Of course, the question wouldn't be answered if asked. But the act of asking it would help make the public aware that more is afoot than meets the eye. Originally, the excuse for Washington's wars was to keep Americans safe from terrorists. Now Washington is endeavoring to turn Syria over to jihad terrorists by helping them to overthrow the secular, non-terrorist Assad government. What is the agenda behind Washington's support of terrorism?

Perhaps the purpose of the wars is to radicalize Muslims and, thereby, destabilize Russia and even China. Russia has large populations of Muslims and is bordered by Muslim countries. Even China has some Muslim population. As radicalization spreads strife into the only two countries capable of being an obstacle to Washington's world hegemony, Western media propaganda and the large number of US financed NGOs, posing as "human rights" organizations, can be counted on by Washington to demonize the Russian and Chinese governments for harsh measures against "rebels."

Another advantage of the radicalization of Muslims is that it leaves former Muslim countries in long-term turmoil or civil wars, as is currently the case in Iraq and Libya, thus removing any organized state power from obstructing Israeli purposes.

Secretary of State John Kerry is working the phones using bribes and threats to build acceptance, if not support, for Washington's war crime-in-the-making against Syria.

Washington is driving the world closer to nuclear war than it ever was even in the most dangerous periods of the Cold War. When Washington finishes with Syria, the next target is Iran. Russia and China will no longer be able to fool themselves that there is any system of international law or restraint on Western criminality. Western aggression is already forcing both countries to develop their strategic nuclear forces and to curtail the Western-financed NGOs that pose as "human rights organizations," but in reality comprise a fifth column that Washington can use to destroy the legitimacy of the Russian and Chinese governments.

Russia and China have been extremely careless in their dealings with the United States. Essentially, the Russian political opposition is financed by Washington. Even the Chinese government is being undermined. When a US corporation opens a company in China, it creates a Chinese board on which are put relatives of the local political authorities. These boards create a conduit for payments that influence the decisions and loyalties of local and regional party members.[116] The US has penetrated Chinese universities and intellectual attitudes. The Rockefeller University is active in China as is Rockefeller philanthropy. Dissenting voices are being created that are arrayed against the Chinese government. Demands for "liberalization" can resurrect regional and ethnic differences and undermine the cohesiveness of the national government.

Once Russia and China realize that they are riven with American fifth columns, isolated diplomatically, and outgunned militarily, nuclear weapons become the only guarantor of their sovereignty. This suggests that nuclear war is likely to terminate humanity well before humanity succumbs to global warming or rising national debts.

WILL OBAMA
DOOM HIMSELF AS
A WAR CRIMINAL?

August 30, 2013

Pushed by his Israeli and neocon masters, especially his National Security Advisor, Susan Rice, who, in effect, functions as an Israeli agent, Obama crawled far out on the limb, only to have it sawed off by the British Parliament.

In response, the "socialist" president of France, Hollande, who lacks French support for France's participation in a US/Israeli orchestrated military attack on Syria, has crawled back off the limb, saying that, while everything is still on the table, he has to see some evidence first.

As Cameron and Obama have made clear, there is no evidence. Even US intelligence has declared that there is no conclusive evidence that Assad used chemical weapons or even has control over the weapons.

Even the US puppet government in Canada has disavowed participating in the Obama/Israeli war crime.

This leaves Obama with support only from Turkey and Israel. Recently, the Turkish government fired on peaceful Turkish protesters. As the entire world is aware, the Israeli government has been committing crimes against the people in Palestine for decades. A distinguished Jewish jurist concluded in an official report that the Israeli government committed war crimes in its attack on the civilian population of Gaza.

No country regards the criminal states of Turkey and Israel as cover for a war crime. If Obama is pushed by Susan Rice and the evil neocons, who are strongly allied with Israel, into going it alone and conducting a military strike on Syria, Obama will have made himself an unambiguous War Criminal under the Nuremberg Standard created by the US Government. Unprovoked military aggression is a war crime under international law. That is completely clear. There are no ifs or buts about it.

If Obama now strikes Syria, when he has no cover from the UN, or from NATO, or from the American people, or from Congress, having ignored the House and Senate, Obama will stand before the entire world, starkly, as a War Criminal. Unless the world is prepared to flush international law, arrest orders for the War Criminal will have to come from a war crimes tribunal. Obama will have to be handed over and put on trial. He will have no more leg to stand on than did the Nazis.

The evil neocons are telling Obama that he must prove that he is a man and go it alone. If Obama does, he will prove that he is a War Criminal.

AMERICA
TOTALLY DISCREDITED

August 30, 2013

An imprudent President Obama and bungling Secretary of State Kerry have handed the United States government its worst diplomatic defeat in history and destroyed the credibility of the Office of the President, the Department of State, and the entire executive branch. All are exposed as a collection of third-rate liars.

Intoxicated with hubris from past successful lies and deceptions used to destroy Iraq and Libya, Obama thought the US "superpower," the "exceptional" and "indispensable" country, could pull it off again, this time in Syria.

But the rest of the world has learned to avoid Washington's rush to war when there is no evidence. Obama was pushed far out on the limb by an incompetent and untrustworthy National Security Advisor, Susan Rice, and the pack of neoconservatives that support her, and the British Parliament cut the limb off.

Would any astute leader put himself in that vulnerable position?

Now Obama stands alone, isolated, trying to back away from his threat to attack a sovereign country without authorization from anyone—not from the UN, not from NATO, not from Congress whom he ignored. Under the Nuremberg Standard military aggression is a war crime. Washington has until now gotten away with its war crimes by cloaking them in UN or NATO approval. Despite these "approvals," they remain war crimes.

If Obama goes it alone, he will be harassed for the rest of his life as a war criminal who dares not leave the US. Indeed, a looming economic collapse could so alter the power and attitude in the United States itself that Obama could find himself being brought to justice for his war crimes.

Regardless, the United States government has lost its credibility throughout the world and will never regain it, unless the Bush and Obama regimes are arrested and put on trial for their war crimes.

Obama's destruction of US credibility goes far beyond diplomacy. It is likely that this autumn or winter, and almost certainly in 2014, the US will face a severe economic crisis.

The long-term abuse of the US dollar's reserve currency role by the Federal Reserve and US Treasury, the never-ending issuance of new debt and printing of dollars to finance it, the focus of US economic policy on bailing out the "banks too big to fail" regardless of the adverse impact on domestic and world economies and holders of US Treasury debt, the continuing political crisis of the unresolved deficit, collapsing job opportunities and a sinking economy all together present the government in Washington with a crisis that is too large for the available intelligence, knowledge, and courage to master.

When the proverbial hits the fan, the incompetent and corrupt Federal Reserve and the incompetent and corrupt US Treasury will have no more credibility than Obama and John Kerry.

The rest of the world—especially Washington's bullied NATO puppet states—will take great delight in the discomfort of "the world's sole superpower" that has been running on hubris ever since the Soviet collapse.

The world is not going to bail out Washington, now universally hated, with currency swaps, more loans, and foreign aid. Americans are going to pay heavily for their negligence, their inattention, their unconcern, and their ignorant belief that nothing can go wrong for them and that anything that does is temporary.

Two decades of jobs offshoring have left the US with a third world labor force employed in lowly paid domestic nontradable services, a workforce comparable to India's of 40 years ago. Already the "world's sole superpower" is afflicted with a large percentage of its population dependent on government welfare for survival. As the economy closes down, the government's ability to meet the rising demands of survival diminishes. The rich will demand that the poor be sacrificed in the interest of the rich. And the political parties will comply.

Is this the reason that Homeland Security, a Nazi Gestapo institution, now has a large and growing paramilitary force equipped with tanks, drones, and billions of rounds of ammunition?

How long will it be before American citizens are shot down in their streets by "their" government as occurs frequently in Egypt, Turkey, Bahrain, Washington's close allies?

Americans have neglected the requirements of liberty. Americans are so patriotic and so gullible that all the government has to do is to wrap itself in the flag, and the people, or too many of them, believe whatever lie the government tells them. And the gullible people will defend the government's lie to their death, indeed, to the death of the entire world.

If Americans keep believing the government's lies, they have no future. If truth be known, Americans have already lost a livable future. The neocons' "American Century" is over before it has even begun.

Update: I have heard from educated and aware friends that the presstitute media on the evening news are beating the drums for war. This shows what a paid whore the US media is and its total disconnect from reality. Anyone who wastes their time on the US media is a brainwashed idiot, and similarly a danger to humanity.

Update 8:52 PM August 30: Is the White House going to be a victim of careless presidential appointments? Does Obama have no one to tell him how to escape the dilemma his bungling Secretary of State and National Security Advisor have put him in? Someone needs to tell him that he must say that he accepts the conclusion of the world community that there is not sufficient evidence for launching a military attack on Syria and killing even more people than were killed in the alleged, but unproven, chemical attack, and that he awaits further and better evidence.

God help him and our unfortunate country.

THE ISOLATION
OF AMERICA

August 31, 2013

Washington preens itself on being "the world's greatest democracy." Washington uses the claim that it is spreading democracy as a justification for its naked aggression—a clear and unambiguous war crime—against other countries. Washington cloaks its illegality in democratic rhetoric despite the obvious fact that its wars are not a consequence of democratic decision.

Washington has used deception and lies to gain acceptance of its extra-constitutional and extra-legal wars— all launched outside the constitutional/democratic framework of the United States.

Obama's war against Libya occurred without the participation of Congress. And now Obama is again revealing that the US is so far removed from democracy that he plans to attack Syria without a vote by Congress. Where is the democracy when a Caesar makes the decisions that the Constitution reserves to Congress?

Polls indicate that 80 percent of US citizens believe that a US military attack on Syria requires approval by the House and Senate. Yet, the Obama regime is purposely avoiding any such vote. The Obama regime has also ignored the letter signed by 162 members of the House of Representatives demanding to see evidence, debate it, and vote prior to any US military strike.

It is an act of treason for the US military to carry out any war orders without congressional authorization. Any military commander who violates his oath to defend the Constitution of the United States has committed high treason against the United States. If the US were truly a lawful democracy, such commanders would be subject to arrest and trial.

The fact that the executive branch and the military operate outside the Constitution and democratic process is proof that the US is not a democracy.

In yesterday's columns I noted that Obama, his media whores, and worshiping Obamabots are overlooking considerations of critical importance. One is that military aggression is a war crime. In the past, Bush and Obama had cloaks for their war crimes, such as a "coalition of the willing," NATO, some limited "congressional consultation" or vague resolution, or a UN resolution that is then stretched to cover the regime's actions.

None of these things are adequate legal cover. Their only worth comes from the fact that other countries and institutions besides the US executive branch are implicated in the war crime. There is safety in the numbers. Charging the entire Western world with war crimes means only that the entire Western world will defend the validity of their excuse.

But this time the regime has no cover. There is no "coalition of the willing," no UN resolution, no NATO support, and Obama has ignored both Congress and the American people. For Obama to proceed with his attack on Syria would be the action of an unaccountable dictator. He would have no cover for his war crime.

Obama's effort to rush to war with Syria has already destroyed whatever remained of the credibility of the US government as a truthful, honest government. The entire world, even Washington's most subservient puppet states, has recognized that Washington has no evidence to back its accusations. No one believes Obama or Kerry. Both have revealed themselves to the entire world as brazen liars.

This has destroyed all trust in the US government. And now Obama seems determined to prove that America has a dictator, not a democracy.

It is difficult to imagine a more serious blow to the US than the one Obama has delivered. All of the important props for Washington's propaganda, such as "the world's greatest democracy," have been kicked out from under what now stands revealed as a criminal enterprise.

Russia's President Putin has openly expressed his contempt for the lies that are flowing nonstop from the mouths of Obama and Kerry. Putin called Obama's claims "utter nonsense." Putin said that if the Americans have any proof, "let them show it to the United Nations inspectors and the Security Council."

For another perspective unreported by the US media, see Ambrose Evans-Pritchard's report in the UK *Telegraph*[117] that Saudi Prince Bandar, head of Saudi intelligence, attempted to bribe and intimidate Putin into abandoning Syria to the Americans. Reportedly, Bandar offered Putin a Saudi-Russian oil cartel and offered Putin protection against Chechen terrorist attacks on Russia's Winter Olympics. Washington's claim that the Syrian "rebels" have no access to chemical weapons is obviously false. On May 30, an Istanbul newspaper reported that Turkish police apprehended al-Nusra "rebels" with sarin gas that al-Nusra planned to use in an attack on Adana.[118] Having repeatedly declared that the use of chemical weapons requires a military response from the US, what will Obama and Kerry do when it comes clear that the "rebels," not Assad, are responsible for the chemical weapons? Will Obama and Kerry attack the "rebels"? Will Obama and Kerry attack Saudi Arabia for giving the chemical weapons to the "rebels"? Don't hold your breath.

My Ph.D. dissertation supervisor, G. Warren Nutter, was brought into the Pentagon by Melvin Laird as Assistant Secretary of Defense for

International Security Affairs and given the task of winding down the Vietnam War. Nutter opposed US foreign policy based on secrecy and deception. He was convinced that US foreign policy had to be transparent, consistent with the country's principles, and carry public support. A policy based on secrecy and deception would undermine democracy and the trust of the public and foreigners in the US government.

Today there are no Warren Nutters in Washington, and there have not been such people in government for many years. As Nutter foresaw, the consequences are the loss of public confidence in government and the isolation of the US in world affairs.

Obama now stands on the verge of military aggression as isolated as Adolf Hitler when Germany attacked Poland.

UPDATE: 4:00 PM US East Coast Time

Learning from the alternative media and not from his clueless advisers that he is isolated in the world and has no cover for his war crime against Syria, Obama has announced that he is going to wait until he gets approval from Congress.

No doubt the White House was also moved by the letter from 161 members of the House of Representatives that to engage in hostilities without congressional authorization is unconstitutional. The letter contains the threat of impeachment:

> We strongly urge you to consult and receive authorization from Congress before ordering the use of U.S. military force in Syria. Your responsibility to do so is prescribed in the Constitution and the War Powers Resolution of 1973.
>
> While the Founders wisely gave the Office of the President the authority to act in emergencies, they foresaw the need to ensure public debate—and the active engagement of Congress—prior to committing U.S. military assets. Engaging our military in Syria when no direct threat to the United States exists and without prior congressional authorization would violate the separation of powers that is clearly delineated in the Constitution.[119]

We can be thankful that at least 161 members of Congress recognize their responsibility to hold the executive branch accountable to the Constitution. Perhaps the lies from the executive branch became so brazen that they lost their effectiveness. Instead of fearing a hyped "terrorist threat," the American people now see the threat of a White House Tyrant.

WILL CONGRESS NOW SAVE OBAMA'S FACE BY SELLING OUT DEMOCRACY?

September 4, 2013

As I observed in previous columns, Obama was pushed out onto the end of the limb by Israel and the neoconservatives. The UN, NATO, the British Parliament, and the rest of the world left the White House flunky there, out on the limb where Israel put him, to make war on Syria all alone.

This proved to be beyond Obama's ability, but instead of crawling back off the limb and finding an excuse to get down, Obama decided to try to buy the Congress and to tell more lies.

The White House and its presstitute media are telling Congress that it is too humiliating for the President of "the world's only superpower" to have to crawl back along the limb and get down just because he told a lie. Congress must "save face" for the liar who is "America's first black president," or the prestige and credibility of the US will be lost.

What this really means, of course, is that the credibility of the Israel Lobby and the neoconservatives will be lost unless America again commits a war crime and destroys the life and prospects of many more people in the Middle East.

Heaven forbid that Washington lose prestige! So money, lots of it, is speaking in Washington and in European capitals. We know that the despicable Cameron will do all in his power to prostitute the British government for Washington.

What has the "socialist" Hollande been promised that makes him so willing to demonstrate that France is Obama's whore?

What larger share of NATO's military budget is Washington promising to underwrite in exchange for NATO's support for another American war crime?

Will bags of money enable Washington to gather support for its latest crime against humanity?

First Congress has to be brought around.

Congress will be pressured "to show a common front" with the White House in order to maintain America's credibility. Members of the House and Senate will be told that now that America has been abandoned by its allies, Congress cannot leave the President of the United States hanging out to dry. Congress must rush to the rescue of America's prestige or Washington will lose its clout and Congress will lose its campaign contributions from the Israel Lobby and the military/security complex.

This argument can even be effective with the strongest opponents to the attack on Syria. Americans have a long tradition of jingoism, and the prospect of lost prestige rankles. But before Congress is pushed into wrapping itself in the flag and giving its OK to another war crime, Congress needs to consider whether endorsing Obama's attack on Syria helps US prestige or hurts it.

It is clear that the American people overwhelming oppose an attack on Syria. Whether Americans have caught on over the years to Washington's endless war lies or whether they simply see no point to the wars and no gain to America from 12 years of costly war, I cannot say. At a time when a large percentage of Americans are having difficulty paying their mortgages, car payments, and putting food on the table, Washington's wars seem an expensive luxury.

It is not only the civilian populations of Afghanistan, Iraq, Libya, Pakistan, Yemen, Somalia, and Syria who have suffered. Tens of thousands of America's young have either been killed, maimed for life, or are suffering permanent post-traumatic stress. Washington's wars have caused thousands of divorces, alcoholism, drug addiction, and homelessness for veterans who were deceived and had their humanity abused by the criminals that rule in Washington.

For Congress, allegedly the representatives of the American people, not the backstop for the executive branch's undeclared agenda, to ignore the people's will and to endorse a war that the American people do not support would be another decisive blow against democracy. If Congress endorses Obama's war, it will prove that American democracy is a hoax.

If the White House were to succeed in using Congress' OK to a military attack on Syria to convince the British Parliament and NATO to go along, despite the strong opposition of the British and European peoples, Western Democracy would everywhere be discredited. Where is the democracy when a few elites at the top can do whatever they want, commit any crime, despite the majority opposition of citizens?

If Congress endorses Obama's transparent lies, American democracy will never recover. If Congress makes itself the handmaiden of the executive branch, Congress will never again have an independent voice. Congress might as well close down. It will have rendered itself superfluous and powerless.

If European governments endorse Obama's lies, it means the end of the West's democratic prestige and will strip away the cloak behind which the West has hidden its crimes against humanity. The voice of the West will never again carry any moral authority.

The loss of Western credibility is a huge price to pay in order to rescue a discredited president whom no one believes, not even his supporters. Essentially Obama is a cipher whose term of office is complete. The Obama regime epitomizes the degeneration of the American state.

Instead of voting on whether to allow Obama to attack Syria, Congress should be voting to impeach Obama and Kerry. Their blatant lies, dictatorial claims, and arrogant inhumanity are powerful arguments for removing them from office.[119]

The lies told by the Obama regime are so transparent that it makes one wonder just how stupid the regime thinks the American people are. Little doubt the White House is relying on its Ministry of Propaganda, a.k.a., the presstitute media, to undermine Americans' confidence in their common sense and to make them accept the latest fiction. The tactic is to use the peer pressure of the prostitute media to silence Americans' conscience.

Media negligence is everywhere. Yesterday NPR calmly reported the lies about Assad that the Obama regime has concocted to cover another act of naked aggression. In the same breath, NPR voiced "the world's outrage" over the rape and murder of one woman in India.

I, of course, do not agree with the raping and killing of anyone, but just imagine the raping and killing that will occur when Obama unleashes the dogs of war on Syria.

NPR is no longer an alternative voice. Yesterday NPR was beating the drums for war. NPR provided a forum for the head of one of the main neoconservative lobbies for war, and in the next hour had Democratic and Republican House and Senate leaders repeating all of Obama and Kerry's lies about how America's prestige cannot tolerate allowing Assad to use "chemical weapons against his own people." No one listening to NPR heard the voice of those demanding peace and truth. NPR was too busy lying for Obama to care about truth and certainly gave truth no voice on the program.

The presstitute media and the House and Senate "leaders" who report to the military/security complex and to the Israel Lobby keep talking about Assad's "own people," but Assad's own people support him. Polls of Syrians show that Assad has more support from the Syrian people than every head of every Western country has from their citizens. Cameron's, Hollande's, Merkel's and Obama's poll numbers are dismal compared to the Syrian peoples' support for Assad.[120]

Just as there was no evidence that Saddam Hussein had "weapons of mass destruction," but the facts did not stop the Bush regime from telling its lies that resulted in massive deaths and destruction of Iraqis, deaths and destruction that continue as I write, Assad has not used chemical weapons "against his own people." All of the evidence points to a false flag event that Obama could seize upon to launch America's 7th war in 12 years.

Moreover, al-Nusra fighters are not Assad's "own people." The al-Nusra front are Islamist extremists recruited from outside Syria and sent in by Washington and Saudi Arabia to overthrow an elected Syrian government, just as Washington used the Egyptian military to overthrow the first elected Egyptian government in history and to shoot down in the streets hundreds of Egyptians who were protesting the military's overthrow of the government that they had elected.

Whether or not Assad used chemical weapons against Washington-supported al-Nusra jihadists, and US Intelligence says that there is "no conclusive evidence," it is nevertheless a war crime for Washington to attack a country that has not attacked, or threatened to attack, the US. Under the Nuremberg standard established by the United States, naked aggression is a war crime regardless of the character of the country attacked or the weapons it uses against forces that attack it.

If Washington succeeds in enabling the al-Nusra terrorists to overthrow the secular Syrian government, how will Washington get Syria away from al-Nusra? In Iraq the death and destruction continues today at the same pace as under the attempted US military occupation. The criminal Bush regime did not bring "freedom and democracy" to Iraq. The Bush regime brought death and destruction that continues long after Washington's exit. In Iraq today, as many people are blown apart and murdered as during the height of Bush's war of aggression.

The chaos in which Washington left Iraq is a far cry from "freedom and democracy." The Obama war criminal did the same to Libya. In Afghanistan Washington added 12 years of war on top of the 10 years of war that Afghans fought with the Red Army. The purpose of Washington's war in Afghanistan has never been stated. No one knows what the war is about or why it continues.

According to the Bush regime, Afghanistan was attacked because the Taliban would not hand over Osama bin Laden without proof that he was responsible for 911. So why does the war continue 12 years after bin Laden died of renal failure and other diseases in December 2001 and then died again in May, 2011, two years and four months ago when Obama claims to have had him killed by Navy SEALs, whose unit was mysteriously wiped out shortly thereafter in Afghanistan. If the purpose of the Afghan war was to get bin Laden, why does the war continue when the man has twice died?

The lies being told by Obama and Kerry are so transparent that it makes one wonder if their strategy is to make such a poor case for war that the control Israel and the neocons have over US foreign policy will be broken. What else is one to make of such absurd statements as John Kerry's claim that "this is our Munich moment!" There is no comparison between Assad's defensive effort to prevent the overthrow of the Syrian government by foreign jihadists supported by Washington and Hitler's aggressive stance toward Czechoslovakia.

The Syrian government has initiated no war and has threatened no one.

America as my generation knew it no longer exists. Criminals have taken over and now rule. Financial policy is in the hands of a small handful of banksters who control the US Treasury, the Federal Reserve, the financial regulatory agencies and who run the world for their own greed and profit. Foreign policy is the preserve of the Israel Lobby and the neoconservatives, every one of which is tightly tied to Israel. Americans have no voice, and no representation. Whatever America is, the government is not influenced by the voices of the American people.

Whatever America is, it most certainly is not a democracy in which government is accountable to the people.

America is a country where a tiny elite has all power and does as it wishes.

If Congress rallies to Obama's war, Congress will have pushed the world closer to nuclear war. Russia and China see that the UN is powerless to prevent aggression and that Washington's aggression is aimed at them. As Russia and China build their nuclear forces, they will draw a starker line at Iran. Iran is Russia's underbelly, and provides 20 percent of China's oil supply.

From what I have been able to discern, both the Russian and Chinese governments have lost all confidence in Washington. Neither government believes any of Washington's lies and both countries are aware of Washington's attempt to isolate them diplomatically and to surround them with military bases. Both countries know that they can expect the same demonization from the presstitute western media as Saddam Hussein, Muammar Gaddafi, and Assad have received. They understand that western demonization is the prelude to destabilization and to military attack.

With the hubris, arrogance, and insanity of Washington an established fact, Russia and China perceive an enemy that intends their destruction. As neither country is going to accept their demise, Congress' acquiescence to Obama's lies in order to save "America's prestige" sets the stage for nuclear war.

However, if Congress refuses to be committed to a war crime based on a lie, rejects Obama's bribes and intimidation, and vetoes the war criminal's attack on Syria, it means the end of the influence of the Israeli

Lobby, the bloodthirsty neoconservatives, and war mongers John McCain and Lindsay Graham.

Without Washington's neoconservative belligerence, the governments of the world might, despite powerful and selfish private interests, be able to come together to sustain life on earth by protecting an increasingly vulnerable ecology from the predations of private capitalism.

If Congress fails to restrain the war that Obama seeks, the world doesn't have long to exist before the life-destroying bombs drop.

HOW TO STOP OBAMA'S MILITARY AGGRESSION AGAINST SYRIA

September 5, 2013

Many are asking what can be done to stop the pending US attack on Syria.

Two things can be done.

One is for the US Congress to realize that it does not save America's face for Congress to endorse a policy that has been rejected by the rest of the world, including Washington's closest ally, Great Britain. For Congress to endorse what the UN Secretary General and the President of Russia have made unequivocally clear would be a war crime under international law harms, not rescues, America's reputation. Doing the wrong thing to save face does not succeed.

In the event that Congress fails to understand the real stakes and votes to support a criminal action, the second thing that can be done to stop the attack is for most other countries in the world—China, India, Japan, Brazil, Australia, Canada, Iran, South Africa, the European and South American countries—to add their clear unequivocal statements to those of the UN General Secretary and President Putin that an American attack on Syria that is not authorized by the UN Security Council is a war crime. Expression by the governments of the world of this truthful statement would make it clear to Washington that it is isolated from the world community. For Obama to proceed in an act of aggression in the face of united opposition would destroy all influence of the US government and make it impossible for any officials of the Obama regime to travel abroad or to conduct business with other governments. What government would conduct business with a war criminal government? It is up to the governments of the world to make it clear to Washington that the US government is not above the law and will be held accountable.

Note the reports from congressional offices of the total lack of any support for Obama's attack on Syria. Calls to Congress are running 499 to 1 against attacking Syria. The entire world is now watching the Obama regime demonstrate its total disregard for the will of the people. The Obama regime is showing that American democracy is a hoax.[121]

THE WEST
DETHRONED

September 7, 2013

"The European race's last three hundred years of evolutionary progress
have all come down to nothing but four words:
selfishness, slaughter, shamelessness and corruption."
Yan Fu

It only took the rest of the world 300 years to catch on to the evil that masquerades as "western civilization," or perhaps it only took the rise of new powers with the confidence to state the obvious. Anyone doubtful of America's responsibility for the evil needs to read *The Untold History of the United States* by Oliver Stone and Peter Kuznick.

The "New American Century" proclaimed by the neoconservatives came to an abrupt end on September 6 at the G20 meeting in Russia. The leaders of most of the world's peoples told Obama that they do not believe him and that it is a violation of international law if the US government attacks Syria without UN authorization.

Putin told the assembled world leaders that the chemical weapons attack was "a provocation on behalf of the armed insurgents in hope of help from the outside, from the countries which supported them from day one." In other words, Israel, Saudi Arabia, and Washington—the axis of evil.

China, India, South Africa, Brazil, Indonesia, and Argentina joined Putin in affirming that a leader who commits military aggression without the approval of the UN Security Council puts himself "outside of law."

In other words, if you defy the world, Obama, you are a war criminal.

The entire world is waiting to see if the Israel Lobby can push Obama into the role of war criminal. Many are betting that Israel will prevail over the weak american president, a cipher devoid of all principle. A couple of decades ago before the advent of the american sheeple, one of the last tough Americans, Admiral Tom Moorer, Chief of Naval Operations and Chairman of the Joint Chiefs of Staff, publicly declared that "no US president can stand up to Israel." America's highest ranking military officer could not get an honest investigation of the Israeli attack on the *USS Liberty*.

We are yet to see an American president who can stand up to Israel. Or, for that matter, a Congress that can. Or a media.

The Obama regime tried to counter its smashing defeat at the G20 Summit by forcing its puppet states to sign a joint statement condemning Syria. However the puppet states qualified their position by stating that they opposed military action and awaited the UN report.

Most of Obama's bought-and-paid-for "supporters" are impotent, powerless. For example Obama counts the UK as a supporting country because of the personal support of the discredited UK prime minister, David Cameron, despite the fact that Cameron was repudiated by the British Parliament in a vote that prohibits British participation in another of Washington's war crimes. So, although Cameron cannot bring the British people and the British government with him, Obama counts the UK as a supporter of Obama's attack on Syria. Clearly, this is a desperate count of "supporting countries."

The Turkish puppet government, which has been shooting its peacefully demonstrating citizens down in the streets, with no protest from Obama or the Israel Lobby, supports "holding Syria accountable," but not itself, of course, or Washington.

The puppet states of Canada and Australia, powerless countries, neither of which carry one ounce of world influence, have lined up to do the bidding of their Washington master. The entire point of having the top government job in Canada and Australia is the payoff from Washington.

The Obama cipher also claims the support of Japan and the Republic of Korea, another two countries devoid of all diplomatic influence and power of any kind. Helpless Japan is on the verge of being destroyed by the Fukushima nuclear disaster, for which it has no solution. As the radiation leaks spread into the aquifer upon which Tokyo and surrounding areas rely, Japan is faced with the possibility of having to relocate 40 million people.

Saudi Arabia, implicated in the transfer to al-Nusra rebels of the chemical weapons used in the attack, supports Washington, knowing that otherwise its own tyranny is toast. Even the neoconservatives headed by Obama's shrill National Security Advisor, Susan Rice, want to overthrow the Saudis.

Obama claims also to have support from France and Germany. However both Hollande and Merkel have stated clearly that a diplomatic solution, not war, is their first choice and that the outcome rests on the UN.

As for Italy and Spain's support, both governments are hoping to be rewarded with the Federal Reserve printing enough dollars to bail out their indebted economies so that both governments are not overthrown in the streets for their acquiescence to the looting of their countries by international banksters. Like so many Western governments, those of Italy and Spain, and, of course, Greece, support the international banksters, not their own citizens.

The president of the European Commission has declared that the European Union, the central overlord over Britain, France, Germany, Italy, and Spain, does not support a military solution to the Syrian Crisis. "The European Union is certain that the efforts should be aimed at a political settlement," Jose Manuel Barroso told reporters at the G20 meeting. The EU has the power to issue arrest warrants for the heads of EU governments that participate in war crimes.

What this reveals is that the support behind the liar Obama is feeble and limited. The ability of the Western countries to dominate international politics came to an end at the G20 meeting. The moral authority of the West is completely gone, eroded and shattered by countless lies and shameless acts of aggression based on nothing but self-interest. Nothing remains of the West's "moral authority," which was never anything but a cover for self-interest, murder, and genocide.

The West has been destroyed by its own governments, who have told too many self-serving lies, and by its capitalist corporations, who offshored the West's jobs and technology to China, India, Indonesia, and Brazil, depriving the Western governments of a tax base and the support of their citizens.

It is difficult to know whether citizens in the West hate their corrupt governments any less than do Muslims, whose lives and countries have been devastated by Western aggression, or than do citizens of third world countries who have been impoverished by being looted by predatory First World financial organizations.

The Western governments have pissed away their clout. There is no prospect whatsoever of the neoconservative fantasy of US hegemony being exercised over Russia, China, India, Brazil, South Africa, South America, Iran. These countries can establish their own system of international payments and finance and leave the dollar standard whenever they wish. One wonders why they wait. The US dollar is being printed in unbelievable quantities and is no longer qualified to be the world reserve currency. The US dollar is on the verge of total worthlessness.

The G20 Summit made it clear that the world is no longer willing to go along with the West's lies and murderous ways. The world has caught on to the West. Every country now understands that the bailouts offered by the West are merely mechanisms for looting the bailed-out countries and impoverishing their peoples.

In the 21st century Washington has treated its own citizens the way it treats citizens of third world countries. Untold trillions of dollars have been lavished on a handful of banks, while the banks threw millions of Americans out of their homes and seized any remaining assets of the broken families.

US corporations had their taxes cut to practically nothing, with few paying any taxes at all, while the corporations gave the jobs and careers of millions of Americans to the Chinese and Indians. With those jobs went US GDP, tax base, and economic power, leaving Americans with massive budget deficits, a debased currency, and bankrupt cities, such as Detroit, which once was the manufacturing powerhouse of the world.

How long before Washington shoots down its own homeless, hungry, and protesting citizens in the streets?

Washington represents Israel and a handful of powerful organized private interests. Washington represents no one else. Washington is a plague upon the American people and a plague upon the world.[122]

TOO MANY YEARS OF LIES: FROM MOSSADEQ TO 9/11

September 10, 2013

Washington has been at war for 12 years. According to experts such as Joseph Stiglitz and Linda Bilmes, these wars have cost Americans approximately $6 trillion, enough to keep Social Security and Medicare sound for years. All there is to show for 12 years of war is fat bank balances for the armament industries and a list of destroyed countries with millions of dead and dislocated people who never lifted a hand against the United States.

The cost paid by American troops and taxpayers is extreme. Secretary of Veteran Affairs Erik Shinseki reported in November 2009 that "more veterans have committed suicide since 2001 than we have lost on the battlefields of Iraq and Afghanistan." Many thousands of our troops have suffered amputations and traumatic brain injuries. At the Marine Corps War College Jim Lacey calculated that the annual cost of the Afghan war was $1.5 billion for each Al Qaeda member in Afghanistan. Many US and coalition troops paid with their lives for every one Al Qaeda member killed. On no basis has the war ever made sense.

Washington's wars have destroyed the favorable image of the United States created over the decades of the Cold War. No longer the hope of mankind, the US today is viewed as a threat whose government cannot be trusted.

The wars that have left America's reputation in tatters are the consequence of 9/11. The neoconservatives who advocate America's hegemony over the world called for "a new Pearl Harbor" that would allow them to launch wars of conquest. Their plan for conquering the Middle East as their starting point was set out in the neoconservative "Project for the New American Century." It was stated clearly by *Commentary* editor Norman Podhoretz and also by many neoconservatives.

The neocon argument boils down to a claim that history has chosen "democratic capitalism" and not Karl Marx as the future. To comply with history's choice, the US must beef up its military and impose the American Way on the entire world.

In other words, as Claes Ryn wrote, the American neoconservatives are the "new Jacobins," a reference to the French Revolution of 1789 that intended to overthrow aristocratic Europe and replace it with "Liberty, equality, fraternity," but instead gave Europe a quarter century of war, death, and destruction.

Ideologies are dangerous, because they are immune to facts. Now that the United States is no longer governed by the US Constitution, but by a crazed ideology that has given rise to a domestic police state more complete than that of Communist East Germany and to a warfare state that attacks sovereign countries based on nothing but manufactured lies, we are left with the irony that Russia and China are viewed as constraints on Washington's ability to inflict evil, death, and destruction on the world.

The two pariah states of the 20th century have become the hope of mankind in the 21st century!

As Oliver Stone and Peter Kuznick prove in their book, *The Untold History of the United States*, the American government has never deserved its white hat reputation. Washington has been very successful in dressing up its crimes in moralistic language and hiding them in secrecy. It is only decades after events that the truth makes the mainstream media.

The latest example is the release of classified documents relating to the overthrow on August 19, 1953, of the democratically elected government of Iran by a coup instigated by the US government.. Sixty years after the event declassified CIA documents detail how the secret CIA operation overthrew a democratic government and imposed Washington's puppet on the people of Iran.

The declassified documents could not have spelled it out any clearer: "The military coup that overthrew Mossadeq and his National Front cabinet was carried out under CIA direction as an act of U.S. foreign policy, conceived and approved at the highest levels of government."[123]

In the 21st century Washington is attempting to repeat its 1953 feat of overthrowing the Iranian government, this time using the faux "green revolution" financed by Washington. When that fails, Washington will rely on military action.

If 60 years is the time that must pass before Washington's crimes can be acknowledged, the US government will admit the truth about September 11, 2001 on September 11, 2061. In 2013, on this 12th anniversary of 9/11, we only have 48 years to go before Washington admits the truth. Alas, the members of the 9/11 truth movement will not still be alive to celebrate their vindication.

But just as it has been known for decades that Washington overthrew Mossadeq, we already know that the official story of 9/11 is hogwash.

No evidence exists that supports the government's 9/11 story. The 9/11 Commission was a political gathering run by a neoconservative White House operative. The Commission members sat and listened to the government's story and wrote it down. No investigation of any kind was made. One member of the Commission resigned, saying that the fix was in. After the report was published, both co-chairmen of the Commission and the legal counsel wrote books disassociating themselves from the report. The 9/11 Commission was "set up to fail," they wrote.

NIST's account of the structural failure of the twin towers is a computer simulation based on assumptions chosen to produce the result. NIST refuses to release its make-believe explanation for expert scrutiny. The reason is obvious. NIST's explanation of the structural failure of the towers cannot survive scrutiny.

There are many 9/11 Truth organizations whose members are high-rise architects, structural engineers, physicists, chemists and nano-chemists, military and civilian airline pilots, firemen and first responders, former prominent government officials, and 9/11 families. The evidence they have amassed overwhelms the feeble official account.

It has been proven conclusively that World Trade Center Building 7 fell at free fall which can only be achieved by controlled demolition that removes all resistance below to debris falling from above so that no time is lost in overcoming resistance from intact structures. NIST has acknowledged this fact, but has not changed its story.

In other words, still in America today official denial takes precedence over science and known undisputed facts.

On this 12th anniversary of a false flag event, it is unnecessary for me to report the voluminous evidence that conclusively proves that the official story is a lie. You can read it for yourself. It is available online. You can read what the architects and engineers have to say. You can read the scientists' reports. You can hear from the first responders who were in the WTC towers. You can read the pilots who say that the maneuvers associated with the airliner that allegedly hit the Pentagon are beyond their skills and most certainly were not performed by inexperienced pilots.

You can read David Griffin's many books. You can watch the film produced by Richard Gage and Architects & Engineers for 9/11 truth. You can read *The 9/11 Toronto Report: International Hearings on 9/11*.[124] You can read *Hijacking America's Mind on 9/11*.[125]

Actually, you do not need any of the expert evidence to know that the US government's story is false. As I have previously pointed out, had a few young Saudi Arabians, the alleged 9/11 hijackers, been capable of outwitting, without support from any government and intelligence service, not only the CIA and FBI, but all sixteen US intelligence services, the intelligence services of Washington's NATO allies and Israel's Mossad, the National Security Council, NORAD, the Joint Chiefs of Staff, Air Traffic Control, and defeat Airport Security four times in one hour on the same morning, the White House, Congress, and the media would have been demanding an investigation of how the National Security State could so totally fail.

Instead, the President of the United States and every government office fiercely resisted any investigation. It was only after a year of demands and rising pressure from the 9/11 families that the 9/11 Commission was created to bury the issue.

No one in government was held accountable for the astonishing failure. The national security state was defeated by a few rag tag Muslims with box cutters and a sick old man dying from renal failure while holed up in a cave in Afghanistan, and no heads rolled.

The total absence of government response to demands for an investigation of an event that is the greatest embarrassment to a "superpower" in world history is a complete give-away that 9/11 was a false flag event. The government did not want any investigation, because the government's cover story cannot stand investigation.

The government could rely on the mega-media corporations in whose hands the corrupt Clinton regime concentrated the US media. By supporting rather than investigating the government's cover story, the media left the majority of Americans, who are sensitive to peer pressure, without any support for their doubts. Effectively, the American Ministry of Propaganda validated the government's false story.

Common everyday experiences of Americans refute the government's story. Consider, for example, self-cleaning ovens. How many American homes have them? Thirty million? More? Do you have one?

Do you know what temperature self-cleaning ovens reach? The self-cleaning cycle runs for several hours at 900 degrees Fahrenheit or 482 degrees Celsius. Does your self-cleaning oven melt at 482 degrees Celsius? No, it doesn't. Does the very thin, one-eighth inch steel soften and your oven collapse? No, it doesn't.

Keep that in mind while you read this: According to tests performed by NIST (National Institute of Standards and Technology), only 2% of the WTC steel tested by NIST reached temperatures as high as 250 degrees Celsius, about half the temperature reached by your self-cleaning oven. Do you believe that such low temperatures on such small areas of the WTC towers caused the massive, thick, steel columns in the towers to soften and permit the collapse of the buildings? If you do, please explain why your self-cleaning oven doesn't weaken and collapse.

In Section E.5 of the Executive Summary in this NIST report it says: "A method was developed using microscopic observations of paint cracking to determine whether steel members had experienced temperatures in excess of 250 degrees C. More than 170 areas were examined . . . Only three locations had a positive result indicating that the steel and paint may have reached temperatures in excess of 250 degrees C."[126] Analysis of steel "microstructures show no evidence of exposure to temperatures above 600 degrees C for any significant time."

In section 3.6 of the NIST report NIST states: "NIST believes that this collection of steel from the WTC towers is adequate for purposes of the investigation."[127]

How did these truths get out? My explanation is that the NIST scientists, resentful of the threat to their jobs and future employment opportunities and chaffing under the order to produce a false report, revealed the coerced deception by including information that their political masters did not understand. By stating unequivocally the actual temperatures, NIST's scientists put the lie to the coerced report.

The melting point of steel is around 1,500 degrees C. or 2,600 degrees F. Steel can lose strength at lower temperatures, but the NIST scientists reported that only a small part of the steel was even subjected to moderate temperatures less than those obtained by the self-cleaning oven in your home.

If you need to think about this a bit more, obtain a copy of *The Making of the Atomic Bomb* by Richard Rhodes. Have a look at the streetcar in photo 108. The caption reads: "The Hiroshima fireball instantly raised surface temperatures within a mile of the hypocenter well above 1,000 degrees F." Is the streetcar a melted lump of steel? No, it is structurally intact, although blackened with burnt paint.

Washington would have you believe that steel that survived intact from an atomic bomb would melt from low temperature, short lived, isolated office fires. What do you think of a government that believes that you are that stupid?

Who would support a government that lies every time it opens its mouth?

The three WTC buildings that were destroyed were massive heat sinks. I doubt that the limited, short-lived, low temperature fires in the buildings even warmed the massive steel structures to the touch.

Moreover, not a single steel column melted or deformed from softening. The columns were severed at specific lengths by extremely high temperature charges placed on the columns.

On this 12th anniversary of 9/11, ask yourself if you really want to believe that temperatures half those reached by your self-cleaning oven caused three massive steel structures to crumble into dust.

Then ask yourself why your government thinks you are so totally stupid as to believe such a fairy tale.

PUTIN STEPS INTO WORLD LEADERSHIP ROLE

September 12, 2013

Putin's article in the September 11 *New York Times* has the stuck pigs squealing. The squealing stuck pigs are just who you thought they would be—all those whose agendas and profits would be furthered by an attack on Syria by the Obama Stasi regime.

Included among the squealing stuck pigs are Human Rights Watch bloggers who seem to be financed out of the CIA's back pocket.

Does any institution remain that has not been corrupted by Washington's money?

Notice that the reason Putin is being criticized is that he has blocked the Obama regime from attacking Syria and slaughtering countless numbers of Syrians in the name of human rights. The stuck pigs are outraged that Obama's war has been blocked. They were so much looking forward to the mass slaughter that they believe would advance their profits and agendas.

Most of Putin's critics are too intellectually challenged to comprehend that Putin's brilliant and humane article has left Putin the leader of the free world and defender of the rule of law and exposed Obama for what he is—the leader of a rogue, lawless, unaccountable government committed to lies and war crimes.

Putin, being diplomatic, was very careful in his criticism of Obama's September 10 speech in which Obama sought to justify Washington's lawlessness in terms of "American exceptionalism." Obama, attempting to lift his criminal regime by the bootstraps up into the moral heavens, claimed that United States government policy is "what makes America different. It's what makes us exceptional."

What Obama told Americans is exactly what Hitler told the Germans. The Russians, having borne more than anyone else the full weight of the German war machine, know how dangerous it is to encourage people to think of themselves as exceptional, unbound by law, the Geneva Conventions, the UN Security Council, and humane concerns for others. Putin reminded Obama that "God created us equal."

If Putin had wanted to give Obama the full rebuke that Obama deserves, Putin could have said: "Obama is correct that the policy of the US government is what makes the US exceptional. The US is the only country in the world that has attacked 8 countries in 12 years, murdering and dispossessing millions of Muslims all on the basis of lies. This is not an exceptionalism of which to be proud."

Putin is obviously more than a match for the immoral, low grade shills that Americans put into high office. However, Putin should not underestimate the mendacity of his enemies in Washington. Putin warned that the militants that Washington is breeding in the Middle East are an issue of deep concern. When these militants return to their own countries, they spread destabilization, as when extremists used by the US in the overthrow of Libya moved on to Mali.

The destabilization of other countries is precisely the main aim of Washington's wars in the Middle East. Washington intends for radicalization of Muslims to spread strife into the Muslim populations of Russia and China. Washington's propaganda machine will then turn these terrorists into "freedom fighters against oppressive Russian and Chinese governments," and use Human Rights Watch and other organizations that Washington has penetrated and corrupted to denounce Russia and China for committing war crimes against freedom fighters. No doubt, chemical weapons attacks will be orchestrated, just as they have been in Syria.

If Washington's NATO puppet states wake up in time, the warmongers in Washington can be isolated, and humanity could be spared WWIII.

WHAT HAPPENS IF THE SHUTDOWN CAUSES THE TREASURY TO RUN OUT OF MONEY?

October 11, 2013

In a speech to the Commonwealth Club, San Francisco, November 23, 2010, Peter Dale Scott gave a history of the various directives concerned with government continuity during a state of emergency. He showed that these directives could be used to supersede the Constitution.[128]

The ease with which both the Bush and Obama regimes were able to set aside the due process protections of the Constitution that prohibit indefinite detention and execution without conviction in a trial indicate that Professor Scott's concern is justified that these directives could result in executive branch rule.

Scott describes how the executive branch efforts to provide government continuity in the aftermath of a nuclear attack dating from the Eisenhower administration were gradually converted into executive or national security (later Homeland Security) orders that confer secret powers to the White House for any event that the executive branch considers to be an emergency.

Generally these various executive orders and directives refer to "national emergencies," or "national disasters." However, President Bush's National Security Presidential Directive/NSPD 51 and Homeland Security Presidential Directive/HSPD-20 issued on May 9, 2007 use the term "Catastrophic Emergency."[129]

The directives speak of "enduring constitutional government" which the president maintains by coordinating "as a matter of comity with respect to the legislative and judicial branches," but it is up to the president and his advisor, the National Continuity Coordinator, to decide what constitutes constitutional government during a catastrophic emergency.

What comprises a catastrophic emergency? It is reasonable for a president to regard a government shutdown, which can threaten everything from national security to default and economic collapse, as a catastrophic emergency, and to take such steps as are necessary to prevent it, such as raising the debt ceiling, on his own authority.

The Federal Reserve also has the power to prevent a government shutdown. If banks are too big to fail, so is the federal government. If the Federal Reserve on its own authority can issue more than $16 trillion in loans to US and European banks in order to prevent their failure, the Federal Reserve can issue a loan to the US government.

I don't expect either of these two possibilities to come into play. A shutdown and default of US debt obligations would terminate the US as a superpower and dethrone the dollar as world reserve currency. Neither Congress nor President Obama desire such an outcome. Also, members of Congress would not want a presidential directive to be implemented that subordinates their position and possibly eliminates their meaningful participation in governance. Therefore, I expect a resolution of the current standoff prior to the Treasury running out of money.

I did interviews on this subject with King World News and with Greg Hunter.[130] The interviews are played to the sensational side, but I do not expect it to go that far.

However, it could.

HOW AMERICA WAS LOST

November 7, 2013

*"No legal issue arises when the United States responds
to a challenge to its power, position, and prestige."*
Dean Acheson, 1962
speaking to the American Society of International Law

Dean Acheson declared 51 years ago that power, position, and prestige are the ingredients of national security and that national security trumps law. In the United States democracy takes a back seat to "national security," a prerogative of the executive branch of government.

National security is where the executive branch hides its crimes against law, both domestic and international, its crimes against the Constitution, its crimes against innocent citizens both at home and abroad, and its secret agendas that it knows that the American public would never support.

"National security" is the cloak that the executive branch uses to make certain that the US government is unaccountable.

Without accountable government there is no civil liberty and no democracy except for the sham voting that existed in the Soviet Union and now exists in the US.

There have been periods in US history, such as President Lincoln's war to prevent secession, World War I, and World War II, when accountable government was impaired. These were short episodes of the Constitution's violation, and the Constitution was reinstated in the aftermath of the wars. However, since the Clinton regime, the accountability of government has been declining—for more than two decades, longer than the three wars combined.

In law there is the concept of adverse possession, popularly known as "squatters' rights." A non-owner who succeeds in occupying a piece of property or someone else's right for a certain time without being evicted enjoys the ownership title conveyed to him. The reasoning is that by not defending his rights, the owner showed his disinterest and in effect gave his rights away.

Americans have not defended their rights conveyed by the US Constitution for the duration of the terms of three presidents. The Clinton regime was not held accountable for its illegal attack on Serbia. The Bush regime was not held accountable for its illegal invasions of Afghanistan and Iraq. The Obama regime was not held accountable for its renewed attack on Afghanistan and its illegal attacks on Libya, Pakistan, and Yemen, and for attacks by its proxies on Syria.

We also have other strictly illegal and unconstitutional acts of government for which the government has not been held accountable. The Bush regime's acts of torture, indefinite detention, and warrantless spying, and the Obama regime's acts of indefinite detention, warrantless spying, and murder of US citizens without due process. As the Obama regime lies through its teeth, we have no way of knowing whether torture is still practiced.

If these numerous criminal acts of the US government spread over the terms of three presidents pass into history as unchallenged events, the US government will have acquired squatters' rights in lawlessness. The US Constitution will be, as President George W. Bush is reported to have declared, "a scrap of paper."

Lawlessness is the hallmark of tyranny enforced by the police state. In a police state law is not a protector of rights but a weapon in the hands of government. [See Roberts & Stratton, *The Tyranny of Good Intentions*] The accused has no recourse to the accusation, which does not require evidence presented to a court. The accused is guilty by accusation alone and can be shot in the back of the head, as under Stalin, or blown up by a drone missile, as under Obama.

As a person aware of the long struggle against the tyrannical state, I have been amazed and disheartened by the acceptance not only by the insouciant American public, but also by law schools, bar associations, media, Congress and the Supreme Court of the executive branch's claim to be above both law and the US Constitution.

As Lawrence Stratton and I show in our book about how the law was lost, liberals and conservatives chasing after their favorite devils, such as child abusers and drug pushers, and prosecutors, judges, and police devoted to conviction and not to justice, have gradually eroded over time the concept of law as a protection of the innocent. With the atmosphere of threat created by 9/11, the final destruction of the protective features of law was quickly achieved in the name of making us safe from terrorists.

The fact that we are no longer safe from our own government did not register.

This is how liberty was lost, and America with it.

Can liberty be regained? Probably not, but there is a chance if Americans have the necessary strength of character. The chance comes from the now known fact that the neoconservative Bush/Cheney regime took America and its puppet states to war in Afghanistan and Iraq entirely on the basis of lies.

As all evidence proves, these wars were not the results of mistaken intelligence. They were the products of intentional lies.

The weapons inspectors told the Bush regime that there were no weapons of mass destruction in Iraq. Despite this known fact, the Bush regime sent Secretary of State Colin Powell to the UN with fabricated evidence to convince the world that Saddam Hussein had "weapons of mass destruction" and was a threat to the world. Even if such weapons had existed in Iraq, many countries have them, including the US and Israel, and the presence of weapons does not under the Nuremberg Laws, justify unprovoked aggression against the possessor. Under the Nuremberg Laws, unprovoked military aggression is a war crime, not the possession of weapons that many countries have. The war crime was committed by the US and its "coalition of the willing," not by Saddam Hussein.

As for the invasion of Afghanistan, we know from the last video of Osama bin Laden in October 2001, attested by experts to be the last appearance of a man dying of renal failure and other diseases, that he declared that he had no responsibility for 9/11 and that Americans should look to their own government. We know as a reported fact that the Afghan Taliban offered to turn over Osama bin Laden to Washington if the Bush regime would provide the evidence that indicated bin Laden was responsible. The Bush regime refused to hand over the (non-existent) evidence and, with support of the corrupt and cowardly Congress and the presstitute media, attacked Afghanistan without any legal justification. Remember, the FBI has stated publicly that it has no evidence that Osama bin Laden was responsible for 9/11 and that that is why the crimes for which the FBI wanted bin Laden did not include responsibility for the 9/11 attack.

The war propaganda campaign was well prepared. Yellow ribbon decals were handed out for cars proclaiming "support the troops." In other words, anyone who raises the obvious questions is not supporting the troops. Still today insouciant Americans sport these decals on their cars unaware that what they are supporting is the murder of foreign women, children and village elders, the death and physical and mental maiming of American soldiers, and the worldwide destruction of the reputation of the United States, with America's main rival, China, now calling for a "de-Americanized world."

A country with a population as insouciant as Americans is a country in which the government can do as it pleases.

Now that we have complete proof that the criminal Bush regime took our country to wars in Afghanistan and Iraq solely on the basis of intentional lies, how can the legal institutions, the courts, the American people possibly tolerate the Obama regime's ignoring of the obvious crimes? How can America simply accept Obama's statement that we mustn't look back, only move ahead? If the US government, which has committed the worst crimes of our generation, cannot be held accountable and punished, how can federal, state, and local courts fill up American prisons with people who smoked pot and with people who did not sufficiently grovel before the police state.

Doubtless, the Obama regime, should it obey the law and prosecute the Bush regime's crimes, would have to worry about being prosecuted for its own crimes, which are just as terrible. Nevertheless, I believe that the Obama regime could survive if it put all the blame on the Bush regime, prosecuted the Bush criminals, and desisted from the illegal actions that it currently supports. This would save the Constitution and US civil liberty, but it would require the White House to take the risk that by enforcing US law, US law might be enforced against its own illegal and unconstitutional acts by a succeeding regime.

The Bush/Cheney/John Yoo neoconservative regime having got rid of US law, no doubt the Obama regime thinks it is best to leave the situation as it is, rid of law.

Without accountability, America is finished. Not only will Americans live in a police state with no civil liberties, but the rest of the world is already looking at America with a jaundiced eye. The US is being reconstituted as an authoritarian state. All it takes is one failure of accountability for the police state to become entrenched, and we have had numerous failures of accountability. Does anyone really believe that some future government is going to make restitution to persecuted truth-tellers, such as Bradley Manning, Julian Assange, and Edward Snowdon, as was done for Japanese Americans?

Now that we know for a certain fact that the invasions of Afghanistan and Iraq were based on propaganda and lies, Congress and the world media should demand to know what was the real secret agenda? What are the real reasons for which Afghanistan and Iraq were invaded?

No truthful explanation for these wars exists.

Paul O'Neill, the Bush regime's first Treasury Secretary, is on public record stating that at the very first cabinet meeting, long prior to 9/11, the agenda was a US attack on Iraq.

In other words, the Bush regime's attack on Iraq had nothing whatsoever to do with 9/11.

What was the Bush regime's secret agenda, kept secret by the Obama regime, that required an illegal, war criminal, attack on a sovereign country, an action for which officials of Hitler's government were executed? What is the real purpose of Washington's wars?

It is totally and completely obvious that the wars have nothing to do with protecting Americans from terrorism. If anything, the wars stir up and create terrorists. The wars create hatred of America that never previously existed. Despite this, America is free of terrorists' attacks except for the ones orchestrated by the FBI. What the fabricated "terror threat" has done is to create a thorough-going domestic police state that is unaccountable.

Americans need to understand that they have lost their country. The rest of the world needs to recognize that Washington is not merely the most complete police state since Stalinism, but also a threat to the entire world. The hubris and arrogance of Washington, combined with Washington's huge supply of weapons of mass destruction, make Washington the greatest threat that has ever existed to all life on the planet. Washington is the enemy of all humanity.

WHAT IS THE REAL AGENDA OF THE AMERICAN POLICE STATE?

November 13, 2013

In my last column I emphasized that it was important for American citizens to demand to know what the real agendas are behind the wars of choice by the Bush and Obama regimes. These are major long term wars each lasting two to three times as long as World War II.

Forbes reports that one million US soldiers have been injured in the Iraq and Afghanistan wars.[131]

RT reports that the cost of keeping each US soldier in Afghanistan has risen from $1.3 million per soldier to $2.1 million per soldier.[132]

Matthew J. Nasuti reports in the Kabul Press that it cost US taxpayers $50 million to kill one Taliban soldier. That means it cost $1 billion to kill 20 Taliban fighters.[133] This is a war that can be won only at the cost of the total bankruptcy of the United States.

Joseph Stiglitz and Linda Bilmes have estimated that the current out-of-pocket and already incurred future costs of the Afghan and Iraq wars is at least $6 trillion.

In other words, it is the cost of these two wars that explains the explosion of the US public debt and the economic and political problems associated with it.

What has America gained in return for $6 trillion and one million injured soldiers, many very severely?

In Iraq there is now an Islamist Shia regime allied with Iran in place of a secular Sunni regime that was an enemy of Iran, one as dictatorial as the other, presiding over war ruins, ongoing violence as high as during the attempted US occupation, and extraordinary birth defects from the toxic substances associated with the US invasion and occupation.

In Afghanistan there is an undefeated and apparently undefeatable Taliban and a revived drug trade that is flooding the Western world with drugs.

The icing on these Bush and Obama "successes" are demands from around the world that Americans and former British PM Tony Blair be held accountable for their war crimes. Certainly, Washington's reputation has plummeted as a result of these two wars. No governments anywhere are any longer sufficiently gullible as to believe anything that Washington says.

These are huge costs for wars for which we have no explanation.

The Bush/Obama regimes have come up with various cover stories: a "war on terror," "we have to kill them over there before they come over here," "weapons of mass destruction," revenge for 9/11, Osama bin Laden (who died of his illnesses in December 2001 as was widely reported at the time).

None of these explanations are viable. Neither the Taliban nor Saddam Hussein were engaged in terrorism in the US. As the weapons inspectors informed the Bush regime, there were no WMD in Iraq. Invading Muslim countries and slaughtering civilians is more likely to create terrorists than to suppress them. According to the official story, the 9/11 hijackers and Osama bin Laden were Saudi Arabians, not Afghans or Iraqis. Yet it wasn't Saudi Arabia that was invaded.

Democracy and accountable government simply does not exist when the executive branch can take a country to wars in behalf of secret agendas operating behind cover stories that are transparent lies.

It is just as important to ask these same questions about the agenda of the US police state. Why have Bush and Obama removed the protection of law as a shield of the people and turned law into a weapon in the hands of the executive branch? How are Americans made safer by the overthrow of their civil liberties? Indefinite detention and execution without due process of law are the hallmarks of the tyrannical state. They are terrorism, not a protection against terrorism. Why is every communication of every American and apparently the communications of most other people in the world, including Washington's most trusted European allies, subject to being intercepted and stored in a gigantic police state database? How does this protect Americans from terrorists?

Why is it necessary for Washington to attack the freedom of the press and speech, to run roughshod over the legislation that protects whistleblowers such as Bradley Manning and Edward Snowden, to criminalize dissent and protests, and to threaten journalists such as Julian Assange, Glenn Greenwald, and Fox News reporter James Rosen?[134]

How does keeping citizens ignorant of their government's crimes make citizens safe from terrorists?

These persecutions of truth-tellers have nothing whatsoever to do with "national security" and "keeping Americans safe from terrorists." The only purpose of these persecutions is to protect the executive branch from having its crimes revealed. Some of Washington's crimes are so horrendous that the International Criminal Court would surely convict if those guilty could be brought to trial. A government that will destroy the constitutional protections of free speech and a free press in order to prevent its criminal actions from being disclosed is a tyrannical government.

One hesitates to ask these questions and to make even the most obvious remarks out of fear not only of being put on a watch list and framed on some charge or the other, but also out of fear that such questions might provoke a false flag attack that could be used to justify the police state that has been put in place.

Perhaps that was what the Boston Marathon Bombing was. Evidence of the two brothers' guilt has taken a backseat to the government's claims. There is nothing new about government frame-ups of patsies. What is new and unprecedented is the lockdown of Boston and its suburbs, the appearance of 10,000 heavily armed troops and tanks to patrol the streets and search without warrants the homes of citizens, all in the name of protecting the public from one wounded 19 year old kid.

Not only has nothing like this ever happened before in the US, but also such a massive intervention could not have been organized on the spur of the moment. It had to have been already in place waiting for the event. This was a trial run for what is to come.

Unaware Americans, especially gullible "law and order conservatives," have no idea about the militarization of even their local police. I have watched local police forces train at gun clubs. The police are taught to shoot first, not once but many times, to protect their lives first at all costs, and not to risk their lives by asking questions. This is why a 13-year old kid with the toy rifle was recently shot to pieces. Questioning would have revealed that it was a toy gun, but questioning the "suspect" might have endangered the precious police who are trained to take no risks whatsoever.

The police operate according to Obama's presidential kill power: murder first then create a case against the victim.

In other words, dear American citizen, your life is worth nothing, but the police whom you pay, are not only unaccountable but also their lives are invaluable. If you get killed in their line of duty, it is no big deal. But don't you injure a police goon thug in an act of self-defense. I mean, who do you think you are, some kind of mythical free American with rights?

Further reading:

http://www.theatlantic.com/politics/archive/2013/11/clemency-for-torturers-but-not-for-edward-snowden/281142/

http://www.policestateusa.com/2013/innocent-man-given-anal-cavity-search-colonoscopy-after-rolling-through-a-stop-sign/

http://www.policestateusa.com/2013/police-tased-arrested-father-as-he-tried-to-save-his-3-year-old-son-from-house-fire/

http://www.policestateusa.com/2013/tube-fed-3-year-old-treated-like-terrorist-by-tsa-family-misses-flight/

http://www.policestateusa.com/2013/john-geer-shot-by-police/

http://www.policestateusa.com/2013/300-pound-officer-shoots-12-pound-terrier-claims-it-threatened-his-life/

http://www.policestateusa.com/2013/innocent-citizens-held-at-gunpoint-in-terrifying-california-checkpoints/

http://www.policestateusa.com/2013/police-perform-simulated-drug-raid-on-5th-graders-child-attacked-by-police-dog/

http://www.policestateusa.com/2013/john-pike-gets-compensation-for-emotional-suffering/

http://www.policestateusa.com/2013/13-year-old-shot-death-police-open-carrying-toy-rifle/

http://www.policestateusa.com/2013/dallas-police-opened-fire-on-unarmed-man-as-he-stood-in-his-doorway/

http://www.informationclearinghouse.info/article36833.htm

BIN LADEN'S OBITUARY NOTICE

November 20, 2013

A Funeral Notice for Osama bin Laden was published on December 26, 2001, in the Egyptian newspaper *al-Ward*. An English translation is provided below. Anyone fluent in Arabic is invited to verify or correct the translation. This item was sent to me from a reader abroad.

Also below is a CNN interview with its medical correspondent who examines the last non-faked video of bin Laden and concludes that bin Laden is seriously ill.

There is also below a 2002 report that Israeli intelligence has concluded that bin Laden is dead.

I cannot attest to the correctness of any of these reports, but it is unclear why there would be so much disinformation from such varied sources about bin Laden's condition or what purpose is served by Israel, Fox News, Egyptian newspapers, Pakistani politicians, and CNN reporting bin Laden's death a decade prior to Obama's claim to have murdered him.

You can use this information to evaluate the Obama regime's unsubstantiated claim that Navy SEALs killed bin Laden in Pakistan a decade later.

Try to identify a single event that the US government has not lied about. Weapons of mass destruction? Iranian nukes? Assad's chemical attack? Spying on Americans? 9/11? The assassination of President John F. Kennedy? The unemployment rate?

Here is the translation of the funeral article on the death of bin Laden which appeared in the Egyptian newspaper, *al-Wafd*.

Osama Bin Laden is dead since December 26, 2001.
al-Wafd, Wednesday, December 26, 2001 Vol 15 No 4633
News of Bin Laden's Death and Funeral 10 days ago
Islamabad -

A prominent official in the Afghan Taleban movement announced yesterday the death of Osama bin Laden, the chief of al-Qa'da organization, stating that bin Laden suffered serious complications in the lungs and died a natural and quiet death.

The official, who asked to remain anonymous, stated to *The Observer* of Pakistan that he had himself attended the funeral of bin Laden and saw his face prior to burial in Tora Bora 10 days ago. He mentioned that 30 of al-Qa'da fighters attended the burial as well as members of his family and some friends from the Taliban.

In the farewell ceremony to his final rest guns were fired in the air. The official stated that it is difficult to pinpoint the burial location of bin Laden because according to the Wahhabi tradition no mark is left by the grave. He stressed that it is unlikely that the American forces would ever uncover any traces of bin Laden.

Here is the original article:

Here is the CNN interview:

Dr. Sanjay Gupta:
Bin Laden would need help if on dialysis
(CNN) 1-21-02

–Speculation about the whereabouts and health of Osama bin Laden picked up over the weekend when Pakistan's president, Gen. Pervez Musharraf, said he thought bin Laden had likely died of kidney failure. CNN medical correspondent Dr. Sanjay Gupta spoke Monday with CNN's Paula Zahn about bin Laden's appearance in recently released videotapes and the possibility that the accused terrorist leader was undergoing kidney treatment.

ZAHN: For a point of reference, I'd like for you to analyze pictures of Osama bin Laden that apparently were taken prior to September 11. Describe to us the color and the tone of his skin, and then I want you to contrast that with pictures we know to have been taken much later.

GUPTA: You can look [at pictures from a December 2001 video] and notice that he has what some doctors refer to as sort of a frosting over of his features—his sort of grayness of beard, his paleness of skin, very gaunt sort of features. A lot of times people associate this with chronic illness. Doctors can certainly look at that and determine some clinical features.

But even more than that, it's sometimes possible to differentiate the specific type of disease or illness that he may be suffering from. The sort of frosting of the appearance is something that people a lot of times associate with chronic kidney failure, renal failure, certainly someone who is requiring dialysis would have that.

He's also not moving his arms. I looked at this tape all the way through its entire length. He never moved his left arm at all. The reason that might be important is because people who have had a stroke—and certainly people are at increased risk of stroke if they also have kidney failure— he may have had a stroke and therefore is not moving his left side. And in the rest of the videotape, he does move his right side a little bit more than he does his left. So those are some of the things that are sort of "of note" here in this more recent videotape.

ZAHN: I think we need to remind the viewers once again that the president of Pakistan talked about [bin Laden] importing two dialysis machines into Afghanistan. Of course, no one other than the president of Pakistan right now is confirming that [bin Laden] in fact needed dialysis.

GUPTA: That's right. And again, renal dialysis—talking about hemodialysis—is something that really is reserved for patients in end-stage renal failure. That means their kidneys have just completely shut down.

The most common cause of something like that would be something like diabetes and hypertension. Once that's happened, if you're separated from your dialysis machine—and incidentally, dialysis machines require electricity, they're going to require clean water, they're going to require a sterile setting—infection is a huge risk with that. If you don't have all those things and a functioning dialysis machine, it's unlikely that you'd survive beyond several days or a week at the most.

ZAHN: If he had all these things you're talking about to keep the dialysis machine running, how much help does he need around him to administer the treatment?

GUPTA: You certainly need someone who really knows how to run that dialysis machine. You have to have someone who's actually assessing his blood, Osama bin Laden's blood, to see what particular dialysate he would need, and to be able to change his dialysate as needed. So you'd need a kidney specialist, a technician — quite a few people around him.

Here is the Israeli article:

Israeli intelligence:
Bin Laden is dead, heir has been chosen
SPECIAL TO WORLD TRIBUNE.COM
Wednesday, October 16, 2002

TEL AVIV: Osama Bin Laden appears to be dead but his colleagues have decided that Al Qaida and its insurgency campaign against the United States will continue, Israeli intelligence sources said.

Al Qaida terrorists have launched a new campaign of economic warfare and are targeting shipping in the Middle East, according to U.S. intelligence officials.

The Israeli sources said Israel and the United States assess that Bin Laden probably died in the U.S. military campaign in Afghanistan in December. They said the emergence of new messages by Bin Laden are probably fabrications, Middle East Newsline reported.

But Bin Laden's heir has been chosen and his colleagues have decided to resume Al Qaida's offensive against the United States and Western allies, the sources said.

They said the organization regards the United States as the main target followed by Israel. "In this case, it doesn't matter whether Bin Laden is alive or not," a senior Israeli intelligence source said. "The organization goes on with help from key people."

The sources said Al Qaida has already determined Bin Laden's heir. They said the heir has not been identified, but is probably not Bin Laden's son, Saad. Saad is said to be in his 20s and ranked within the top 20 members of Al Qaida.

Earlier this week, Bin Laden's deputy, Ayman Zawahiri, was said to have released a videotape in which he claims that the Al Qaida leader is alive and functioning. Bin Laden's voice was not heard on the tape.

A senior Bush administration economic official said last week that another major Al Qaida attack anywhere in the world could have devastating economic repercussions.

The FBI warned last week that Al Qaida may be preparing for a major attack. The warning followed the release of an audio tape featuring the voice of Zawahiri.

Bombings in Bali aimed at tourists, an attack on U.S. soldiers training in Kuwait and the bombing of a French tanker in Yemen are signs of the new campaign, Geostrategy-Direct.com reported in its Oct. 22 edition.

The first attack was carried out last week with the Al Qaida terrorist attack on the French tanker Limburg, a 157,000-ton ultra large crude oil carrier, that was bombed as it picked up a pilot before mooring at the Yemeni port of al Shihr.

One crew member was killed and others were injured in the blast.

According to intelligence officials, a small boat approached at high speed from the starboard side of the ship and detonated a large explosive device.

A week earlier, the Office of Naval Intelligence issued an alert to ships in the Middle East to be alert for Al Qaida terrorist attacks.

Fox News, along with a number of international news sources, such as *The Pakistan Observer,* reported bin Laden's death on Dec. 26, 2001.[135] But this didn't stop Fox News from joining in the hype about "CIA-Led SEALs Team Delivers Blow To Al Qaeda" ten years later on May 2, 2011.

THE KENNEDY ASSASSINATION
(NOVEMBER 22, 1963)
50 YEARS LATER

November 22, 2013

November 22, 2013 is the 50th anniversary of the assassination of President John F. Kennedy. The true story of JFK's murder has never been officially admitted, although the conclusion that JFK was murdered by a plot involving the Secret Service, the CIA, and the Joint Chiefs of Staff has been well established by years of research, such as that provided by James W. Douglass in his book, *JFK and The Unspeakable*, published by Simon & Schuster in 2008. Ignore Douglass' interest in the Trappist monk Thomas Merton and Merton's prediction, and focus on the heavily documented research that Douglass provides.

Or just turn to the contemporary films taken by tourists watching JFK's motorcade that are available on YouTube, which show clearly the Secret Service pulled from President Kennedy's limo just prior to his assassination, and the Zapruder film that shows the killing shot to have come from President Kennedy's right front, blowing off the back of his head, not from the rear as postulated in the Warren Commission Report, which would have pushed his head forward, not rearward.

I am not going to write about the assassination to the extent that the massive information permits. Those who want to know already know. Those who cannot face the music will never be able to confront the facts regardless of what I or anyone else write or reveal.

To briefly review, the facts are conclusive that JFK was on terrible terms with the CIA and the Joint Chiefs. He had refused to support the CIA organized Bay of Pigs invasion of Cuba. He had rejected the Joint Chiefs' "Operation Northwoods," a plan to commit real and faked acts of violence against Americans, blame Castro and use the false flag events to bring regime change to Cuba. He had rejected the Joint Chiefs' case that the Soviet Union should be attacked while the US held the advantage and before the Soviets could develop delivery systems for nuclear weapons. He had indicated that after his reelection he was going to pull US troops out of Vietnam and that he was going to break the CIA into a thousand pieces. He had aroused suspicion by working behind the scenes with Khrushchev to defuse the Cuban Missile Crisis, leading to claims that he was "soft on communism." The CIA and Joint Chiefs' belief that JFK was an unreliable ally in the war against communism spread into the Secret Service.

It has been established that the original autopsy of JFK's fatal head wound was discarded and a faked one substituted in order to support the official story that Oswald shot JFK from behind. FBI director J. Edgar Hoover and President Johnson knew that Oswald was the CIA's patsy, but they also understood, as did members of the Warren Commission, that to let the true story out would cause Americans to lose confidence in their own government at the height of the Cold War.

Robert Kennedy knew what had happened. He was on his way to being elected president and to holding the plotters accountable for the murder of his brother when the CIA assassinated him. A distinguished journalist, who was standing behind Robert Kennedy at the time of his assassination, told me that the killing shots came from behind past his ear. He submitted his report to the FBI and was never contacted.

Acoustic experts have conclusively demonstrated that more shots were fired than can be accounted for by Sirhan Sirhan's pistol and that the sounds indicate two different calibers of firearms.

I never cease to be amazed by the gullibility of Americans, who know nothing about either event, but who confidently dismiss the factual evidence provided by experts and historians on the basis of their naive belief that "the government wouldn't lie about such important events" or "someone would have talked." What good would it do if someone talked when the gullible won't believe hard evidence?

Secret Service pulled from JFK's limo[136]

Zapruder film[137]

James W. Douglass, *JFK and the Unspeakable*, Simon & Schuster, 2008

Operation Northwoods[138]

PROTESTS
IN UKRAINE

December 4, 2013

The days of organized protests in Ukraine are notable for the absence of the high level of police violence that protesters encounter in the US, Canada, Thailand, Greece, and Spain, where peaceful protesters are beaten, tear gassed, water cannoned, and tasered, or in Egypt, Palestine, and Bahrain where protesters are fired upon with live ammunition. The restraint of the Ukrainian government and police in the face of provocations and attacks on the police is unusual. Apparently, Ukrainian police have not been militarized by US Homeland Security and taught that the public is the enemy.

What are the Ukrainian protests about? On the surface, the protests don't make sense. The Ukrainian government made the correct decision to stay out of the EU. Ukraine's economic interests lie with Russia, not with the EU. This is completely obvious.

The EU wants Ukraine to join so that Ukraine can be looted, like Latvia, Greece, Spain, Italy, Ireland, and Portugal. The situation is so bad in Greece, for example, that the World Health Organization reports that some Greeks are infecting themselves with HIV in order to receive the 700 euro monthly benefit for the HIV-infected.

The US wants Ukraine to join so it can become a location for more of Washington's missile bases against Russia.

Why would Ukrainians want to be looted?

Why would Ukrainians want to become targets for Russia's Iskander Missiles by becoming a host country for Washington's aggression against Russia?

Why would Ukrainians, having gained their sovereignty from Russia, want to lose it to the EU or become Washington's puppet state?

Obviously, an intelligent, aware, Ukrainian population would not accept these costs of joining the EU.

So why the protests?

Part of the answer is Ukrainian nationalists' hatred of Russia, especially in the Western Catholic part of Ukraine as opposed to the Eastern Orthodox part. With the Soviet collapse, Ukraine became a country independent of Russia. When empires break up, other interests can seize power. Various secessions occurred producing a collection of small states such as Georgia, Azerbaijan, the former central Asian Soviet Republics, Ukraine, the Baltics, and the pieces into which Czechoslovakia and Yugoslavia were broken by "nationalism." The governments of these weak states were easy for Washington to purchase. The governments of these powerless states are more responsive to Washington than to their own people. Much of the former Soviet Empire is now part of Washington's Empire. Georgia, the birthplace of Joseph Stalin, now sends its sons to die for Washington in Afghanistan, just as Georgia did for the Soviet Union,

These former constituent elements of the Russian/Soviet Empire are being incorporated into Washington's Empire. The gullible nationalists, naifs really, in these American colonies might think that they are free, but they simply have exchanged one master for another.

They are blind to their subservience, because they remember their subservience to Russia/Soviet Union and have not yet realized their subservience to Washington, which they see as a liberator with a checkbook. When these weak and powerless new countries, which have no protector, realize that their fate is not in their own hands, but in Washington's hands, it will be too late for them.

With the collapse of the Soviet Union, Washington quickly stepped into the place of Russia. The new countries were all broke, as was Russia at the time and, thus, helpless. Washington funded and used NGOs and its EU puppets to create anti-Russian, pro-American, pro-EU movements in the former constituent parts of Soviet Russia. The gullible peoples were so happy to have escaped the Soviet thumb that they did not realize that they now had new masters.

It is a good bet that the Ukrainian protests are a CIA organized event, using the Washington and EU funded NGOs and manipulating the hatred of Ukrainian nationalists for Russia. The protests are directed against Russia. If Ukraine can be realigned and brought into the fold of Washington's Empire, Russia is further diminished as a world power.

To this effect NATO conducted war games against Russia last month in operation Steadfast Jazz 2013.[139] Finland, Ukraine, Georgia, and neutral Sweden have offered their military participation in the next iteration of NATO war games close to Russia's borders despite the fact that they are not NATO members.

The diminishment of Russia as a powerful state is critical to Washington's agenda for world hegemony. If Russia can be rendered impotent, Washington's only concern is China.

The Obama regime's "Pivot to Asia" announced Washington's plan to surround China with naval and air bases and to interject Washington into every dispute that China has with Asian neighbors. China has responded to Washington's provocation by expanding its air space, an action that Washington calls destabilizing when in fact it is Washington that is destabilizing the region.

China is unlikely to be intimidated, but could undermine itself if its economic reform opens China's economy to western manipulation. Once China frees its currency and embraces "free markets," Washington can manipulate China's currency and drive China's currency into volatility that discourages its use as a rival to the dollar. China is disadvantaged by having so many university graduates from US universities, where they have been indoctrinated with Washington's view of the world. When these American-programmed graduates return to China, some tend to become a fifth column whose influence will ally with Washington's war on China. JP Morgan's "Sons and Daughters program" of gaining influence over the Chinese government by hiring the sons and daughters of senior Chinese officials is just one of many threats that US gangster institutions pose to the integrity of the Chinese government.

So where does this leave us? Washington will prevail until the US dollar collapses.

Many support mechanisms are in place for the dollar. The Federal Reserve and its dependent bullion banks have driven down the price of gold and silver by short-selling in the paper futures market, allowing bullion to flow into Asia at bargain prices, but removing the pressure of a rising gold price on the exchange value of the US dollar.

Washington has prevailed on Japan and, apparently, the European Central Bank, to print money in order to prevent the rise of the yen and euro to the dollar.

The Trans-Pacific and Trans-Atlantic Partnerships are designed to keep countries in the US dollar payments system, thus supporting the dollar's value in currency markets.

Eastern European members of the EU that still have their own currencies have been told that they must print their own currencies in order to prevent a rise in their currency's value relative to the US dollar that would curtail their exports.

The financial world is under Washington's thumb. And Washington is printing money for the sake of 4 or 5 mega-banks.

That should tell the protestors in Ukraine all they need to know.

WASHINGTON DRIVES THE WORLD TOWARD WAR

December 14, 2013

Washington has had the US at war for 12 years: Afghanistan, Iraq, Somalia, Libya, Pakistan, Yemen, and almost Syria, which could still happen, with Iran waiting in the wings. These wars have been expensive in terms of money, prestige, and deaths and injuries of both US soldiers and the attacked civilian populations. None of these wars appears to have any compelling reason or justifiable explanation. The wars have been important to the profits of the military/security complex. The wars have provided cover for the construction of a Stasi police state in America, and the wars have served Israel's interest by removing obstacles to Israel's annexation of the entire West Bank and southern Lebanon.

As costly and destructive as these wars have been, they are far below the level of a world war, much less a world war against nuclear armed opponents.

The fatal war for humanity is the war with Russia and China toward which Washington is driving the US and Washington's NATO and Asian puppet states. There are a number of factors contributing to Washington's drive toward the final war, but the overarching one is the doctrine of American exceptionalism.

According to this self-righteous doctrine, America is the indispensable country. What this means is that the US has been chosen by history to establish the hegemony of secular "democratic capitalism" over the world. The primacy of this goal places the US government above traditional morality and above all law, both its own and international.

Thus, no one in the US government has been held accountable for unprovoked aggression against other countries and for attacking civilian populations, unambiguous war crimes under international law and the Nuremberg standard. Neither has anyone in the US government been held accountable for torture, a prohibited crime under US law and the Geneva

Conventions. Neither has anyone been held accountable for numerous violations of constitutional rights—spying without warrants, warrantless searches, violations of habeas corpus, murder of citizens without due process, denial of legal representation, conviction on secret evidence. The list is long.

A person might wonder what is exceptional and indispensable about a government that is a reincarnation of Nazi Germany in every respect. People propagandized into the belief that they are the world's special people inevitably lose their humanity. Thus, as the US military video released by Bradley Manning reveals, US troops get their jollies by mowing down innocent people as they walk along a city street.

With the exception of the ACLU, constitutional rights groups and independent Internet voices, the American people including the Christian churches have accepted their government's criminality and immorality with scant protest.

The absence of moral denunciation emboldens Washington which is now pushing hard against Russia and China, the current governments of which stand in the way of Washington's world hegemony.

Washington has been working against Russia for 22 years ever since the collapse of the Soviet Union in 1991. In violation of the Reagan-Gorbachev agreement, Washington expanded NATO into Eastern Europe and the Baltic states and established military bases on Russia's borders. Washington is also seeking to extend NATO into former constituent parts of Russia itself such as Georgia and Ukraine.

The only reason for Washington to establish military and missile bases on Russia's frontiers is to negate Russia's ability to resist Washington's hegemony. Russia has made no threatening gestures toward its neighbors, and with the sole exception of Russia's response to Georgia's invasion of South Ossetia, has been extremely passive in the face of US provocations.

This is now changing. The George W. Bush regime's alteration of US war doctrine, which elevated nuclear weapons from a defensive, retaliatory use to pre-emptive first strike, together with the construction on Russia's borders of US anti-ballistic missile bases and Washington's weaponization of new technologies, has made it clear to the Russian government that Washington is setting up Russia for a decapitating first strike.

In his presidential address to the Russian National Assembly (both chambers of parliament) on December 12, Vladimir Putin addressed the offensive military threat that Washington poses to Russia. Putin said that Washington calls its anti-ballistic missile system defensive, but "in fact it is a significant part of the strategic offensive potential" and designed to tip the balance of power in Washington's favor. Having acknowledged the threat, Putin replied to the threat: "Let no one have illusions that he can achieve military superiority over Russia. We will never allow it."

Faced with the Obama regime's nullification of the START nuclear weapons reduction treaty, Putin said: "We realize all this and know what we need to do."

If anyone remains to write a history, the Obama regime will be known as the regime that resurrected the Cold War, which President Reagan worked so hard to end, and drove it into a hot war.

Not content to make Russia an enemy, the Obama regime has also made an enemy of China. The Obama regime declared the South China Sea to be an area of "US national security interest." This is akin to China declaring the Gulf of Mexico to be an area of Chinese national security interest.

To make clear that the claim to the South China Sea was not rhetorical, the Obama regime announced its "Pivot to Asia," which calls for the redeployment of 60% of the US fleet to China's zone of influence. Washington is busy at work securing naval and air bases from the Philippines, South Korea, Vietnam, Australia, and Thailand. Washington has increased the provocation by aligning itself with China's neighbors who are disputing China's claims to various islands and an expanded air space.

China has not been intimidated. China has called for "de-americanizing the world." Last month the Chinese government announced that it now possesses sufficient nuclear weapons and delivery systems to wipe the US off of the face of the earth. A couple of days ago, China aggressively harassed a US missile cruiser in the South China Sea.

The militarily aggressive stance that Washington has taken toward Russia and China is indicative of the extreme self-assuredness that usually ends in war. Washington is told that US technological prowess can prevent or intercept the launch of Russian and Chinese missiles, thus elevating a US pre-emptive attack to slam-dunk status. Yet the potential danger from Iran acquiring nuclear weapons is said to be so great that a pre-emptive war is necessary right now, and a massive Department of Homeland Security is justified on the grounds that the US remains vulnerable to a few stateless Muslims who might acquire a nuclear weapon. It is an anomalous situation that the Russian and Chinese retaliatory response to US attack is considered to be inconsequential, but not nuclear threats from Iran and stateless Muslims.

Not content with sending war signals to Russia and China, Washington has apparently also decided to torpedo the Iranian settlement by announcing new sanctions against companies doing business with Iran. The Iranians understood Washington's monkey wrench as Washington probably intended, as a lack of Washington's commitment to the agreement, left Geneva and returned to Iran. It remains to be seen whether the agreement can be resurrected or whether the Israel Lobby has succeeded in derailing the agreement that promised to end the threat of war with Iran.

American citizens seem to have little, if any, influence on their government or even awareness of its intentions. Moreover, there is no organized opposition behind which Americans could rally to stop Washington's drive toward world war. Hope, if there is any, would seem to lie with Washington's European and Asian puppets. What interests do these governments have in putting the existence of their countries at risk for no other purpose than to help Washington acquire hegemony over the world? Can't they realize that Washington's game is a death-dealing one for them?

Germany alone could save the world from war while simultaneously serving its own interests. All Germany has to do is to exit the EU and NATO. The alliance would collapse, and its fall would terminate Washington's hegemonic ambition.

UPDATE: In their annual End of Year survey, Win/Gallup International[140] found that the United States is considered the number one "greatest threat to peace in the world today" by people across the globe. The poll of 67,806 respondents from 65 countries found that the U.S. won this dubious distinction by a landslide, as revealed in the chart below.

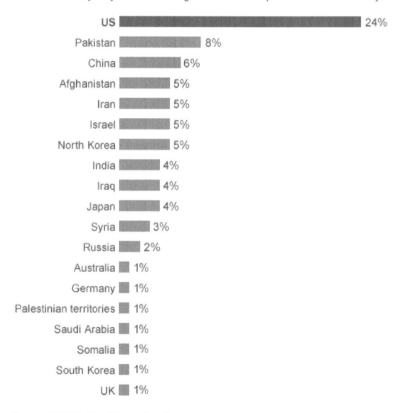

Q: Which country do you think is the greatest threat to peace in the world today?

Country	Percent
US	24%
Pakistan	8%
China	6%
Afghanistan	5%
Iran	5%
Israel	5%
North Korea	5%
India	4%
Iraq	4%
Japan	4%
Syria	3%
Russia	2%
Australia	1%
Germany	1%
Palestinian territories	1%
Saudi Arabia	1%
Somalia	1%
South Korea	1%
UK	1%

Source: WIN/Gallup International

WASHINGTON HAS DISCREDITED AMERICA

December 19, 2013

Years ago when I described the George W. Bush regime as a police state, right-wing eyebrows were raised. When I described the Obama regime as an even worse police state, liberals rolled their eyes. Alas! Now I am no longer controversial. Everybody says it.

According to the UK newspaper, *The Guardian*, the Chancellor of Germany, Angela Merkel, had an angry exchange with Obama in which Merkel compared Obama's National Security Agency (NSA) with the East German Communist Stasi, which spied on everyone through networks of informers.[140]

Merkel grew up in Communist East Germany where she was spied upon by the Stasi, and now that she has risen to the highest political office in Europe's most powerful state, she is spied upon by "freedom and democracy" America.

A former top NSA official, William Binney, declared that "We (the US) are now in a police state." The mass spying conducted by the Obama regime, Binney says "is a totalitarian process."[141]

Perhaps my best vindication, after all the hate mail from "super patriots," who wear their ignorance on their sleeves, and Obama-worshipping liberals, whose gullibility is sickening, came from federal judge Richard Leon, who declared the Obama-sanctioned NSA spying to be "almost Orwellian." As the American Civil Liberties Union realized, federal judge Leon's decision vindicated Edward Snowden by ruling that the NSA spying is likely outside what the Constitution permits, "labeling it 'Orwellian'—adding that James Madison would be 'aghast.'"

If only more Americans were aghast. I sometimes wonder whether Americans like being spied upon, because it makes them feel important. "Look at me! I'm so important that the government spends enough money to wipe out US poverty spying on me and my Facebook, *et. al.*, friends. I bet they are spending one billion dollars just to know who I connected with today. I hope it didn't get lost in all the spam."

Being spied upon is the latest craze of people devoid of any future but desperate for attention.

Jason Ditz at the FBI spied-upon Antiwar.com says that Judge Leon's ruling is a setback for Obama, who was going to restore justice and liberty but instead created the American Stasi Spy State. Congress, of course, loves the spy state, because all the capitalist firms that make mega-millions or mega-billions from it generously finance congressional and senatorial campaigns for those who support the Stasi state.

The romance that libertarians and "free market economists" have with capitalism, which buys compliance with its greed and cooperates with the Stasi state, is foolish.

Let's move on. It was only a few weeks ago that Obama and his Secretary of State John Kerry were on the verge of attacking Syria on the basis of faked evidence that Syria had crossed the "red line" and used weapons of mass destruction against the American organized, armed, and financed "rebels," almost all of whom come from outside Syria.

Only the bought-and-paid-for-by-Washington French president made a show of believing a word of Washington's lies against the Assad government in Syria. The British Parliament, long a puppet of Washington, gave Obama the bird and voted down participating in another American war crime. That left UK prime minister, David Cameron, hanging. Where do the British get prime ministers like Cameron and Blair?

Washington's plan for Syria, having lost the cover of its British puppet, received a fatal blow from Russian President Putin, who arranged for Syria's chemical weapons to be delivered to foreign hands for destruction, thus putting an end to the controversy.

In the meantime it became apparent that the "Syrian rebellion" organized by Washington has been taken over by Al Qaeda, an organization allegedly responsible for 9/11. Even Washington was able to figure out that it didn't make sense to put Al Qaeda in charge of Syria. Now the headlines are: "West tells Syria rebels: Assad must stay."

Meanwhile, Washington's arrogance has managed to make an enemy of India. The TSA, a component of Homeland Security, subjected a female diplomat from India to multiple strip searches, cavity searches and ignored her protestations of consular immunity.[143]

There was no justification whatever for this abuse of an Indian diplomat. To indicate its displeasure, the Indian government has removed barriers that prevent truck bombs from being driven into the US embassy.

Washington has managed to recreate the arms race. More profits for the military/security complex, and less security for the world. Provoked by Washington's military aggressiveness, Russia has announced a $700 billion upgrade of its nuclear ballistic missiles. China's leaders have also made it clear that China is not intimidated by Washington's intrusion into China's sphere of influence. China is developing weapon systems that make obsolete Washington's large investment in surface fleets.

Recently, Pat Buchanan, Mr. Conservative himself, made a case that Russia's Putin better represents traditional American values than does the President of the United States.[144]

Buchanan has a point. It is Washington, not Moscow or Beijing, that threatens to bomb countries into the stone age, that forces down airplanes of heads of state and subjects them to searches, and that refuses to honor grants of political asylum.

Certainly, Washington's claim to be "exceptional" and "indispensable" and, therefore, above law and morality contrasts unfavorably with Putin's statement that "we do not infringe on anyone's interests or try to teach anyone how to live."

Washington's arrogance has brought America disrepute. What damage will Washington next inflict on us?

NO NEED FOR NATO

December 2013, *Trends Journal*

NATO has gone on too long. The North Atlantic Treaty Organization was established on April 4, 1949, as a defensive alliance whose purpose was to defend Western Europe in the event of a Soviet invasion. As NATO's first secretary general put it, NATO was formed in order to keep the Russians out of Western Europe and the Americans in.

NATO was resurrected as America's Imperial Army. Instead of disbanding NATO when the Soviet Union collapsed in 1991, Washington dramatically expanded NATO. In violation of the Reagan-Gorbachev agreements, the Clinton and George W. Bush regimes added constituent parts of the former Soviet empire to NATO—Hungary, Czech Republic, Poland, Estonia, Latvia, Lithuania, Slovenia, Slovakia, Bulgaria, and Romania. France, taken out of NATO by General de Gaulle, rejoined in April 2009 eighteen years after the collapse of the Soviet Union along with Croatia and Albania. Currently the Obama regime is working to incorporate into NATO two former Soviet Republics—Ukraine and Georgia.

Efforts are currently underway to expand this structure to Japan. On April 15, 2013, NATO Secretary General Rasmussen and Japanese Prime Minister Abe signed the Joint Political Declaration. The Joint Political Declaration acknowledges that Japan and NATO face the same security challenges and have been brought together by shared values. Washington, it appears, is using Japan to bring the NATO threat to China.

In addition, the Bush regime initiated the US Africa Command, which began operations in 2007. This new command's mission is to "protect and defend the national security interests of the United States by strengthening the defense capabilities of African states. . . in order to deter and defeat transnational threats."

The military-security complex has grown fabulously wealthy by identifying threats to America in every corner of the earth and putting in place hundreds of US military bases.

The "war on terror" has served as the cover for organizing much of the world into America's Empire Army. The main purpose of the imperial army is to establish US hegemony over the world. American hegemony is the ideology of the neoconservatives who are still angry that President Reagan ended the cold war with diplomacy instead of winning it with a military victory. Reagan repeatedly declared that his goal was to end the cold war, not to win it. I know. I was there. I was part of it.

When the Soviet Union collapsed, the neoconservatives renewed their push for American supremacy. Security against a vague stateless "terrorist threat" became the new source of money for the military-security complex. The US and Europe are struggling with faltering economies, unable to maintain social infrastructure, health and pensions systems or to stem the flow of new public debt, sacrificing all to the funding of a massive imperial army to defend against a few stateless terrorists.

What does it mean to exercise world hegemony while your society comes apart at the seams? The internal collapse of Western society is a far greater threat than a few stateless terrorists. It makes no sense for Washington to build up military commands when Washington cannot pay Medicare bills or Veterans Benefits.

The formation of NATO was one of the first acts of the Cold War. There was no evidence that the Soviet Union intended to invade Western Europe. Despite Stalin's refusal to support the indigenous communist insurgency in Greece in 1948, President Truman and his advisors saw the Greek uprising as part of a Soviet plan for world domination, just as later US administrations saw the same thing in Vietnam.

Stalin had buried any prospect of world revolution when he defeated its advocate, Leon Trotsky, the founder and commander of the Red Army in the Russian civil war, who defined the communist purpose as international "permanent revolution." Stalin declared, "revolution in one country." But the myth of the Soviet Union pursuing world revolution persisted from the Truman administration right through President Reagan's first press conference on January 29, 1981.

The cultivation of this myth was very beneficial for the profits and power of the US military/security complex. When the Soviet collapse disposed of "the threat," the military/security complex came up with a new threat—Muslim Terrorism—and has used this threat to expand the military/ security budget and the infringement of civil liberty beyond what was achieved by hyping the Soviet threat. Evidently, Muslims with box cutters are more frightening to Americans than Soviets with nuclear weapons.

To the Soviets, who had no military designs on Western Europe, the formation of NATO looked like Anglo-American encirclement of the Soviet Union. The Soviet Union's response was to form the Warsaw Pact with Eastern Europe in 1955—six years after the formation of NATO. The Warsaw Pact was immediately misrepresented by Western cold warriors as evidence of Soviet military designs on Europe.

In those days US news magazines were full of maps of Warsaw Pact divisions arrayed against NATO divisions. The troop disparity so greatly favored the Soviet side that President Eisenhower despaired of the financial cost of matching the Soviets in troops and conventional weapons. Deciding in favor of more bang for the buck, Eisenhower shifted US military doctrine to reliance on nuclear weapons. Republicans, then as now, were fixated on budget deficits, and Eisenhower found budget deficits to be greater threats than nuclear war.

It is doubtful that NATO ever served any purpose commensurate with the risk. Regardless, NATO lost its purpose 22 years ago when the Soviet Union collapsed. NATO exists today because Washington stood NATO on its head and reconstituted it as an offensive military alliance serving Washington's wars for world hegemony.

The Russian government understands that the expansion of NATO into former Warsaw Pact countries and also into former Soviet Republics that were part of the Soviet Union constitutes encirclement. This bold and reckless encirclement of Russia by Washington and its NATO puppet states is underlined by Washington's establishment of missile bases on former Warsaw Pact territory. The purpose of these missile bases is to neutralize or to degrade Russia's nuclear deterrent. No one believes Washington's claim that the anti-ballistic missile bases on Russia's frontier are directed at Iran. Washington's encirclement of Russia is reckless and dangerous.

Present day Russia is not the Soviet Union, but Russia possesses sufficient nuclear weapons and delivery systems to destroy Western Europe and the US. What purpose is being served by Washington's aggressive use of NATO against Russia?

Is the purpose worth the risk of nuclear war? Why has Washington raised tensions to the point that the Deputy Defense Minister of Russia, Anatoly Antonov, felt compelled to state publicly on July 2, 2013, that no country will be able to attack Russia's strategic nuclear forces with impunity?

Why have policymakers in Washington, wallowing in their hubris, caused the Russians to perceive such a high level of threat? The answer is that Washington's commitment to the US military/security complex places profits above life. As far as the military/security complex is concerned, Americans cannot have enough enemies. Protecting America's security is a profitable business.

Washington used NATO for the first time as an offensive weapon to break apart Yugoslavia during 1993-95. NATO air strikes and bombings frustrated the Yugoslavian government's attempt to prevent the breakup of the country into its constituent parts. In 1999 Washington again used NATO to strip from Serbia its historic homeland of Kosovo and deliver it into Muslim hands.

In 2001 Washington pretended that the 9/11 attack was the work of Afghanistan and forced NATO to invoke Article 5. This article says that an attack on one member is an attack on all, requiring every NATO country to come to Washington's aid. By forcing NATO to invoke Article 5, Washington provided cover for its war of aggression against Afghanistan, now in its twelfth year. It is extraordinary that Congress has allowed the executive branch to squander trillions of dollars on wars in Afghanistan and Iraq when Washington is dependent on the Federal Reserve to finance its annual budget deficits by printing money and is considering curtailing Social Security, Medicare, and veterans' benefits in order to reduce the federal budget deficit.

In 2011 the Obama regime used NATO to overthrow the government of Libya. Until blocked by Russia and the British Parliament, the Obama regime tried to get NATO involved in the Syrian conflict that Washington initiated by having Saudi Arabia and the oil emirates arm the Islamists who wish to overthrow the secular Assad government.

In 2008, egged on by Washington, the former Soviet Republic of Georgia attacked Russian peacekeeping troops and the Russian population of South Ossetia. In reassuring the Georgian government, Washington miscalculated the Russian response. The Russian military made short work of the US and Israeli trained and armed Georgian army and could easily have reincorporated Georgia back into Russia, where it was for 200 years and where many believe it belongs. However, with the point made, Russia withdrew its victorious forces.

Thirsting for revenge, which seems to be the main motivation of Washington throughout its history, Washington is trying to convince NATO to extend membership to Georgia, a country located in Asia between the Black and Caspian Seas far removed from the North Atlantic. NATO membership would make Georgia a treaty protectorate of Washington and NATO, which is Washington's way of sticking its finger into Putin's eye and telling Russia that it will have to acquiesce in Georgia's next act of aggression or risk general war with the West.

No clearer statement could be made that Washington is reckless and willing to risk war for prestige reasons alone. But for Washington's NATO puppets, the stakes are extremely high—every capital city of Europe and the very existence of the European population.

It is NATO that enables Washington to be reckless and aggressive. Without the cover NATO provides and the bases NATO makes available, Washington would have to transform itself from an aggressive warmongering bully into a good neighbor. Europeans have resisted Georgia's NATO membership precisely for the reasons outlined above, but Washington is persistent and usually prevails with bribes, threats, and political pressure.

To the extent that the US media reports on any of these dangerous developments, it is usually along the lines of a partisan sports announcer cheering that his team is winning. Washington's aggressive use of NATO against Russia's security can easily lead to miscalculation.

Washington is using NATO to incorporate the military forces of the 27 NATO countries into Washington's Empire Army. For example, Spanish navy ships are armed with US weapons systems, such as AEGIS, and are integrated into US forces under the rubric of "interoperability between NATO member nations." In other words, European governments are losing control over their own armed forces which are increasingly unable to operate outside the US dominated NATO structure.

Following their defeat in World War II, both Germany and Japan were prohibited from having any offensive military capability. Now both countries are being incorporated into the forces supporting Washington's wars for world hegemony.

NATO is expensive as well as an enabler of US aggression. The military budgets of NATO countries account for 70% of world expenditures on military forces. Because of disputed sovereignty, the number of countries in the world cannot be precisely stated, but the boundaries are 190-206 separate countries.

If we take the lower number, then 15 percent of the countries in the world—the NATO members—account for 70 percent of world military expenditures.

In contrast, 85 percent of the countries in the world, including China, India, Iran, and Russia, account for 30 percent of military expenditures.

Obviously, Washington has honed NATO into a tool for military aggression.

Europe cannot afford to fight for Washington in the Middle East, Africa, and Asia. Europe lacks the resources to deal with its sovereign debt problems and is having to resort to severe austerity imposed on European populations. Unemployment and poverty are rising in Europe. Yet, European countries that cannot afford to pay their police and teachers and run their medical services are spending money they do not have in order to fight for American hegemony in distant areas of the world where Europeans have no national interests.

The Poles, Hungarians, and Czechs revolted against their Soviet overlords. Washington preempts revolt by paying off the European governments. By enabling Washington, NATO is setting the course for World War III. Poland's decision to accept US missile bases on its border with Russia might be a fatal step on the path to World War III.

Today the US faces no hostile military power. Although Russia and China have substantial military capability and the governments of both countries are described as "authoritarian" by Western propagandists, neither government represents a communist ideology hostile to the West. The governments of both countries are striving to avoid conflict with the US and to improve the wellbeing of citizens.

The only dangerous ideology in the world today is Washington's ideology of neoconservatism. This ideology proclaims the US to be the "indispensable nation," with the right and responsibility to impose its economic and political system on the world. Claes Ryn calls neoconservatism "the New Jacobinism," the French Revolution all over again, only this time the target is not merely Europe but the entire world.

Neoconservatism is an aggressive ideology and foments self-righteousness and militarism. The aggressiveness of the ideology is reflected in the Pentagon's June 19, 2013, report to Congress outlining US nuclear war strategy. The report shows that more than two decades after the collapse of the "Soviet threat" Washington is still preparing for waging nuclear war.

The report attempts to lull Russia by stating that "it is not our intent to negate Russia's strategic nuclear deterrent, or to destabilize the strategic military relationship with Russia." However, the report backtracks on the 2010 Nuclear Posture Review that set the goal of limiting the purpose of US nuclear weapons to deterrence of nuclear attack.

The June 2013 report says: "we cannot adopt such a policy today."

Washington's excuse for retaining the right to initiate a nuclear attack is the threat of "nuclear terrorism" by "Al Qaeda and their extremist allies." Al Qaeda is not a state or a country. The report does not say how a preemptive US nuclear attack can be used against Al Qaeda. Indeed, the extremism of Al Qaeda is the product of Washington's imperialism. If Washington would leave Muslims alone, the extremism would be internalized between Sunni and Shi'ites and between secular rulers and Islamists.

If the US would renounce its interventionist policies, the terrorist threat would abate.

Even the present level of hostility does not prevent Chechen terrorists from cooperating with Washington in efforts to destabilize the Russian North Caucasus region.

Washington's use of Muslim extremists against the Russian state dates to the Soviet invasion of Afghanistan. When Gorbachev became General Secretary, he informed Washington that he was withdrawing Soviet troops from Afghanistan. In their 2012 book, The Untold History of the United States, Oliver Stone and Peter Kuznick report that instead of facilitating the end of the conflict, Washington worked to tie down Soviet forces in Afghanistan as long as possible by supplying Osama bin Laden and Ayman al-Zawahiri with money and weapons and by blocking UN attempts to broker a settlement.

The neoconservatives are bitter that the Cold War ended without a US military triumph over Russia. It is a triumph that the dangerous warmongers still hope to achieve.

CONCLUSION

As at the conclusion of this writing in December, 2013, it appears that Washington might have lost the initiative in fomenting wars in the Middle East. Most of the world has concluded, along with the Russian government, that the use of chemical weapons in Syria was an orchestrated pretext for US military intervention in behalf of the Islamist attempt to overthrow the secular Assad government. The diplomatic offensive by Iran's president, Dr. Hassan Rouhani, has further constrained Washington's ability to obtain support from other countries as a cover for Washington's wars of aggression.

Washington, of course, is unhappy with these restraints, but the risk to Washington of initiating naked aggression without some kind of cover, such as a UN resolution, NATO support, or a "coalition of the willing," is to be branded a war criminal. Washington's ability to continue its march through the neoconservatives' list of governments to be overthrown lacks the necessary support both at home and abroad. Washington might possibly use a false flag event in order to regain support for remaking the Middle East, but this would be risky considering the high level of skepticism that now exists related to the US government's account of 9/11.[145]

During the twelve years of Washington's focus on the "war on terror," other developments have occurred that Washington now regards as greater threats to its hegemony. Under the leadership of Putin and Medvedev, Russia has emerged as a diplomatic force independent of foreign financial control, and China has emerged as an industrial and manufacturing powerhouse that eclipses the US economy.

After a costly decade of wars in the Middle East with no offsetting gains, the Obama regime announced the "Pivot to Asia," a policy of encircling China with military bases.

The Pivot to Asia calls for shifting 60 percent of the US fleet to positions from which the US can both control choke points, such as the Straits of Malacca, through which China's vital trade and energy imports flow, and bolster other countries in their disputes with China over resource rich islands.

To accommodate and to protect the fleet, Washington is seeking air and naval bases in the Philippines, Thailand, Vietnam, Singapore and Myanmar. Additionally, Washington is pushing a Trans-Pacific Partnership designed to further dollar imperialism and to counter China's growing trade with Asian countries.

Washington intends to offset Russia and China's ability to constrain US hegemony with military encirclement and by fomenting internal instability. Washington has surrounded Russia with military bases and anti-ballistic missile sites and is attempting to make NATO members of former constituent parts of the Russian empire, such as Georgia and Ukraine. Washington has targeted Russia and China with Washington-financed Non-Governmental Organizations (NGOs) and covertly supports Muslim separatists in both countries.

Washington's policy is financially and diplomatically expensive and increases the risk of nuclear war. It is a very ambitious policy for the US, which is financially and diplomatically impaired from twelve years of war and which is unable to recover from five years of economic weakness despite unprecedented monetary and fiscal stimulus.

Washington now suffers from its own economic and political divisions, with the bulk of the population failing to advance and even regressing, while income and wealth have been concentrated in fewer hands. Washington's superpower ambitions do not seem to be matched by its capabilities. The large disparity between Washington's goals and capabilities implies failure. If Washington is unable to accept failure, Washington will resort to war.

The prospect of war is only one of the dangers emanating from Washington that confronts Americans and the rest of the world. The 21st century transformation of the United States from a democratic accountable government to a lawless tyranny is a threat not only to Americans but also to peoples everywhere.

The Bush and Obama regimes set themselves up as higher than law, declaring their independence from international law and the Geneva Conventions and from US statutory law and the Constitution. The hoax "war on terror" is used to provide legal legitimacy for these spurious claims.

Among all the democratic countries in the world, only the president of the United States proclaims that he has the right to murder citizens without due process of law, without charges presented to a court, without trial and conviction for a capital offense. Only the president of the United States claims the legal right to indefinitely imprison citizens without cause being presented to a court and conviction obtained in a court. Only the president of the United States has declared that he has the right to violate peremptory norms of international law by torturing detainees. Only the president of the United States declares that he has the right to spy not only on Americans in violation of their Constitutional right to privacy and statutory US law, but also on all the peoples of the world.

Little doubt but that brutal dictators murder people and throw them in dungeons without trial or conviction. Are these dictators behaving illegally and unconstitutionally, or are they ruling in countries in which there is no rule of law?

Certainly, no other government that claims to be democratic is equipped with a Department of Justice, as Obama is and Bush was, that concocts legal justification for the head of the executive branch to be elevated above law despite the Constitution's prohibition of any such elevation. To rule independently of a rule of law is to be lawless.

In America the federal courts, both houses of Congress, law schools, the public and presstitute media have accepted the claims that the head of the executive branch, the president, has "unitary powers" that place him above accountability in certain circumstances such as war--thus the orchestration of "the war on terror." Although the president fallaciously claims to be unaccountable, there is no provision in international law that provides exceptions for war crimes, and the US Military Code does not extend this protection to soldiers and military officers.

The Bush and Obama regimes have committed crimes against numerous peoples and laws comparable to those committed by members of Germany's National Socialist government who were executed for their crimes. It was US prosecutors who established the basis for the capital crimes for which Germans were held accountable. Yet Bush and Obama have contrived legal arguments that seek to make them exempt from accountability, and the judiciary, Congress, and the media have failed to challenge the claims.

Is this what is meant when neoconservatives declare that the US government is "exceptional" and "indispensable"? Is America exceptional only because Washington can ignore both US statutory law and international law and avoid accountability?

A government cannot be both unaccountable and democratic. The 21st century Bush/Obama regimes have brought lawlessness and tyranny to America and to the world.

ENDNOTES

1   <http://rt.com/news/syria-resolution-force-lavrov-485/>

2   <http://news.antiwar.com/2009/05/25/obama-calls-on-world-to-stand-up-to-north-korea/>

3   <http://www.lewrockwell.com/lrc-blog/who-put-the-green-in-the-green-revolution/>

4   <http://www.theguardian.com/commentisfree/cifamerica/2009/sep/25/iran-secret-nuclear-plant-inspections>

5   <http://www.haaretz.com/news/american-jews-eye-obama-s-anti-israel-appointees-1.2773>

6   Alexandr Solzhenitsyn, The First Circle, Harper Perennial, 2009.

7   Chris Hedges, "One Day We'll All Be Terrorists", Truthdig, Dec. 28, 2009.

8   Glenn Greenwald, "Binding U.S. law requires prosecution for those who authorize torture," Salon, January 18, 2009.

9   <http://www.salon.com/2009/01/18/prosecutions_2/>

10   <http://ccrjustice.org/files/Rasul_AppealsCourtDecision_01_08.pdf>

11   <http://www.informationclearinghouse.info/article24605.htm>

12   See <http://www.globalresearch.ca/index.php?context=va&aid=17709 >

13   <http://www.heraldscotland.com/news/world-news/final-destination-iran-1.1013151>

14   <http://100777.com/node/106>

15   <http://original.antiwar.com/giraldi/2010/03/10/the-rogue-nation/>

16   <http://news.antiwar.com/2010/07/06/us-demands-north-waziristan-offensive/>

17   <http://www.boston.com/news/nation/washington/articles/2010/01/02/group_slams_chertoff_on_scanner_promotion/>

18   <http://www.sourcewatch.org/index.php?title=Gay_Hart_Gaines>

19   <http://www.washingtonpost.com/wp-dyn/content/article/2005/07/14 AR2005071402099.html>

20   <http://www.sott.net/article/184730-The-Tortured-and-Manipulated-Terrorist-Threat-Evidence>

21   <http://www.npr.org/2010/11/24/131574360/obama-administration-weighs-indefinite-detention>

22   <http://news.antiwar.com/2010/11/30/mike-huckabee-demands-bradley-mannings-execution/>

23   <http://news.antiwar.com/2010/11/30/brown-govt-pledged-to-foil-its-own-iraq-probe-for-us/>

24   <http://news.antiwar.com/2010/11/30/state-dept-warned-spain-us-running-out-of-patience-with-antiwar-positions/>

25   <http://news.antiwar.com/2010/12/01/facing-lieberman-boycott-amazon-ousts-wikileaks/>

26   <http://news.antiwar.com/2010/12/28/citing-facebook-posts-fox-news-turns-in-indiana-grandmother-for-terror-link/>

27   <http://www.theguardian.com/world/2008/feb/28/iraq.afghanistan>

28   <http://www.globalresearch.ca/war-on-libya-and-control-of-the-mediterranean/23940>

29.   <http://www.energyinsights.net/cgi-script/csArticles/uploads/6630/Libya%20Oil.gif>

30   <http://www.defense.gov/news/newsarticle.aspx?id=43817>

31   <http://www.foxnews.com/story/0,2933,41576,00.html>

32   <http://www.dailymail.co.uk/news/article-1387625/IMF-chief-Dominique-Strauss-

Kahn-feared-political-enemy-pay-woman-allege-rape.html>

33 <http://www.unitar.org/gls/sites/unitar.org.gls/files/Mr_Strauss_Kahn_speech%20_English.pdf>

34 <http://www.marketwatch.com/story/imf-bombshell-age-of-america-about-to-end-2011-04-25>

35 <http://www.vdare.com/pb/death_of_due_process.htm>

36 <http://rt.com/usa/gibson-guitar-raid-wood-489/>

37 <http://rt.com/usa/food-agents-year-milk/>

38 <http://rt.com/usa/fbi-family-adams-home/>

39 <http://rt.com/usa/swat-kills-american-hero/>

40 <http://www.defense.gov/news/newsarticle.aspx?id=43817

41 <http://www.informationclearinghouse.info/article28970.htm>

42 <http://rt.com/usa/fbi-terror-report-plot-365-899/>

43 <http://usatoday30.usatoday.com/news/washington/story/2011-09-28/DC-terrorist-plot-drone/50593792/1>

44 <http://news.antiwar.com/2011/09/30/cia-assassinates-two-american-citizens-in-yemen/print/>

45 <http://news.antiwar.com/2011/09/30/us-officials-work-to-posthumously-promote-anwar-awlaki/print/>

46 <http://www.informationclearinghouse.info/article29269.htm>

47 <http://www.whitehouse.gov/sites/default/files/omb/legislative/sap/112/saps1867s_20111117.pdf>

48 <http://www.paulcraigroberts.org/2012/01/11/the-next-war-on-washingtons-agenda/>

49 <http://www.paulcraigroberts.org/2012/01/14/news-alert/>

50 <http://www.mcclatchydc.com/2012/01/13/135861/spanish-judge-reopens-guantanamo.html>

51 <http://www.freenations.freeuk.com/news-2012-02-19.html>

52 <http://www.youtube.com/watch?v=suJCvkazrTc>

53 <http://www.informationclearinghouse.info/article31151.htm>

54 <http://www.andyworthington.co.uk/>

55 <http://www.nydailynews.com/new-york/occupy-wall-street-numbers-article-1.978990>

56 <http://www.foxnews.com/us/2011/10/01/500-arrested-after-wall-street-protest-on-nys-brooklyn-bridge/>

57 <http://www.chicagojournal.com/News/05-23-2012/NATO_protester_arrests>

58 <http://www.informationclearinghouse.info/article31413.htm>

59 <http://www.dailytimes.com.pk/default.asp?page=2012\05\25\story_25-5-2012_pg7_14>

60 <http://www.trust.org/item/?map=un-report-says-both-sides-in-syria-abuse-rights/>

61 <http://www.icrc.org/applic/ihl/ihl.nsf/INTRO/390>

62 <http://www.spiegel.de/international/world/pew-study-finds-steep-declines-in-faith-in-politicians-and-capitalism-a-844127.html >

63 <http://www.guardian.co.uk/business/2012/aug/10/illinois-workers-bain-outsourcing>

64 <http://www.globalresearch.ca/anglo-american-1957-secret-plan-to-assassinate-the-syrian-president-d-j-vu/32254>

65 <http://rt.com/usa/dhs-ammo-rounds-security-560/>

66 <http://www.nytimes.com/2012/08/17/world/americas/ecuador-to-let-assange-stay-in-its-embassy.html>

67 <http://www.bordc.org/newsletter/2012/08/>

68 <http://www.infowars.com/army-manual-outlines-plan-to-kill-rioters-in-america/>

69 <http://rt.com/usa/news/ndaa-injunction-tangerine-detention-376/>

70 <http://news.antiwar.com/2012/08/15/report-obama-to-tell-israel-us-will-attack-iran-by-june-2013-if-diplomacy-fails/>

71 <http://www.washingtonsblog.com/2012/08/major-general-why-have-government-

agencies-recently-purchased-enough-specialized-for-killing-ammunition-to-put-5-rounds-in-every-american.html>

72   <http://www.bbc.co.uk/news/world-us-canada-20634768>
73   <http://rt.com/politics/prepares-russias-reply-magnitsky-705/>
74   <http://www.armytimes.com/news/2013/01/ap-judge-limits-motive-evidence-wikileaks-case-bradely-manning-011613/>
75   <http://www.wrmea.org/wrmea-archives/541-washington-report-archives-2011-2015/january-february-2013/11611-why-all-americans-should-care-about-the-holy-land-foundation-case.html>
76   <www.ahherald.com/newsbrief-mainmenu-2/monmouth-county-news/14849-public-says-its-illegal-to-target-americans-abroad-as-some-question-cia-drone-attacks>
77   <http://www.theonion.com/articles/american-citizens-split-on-doj-memo-authorizing-go,31207/>
78   <http://www.globalresearch.ca/record-numbers-of-us-military-and-veteran-suicides/5322544>
79   <http://www.wired.com/dangerroom/2013/02/cost-of-war/>
80   <http://news.antiwar.com/2013/02/10/lawmakers-push-plans-to-advance-drone-strikes/>
81   <http://www.informationclearinghouse.info/article33894.htm>
82   <http://antiwar.com/blog/2013/02/11/is-obama-already-holding-us-citizens-in-indefinite-detention/>
83   <http://www.theguardian.com/commentisfree/2013/feb/11/progressives-defend-obama-kill-list>
84   <http://www.counterpunch.org/2013/03/08/obituaries-for-hugo-chavez/ and also <http://fair.org/take-action/media-advisories/in-death-as-in-life-chavez-target-of-media-scorn/>
85   <http://www.fair.org/blog/2013/03/06/ap-chavez-wasted-his-money-on-healthcare-when-he-could-have-built-gigantic-skyscrapers/>
86   <http://en.wikipedia.org/wiki/Operation_Northwoods>
87   <http://www.informationclearinghouse.info/article34259.htm> and <http://www.forbes.com/sites/ralphbenko/2013/03/11/1-6-billion-rounds-of-ammo-for-homeland-security-its-time-for-a-national-conversation/>
88   <http://www.globalresearch.ca/the-militarization-of-law-enforcement-in-america-use-of-military-technology-and-tactics-by-local-level-police/5326303>
89   <http://www.youtube.com/watch?v=FfkZ1yri26s> and <http://info.publicintelligence.net/USArmy-InternmentResettlement.pdf>
90   John W. Dower, Cultures of War: Pearl Harbor / Hiroshima / 911 / Iraq, W.W. Norton, 2011.
91   <http://www.reuters.com/article/2013/03/14/iraq-war-anniversary-idUSL1N0C5FBN2010314>
92   <http://nationalinterest.org/blog/paul-pillar/still-peddling-iraq-war-myths-ten-years-later-8227>
93   <http://www.pbs.org/wgbh/pages/frontline/homefront/interviews/klein.html>
94   <http://news.antiwar.com/2013/06/07/us-spy-chief-slams-reprehensible-leak-of-nsa-surveillance-scheme/>
95   <http://www.whitehouse.gov/the-press-office/2013/06/19/remarks-president-obama-brandenburg-gate-berlin-germany>
96   <http://www.spiegel.de/international/world/europe-must-stand-up-to-american-cyber-snooping-a-906250.html>
97   <http://www.globalresearch.ca/follow-the-money-the-secret-heart-of-the-secret-state-the-deeper-implications-of-the-snowden-revelations/5340132>
98   <http://www.opednews.com/populum/printer_friendly.php?content=a&id=167695>
99   <http://yalejournal.org/2013/06/12/who-authorized-preparations-for-war-with-china/>
100   <http://www.bloomberg.com/news/2013-07-30/al-qaeda-backers-found-with-u-s-

contracts-in-afghanistan.html>
101   <http://www.nytimes.com/cq/2006/11/08/cq_1916.html>
102   <http://www.thewire.com/national/2013/08/government-knocking-doors-because-
       google-searches/67864/>
103   <http://www.informationclearinghouse.info/article35773.htm>
104   <http://www.theguardian.com/commentisfree/2013/aug/10/james-risen-prison-
       journalism-criminalised>
105   <http://news.antiwar.com/2013/08/11/us-drones-pound-yemen-but-targets-arent-all-
       militants/print/>
106   <http://www.manufacturingnews.com/news/TAA0731131.html>
107   <http://rt.com/op-edge/uk-gay-greenwald-freedom-police-679/>
108   <http://rt.com/news/uk-parliament-vote-syria-181/>
109   <http://rt.com/op-edge/syria-un-war-investigation-006/>
110   <http://www.independent.co.uk/news/world/middle-east/syria-un-weapons-inspectors-
       attacked-as-they-try-to-enter-poison-gas-attack-site-8784435.html>
111   <http://news.antiwar.com/2013/08/25/obama-administration-accepts-rebels-account-
       on-syria-prepares-for-war/> See also <http://news.antiwar.com/2013/08/25/syria-
       accepts-un-inspectors-us-spurns-call-as-too-late/>
112   <http://rt.com/news/un-chemical-oservers-shot-000/>
113   <http://news.yahoo.com/syria-war-escalates-americans-cool-u-intervention-re
       uters-003146054.html>
114   <http://rt.com/usa/carter-comment-nsa-snowden-261/>
115   <http://rt.com/news/uk-response-without-un-backing-979/>
116   <http://www.businessinsider.com/jp-morgan-investigated-for-bribing-china-2013-8>
117   <http://www.telegraph.co.uk/finance/newsbysector/energy/oilandgas/10266957/
       Saudis-offer-Russia-secret-oil-deal-if-it-drops-Syria.html>
118   <http://www.todayszaman.com/news-316966-report-police-foil-al-nusra-bomb-attack-
       planned-for-adana.html>
119   <http://antiwar.com/blog/2013/08/31/impeachment-congress-fires-opening-shot-
       across-obamas-bow/>
120   <http://www.worldtribune.com/2013/05/31/nato-data-assad-winning-the-war-for-
       syrians-hearts-and-minds/>
121   <http://www.wnd.com/2013/09/calls-to-congress-244-to-1-against-syria-war/>
122   <http://rt.com/news/g20-against-syria-strike-527/>
123   <http://www.cnn.com/2013/08/19/politics/cia-iran-1953-coup>
124   <http://www.amazon.com/9-11-Toronto-Report/dp/1478369205/ref=sr_1_1?s=book
       s&ie=UTF8&qid=1376960447&sr=1-1&keywords=The+Toronto+Report>
125   <http://www.international.to/index.php?option=com_content&view=article&id=93
       19:hijacking-americas-mind-on-911-counterfeiting-evidence&catid=66:oped&Item
       id=151>
126   <http://www.nist.gov/customcf/get_pdf.cfm?pub_id=101019>
127   <http://www.nist.gov/customcf/get_pdf.cfm?pub_id=860495>
128   <http://www.globalresearch.ca/continuity-of-government-is-the-state-of-emergency-
       superseding-our-constitution/22089>
129   <http://georgewbush-whitehouse.archives.gov/news/releases/2007/05/20070509-12.
       html>
130   My interview with King World News is relatively short, but Eric King knows how
       to bring it to the most controversial point. What everyone should wonder is, "How
       did we, a free people protected by the US Constitution, become one step away from
       rule by Caesar? <http://kingworldnews.com/kingworldnews/KWN_DailyWeb/Entries/
       2013/10/8_Former_US_Treasury_Official_-_President_To_Seize_Total_Power.html>
       My interview with Greg Hunter of USA Watchdog is, in my opinion, one of my best.
       The interview covers a broad range of issues or possibilities and makes it unnecessary
       for me to write a column about the government shutdown and its implications and

possible consequences. <http://usawatchdog.com/paul-craig-roberts-obama-could-govern-as-a-dictator/>

131   <http://www.forbes.com/sites/rebeccaruiz/2013/11/04/report-a-million-veterans-injured-in-iraq-afghanistan-wars/>

132   <http://rt.com/usa/us-afghanistan-pentagon-troops-budget-721/>

133   <http://kabulpress.org/my/spip.php?article32304>

134   <http://www.nytimes.com/2013/05/22/opinion/another-chilling-leak-investigation.html?_r=0 >

135   <http://www.foxnews.com/story/2001/12/26/report-bin-laden-already-dead/>

136   <http://www.lewrockwell.com/2013/11/james-huang/must-watch-video/>

137   <http://www.youtube.com/watch?v=ufvmHYqfdbU> and <http://www.youtube.com/watch?v=1q91RZko5Gw>

138   <http://en.wikipedia.org/wiki/Operation_Northwoods>

139   <http://www.strategic-culture.org/news/2013/10/17/nato-steadfast-jazz-exercise-chill-of-cold-war.html>

140   <http://www.wingia.com/en/services/about_the_end_of_year_survey/7/>

141   <http://www.theguardian.com/world/2013/dec/17/merkel-compares-nsa-stasi-obama>

142   <http://www.washingtonsblog.com/2013/12/former-top-nsa-official-now-police-state.html>

143   <http://news.nationalpost.com/2013/12/18/devyani-khobragade-reveals-how-she-broke-down-after-stripping-and-cavity-searches-as-row-between-u-s-and-india-deepens/>

144   <http://www.unz.com/pbuchanan/is-putin-one-of-us/>

145   <http://rt.com/op-edge/questioning-9-11-conspiracy-acceptable-708/>

INDEX

29099384R00261

Made in the USA
Charleston, SC
01 May 2014